Lecture Notes in Computer Science 612

Edited by G. Goos and J. Hartmanis

Advisory Board: W. Brauer   D. Gries   J. Stoer

M. Tokoro O. Nierstrasz P. Wegner (eds.)

Object-Based
Concurrent Computing

ECOOP '91 Workshop
Geneva, Switzerland, July 15-16, 1991
Proceedings

Springer-Verlag
Berlin Heidelberg New York
London Paris Tokyo
Hong Kong Barcelona
Budapest

M. Tokoro   O. Nierstrasz   P. Wegner (Eds.)

Object-Based Concurrent Computing

ECOOP '91 Workshop
Geneva, Switzerland, July 15-16, 1991
Proceedings

Springer-Verlag

Berlin Heidelberg New York
London Paris Tokyo
Hong Kong Barcelona
Budapest

Series Editors

Gerhard Goos
Universität Karlsruhe
Postfach 69 80
Vincenz-Priessnitz-Straße 1
W-7500 Karlsruhe, FRG

Juris Hartmanis
Department of Computer Science
Cornell University
5149 Upson Hall
Ithaca, NY 14853, USA

Volume Editors

Mario Tokoro
Department of Computer Science, Keio University
3-14-1 Hiyoshi, Kohoku-ku, Yokohama 223, Japan

Oscar Nierstrasz
Centre Universitaire d'Informatique, University of Geneva
24, rue du Général-Dufor, CH-1211 Geneva 4, Switzerland

Peter Wegner
Department of Computer Sciene, Brown University
P. O. Box 1910, Providence, Rhode Island 02912-1910, USA

CR Subject Classification (1991): D.1.3, D.1.5, D.3.2-3, F.3.2-3

ISBN 3-540-55613-3 Springer-Verlag Berlin Heidelberg New York
ISBN 0-387-55613-3 Springer-Verlag New York Berlin Heidelberg

Typesetting: Camera ready by author/editor
Printing and binding: Druckhaus Beltz, Hemsbach/Bergstr.
45/3140-543210 - Printed on acid-free paper

Preface

Background

The world we live in is concurrent, persistent, dynamic, distributed, and open-ended in its very nature. Besides, computation can be envisaged as simulation of a part of the real or an imaginary world, by computers. As hardware facilities for parallel and distributed computation, such as distributed computer networks and various multiprocessors, become more and more popular, large demands arise for providing users with computational frameworks, or tools of abstraction, for concurrent, distributed, and open-ended worlds.

The notion of objects gives us the framework of computation that provides the properties of boundary, identity, and persistence. If we examine these properties very carefully, we come to the conclusion that objects are inherently active, concurrent, and distributed, rather than passive, sequential, and centralized. Thus, a world can naturally be mapped onto a collection of objects and simulated as the mutual effects of objects.

Various attempts have been made, starting from sequential objects, to extend them to be concurrent. There has also been a view in which people look at computing as concurrent activities from the beginning, and regard a sequential one as a constrained form. Either way, concurrency has brought about a lot of new problems. However, attacking concurrency is inevitable and indispensable for establishing the basis of new computer science. We believe that concurrent object-based computing will open a new computational paradigm for the 1990s and beyond.

The Workshop

The ECOOP'91 Workshop on Object-Based Concurrent Computing was organized to provide a forum on concurrent, distributed, and open-ended computing. We put some emphasis on conceptual, theoretical, or formal aspects, as well as practical requirements and sound experience, since we deem that such a viewpoint is indispensable at this stage in order to investigate and to establish a common agreed-upon theoretical basis for further development.

The workshop was held on July the 15th and 16th, 1991 in the University of Geneva as a pre-conference workshop of ECOOP'91. The workshop comprised two invited lectures, twenty-five technical presentations, and a panel. We invited Professor Robin Milner of the University of Edinburgh and Professor Joseph Goguen of Oxford University to give special lectures, and they both kindly accepted our invitation.

Professor Milner's lecture was entitled *Concurrent Processes as Objects*. He presented his constructive view of concurrent computing and explained π-calculus which had been extended from CCS. He alluded to passing references, process migration, interpretation of λ-calculus by π-calculus, and the relationship between process creation and linear logic.

Professor Goguen's lecture was entitled *Semantics of the Object-Oriented Paradigm*. Based on his equilibrium view of concurrent computing, Goguen proposed the sheaf theory as a unified theoretical basis of concurrent and parallel computing. He explained how the sheaf theory is practically used by giving an example of logic design.

Unfortunately, we could not include the manuscripts or transcripts of the invited lectures. Professor Milner, however, participated in the panel discussion which was recorded and transcribed, so readers may capture his thought by tracing these arguments. Professor Goguen, upon our request after the workshop, submitted a technical paper on his related work, which was included in this volume. In this way, the readers can learn at least part of what he intended to convey in his lecture.

About this Volume

We selected 12 presentations out of 25 and asked the authors to revise their papers according to editors' comments. Thus, including Professor Goguen's paper, we gathered 13 papers and one transcribed panel discussion in this volume. The papers are classified into four categories: Formal Methods (1), Formal Methods (2), Concurrent Programming, and Models.

Formal Methods (1): The first three papers are concerned with the formal semantics of concurrent objects based on process calculi. The first paper, by Oscar Nierstrasz, is entitled *Towards an Object Calculus*. Nierstrasz first put his stress on the importance of the notions of concurrency, distribution and persistence in the study of object-oriented computing. He also deals with the computational and compositional aspects of concurrent programs and proposes an *object calculus* that integrates the concept of agents in process calculi with that of functions in λ-calculus.

The second paper is *On Asynchronous Communication Semantics* by Kohei Honda and Mario Tokoro. The authors first discuss the similarity and difference between synchronous and asynchronous systems, and then propose an equational theory called *asynchronous bisimulation* which is based on Milner's π-calculus. They also show that asynchronous bisimilarity is strictly more general than its synchronous counterpart.

The third paper is *A Unifying Framework for Process Calculus Semantics of Concurrent Object-Oriented Languages* by Michael Papathomas. From the viewpoint of designing better concurrent object-oriented languages, Papathomas claims the necessity of a common framework to discuss object-oriented features including encapsulation, object identity, class and inheritance, and concurrency. He proposes a framework for semantic definition of concurrent object-based languages by its translation to CCS, so that various concurrent object-oriented languages can be defined and compared. The framework also supports class and inheritance.

Formal Methods (2): The next four papers are concerned with various formal approaches to the semantics of concurrent programs. The first paper is an extended abstract entitled *A Sheaf Semantics for FOOPS Expressions* written by D. A. Wolfram and Joseph A. Goguen. They present a sheaf semantics for concurrent method expression evaluation in a concurrent object-oriented language called FOOPS, so that evaluations of functions, methods, and attributes are treated in a uniform way.

The next paper is *Semantic Layers of Object-Based Concurrent Computing* by Etsuya Shibayama. He proposes a layered semantics model for an object-based concurrent programming language. The bottom layer semantics is defined based on a transition system, the middle layer is defined based on an object diagram, and the top layer is defined based on the notion of program transformation. The model provides a means of reasoning about object composition.

The third paper is *Formal Techniques for Parallel Object-Oriented Languages* by Pierre America. It gives an overview of the formal techniques that have been developed to deal with the family of parallel object-oriented languages which are generally referred to as POOL. This is a slightly revised version of an invited paper for the Concur'91 Conference published in LNCS Vol. 527.

The last paper in this set is by Vasco Vasconcelos and Mario Tokoro, and is entitled *Trace Semantics for Actor Systems*. This paper describes their attempt to give concurrent semantics to Actor-like concurrent systems by using the theory of traces. They also develop a notion of composition of actor systems that allows the derivation of the semantics of a system from the semantics of its components.

Concurrent Programming: The third set is composed of three papers related to concurrent programming. The first one is written by Jean-Marc Andreoli, Remo Pareschi, and Marc Bourgois, and is entitled *Dynamic Programming as Multiagent Programming*. This paper is concerned with the well-known operations research technique of dynamic programming. The authors view the technique as a concurrent and truly dynamic system, and map the problem onto concurrent programs described in their LO (Linear Objects) programming language. For a given directed acyclic graph with weighted edges, the best path is found by cooperation and competition of multiple agents in a concurrent program.

The second paper is *Scheduling Predicate* by Ciaran McHale, Bridget Walsh, Sean Baker, and Alexis Donnelly. The authors describe a new synchronization mechanism intended to provide programmers with a facility for describing the scheduling of operations based on relative arrival times, values of parameters, and built-in synchronization counters.

The last paper in this set is *A Concurrency Control Mechanism for C++ Objects* by Hayssam Saleh and Philippe Gautron. They first study various synchronization mechanisms which were introduced into class-based languages and then propose a mechanism called *conditional wait* which is incorporated with C++. The incorporation is achieved orthogonally to the base language in such a way that it does not interfere with encapsulation, inheritance, and component reusability.

Models: The fourth set is composed of three papers concerned with models for concurrent systems. The first paper is written by Satoshi Matsuoka, Takuo Watanabe, Yuuji Ichisugi, and Akinori Yonezawa and is entitled *Object-Oriented Concurrent Reflective Architectures*. They introduce the notion of *reflection* into a concurrent language. Reflection provides the abilities of reasoning about and altering the dynamic behavior of computation from within the language framework. This paper first discusses the benefits of reflective architectures and then classifies previously proposed architectures into some categories. Then they present the current state of their work on ABCL/R and its future extensions.

The second paper is *Abstract Description of Distributed Object Systems* by Ralf Jungclaus and Thorsten Hartmann. They first propose an object-oriented model to describe distributed systems, called the Basic Object Model. The model consists of base objects for representing entities as processes and channels for communication. A language which describes distributed systems based on the Basic Object Model is presented.

In the last paper, *Design Issues for Object-Based Concurrency* by Peter Wegner, the author first examines the design space for object-based concurrent programming. Then, he considers the role of abstractions, distribution, and synchronization, and introduces the notion of *relative persistence* of operations and data for functions, objects, and transactions.

The Panel: This volume concludes with a panel discussion, transcribed and edited by Kohei Honda and Satoshi Matsuoka. We had Peter Wegner as the chair and Pierre America, Robin Milner, Oscar Nierstrasz, Mario Tokoro, and Akinori Yonezawa as panelists. The title of the panel was *What is an Object?* Discussions ranged over various issues regarding objects including the definition of objects, identity, persistence, and concurrency. The readers of this volume may be able to discover and appreciate the underlying concepts of the panelists who have been leading research on Concurrent Object-Based Computing.

Acknowledgments

Lastly, but not least, we would like to thank Professor Dennis Tsichritzis, who served as the ECOOP'91 General Chair, for his support in organizing this workshop, Michael Papathomas for his devotion to local arrangements, Professors Robin Milner and Joseph Goguen for their insightful lectures, and all the authors and panelists who really materialized this volume . We are also grateful to Kohei Honda and Ichiro Satoh for their help in editing this volume.

April 1992

Mario Tokoro
Oscar Nierstrasz
Peter Wegner

Contents

Models

Moderator:	Peter Wegner
Panelists:	Pierre America
	Robin Milner
	Oscar Nierstrasz
	Mario Tokoro
	Akinori Yonezawa

Towards an Object Calculus

Oscar Nierstrasz
University of Geneva*

Abstract

The development of concurrent object-based programming languages has suffered from the lack of any generally accepted formal foundations for defining their semantics. Furthermore, the delicate relationship between object-oriented features supporting reuse and operational features concerning interaction and state change is poorly understood in a concurrent setting. To address this problem, we propose the development of an *object calculus*, borrowing heavily from relevant work in the area of process calculi. To this end, we briefly review some of this work, we pose some informal requirements for an object calculus, and we present the syntax, operational semantics and use through examples of a proposed object calculus, called OC.

1 Introduction

In order for object-oriented languages to be an effective medium for implementing reusable software components for reactive applications, they must be able to cope with concurrency, distribution and persistence. Although distribution and persistence can arguable be considered as being purely run-time concerns, concurrency cannot, for it directly concerns the semantics of software composition. There have been numerous attempts in recent years to integrate concurrency features into object-oriented languages (see [33] for a survey). As a result of these experiences, a number of difficulties have become apparent:

1. Most concurrent object-oriented languages lack a well-defined semantic foundation. There is no generally accepted semantic domain or computational model for specifying such languages or for comparing their features. This naturally makes it quite difficult to reason about the abstract properties of any software component.

2. The clean integration of concurrency features with object-oriented features supporting encapsulation and reuse is difficult to achieve. In the particular case of inheritance, difficulties that arise in sequential languages due to confusion between

---

Mailing address: Centre Universitaire d'Informatique. 12 Rue du Lac. CH-1207 Geneva, Switzerland. *E-mail:* oscar@cui.unige.ch

encapsulation of instances relative to their clients and encapsulation of classes relative to subclasses are aggravated in the concurrent case [22].

3. Compositionality of concurrent objects is poorly understood. Standard notions of polymorphism do not carry over very well to the world of concurrent objects that may exhibit non-uniform service availability [29, 31].

To address these issues, we propose the development of an *object calculus* that integrates the concept of *agents* present in process calculi with that of *functions* present in λ calculi. An (active) object can then be viewed as a function (agent) with state. Mechanisms for software composition can be viewed as functional composition of agents. The semantics of concurrent object-oriented languages can then be understood within a uniform framework that addresses both computational and compositional issues.

We shall first briefly review the status of current work in semantics of concurrent object-oriented languages and trends in process calculi, and summarize our requirements for an object calculus. We shall then proceed by presenting and exploring an attempt at the definition of such a calculus. We conclude with some remarks on various theoretical and practical considerations for future exploration.

2 The Search for an Object Calculus

2.1 Semantics of Concurrent Object-Oriented Languages

Until recently, much of the work on models of concurrency has proceeded independently of the development of concurrent object-oriented languages. Perhaps the earliest attempts to provide semantic foundations for these languages has been by means of the actor model [1, 12]. (Which helps to explain why many concurrent object-oriented languages either are, or claim to be, actor languages.) More recently, both operational and denotational semantics have been developed for POOL, based respectively on transition systems [3] and on complete metric spaces [4]. Rewriting logics have been used to provide an operational semantics for Maude [23] (with a corresponding denotational semantics based on category theory).

Another promising direction is to use process calculi as a semantic foundation for concurrent object-oriented languages. In this case, the approach is to view objects as "patterns" of agents that obey the higher-level protocols established by the programming language. One may view the specification of a programming language as a mapping from syntactic patterns representing language constructs to the behavioural patterns that they stand for [29, 30]. The choice of the underlying computational model is critical if the semantic mapping is to be as simple as possible. As such, one would like the primitives of the process calculus to be as natural as possible for modelling the concepts of the programming language.

Difficulties with the semantics of inheritance in object-oriented languages, and in particular, difficulties with the conflict between inheritance of code versus inheritance of specification [14], have led to interest in formal semantics for inheritance [10, 13]. Although there have been many attempts to unify inheritance of code and specification, there is some consensus that the two concepts should be kept separate [5]. On the one hand, there is some feeling that inheritance is not the right way to approach software composition as the complex mechanics of inheritance are not made explicit [16, 35, 37], and on the other hand there are some ongoing attempts to "unbundle" inheritance to make its mechanics more explicit [9, 17]. In either case, object-oriented software composition is essentially being viewed as *functional composition* of the software components that make up an object.

We feel that these trends lend weight to our conviction that an integration of functions and agents will lead to calculus suitable for modelling both the computational aspects of active objects as well as the compositional aspects of mechanisms for software reuse.

2.2   Trends in Process Calculi

During the 1980s there has been a great deal of relevant work in the development of models of concurrency based on synchronously communicating concurrent *agents* (also called "processes"). The most familiar and accessible work has been on Milner's Calculus of Communicating Systems (CCS) [24] and Hoare's Communicating Sequential Processes (CSP) [19].

The Actor model of computation [1] bears comparison to the agent-based models, but is based on asynchronous communication, and its theoretical foundations are less well-developed (there is, for example, no commonly accepted notion of actor equivalence). More recently there has been work by Honda and Tokoro on the development of a process calculus for actor-like objects [20] and, within this framework, a notion of actor equivalence that is closely related to, but distinguishable from, usual notions of process equivalence [21].

There has been renewed interest in extending process calculi to cope with the communication of "labels" (i.e., the name, or *port* by which one may address a communication to a particular agent) and the communication of *agents* themselves. CCS did not originally permit label passing because of technical difficulties in controlling the scope of names, but this meant that only static interconnections between agents could be modelled. Label passing is important for modelling the semantics of active objects because (1) object identifiers can in general be communicated between objects, and (2) reflective capabilities, which are especially important in persistent object systems, are more easily modelled if we can manipulate and communicate behaviours (just as we can manipulate and communicate functions in the λ calculus). Since the label of an agent provides access to the agent itself, both research directions can be seen as attempts to integrate process calculi and λ calculi (i.e., where function application is analogous to communication and functions are first class communicable values).

The original work on extending CCS to accommodate label passing is by Engberg [15]. More recently, there has been the development of the π calculus [25], Thomsen's Calculus of Higher Order Communicating Systems (CHOCS) [38], Nielsen's λ calculus with first-class processes [28], Boudol's proposal for a concurrent λ calculus [8], and Berry and Boudol's Chemical Abstract Machine (CHAM) [7]. The most important contributions in these developments appear to be:

1. The notion of *migration* in the π calculus which facilitates the creation and visibility of names analogously to the substitution and conversion rules of the λ calculus [6].

2. The *structural congruence* of CHAM that simplifies the expression of the semantic reduction rules.

Although various authors have demonstrated how λ calculi can be accurately encoded or embedded in these process calculi [8, 26, 38], a single calculus that truly unifies the notions of functions and agents in a convincing way remains a topic for active research. In particular, the theoretical foundations of HOπ, a higher-order variant of the π calculus in which not only labels but also processes may be communicated, are being explored by means of translation to the (first-order) π calculus [36].

2.3 Some Requirements for an Object Calculus

There are three fundamental aspects of concurrent object-oriented languages that we would like to capture through the formalism of an object calculus:

Encapsulation:

- *Objects* are processes that encapsulate services. Each communication is typically either a *request* or a *reply*, and every communication of a request eventually results in a reply.

- Objects have an internal state which may (or may not) change. This state is accessible only indirectly through the services provided.

- Objects (usually) have a unique *identity* or name which is needed to gain access to its services.

Active objects:

- Objects are autonomous entities that have full control over which communications they will send or accept at any time.

- Objects may be internally concurrent.

- An object may simultaneously service multiple pending requests.

Composition:

- Objects may be composed of systems of more primitive objects.

- Objects may be specified as a functional composition of (higher-order) abstractions over objects, services and other object parts. In composing objects, it is possible to override "inherited" services with new ones.

If we take process calculi as a natural starting point for modelling active objects as processes, it quickly becomes clear that a unification of functions and processes is needed in order to express object composition. An *agent* can be either viewed as a process (when communicating by message passing) or as a "function with state" (when accepting input by local application). Objects can then be seen either as primitive agents or as compositions of lower-level agents.

We can now translate our requirements to specific features that would be desirable in an object calculus:

1. *Concurrency:* as in process calculi.

2. *Tuple-based communication:* to model complex messages.

3. *Local and remote communication:* unifying the functional and process paradigms.

4. *Recursion:* to express non-terminating agents and state change.

5. *Higher-order agents:* to express agent composition.

6. *Name creation:* as in the π calculus, to create unique identifiers for objects.

7. *Left-preferential choice:* to express overriding of services.

In the following we will present an attempt to define such an object calculus and explore some of its properties.

3 OC — An Object Calculus

The object calculus (OC) we present here is an evolution of Abacus [29, 30], an executable notation based on CCS and intended for specifying and prototyping object-based concurrent languages. OC bears the same relationship to Abacus that the π calculus does to CCS — we have tried to take advantage of recent developments in process calculi to simplify and generalize the notation, and we have tried to recover the higher-order expressiveness of the λ calculus. In fact, as we shall see, OC is effectively a unification of the π and λ calculi, with communication generalized to tuples. OC is an experimental calculus — by applying OC to concrete examples in object-based concurrency, we hope to arrive at a practical calculus and also to motivate strongly further theoretical explorations.

The terms of OC consist of a set of expressions representing *agents*, $\mathcal{A}$. Agents are composed of a set of *names*, $\mathcal{N}$, a set of *output patterns* (or *values*), $\mathcal{V}$, and a set of *input patterns*, $\mathcal{X}$. We let a, b, c range over $\mathcal{A}$, n, m over $\mathcal{N}$, v over $\mathcal{V}$ and x over $\mathcal{X}$.

The syntax of agents is as follows:

$$a ::= a \& a \mid n := a \mid a|a \mid x \rightarrow a \mid v \wedge a \mid a@v \mid n \backslash a \mid n \mid \text{nil}$$

The operators are given from loosest to tightest binding. Concurrent composition is $\&$, recursion is $:=$, (left-preferential) choice is $|$, abstraction (input) is $\rightarrow$, output is $\wedge$, (functional) application is $@$, restriction (of local names) is $\backslash$ and the inactive agent is given by nil. A name n stands for an agent only if it has been bound to an agent expression by a communication or by a recursive definition. Our syntax differs slightly from that of the π calculus, partly because OC is executable (so we prefer to use typable characters), but mainly because we adopt a tuple-based rather than a channel-based approach to communication. As we shall see, we have chosen $\rightarrow$ to denote an input guard as it will serve for accepting both remote and local (functional) communications.

The operators $\&$, $|$, $\rightarrow$, $\wedge$ and $\backslash$ associate to the right, and $@$ associates to the left. So $x \rightarrow y \rightarrow a$ is parsed as $x \rightarrow (y \rightarrow a)$ and $a@b@v$ as $(a@b)@c$.

Agents communicate by sending messages, which are tuples containing names, agents or other tuples:

$$v ::= n \mid a \mid (v, ..., v)$$

In general, communications may only take place when an output matches an input pattern of another agent. Input patterns are tuples of names and local variables:

$$x ::= n \mid n? \mid (x, ..., x)$$

The construct $n?$ occurring in x binds the name n locally within a in the expression $x \rightarrow a$. These locally bound names act as variables in communications, whereas the free names (i.e., not annotated by ?) serve to match input and output patterns.

Definition 1 *Matching of outputs and inputs is denoted by $\sim$, defined as follows:*

$$
\begin{aligned}
n &\sim n \\
v &\sim n? \\
\vec{v} &\sim \vec{x} \qquad \Leftrightarrow \forall i, v_i \sim x_i \qquad \square
\end{aligned}
$$

We will make use of a slightly special substitution function, $a\{v/x\}$ to substitute free occurrences in a of variables introduced in x by their matching values in v. Free names in x are ignored as they must match exactly the corresponding names in v, so no substitution is required. So $a\{(b,m)/(n?,m)\}$ causes (free) instances of n in a to be substituted by b. On the other hand, a substitution such as $a\{(b,m)/(n,m)\}$ is invalid, since $(b,m) \not\sim (n,m)$.

As in CHAM and the π calculus, we start by defining the structural congruence, $\equiv$:

Definition 2 *Structural congruence* for agents is the smallest congruence $\equiv$ over $\mathcal{A}$ satisfying:

1. $a\&b \equiv b\&a$, $a\&(b\&c) \equiv (a\&b)\&c$, $a\&nil \equiv a$

2. $n := a \equiv a\{(n := a)/n?\}$

3. $n\backslash a \equiv a$, $n \notin fn(a)$

4. $n\backslash m\backslash a \equiv m\backslash n\backslash a$

5. $n\backslash a \star b \equiv n\backslash(a \star b)$, $n \notin fn(b)$, $\star$ is any of $\&$, $|$ or $@$
   $a|n\backslash b \equiv n\backslash(a|b)$, $n \notin fn(a)$

6. $n := a \equiv n' := a\{n'/n?\}$, $n' \notin fn(a)$

7. $n\backslash a \equiv n'\backslash a\{n'/n?\}$, $n' \notin fn(a)$

8. $x \to a \equiv x\{n'/n?\} \to a\{n'/n?\}$, $n' \notin fn(x, a)$ □

A few words of explanation are in order. The first set of equations simply tells us that concurrent composition is commutative and associative, and that nil contributes nothing. The second equation tells us how to expand recursive agents (i.e., substitute all free occurrences of n in a by $n := a$). The third allows us to discard a restriction of an unused name ($fn(a)$ is the set of *free names* in a). The fourth equation tells us that the order of restriction is unimportant. The fifth equation allows us to expand the scope of a restriction to nearby agents (called *scope extrusion* [25]), if the restricted name is new. The last three equations define α-convertibility for agents. They are needed for substituting local names by globally unique names prior to scope extrusion.

Definition 3 *Communication offers*, denoted by $\xrightarrow{c}$, where c is either v (for input) or $\bar{v}$ (for output), and *Reduction*, written $\longrightarrow$, are induced by the following rules:

$$\text{Out}: \frac{}{v \wedge a \xrightarrow{\bar{v}} a} \qquad \text{In}: \frac{v \sim x}{x \to a \xrightarrow{v} a\{v/x\}} \qquad \text{Conc}: \frac{a \xrightarrow{c} a'}{a\&b \xrightarrow{c} a'\&b}$$

$$\text{If}: \frac{a \xrightarrow{c} a'}{a|b \xrightarrow{c} a'} \qquad \text{Else}: \frac{a \not\xrightarrow{} , \; a \not\xrightarrow{c} , \; b \xrightarrow{c} b'}{a|b \xrightarrow{c} b'}$$

$$\text{Apply}: \frac{a \xrightarrow{v} a'}{a@v \longrightarrow a'} \qquad \text{Comm}: \frac{a \xrightarrow{v} a', \; b \xrightarrow{\bar{v}} b'}{a\&b \longrightarrow a'\&b'}$$

$$\text{Left}: \frac{a \longrightarrow a'}{a \star b \longrightarrow a' \star b} \; [\star \text{ is } \&, | \text{ or } @] \qquad \text{Right}: \frac{b \longrightarrow b'}{a \star b \longrightarrow a \star b'} \; [\star \text{ is } \&, | \text{ or } \backslash]$$

$$\text{Struct}: \frac{a \equiv b, \; b \longrightarrow b', \; b' \equiv a'}{a \longrightarrow a'} \qquad □$$

Note that the left argument of the choice operator has priority over the right argument, so we must first be sure (in **Else**) that a cannot be further reduced.

The rules **Apply** and **Comm** define local and remote communication. In an expression such as $a@v$, the agent a is *required* to (eventually) accept the input v, if it can. By rule **Left**, a may first reduce to some form a' before accepting v, but it may not communicate with any external agent until it has done so (since $\xrightarrow{c}$ is not defined for the form $a@v$). If a is incapable of accepting v at any time, then $a@v$ is effectively dead. With remote communication, on the other hand, in $a\&b\&c$, a is free to communicate with either b or c, should their offers match.

As a matter of convenience, we will also overload the operator $:=$ to stand for $\overset{def}{\equiv}$.

4 Using OC

4.1 Concurrency, Communication and Synchronization

Let us consider first the very simple example of a binary semaphore:

bsem := p→v→bsem | v→bsem

bsem would like to accept as input a p (from an agent claiming a resource) and then accept a v (when the agent releases it). Note that any attempts to release the resource when it has not yet been claimed are discarded.

We may similarly define a printer that accepts print requests:

printer := print→printer

and a couple of clients:

c1 := p∧print∧print∧v∧nil

c2 := p∧print∧print∧v∧nil

Each client attempts to grab the semaphore, communicates twice with the printer, and then releases it.

Now, if we start with the system bsem & printer & c1 & c2, we may reach after the communication of a p the following configuration:

$\longrightarrow$ v→bsem & printer & print∧print∧v∧nil & p∧print∧print∧v∧nil

Note that the second client is unable to claim the resource since it is waiting to send a p that the semaphore is not yet prepared to accept. Let us trace through the rest of the computation.

$\longrightarrow$ v→bsem & printer & print∧v∧nil & p∧print∧print∧v∧nil

$\longrightarrow$ v→bsem & printer & v∧nil & p∧print∧print∧v∧nil

$\longrightarrow$ bsem & printer & p∧print∧print∧v∧nil

$\longrightarrow$ v→bsem & printer & print∧print∧v∧nil

$\longrightarrow$ v→bsem & printer & print∧v∧nil

$\longrightarrow$ v→bsem & printer & v∧nil

$\longrightarrow$ bsem & printer

At this point the system is *stable*, as it can be reduced no further. Note that exactly two possible computation paths were possible, depending on which client grabbed the resource first.

4.2   Composition

So far we have seen only pure synchronization and remote communication. We shall now show how an agent can also be treated as a function.

Let us consider an agent that models the behaviour of the Linda *tuple space* [11]. Linda provides a small set of primitives to allow concurrent processes to communicate and synchronize by writing and reading tuples to a so-called tuple space. A process may write a tuple using the non-blocking *out* primitive, and may read a tuple either destructively with the *in* primitive, or non-destructively with the *rd* primitive. Both read primitives block if no matching tuple exists. The following agent, linda, supports these three primitives:

linda := (out,t?) → (linda & tuple@t)

tuple := t? → ((in,t)∧nil | (rd,t)∧tuple@t)

When linda receives a request to create a new tuple, it replaces itself by a system including a copy of itself and an agent that implements the behaviour of a tuple. tuple is in fact an abstraction over the possible set of tuple values. To instantiate it, the value t must be applied to tuple.

With this agent, we may re-specify our clients of the previous example as follows:

c1 := (in,sem) → print∧print∧(out,sem)∧ nil

c2 := (in,sem) → print∧print∧(out,sem)∧ nil

and the system to evaluate is now:

linda & (out,sem)∧nil & printer & c1 & c2

Note that tuple is not just a function but is in fact an agent. It is a little unusual in that it contains no free names in its input pattern. In a sense, it is an "anonymous" agent in that t? will match any output whatsoever. We can force it to accept a particular communication as input only through the use of @.

In the Linda example, only names were communicated. The following example, of a stack, makes use of agent communication to define an abstraction of a stack:

empty := (push,x?) → stack@(x,empty)

```
stack  := (top?,rest?) → ( (pop,top) ∧ rest
                          | (push,x?) → stack@(x,stack@(top,rest)))
```

The agent stack accepts two values as input: top, which is the value to be popped off, and rest, which is the agent (i.e., stack) to be revealed when the top is popped off. Note that it is imperative that rest be bound to an agent, whereas top may be any value. If we incorrectly try to evaluate stack@(n,m) & (pop,x?)→nil then we will eventually reduce to a term (namely m) which is not an agent. This suggests that communications have sorts, and agents have types associated with them, as is the case in the π calculus [27].

4.3 Encapsulation

Up to now our agents have communicated only through a fixed set of names. Let us now consider the standard example of a sequence of linked agents that implement a queue:

```
queue := (put,x?) → done\(head@(x,done) & tail@done)
head  := (x?,done?) → (get,x)∧done∧nil
tail  := ready? → ( (put,x?) → done\(ready→head@(x,done) & tail@done)
                  | ready → queue )
```

The empty queue can only accept requests to put a new value. When it receives the first value, it turns into a head agent containing this value, linked to a tail that accepts further put requests. head is an abstraction over x, the value to remember, and done, a private name to communicate to the next agent in the queue when it has yielded its value. tail takes as an argument the name of the link to the last head cell in the queue. When the tail receives a new put request, it creates a new head cell that waits to be receive this name as input before being ready to output its value. A new name done is introduced to link the tail to this new head agent. When the tail itself comes to the real head of the queue, it simply becomes an empty queue, since this means there are no more values to get.

Let us see just a few intermediate states resulting from the following system:

```
queue & (put,a)∧(put,b)∧nil
```

with (put,a) we reduce to:

```
done\( head@(a,done)
     & tail@done)
& (put,b)∧nil
```

which further reduces to:

```
done\(( (get,a)∧done∧nil
      & (put,x?) → done'\ ( done→head@(x,done') & tail@done')
        | done→queue )
      & (put,b)∧nil)
```

With (put,b) we get:

done\ ((get,a)∧done∧nil
      & done'\ (done→head@(b,done')
          & tail@done'))

which finally reduces to:

done\done'\((get,a)∧done∧nil
      & done→head@(b,done')
      & (put,x?) → done\ (done' →head@(x,done) & tail@done)
      | done' →queue)

Note that the local name done in tail is α-converted to done' to avoid the conflict with the free name done in the expression tail@done. Also, the scope of done has expanded as well to permit the communication (put,b). If a further put were required, the innermost done would have to be α-converted to done'' and migrated outward to permit the communication.

4.4 Numbers

Our examples so far have avoided arithmetic. We could have provided numbers as primitives in our calculus, but it is more satisfying to provide an encoding that allows us to view them just as any other kind of agent. A natural place to look is at the standard encodings into the λ calculus [6].

First, we need Boolean values encoded as agents. Booleans are used in practice for making a choice between two alternatives, so:

true := (a?,b?) → a

false := (a?,b?) → b

With this interpretation, we can also define:

neg := a? → a@(false,true)

and := (a?,b?) → a@(b,a)

or := (a?,b?) → a@(a,b)

So, for example,

neg@true   ⟶   false

Our encoding of natural (non-negative) numbers differs only slightly from the standard one. Instead of viewing an expression such as $1 + 2$ as a function $+$ applied to the values 1 and 2, we interpret it as syntactic sugar for applying the tuple $(+, 2)$ to the agent 1, i.e., as $1@(+, 2)$. That is, $+$ is not a function but merely a name serving as a *message selector.* In this way we are later free to define other kinds of agents that are not numbers, but that also understand messages of the form $(+, a)$, exactly as one would when defining new classes in an object-oriented programming language.

We now encode the natural numbers as an abstraction over two values: a Boolean value indicating if the number is 0, and the number's predecessor, if any:

$$
\begin{aligned}
\text{nat} := (z?,p?) \rightarrow (\ &\text{iszero} \rightarrow z \\
&|\ \text{pred} \rightarrow p \\
&|\ \text{succ} \rightarrow \text{nat@(false,nat@(z,p))} \\
&|\ (+,n?) \rightarrow z@(n,\ (p+(n@\text{succ}))) \\
&|\ (\times,n?) \rightarrow z@(0,\ (n+(p\times n))) \\
&|\ ...\ )
\end{aligned}
$$

where $0 := \text{nat@(true,nil)}$.

Now it is easy to see that $0@\text{iszero} \longrightarrow$ true and $0@\text{succ@iszero} \longrightarrow$ false. Addition and multiplication are defined in the usual way. If m is zero then m+n evaluates to n, otherwise it evaluates to p plus the successor of n, where p is m's predecessor. Note how the Boolean value z is used to choose between the two possible continuations.

4.5 Actors

As a final example, let us consider the problem of modelling actors. Actors are computational entities that communicate by asynchronous message-passing [1, 18]. An actor consists of a queue of pending messages and a "behaviour" that accepts and responds to messages. Every actor is associated with a unique "mail address" used to receive messages. An actor may know the mail addresses of other actors which are its acquaintances. When an actor accepts a message, it can do three things:

1. Create new actors.

2. Send messages to its acquaintances.

3. Specify the replacement behaviour to handle the next message.

The replacement behaviour may be specified at any time, thus permitting an actor to begin processing the next message concurrently with the processing of the current one.

Let us consider Hewitt's standard example of a factorial actor written in a version of Agha's Simple Actor Language, SAL [1, 30].

```
def recFact accept fact:[n,client] ⇒
              become self ;
              if (n=0)
              then send result:[1] to client
```

```
        else  let c = new factCust with [n,client]
                 in { send fact:[n−1,c] to self }
def factCust with [n,c] accept result:[k] ⇒ send result:[n×k] to c
```

The behaviour recFact accepts requests of the form fact:[n,client] to compute the factorial of n and eventually causes the message: result:[*factorial of n*] to be sent back to the client. If the request is for the factorial of 0, the factorial actor responds immediately. Otherwise it dynamically creates a customer whose acquaintances are n and client, and it sends itself a request to compute the factorial of n−1 and send the result to the customer. The customer will eventually receive this result, compute the product of n and the factorial of n−1 and it will send the value to the client. For a request to compute n factorial, then, recFact will end up creating n customers, thus simulating an execution stack. Since recFact maintains no state information itself (it uses the customer to remember the original client) it immediately specifies its replacement as self to begin processing the next message. As a consequence, the factorial actor may service multiple requests concurrently.

A plausible and straightforward translation of recFact into OC is as follows:

```
recFact := id? → (id,fact,n?,client?) → ( recFact@id
                                        & n @ iszero @
                                          ( ((client,result,1)∧nil),
                                            (new\( factCust@(new,n,client)
                                                 & (id,fact,n-1,new)∧nil)))))
factCust := (id?,n?,c?) → (id,result,k?) → (c,result,n×k)∧nil
```

A behaviour is simply an abstraction whose arguments are the actor's id and its acquaintances, if any. Actor messages are represented as tuples in which the first argument is the actor's id, the second the message selector, and the remaining arguments the contents of the message. An actor may become self by spawning a copy of its behaviour, as recFact does immediately upon receiving a request. A new actor is created by introducing a new name, new, and binding it to a new instance of factCust.

Note that we have opted for a lazy interpretation. The agents that will evaluate the resulting arithmetic expressions are passed around rather than the final results.

5   Our Requirements, Reconsidered

Although a full treatment of how to model features of various concurrent object-oriented languages is beyond the scope of this paper (see, however, [34] for a CCS framework for modelling such languages), let us briefly review our informal requirements to see how OC addresses them.

First, we wish to view objects as agents encapsulating services. Let us suppose that all remote communications take one of the following two forms:

1. (request, *oid, selector, contents, reply-address*)

2. (reply, *reply-address, reply*)

Then, to send a message m with contents a to object x and obtain a reply, one may use the following protocol:

rid\(((request,x,m,a,rid)∧(reply,rid,val?)→...)

More precisely, since the value obtained should be passed on to some expression continuation, we may abstract the calling sequence as follows:

call := (x?,m?,a?,econt?) → rid\(((request,x,m,a,rid) ∧ (reply,rid,val?) → econt@val))

Thus, to call x as before with the continuation c, we simply instantiate call@(x,m,a,c).

State change can clearly be modelled, as shown even in the semaphore examples. Unique object identifiers are provided by restriction and scope extrusion. As objects are agents, they have full control over their communications. Non-uniform service availability can be readily specified, as shown by the stack and queue examples. Internal concurrency and multiple pending requests are illustrated by the recursive factorial agent. The ability to generate unique reply addresses is essential for managing multiple pending requests. Finally, objects as systems of more primitive objects and as functional compositions of various abstractions has been shown in several of the examples.

We have not yet demonstrated how inheritance and overriding can be accurately modelled, but we conjecture that the approach of Cook [13] will work well here. To give a flavour of this approach, let us abstract from the stack example given earlier and introduce *generators* for stacks:

emptyGen := sub? → (sub@nil
             | (push,x?) → stackGen@sub@(x,emptyGen@sub))

stackGen := sub? → (top?,rest?) →
                         (sub@(top,rest)
                         | (pop,top) ∧ rest
                         | (push,x?) → stackGen@sub@(x,stackGen@sub@(top,rest)))

The new variable sub may be bound to an abstraction of a new service in order to extend or override the services already provided. It is provided with the top of the stack and the rest of the stack as parameters. Now, to obtain the original stack from the generator, we may define:

empty := emptyGen@nil

Note that nil@(top,rest) behaves like nil, and so adds nothing to the behaviour of emptyGen or stackGen. Now suppose that we want to add a new service peek that allows a client to peek at the top of the stack without popping the value off.

We may define the new service as:

peek := (top?,rest?) → (peek,top) ∧ stackGen@peek@(top,rest)

and the new empty stack as:

newempty := emptyGen@peek

Of course peek@nil is incapable of any action, which is correct for the case when the stack is empty.

The same approach could be use to define natGen, a generator for natural numbers. New message selectors to be understood by numbers could thus be defined, and existing ones could be overridden, as long as the parameter sub appears as the first choice.

6   Some Theoretical Considerations

Although we have provided operational semantics for OC, we have not shown that we can prove any interesting properties about OC agents, such as when two expressions denote the same behaviour, nor have we shown that any standard results from other process calculi carry over to OC. As we hope to recover as much as possible from previous work, let us briefly resume the differences between OC and other process calculi (mainly the π calculus), and summarize the problems to be resolved.

- *Tuple-based communication:* communications in OC are tuples of names and agent terms. Synchronization is by matching of free names to free names and names or agents to locally bound names (introduced by a ?). Free names in input patterns serve essentially the same function as ports in the π calculus, except that one may synchronize with respect to several free names instead of just a single port name. It is also possible to have input patterns containing no free names at all, permitting anonymous ("port-less") communications.

- *Functions are agents:* although several other higher-order process calculi have been proposed, and accurate encodings of the λ calculus into first-order process calculi have been demonstrated, to our knowledge only OC has proposed the unification of functions and processes through a single abstraction mechanism. (Though it should be noted that Boudol [8] has proposed a *cooperation* operator ⊙ which can be used to similar effect: $p \odot q$ forces p and q to interact until one of them is exhausted (i.e., equal to nil). Then a@v can be expressed by a⊙(v∧nil).)

- *Left-preferential choice:* the choice operator of OC is purely deterministic, preferring left-hand interactions to right-hand ones in the case of conflicts. This suggests that we lose some expressive power with respect to the summation operator of CCS or the π calculus, but in practice we are interested only in non-determinism arising from concurrency. Left-preferential choice makes it possible to override interactions in composing new agents much in the same way that we can override default behaviour when inheriting from a superclass in an object-oriented language. (A similar effect can be obtained using the restriction operator of CCS [34]). Furthermore, choice in OC is insensitive to internal actions, which is essential when expressing summands as compositions of other agents. We also suspect that this will help in developing a behavioural equivalence which is also a congruence, since we wish to distinguish agents only on the basis of their visible interactions.

There appears to be a faithful translation of the π calculus into OC. We offer (without proof) the following mapping (taking the version of the π calculus presented in [26]):

$$
\begin{aligned}
\Pi(\bar{x}yP) &= (x,y) \wedge \Pi(P) \\
\Pi(x(y).P) &= (x,y?) \to \Pi(P) \\
\Pi(0) &= \text{nil} \\
\Pi(P|Q) &= \Pi(P)\&\Pi(Q) \\
\Pi(!P) &= n := n\&\Pi(P), \quad n \notin fn(\Pi(P)) \\
\Pi((y)P) &= y\backslash\Pi(P)
\end{aligned}
$$

The reverse problem, of demonstrating a translation of OC to the π calculus appears to be more difficult, especially as there is no simple way to simulate the tuple-based communication of OC using ports. For example, in the system

$$(a,b)\wedge\text{nil} \ \& \ (a,x?)\to\text{nil} \ \& \ (x?,b)\to\text{nil}$$

a and b are used simultaneously as ports and as values to be passed. For arbitrary communications, any subset of the free names of the message may be needed to match an input pattern. This suggests that there will be an explosion of port names to model the various possible matchings. We expect, however, that an encoding exists, and that it can be closely modelled after the translation of the higher-order π calculus, HOπ, into the first-order one.

The translation of the lazy λ calculus is straightforward:

$$
\begin{aligned}
\Lambda(\lambda x.E) &= x? \to \Lambda(E) \\
\Lambda(E_1E_2) &= \Lambda(E_1)@\Lambda(E_2)
\end{aligned}
$$

Eager evaluation cannot be directly expressed in OC since there are no rules for reducing active sub-expressions of v in $a@v$ (or, for that matter, in $v \wedge a$). We could alter **Left** and **Right** to permit eager evaluation, but this would introduce an unwanted aspect of non-determinism since the Church-Rosser property (i.e., that evaluation order does not matter) does not hold in general for OC. Intuitively it seems as if it should hold, since any reduction within an output pattern is purely local and independent of context, but if the reductions are due to **Comm**, then we may lose something. Consider, for example: $(x?\to x)@(n\to\text{nil} \ \& \ n\wedge\text{nil})$. Lazy evaluation reduces this to $(n\to\text{nil} \ \& \ n\wedge\text{nil})$, which permits further interactions with the environment, whereas eager evaluation would reduce it in two steps to nil. As a consequence, we must either explicitly evaluate expressions *before* communicating them, if strictness is desired, or we must demonstrate for a particular case that evaluation order does not matter.

Note that these translations suggest that OC is actually a merge of the π and λ calculi, extended by | and $\sim$. Furthermore, since we can simulate the λ calculus, we may express Curry's fixed-point combinator as an agent:

$$\mathsf{fix} \stackrel{def}{\equiv} \mathsf{f?} \rightarrow (\mathsf{x?} \rightarrow \mathsf{f@(x@x)}) \; @ \; (\mathsf{x?} \rightarrow \mathsf{f@(x@x)})$$

which means that := is not strictly needed. For example, we can then express the ! operator of the π calculus as

$$\mathsf{fix@(bang?} \rightarrow \mathsf{p?} \rightarrow (\mathsf{p} \; \& \; \mathsf{bang@p}))$$

The principle problems to be explored are:

- Is there a translation of OC to the π calculus (or to another established process calculus) that preserves its operational semantics? If not, what conclusions can be drawn?

- What notion of behavioural equivalence is appropriate for OC? Since we should also factor out equivalent agents appearing in communications, perhaps the higher-order bisimulation of CHOCS [38] is called for.

- Can we develop a type theory for agents that allows us to reason about compositionality? How is type conformance related to the (stronger) notion of behavioural equivalence?

- Under what circumstances are eager and lazy evaluation equivalent for reducible terms appearing in communications?

7   Concluding Remarks

We have put forward some informal requirements for a calculus suitable for specifying the behaviour of active objects, and we have presented the syntax and operational semantics of a proposed object calculus, OC. We have illustrated the use of OC through a series of examples that highlights the requirements we have posed. The interesting formal properties of OC are unknown as yet, but we have indicated some of the key differences with existing process calculi and outlined a program of topics for further study.

In a larger context, we wish to use OC to explore:

1. *Integration of language features* for concurrent object-oriented languages, particularly reuse features and concurrency mechanisms.

2. *A type theory for active objects* in which a type is a specification of a "software contract" between an object and its clients, and a subtype is just a stronger specification.

3. *Language design and prototyping* by translation to executable specifications in OC.

An interpreter for the version of OC presented here has been implemented in Prolog. The implementation is very similar to the earlier one of Abacus [30], but all dependency on Prolog variables has been eliminated since the semantics of unification in Prolog is incompatible with that of communication in OC. In particular, α-conversion and variable substitution are directly implemented. If and when OC stabilizes, a more efficient implementation is planned as the Prolog version is impractical for large examples.

In the long term, we hope to use OC as the foundation for a new programming language — a "pattern language" for active objects — in which applications are constructed by composing reusable software patterns, much in the way that architectural designs can be composed from established architectural patterns [2]. Such a language would be used in two complementary ways: first, to design and develop reusable patterns of objects, and second, to compose applications from pre-designed patterns [32]. An object calculus is the first step to defining such a pattern language.

Acknowledgements

Many thanks to Michael Papathomas and Laurent Dami who offered considerable improvements to the presentation of this paper.

References

[1] G.A. Agha, *ACTORS: A Model of Concurrent Computation in Distributed Systems*, The MIT Press, Cambridge, Massachusetts, 1986.

[2] C. Alexander, S. Ishakawa and M. Silverstein, *A Pattern Language*, Oxford University Press, New York, 1977.

[3] P. America, J. de Bakker, J.N. Kok and J. Rutten, "Operational Semantics of a Parallel Object-Oriented Language," in *Proceedings POPL '86*, pp. 194-208, St. Petersburg Beach, Florida, Jan 13-15, 1986.

[4] P. America, J. de Bakker, J. Kok and J. Rutten, "Denotational Semantics of a Parallel Object-Oriented Language," Information and Computation, vol. 83, no. 2, pp. 152-205, Nov 1989.

[5] P. America, "A Parallel Object-Oriented Language with Inheritance and Subtyping," ACM SIGPLAN Notices, Proceedings OOPSLA/ECOOP '90, vol. 25, no. 10, pp. 161-168, Oct 1990.

[6] H.P. Barendregt, *The Lambda Calculus – Its Syntax and Semantics*, Studies in Logic and the Foundations of Mathematics, 103, North-Holland, 1984, (Revised edition).

[7] G. Berry and G. Boudol, "The Chemical Abstract Machine," in *Proceedings POPL '90*, pp. 81-94, San Francisco, Jan 17-19, 1990.

[8] G. Boudol, "Towards a Lambda-Calculus for Concurrent and Communicating Systems," in *Proceedings TAPSOFT '89*, ed. Díaz and Orejas, LNCS 351, pp. 149-161, Springer-Verlag, 1989.

[9] G. Bracha and Wm. Cook, "Mixin-based Inheritance," ACM SIGPLAN Notices, Proceedings OOPSLA/ECOOP '90, vol. 25, no. 10, pp. 303-311, Oct 1990.

[10] L. Cardelli, "A Semantics of Multiple Inheritance," Information and Computation, vol. 76, pp. 138-164, 1988.

[11] N. Carriero and D. Gelernter, "How to Write Parallel Programs: A Guide to the Perplexed," ACM Computing Surveys, vol. 21, no. 3, pp. 323-357, Sept 1989.

[12] W.D. Clinger, "Foundations of Actor Semantics," AI-TR-633, MIT Artificial Intelligence Laboratory, May 1981.

[13] Wm. Cook, "A Denotational Semantics of Inheritance," ACM SIGPLAN Notices, Proceedings OOPSLA '89, vol. 24, no. 10, pp. 433-443, Oct 1989.

[14] Wm. Cook, W. Hill and P. Canning, "Inheritance is not Subtyping," in *Proceedings POPL '90*, San Francisco, Jan 17-19, 1990.

[15] U. Engberg and M. Nielsen, "A Calculus of Communicating Systems with Label Passing," DAIMI PB-208, University of Aarhus, 1986.

[16] R. Helm, I.M. Holland and D. Gangopadhyay, "Contracts: Specifying Behavioural Compositions in Object-Oriented Systems," ACM SIGPLAN Notices, Proceedings OOPSLA/ECOOP '90, vol. 25, no. 10, pp. 169-180, Oct 1990.

[17] A.V. Hense, "Denotational Semantics of an Object Oriented Programming Language with Explicit Wrappers," Technical report A11/90, FB 14, Universität des Saarlandes, Nov. 5, 1990, submitted for publication.

[18] C. Hewitt, "Viewing Control Structures as Patterns of Passing Messages," Artificial Intelligence, vol. 8, no. 3, pp. 323-364, June 1977.

[19] C.A.R. Hoare, *Communicating Sequential Processes*, Prentice-Hall, 1985.

[20] K. Honda and M. Tokoro, "An Object Calculus for Asynchronous Communication," in *Proceedings ECOOP '91*, ed. P. America, LNCS 512, pp. 133-147, Springer-Verlag, Geneva, Switzerland, July 15-19, 1991.

[21] K. Honda and M. Tokoro, "On Asynchronous Communication Semantics," in *Proceedings of the ECOOP '91 Workshop on Object-Based Concurrent Computing*, ed. M. Tokoro, O. Nierstrasz, P. Wegner, A. Yonezawa, LNCS, Springer-Verlag, Geneva, Switzerland, July 15-16, 1991, to appear.

[22] D.G. Kafura and K.H. Lee, "Inheritance in Actor Based Concurrent Object-Oriented Languages," in *Proceedings ECOOP '89*, pp. 131-145, Cambridge University Press, Nottingham, July 10-14, 1989.

[23] J. Meseguer, "A Logical Theory of Concurrent Objects," ACM SIGPLAN Notices, Proceedings OOPSLA/ECOOP '90, vol. 25, no. 10, pp. 101-115, Oct 1990.

[24] R. Milner, *Communication and Concurrency*, Prentice-Hall, 1989.

[25] R. Milner, J. Parrow and D. Walker, "A Calculus of Mobile Processes, Parts I and II, " Reports ECS-LFCS-89-85 and -86, Computer Science Dept., University of Edinburgh, March 1989.

[26] R. Milner, "Functions as Processes," in *Proceedings ICALP '90*, ed. M.S. Paterson, LNCS 443, pp. 167-180, Springer-Verlag, Warwick U., July 1990.

[27] R. Milner, "Sorts and Types in the π Calculus," manuscript (RM15), Computer Science Dept., University of Edinburgh, December 1990.

[28] F. Nielson, "The Typed Lambda-Calculus with First-Class Processes," in *Proceedings PARLE '89, Vol II*, ed. E. Odijk, J-C. Syre, LNCS 366, pp. 357-373, Springer Verlag, Eindhoven, June 1989.

[29] O.M. Nierstrasz and M. Papathomas, "Viewing Objects as Patterns of Communicating Agents," ACM SIGPLAN Notices, Proceedings OOPSLA/ECOOP '90, vol. 25, no. 10, pp. 38-43, Oct 1990.

[30] O.M. Nierstrasz, "A Guide to Specifying Concurrent Behaviour with Abacus," in *Object Management*, ed. D.C. Tsichritzis, pp. 267-293, Centre Universitaire d'Informatique, University of Geneva, July 1990.

[31] O.M. Nierstrasz and M. Papathomas, "Towards a Type Theory for Active Objects," ACM OOPS Messenger, Proceedings OOPSLA/ECOOP 90 workshop on Object-Based Concurrent Systems, vol. 2, no. 2, pp. 89-93, April 1991.

[32] O. Nierstrasz, "The Next 700 Concurrent Object-Oriented Languages – Reflections on the Future of Object-Based Concurrency," in *Object Composition*, ed. D.C. Tsichritzis, pp. 165-187, Centre Universitaire d'Informatique, University of Geneva, June 1991, Submitted for publication.

[33] M. Papathomas, "Concurrency Issues in Object-Oriented Programming Languages," in *Object Oriented Development*, ed. D.C. Tsichritzis, pp. 207-245, Centre Universitaire d'Informatique, University of Geneva, July 1989.

[34] M. Papathomas, "A Unifying Framework for Process Calculus Semantics of Concurrent Object-Based Languages," in *Proceedings of the ECOOP '91 Workshop on Object-Based Concurrent Computing*, ed. M. Tokoro, O. Nierstrasz, P. Wegner, A. Yonezawa, LNCS, Springer-Verlag, Geneva, Switzerland, July 15-16, 1991, to appear.

[35] R.K. Raj and H.M. Levy, "A Compositional Model for Software Reuse," in *Proceedings ECOOP '89*, pp. 3-24, Cambridge University Press, Nottingham, July 10-14, 1989.

[36] D. Sangiorgi, forthcoming Ph.D. thesis, Computer Science Dept., University of Edinburgh, 1992.

[37] D. Taenzer, M. Ganti and S. Podar, "Problems in Object-Oriented Software Reuse," in *Proceedings ECOOP '89*, pp. 25-38, Cambridge University Press, Nottingham, July 10-14, 1989.

[38] B. Thomsen, "A Calculus of Higher Order Communicating Systems," in *Proceedings POPL '89*, pp. 143-154, Austin, Texas, Jan 11-13, 1989.

On Asynchronous Communication Semantics

Kohei Honda and Mario Tokoro*

Department of Computer Science,
Keio University,
3-14-1 Hiyoshi, Kohoku-ku, Yokohama, 223,
Japan

Abstract

This paper presents some results concerning equational theories for an elementary calculus based on a fragment of Milner's π-calculus. The system is interesting because it realises asynchronous message passing not by extending but reducing the original fragment, while preserving the computational power. The bisimulation based on a novel asynchronous transition system is introduced and studied. Presented results include congruence of the bisimilarity for the calculus, its relationship with two other asynchronous theories based on traces and failures, strict inclusion of its synchronous counterpart in the asynchronous theory, and the method called the $\mathcal{I}$ completion that transforms two asynchronously bisimilar terms into synchronously bisimilar ones.

1 Introduction

This paper presents some results concerning equational theories for an elementary calculus based on a fragment of Milner's π-calculus [22]. The calculus, which first appeared in its present form in [12], expresses asynchronous communication not by adding extra machinery to the original synchronous communication mechanism, but by *reducing* the original one. It is capable of expressing synchronous (or handshake) communication quite concisely in terms of its reduced set of constructs and can express various computational structures elegantly (cf. [12, 13]). These and other interesting findings prompted our investigation to construct a theory of concurrent computation purely based on asynchronous message passing.

The asynchronous communication considered here, is in its most unconstrained form. That is, we assume that a "sender" can freely send messages with no bound in the number of pending messages, and the "receiver" will consume a message out of many targeted to it in a quite arbitrary fashion (i.e. nondeterminism in the arrival order). The framework can be thought of as a kind of abstract representation of real-life distributed computing

---

*Also with Sony Computer Science Laboratory Inc. 3-14-13 Higashi-Gotanda, Shinagawa-ku, Tokyo, 141, Japan

environments [28, 15], or as a logically extreme communication framework where the other extreme is pure synchronous interaction in the form of, say, CCS [17]. The fact that a basic formal construct originally developed for synchronous interaction in process calculi can handle asynchronous interaction comes as a pleasant surprise.

The difference between asynchrony and synchrony in communication lies in whether the event of reception of communication is tied to the output (sender) system or not. Separating the sender from the event of reception abstractly represents the notion of *distance* between two communicating parties. From this viewpoint, the synchronous communication may be considered as a special case where this distance is always zero. Another viewpoint is that asynchronous communication *is* a special case of synchronous communication because it can be formulated using buffers composed of synchronously communicating agents. We do not, however, intend to give arguments for or against these standpoints. Our goal is to pursue formal computational and semantic constructions based purely on asynchronous interaction, and deepen our understanding of the true significance of this theoretically neglected communication paradigm in a formal setting.

In this context, the paper introduces an equational theory called *asynchronous bisimulation* defined for the elementary calculus, and studies its basic properties. The equational theory forms the basis of various investigation related with the calculus exposed elsewhere (cf. e.g. [13, 14]). Section 2 introduces the basic notions of the calculus. The way of presenting the basic transition relation is much simpler than our original formulation [12] due to the normal form representation of term expressions. Section 3 then defines the *asynchronous bisimulation* and studies its basic properties. We prove that the bisimulation is a congruence relation, show several alternative characterizations for the equivalence relation, and position it among other asynchronous theories. Section 4 tries to understand the asynchronous theory in relationship with its synchronous counterpart. We prove that the asynchronous bisimilarity is strictly more general than the synchronous one, and show that a method called the $\mathcal{I}$ *completion* can transform any asynchronously bisimilar pair of terms into synchronously bisimilar pair, without changing their (asynchronous) meaning. The method is effective to weak theories in general. Finally Section 5 concludes the paper.

Note. Throughout the exposition, $\stackrel{\text{def}}{=}$ denotes definitional equality.

2   The Calculus

This section introduces the reader to the basic definitions of the calculus, the semantic construction for which is the subject of the present exposition. There are some novel points in the formulation of transition rules, which is surprisingly simple because of the normal form representation of terms.

Syntax

The elementary calculus has its origin in a computationally complete fragment of the π-calculus presented in [22] (cf. [24, 19, 20]). Inheriting important construction by Milner, small syntactic changes given to the original formalism are the contraction of an output-guarded term to a message (i.e. $\bar{a}v.P$, a process which offers v through a port a, becomes $\leftarrow av$, a message to a target a with a value v), and introduction of a restricted form of recursive structure, in place of replication. These changes make the formalism smaller than the original, while retaining the same expressive power [12, 14], and let it embody the notion of *asynchrony* both in computation and communication. Various aspects of the calculus are currently being investigated (see e.g. [12, 13, 14]).

Definitions 2.1 *Syntax.* $\mathbf{N}$, $\widetilde{\mathbf{N}}$, and $\mathbf{V}$ are the sets of infinite (port) names, the set of finite sequences of names, and the set of infinite (structure) variables[1], respectively. Then the set of term expressions (or simply terms) $\mathbf{C}$ is given by the following abstract syntax.

$$
\begin{array}{llr}
\mathbf{C} \;=\; & \leftarrow \mathbf{NN} & \text{(a message)} \\
\mid & \mathbf{NN}.\mathbf{C} & \text{(a receptor)} \\
\mid & \{\mathbf{V}(\widetilde{\mathbf{N}}) = \mathbf{NN}.\mathbf{C}\}(\widetilde{\mathbf{N}}) & \text{(a recursively defined receptor)} \\
\mid & \mathbf{V}(\widetilde{\mathbf{N}}) & \text{(a variable with a parameter)} \\
\mid & |\mathbf{N}|\mathbf{C} & \text{(scope restriction)} \\
\mid & \mathbf{C}, \mathbf{C} & \text{(concurrent composition)} \\
\mid & \Lambda & \text{(the null term)} \quad \blacksquare
\end{array}
$$

Conventions 2.2

   (i) $a, b, c, ..$ range over $\mathbf{N}$.
   (ii) $\tilde{a}, \tilde{b}, \tilde{c}, ..$ range over $\widetilde{\mathbf{N}}$.
   (iii) $X, Y, Z, ..$ range over $\mathbf{V}$.
   (iv) $P, Q, R, ..$ range over $\mathbf{C}$. $\qquad\qquad\qquad\qquad\qquad\qquad\qquad\blacksquare$

We will assume that the constructor "," is the weakest in association, others being of the same precedence. When some ambiguity arises, we will use parenthesis as usual. Top level terms are often called *configurations*. For convenience, some parts of syntactic structures are given their respective names, as below.

Definitions 2.3

   (i) In $\leftarrow av$, a is called a *target* and v is called a *value*. When the value is insignificant, we will sometimes write $\leftarrow a$.
   (ii) In $ax.P$, a is called an *input port*, x is called a *formal parameter*, and P is called a *body*. When the formal parameter is insignificant, we will sometimes write $a.P$.
   (iii) In $\{X(\tilde{x}) = by.P\}(\tilde{a})$, the part $\{X(\tilde{x}) = by.P\}$ is called a *recursive structure*, of which $X(\tilde{x})$ and $by.P$ are called a *head* and a *body*, respectively. $\tilde{a}$ is called a *parameter* to the recursive structure.
   (iv) In $X(\tilde{a})$, X is a (structure) variable and $\tilde{a}$ is a parameter to the variable.
   (v) In $|v|P$, $|v|$ is called a *(scope) restrictor* and P is called a *body*. $|xyz|P$ denotes $|x|(|y|(|z|P))$. $\qquad\qquad\qquad\qquad\qquad\qquad\qquad\blacksquare$

Some intuitive understanding of each syntactic form will help. First, $\leftarrow av$ represents a message in transit, carrying a name v to a receptor which owns a as its input port name. A message resembles an argument for functional application. Then a receptor, say

---
[1]In [12], they are called *term variables*.

$ax.P$, resembles a function body, which receives (at the port a) a message and instantiate free occurences of x in P with the received value. A term such as $\{X(\tilde{x}) = by.P\}(\tilde{a})$ is a recursive variant of a receptor. Now an important construction $|v|P$ implies that free occurrences of v in P are *local* to P, or, in other words, different from any other v out of its scope. Combined with recursive structures, it gives to the formalism capability to generate new port names unboundedly. P, Q is a *concurrent composition* of P and Q, written $P|Q$ in CCS and π-calculus. Finally Λ is syntactic convention to express "nothing".

Three kinds of bindings play essential roles in the calculus.

Definitions 2.4 *Bindings.*

(i) In $ax.P$, the formal parameter x, occurring bound itself, binds free occurrences of the same name in the body.

(ii) In $\{X(\tilde{x}) = by.P\}(\tilde{a})$, names in $\tilde{x}$ at the head, occurring bound themselves, bind their free occurrences in the body. The variable X at the head, occurring bound, binds its free occurrences in the body. We hereafter assume that the names and the variables occurring free in the body is the subset of the names and the variable occurring in the head, and names in the head are pairwise distinct.

(iii) In $|v|P$, v of $|v|$, occurring bound, binds its free occurrences in the body.

$\mathcal{BN}(P)$ (resp. $\mathcal{FN}(P)$) is a set of bound (resp. free) names in P. $\mathcal{N}(P)$ is the union of these two. ∎

Then we have two kinds of *substitutions*. One is a name to a name, the other is a variable to a structure. Note the difference from e.g. the λ calculi, where we have no such decomposition.

Definitions 2.5 *Substitutions.*

(i) $P[v/x]$ denotes the result of substituting free occurrences of x in P for v, taking care of name collision as usual. α-convertibility among terms is defined in the standard way.

(ii) $P[\Upsilon/X]$ where Υ stands for some recursive structure, denotes the result of substituting free occurrences of X for the structure. ∎

Let us list some basic facts about substitution (cf. Chapter 1 of [10]).

Lemma 2.6 In (iv) and (v) let x and v be distinct.

(i) $P[x/x] \stackrel{\text{def}}{=} P$

(ii) $z \notin \mathcal{FN}(P) \Rightarrow P[w/z] \stackrel{\text{def}}{=} P$

(iii) $z \notin \mathcal{FN}(P) \Rightarrow P[z/x][y/z] \stackrel{\text{def}}{=} P[y/x]$

(iv) $P[w/x][v/y] \stackrel{\text{def}}{=} P[v/y][(w[v/y])/x]$

(v) $P[v/x][w/x] \stackrel{\text{def}}{=} P[v/x]$

(vi) $z \notin \mathcal{FN}(P) \cup \mathcal{FN}(Q) \Rightarrow (P[v/x], Q) \stackrel{\text{def}}{=} (P, Q[z/x])[v/x][x/z]$ ∎

We omit the proof. To prove (vi), one needs (ii), (iii) and (i) (in this order).

Finally the notion of the set of free input port names of a configuration, by which receptors in it are "ready to interact" with messages from outside, will become important later.

Definitions 2.7 The set of free input names of P, denoted $\mathcal{FI}(P)$, are inductively given by: $\mathcal{FI}(ax.P) \stackrel{\text{def}}{=} \{a\}$, $\mathcal{FI}(|x|P) \stackrel{\text{def}}{=} \mathcal{FI}(P) \backslash \{x\}$, $\mathcal{FI}(\{X(\tilde{x}) = by.P\}(\tilde{a})) \stackrel{\text{def}}{=} \{b[\tilde{a}/\tilde{x}]\}$, $\mathcal{FI}(P,Q) \stackrel{\text{def}}{=} \mathcal{FI}(P) \cup \mathcal{FI}(Q)$, and if P is in other syntactic forms we have $\mathcal{FI}(P) \stackrel{\text{def}}{=} \emptyset$. ∎

Structural Equivalence

The following structural rules define equivalence over syntactic representation. It was Milner [22] who first introduced the set of structural rules for formulation of the π-calculus and successfully utilized it. The spirit is that we let tacit and static semantics of various constructors represented in the structural rules, while expressing truly dynamic aspects of the system by transition rules. For port-passing calculi, structural rules play an essential role for tractable formulation of transition rules. The set of rules below basically follow Milner's construction, but are substantially weakened to make computational aspects as explicit as possible (it is even weaker than $\equiv$ in [12]).

Definitions 2.8 *Structural Equivalence.* $\equiv$ is the smallest equivalence relation over terms defined by:

(i) $P \equiv Q$ (where P is α-convertible to Q)

(ii) $(P,Q), R \equiv P, (Q, R)$

(iii) $|x|P, Q \equiv |x|(P,Q)$ $(x \notin \mathcal{FN}(Q))$

(iv) $P, \leftarrow av \equiv \leftarrow av, P$

(v) $\{X(\tilde{x}) = yz.P\}(\tilde{a}) \equiv yz.P[\tilde{a}/\tilde{x}][\{X(\tilde{x}) = yz.P\}/X]$

(vi) $P \equiv Q$ then $P, R \equiv Q, R$ and $|x|P \equiv |x|Q$. ∎

Note that $\equiv$ preserves basic properties of terms, i.e.

Lemma 2.9 For any P, Q, x, v,

(i) $P \equiv Q \Rightarrow \mathcal{FN}(P) \equiv \mathcal{FN}(Q) \wedge \mathcal{FI}(P) \equiv \mathcal{FI}(Q)$.

(ii) $P \equiv Q \Rightarrow P[v/x] \equiv Q[v/x]$. ∎

Proof Based on the inductive properties of $\mathcal{FN}(P)$, $\mathcal{FI}(P)$, and $[v/x]$. ∎

Another fact is that we can always transform a term expression into what we call a *normal form representation.*

Proposition 2.10 Let us call terms of the forms $\leftarrow av$, $ax.P$, and Λ, *primitive terms.* Then, for any $P \in \mathbf{C}$, we have $P' \equiv P$ such that, for some $m \geq 0$,

$$P' \stackrel{\text{def}}{=} |\tilde{w}|(P_1, P_2, ..., P_m)$$

where $P_1, ..P_m$ denote primitive terms. We call such P' (usually not unique) a *normal form representation* of P. Above we say $P_1, ..P_m$ are *active* in P'. ∎

Proof By simple application of structural rules based on the structure of terms. ∎

In the proposition above, we can write $P_1, P_2, \ldots$ etc. without any ambiguity (up to $\equiv$), due to the rule (ii) of Definition 2.8. Also note that, with P in a normal form, $\mathcal{FI}(P)$ is by definition the set of free input port names of active receptors in P.

 In reasoning about terms in normal form representation, the following notation is convenient.

Conventions 2.11 Γ, Δ, etc. range over a sequence of concurrent composition of primitive terms. ∎

The Transition

The essence of the notion of asynchronous communication lies in that, at the time of consumption of a message, its "sender" is not participating in the event any more. Intuitively, then, the sender side *cannot* observe how the messages it sends will be treated by the other party. This changes the foregoing semantic scenario based on "experiments by the outside synchronous experimenter" (cf. [17]) into the new one with an asynchronous experimenter, where one can always proceed one's experiments as far as sending to the target system is concerned, while generation of messages from the target is beyond his control. This notion is formally represented in our labelled transition relation.

 We first introduce *labels* for the transition.

Definitions 2.12 *Labels.* The set of labels **L** for interaction is given by the following abstract syntax.

$$\mathbf{L} \ = \ \tau \mid \downarrow\!\mathbf{NN} \mid \uparrow\!\mathbf{NN}\,. \ \ \blacksquare$$

Conventions 2.13 $l, l', \ldots$ range over **L**. Sometimes $\downarrow\!\alpha$, $\uparrow\!\beta$, etc. range over **L**. ∎

Definitions 2.14

 (i) $l[v/x]$ is defined as in the case of term expressions.
 (ii) $\mathcal{N}(l)$ is the set of names occurring in labels, where $\mathcal{N}(\tau) = \emptyset$.
 (iii) Two functions on labels are defined as: $\pi_1(\uparrow\!av) = \pi_1(\downarrow\!av) = \{a\}$,
  $\pi_2(\uparrow\!av) = \pi_2(\downarrow\!av) = \{v\}$, and $\pi_1(\tau) = \pi_2(\tau) = \emptyset$. ∎

From the viewpoint of "semantics by experiments", we can give the following intuitive meaning to three kinds of labels.

 (1) τ denotes the internal computation, i.e. communication occurring inside the configuration, thus unseen from the outside.
 (2) $\downarrow\!av$ means that the experimenter sends a message to the configuration.
 (3) $\uparrow\!av$ means the experimenter receives such a message.

Now the *interaction relation* defined below, shows how a configuration, after an experiment or an observation, evolves to the next stage. The element of the relation is of the form (P, l, P'), written as $P \xrightarrow{l} P'$.

Definitions 2.15 *Asynchronous Interaction.* Let $\tilde{w} \setminus v$ denote a sequence of names where the occurrences of v are taken away from $\tilde{w}$, $\{\tilde{w}\}$ a set of names in the sequence $\tilde{w}$. Then *interaction of terms*, denoted $\overset{l}{\longrightarrow}$, is the smallest relation inferred by:

IN :
$$|\tilde{w}|(\Gamma, \Delta) \overset{\downarrow av}{\longrightarrow} |\tilde{w}|(\Gamma, \leftarrow av, \Delta) \qquad (a, v \notin \{\tilde{w}\})$$

OUT :
$$|\tilde{w}|(\Gamma, \leftarrow av, \Delta) \overset{\uparrow av}{\longrightarrow} |\tilde{w} \setminus v|(\Gamma, \Delta) \qquad (a \notin \{\tilde{w}\})$$

COM :
$$|\tilde{w}|(\Gamma, \leftarrow av, ax.P, \Delta) \overset{\tau}{\longrightarrow} |\tilde{w}|(\Gamma, P[v/x], \Delta)$$

STRUCT :
$$\frac{P_1' \equiv P_1,\; P_1 \overset{l}{\longrightarrow} P_2,\; P_2 \equiv P_2'}{P_1' \overset{l}{\longrightarrow} P_2'}$$

where in COM we call $\leftarrow av, ax.P$ a *redex pair* or simply a *redex*. ∎

Note that:

(1) The presentation of the transition rules is surprisingly simpler than its first version in [12] (cf. [22]). The use of normal form representation and the lack of bound labels are the main source of its simplicity. However it is consistent with the original formulation, as shown in Appendix A.

(2) Intuitively, the transition system defines behaviour of a configuration as asynchronous interaction with the outside world or an experimenter. In this regard IN rule is essential in that it directly represents the asynchronous character of experiments. It says that the experimenter can send *any* messages he wants at *any* occasion. The notion is in sharp contrast with a usual input rule in process calculi, where the experiment can proceed only when some agent in the configuration is ready to interact with the experimenter's action (cf. Definition 4.1 later).

(3) From *computational* point of view, only τ transition is substantial, defining the mechanism of computation in this formalism. In this regard we may say that IN and OUT rules define *semantic* transitions (cf. [22, 12]). Thus consistency of these semantic rules with the computational rule becomes an intriguing question (see [14] for more discussions).

The second point is represented in the following proposition.

Proposition 2.16 For any $P \in C$ and a, v, $P \overset{\downarrow av}{\longrightarrow} (P, \leftarrow av)$. ∎

Several other facts regarding $\overset{l}{\longrightarrow}$ (cf. Lemmas 1-3 in [20]) will be useful for our later discussions. The first shows how free names in the configuration can be affected by transitions.

Lemma 2.17 *Free name lemma for* $\overset{l}{\longrightarrow}$.

(1) $P \overset{\downarrow av}{\longrightarrow} P' \;\Rightarrow\; \mathcal{FN}(P) \cup \{a, v\} = \mathcal{FN}(P')$

(2) $P \overset{\uparrow av}{\longrightarrow} P' \;\Rightarrow\; \mathcal{FN}(P) \cup \{v\} = \mathcal{FN}(P') \cup \{a, v\}$

(3) $P \xrightarrow{\tau} P' \Rightarrow \mathcal{FN}(P) \supset \mathcal{FN}(P')$ ∎

Proof Easy case analysis based on name occurrences in the initial and derived terms, using Lemma 2.9 for the rule STRUCT. The addition of $\{v\}$ in (2) corresponds to the possible removal of a name in the binding in OUT rule of Definition 2.15. ∎

The second lemma shows how substitution affects transitions.

Lemma 2.18 *Substitution lemma for* $\xrightarrow{l}$. For any P, P' and l,

$$P \xrightarrow{l} P' \Rightarrow P[v/x] \xrightarrow{l[v/x]} P'[v/x] \ .$$

with if $x \notin \mathcal{FN}(P)$ then $v \notin \mathcal{FN}(P)$. ∎

Proof By checking each transition rule and using Lemma 2.9. ∎

3 The Asynchronous Bisimulation

This section introduces the equivalence relation called *asynchronous bisimulation* and studies its basic properties.

Bisimulation in the Context of Asynchronous Interaction

In the synchronous communication setting of process calculi, several equivalence notions have been proposed, i.e. bisimulation [21, 27], failure equivalence (or testing equivalence) [11, 23], and trace equivalence (for comprehensive treatment, see [1]). All of them can be defined over an arbitrary labeled transition system. Yet it is both surprising and pleasing that these notions are proven to be quite robust even in the setting of asynchronous interaction, for the underlying operational context is quite different here. For example, just as in the synchronous setting, the traces are not adequate to capture the operational behaviour of systems.

Definitions 3.1 *Traces*[2]. Let $\tilde{l}\backslash l_0$ be the result of taking away all occurrences of l_0 from a sequence of labels $\tilde{l}$. Then the set of (weak) *traces* of a term P, denoted $tr\langle P \rangle$, is given as follows.

$$tr\langle P \rangle \stackrel{\text{def}}{=} \{l_1..l_n\backslash\tau \mid \exists P_1..P_n.\ P \xrightarrow{l_1} P_1 \xrightarrow{l_2} .. \xrightarrow{l_n} P_n\} \cup \{\varepsilon\} \ ∎$$

An example which shows traces do *not* characterize the behaviour of communicating agents can be given using the nondeterministic summation operator defined below.

Definitions 3.2 *Nondeterministic summation.* With $c \notin \mathcal{FN}(P) \cup \mathcal{FN}(Q)$,

$$P \oplus Q \stackrel{\text{def}}{=} |c|(\leftarrow c,\ c.P,\ c.Q) \ . \quad ∎$$

With this definition, $P \oplus Q$ behaves like P or like Q nondeterministically. Easily we have:

---

[2]cf. Definition 3.27 later.

Proposition 3.3 $tr\langle P \oplus Q \rangle \stackrel{\text{def}}{=} tr\langle P \rangle \cup tr\langle Q \rangle$. ∎

Hence:

Fact 3.4 $tr\langle \leftarrow av \oplus (\leftarrow av, \leftarrow bw) \rangle = tr\langle \leftarrow av, \leftarrow bw \rangle$. ∎

But they should be differentiated since, put in a context

$$C[\cdot] \stackrel{\text{def}}{=} |ab|(ax.(by. \leftarrow xy), [\cdot]),$$

one may or may not emit $\leftarrow vw$ while the other surely does so. Thus the standard argument for the equivalence relation stronger than traces (cf. e.g. [17]) is still valid in the asynchronous setting, leading us to the definition of *asynchronous bisimulation*.

The Bisimulation

To formulate the bisimulation for our calculus, we need the notion of soundness of labels to avoid unnecessary collision between a newly created name and free names of terms.

Definitions 3.5 A label l of P is sound with respect to Q if and only if either $l = \tau$, $l = \downarrow \alpha$, or $l = \uparrow av$ with either $v \in \mathcal{FN}(P)$ or $v \notin \mathcal{FN}(P) \cup \mathcal{FN}(Q)$. ∎

Also let us have:

Definitions 3.6 $P \stackrel{l}{\Longrightarrow} Q$ is defined as $P \stackrel{\tau}{\longrightarrow}{}^* \stackrel{l}{\longrightarrow} \stackrel{\tau}{\longrightarrow}{}^* Q$ with $l \neq \tau$ and $P \stackrel{\tau}{\longrightarrow}{}^* Q$ with $l = \tau$, where $(\mathcal{R})^*$ denotes the reflexive transitive closure of a relation $\mathcal{R}$. ∎

Now we can define the notion of *asynchronous bisimulation* as follows[3].

Definitions 3.7 *Asynchronous bisimulation*[4]. P_1 and Q_1 are asynchronously bisimilar, denoted by $P_1 \approx_a Q_1$, if and only if $(P_1, Q_1) \in \mathcal{R}$ with

(i) For any $(P, Q) \in \mathcal{R}$, whenever $P \stackrel{l}{\longrightarrow} P'$ where l is sound with respect to Q, there exists Q' such that $Q \stackrel{l}{\Longrightarrow} Q'$ and $(P', Q') \in \mathcal{R}$.

(ii) $\mathcal{R}$ is symmetric[5]. ∎

We call $\mathcal{R}$ as above an *asynchronous bisimulation*. Then $\approx_a$ (the *asynchronous bisimilarity*) is the union of all the bisimulations. The closure property of bisimulation is useful for verifying various theoretical and practical properties.

The below shows several examples of bisimilar and non-bisimilar terms. (ii) is the example in Fact 3.4. In (iii) we see a pair which cannot be equated by the bisimilarity but still seem indistinguishable from one another in any context (cf. Proposition 3.30).

---

[3] *Weak* asynchronous bisimulation, to be strict.

[4] We replace Definition 10 in [12] with the present one.

[5] The requirement for symmetry (cf. [27]) can be weakened as shown in [22], but no difference comes about as a semantic theory.

Examples 3.8 *Examples of asynchronous (non-)bisimilarity.*

(i) $|c|(cx.P) \approx_a |a|(\leftarrow av) \approx_a \Lambda$.

(ii) $\leftarrow av \oplus (\leftarrow av, \leftarrow bw) \not\approx_a \leftarrow av, \leftarrow bw$.

(iii) $(\leftarrow av_1, \leftarrow bv_2) \oplus (\leftarrow av_1, \leftarrow cv_3) \not\approx_a \leftarrow av_1, \leftarrow bv_2 \oplus \leftarrow cv_3$. ∎

For other examples and applications of the bisimulation, see [12, 13, 14].

Finally, we need to extend $\approx_a$ to make it applicable to subexpressions in general. The extended $\approx_a$ can equate two expressions in the body of recursively defined receptors where structure variables may occur free. With this extension, we can discuss equivalence between any subexpressions of legitimate terms.

Definitions 3.9 Given $\{X(\tilde{x}) = yz.P\}(\tilde{a})$ and $\{X(\tilde{x}) = yz.Q\}(\tilde{a})$, we define

$$P \approx_a Q \quad \Leftrightarrow_{\text{def}} \quad P[\{X(\tilde{x}) = yz.P\}/X] \approx_a Q[\{X(\tilde{x}) = yz.Q\}/X]$$

and similarly for any subexpressions of P and Q. ∎

Now we are ready to discuss basic properties of $\approx_a$.

Substitutivity of Term Expressions

In CCS and other process calculi with general summation, the bisimulation is not a congruence relation because of the pre-emptive τ transition. That is, though we have $\tau.\Lambda \approx \Lambda$, $\tau.\Lambda + P \approx P$ does not usually hold. Our system lacks summation as a primitive[6], so that we may hope $\approx_a$ is preserved within any context. Name substitution presents subtle issues, but the following development validates the congruence of $\approx_a$.

First, Definition 3.7 almost directly tells us that:

Proposition 3.10 $\approx_a$ is an equivalence relation. That is, it is symmetric, reflexive and transitive. ∎

To show that $\approx_a$ is closed under every syntactic construction, one essential fact is that $\approx_a$ is preserved under concurrent composition with arbitrary messages. The form of composition itself is also often used in proving or disproving the asynchronous bisimilarity (cf. Proposition 3.15), which reflects its special position in our semantic theory (also see Proposition 3.19).

Proposition 3.11 With M being an arbitrary sequence of concurrent composition of messages, i.e. $M \equiv (\leftarrow a_1v_1, \leftarrow a_2v_2, .., \leftarrow a_nv_n)$ $(n \geq 0)$, we have

$$P \approx_a Q \quad \Rightarrow \quad (P, M) \approx_a (Q, M) \quad \blacksquare$$

---

[6]which does not mean that it cannot express branching structures [12, 13].

Proof By proving that the relation $\mathcal{R} \overset{\text{def}}{=} \{((P,M),\,(Q,M)) \mid P\approx_a Q\}$ is an asynchronous bisimulation. The only non-trivial case is when $(P,M) \overset{\tau}{\longrightarrow} P''$ and one of the redex for this τ transition is in M. Then there should be a message, say $\leftarrow av$, in M, so that $M \equiv (M', \leftarrow av)$ and that $P \overset{\downarrow av}{\longrightarrow} (P, \leftarrow av) \overset{\tau}{\longrightarrow} P'$ with $P'' \equiv (P', M')$. But because $P \approx_a Q$, we have, for some $Q' \approx_a P'$, $Q \overset{\downarrow av}{\Longrightarrow} Q'$, and $((P', M'), (Q', M')) \in \mathcal{R}$ as required. ∎

Note that the converse is not true, that is,

Proposition 3.12 $(P, \leftarrow av) \approx_a (Q, \leftarrow av)$ does not imply $P \approx_a Q$. ∎

Proof Take a pair

$$P \overset{\text{def}}{=} \leftarrow b, b.Q, \qquad Q \overset{\text{def}}{=} \{X(xy) = xz.(\leftarrow xz, \leftarrow y, y.X(xy))\}(ab)$$

and show that $(P, \leftarrow av) \approx_a (Q, \leftarrow av)$ but $P \not\approx_a Q$. ∎

The above implies that pending messages in a configuration play an essential role in our semantic framework.

Now the substitutivity for concurrent composition and scope restriction can easily be obtained.

Proposition 3.13 For any P, Q, R and x,

(i) $P \approx_a Q \;\Rightarrow\; |x|P \approx_a |x|Q$.
(ii) $P \approx_a Q \;\Rightarrow\; (P, R) \approx_a (Q, R)$ ∎

Proof

(i) Take the relation $\{(|x|P, |x|Q) \mid P \approx_a Q\} \cup \approx_a$. For input, we use Proposition 3.11 above.
(ii) Take the relation $\{((P, R), (Q, R)) \mid P \approx_a Q\}$ where R is an arbitrary term. We use (i) above for τ transitions. ∎

What is subtle is the substitutivity of expressions for a body of a receptor. The following non-trivial lemma, established by extensively using Lemmas 2.6 and 2.18, is essential for proving it.

Lemma 3.14 For any P, Q, v and x, $P \approx_a Q \;\Rightarrow\; P[v/x] \approx_a Q[v/x]$. ∎

Proof See Appendix B. ∎

Now we can show that the asynchronous bisimulation is indeed preserved by the prefix operation in constructing a receptor, and consequently also by recursively defined receptors.

Proposition 3.15 For any P, Q and a, x,

$$P \approx_a Q \;\Rightarrow\; ax.P \approx_a ax.Q \;.\; ∎$$

Proof We take the relation

$$\mathcal{R} = \{((ax.P,\ M),\ (ax.Q,\ M))\} \cup \approx_a$$

where $P \approx_a Q$ and M is zero or more messages. For input and output, the resulting pair is still in $\mathcal{R}$. For τ transition, we should consider the pair $((P[v/x], M'),\ (Q[v/x], M'))$ where $P \approx_a Q$. But we know by Lemma 3.14 and Proposition 3.13 that they are in $\approx_a$, i.e. in $\mathcal{R}$. Thus $\mathcal{R}$ is a bisimulation, concluding the proof. ∎

Proposition 3.16 Given any well-formed $\{X(\tilde{x}) = yz.P\}(\tilde{a})$ and $\{X(\tilde{x}) = yz.Q\}(\tilde{a})$,

$$P \approx_a Q \ \Rightarrow \ \{X(\tilde{x}) = yz.P\}(\tilde{a}) \approx_a \{X(\tilde{x}) = yz.Q\}(\tilde{a}) \ .$$

with $P \approx_a Q$ as defined in Definition 3.9. ∎

Proof With $\Upsilon_1 \overset{\text{def}}{=} \{X(\tilde{x}) = yz.P\}$ and $\Upsilon_2 \overset{\text{def}}{=} \{X(\tilde{x}) = yz.Q\}$, and also using the structural rule for recursion (cf. Definition 2.8), what we should prove is

$$P[\Upsilon_1/X] \approx_a Q[\Upsilon_2/X] \ \Rightarrow \ (yz.P[\Upsilon_1/X])[\tilde{a}/\tilde{x}] \approx_a (yz.Q[\Upsilon_2/X])[\tilde{a}/\tilde{x}] \ .$$

It is easy to see that the above case is reduced to the substitutivity of expressions in prefix operation and substitution, already proved in Proposition 3.15 and Lemma 3.14. ∎

Summarising Propositions 3.13, 3.15 and 3.16, we have:

Proposition 3.17 $\approx_a$ *is a congruence relation.* ∎

Thus two asynchronously bisimilar expressions can be used interchangeably as a part of any composite systems as far as we are based on our asynchronous semantic theory. Moreover another study not presented here shows that such a pair *does* behave quite compatibly in any context (in the sense that they will affect their environment identically). In this context, discussions in Section 4 provide an interesting comparison between the asynchronous theory and its synchronous counterpart in regard of the discernibility of a pair of terms apparently indistinguishable in their behaviour (see also [14] for related discussions).

Alternative Characterizations

In the following, we give a series of characterization results for the asynchronous bisimilarity. They shed light on various aspects of this bisimulation, as well as providing us with alternative proof methods.

Input-less Bisimulation

The following definition and proposition are based on the observation that the preservation of equivalence under composition with arbitrary messages is the crucial element for $\approx_a$.

Definitions 3.18   We define $\xrightarrow{\lceil a,\tau}$ where l is the subset of $\xrightarrow{l}$ as the smallest relation inferred by the rules in Definition 2.15 minus IN rule.   ∎

Proposition 3.19 $P_1 \approx_a Q_1$ if and only if $(P_1, Q_1) \in \mathcal{R}$ where for any $(P, Q) \in \mathcal{R}$ we have, in terms of $\xrightarrow{\lceil a,\tau}$, whenever $P \xrightarrow{l} P'$ where l is sound with respect to Q, there exists Q' such that $Q \xRightarrow{l} Q'$ and $(P', Q') \in \mathcal{R}$, and:

(i) $\mathcal{R}$ is symmetric.

(ii)   For any P, Q and $\leftarrow av$, $(P, Q) \in \mathcal{R} \;\Rightarrow\; ((P, \leftarrow av), (Q, \leftarrow av)) \in \mathcal{R}$.   ∎

Proof   The clause (ii) above is exactly what IN transition means for the bisimulation property.   ∎

The result is a repercussion of Proposition 2.16 which says every term is capable of performing *any* input transition. Thus, naturally, to check whether one party can simulate an input transition of the other is vacuous as a verification of the capability itself, but is significant only in terms of the constraint that *the resulting configurations are still in the closure*, hence Proposition 3.19. The fact is well reflected in the construction of the relation in e.g. the proof of Propositions 3.15.

Restricting Input Labels

Another and possibly more enlightening characterization comes from a question asking whether we really need all the possible labels for input. As we noted, the significance of IN rule does not lie in expressing the concerned term's capability (to perform the transition), but as a probe to know potential behaviour of the expression by putting a message in it (cf. Proposition 2.16). The following result is significant in this respect. The proof is direct from the definition of $\xrightarrow{l}$ and omitted.

Proposition 3.20   Suppose $P' \equiv (P, \leftarrow av)$, or equivalently $P \xrightarrow{\downarrow av} P'$, with $a \notin \mathcal{FI}(P)$. Then the following holds.

(i) $P' \xrightarrow{\downarrow bw} Q' \;\Leftrightarrow\; P \xrightarrow{\downarrow bw} Q \wedge Q' \equiv (Q, \leftarrow av)$.

(ii) $P' \xrightarrow{\uparrow bw} Q' \;\Leftrightarrow\; P \xrightarrow{\uparrow bw} Q \wedge Q' \equiv (Q, \leftarrow av) \;\vee\; \leftarrow bw \stackrel{\text{def}}{=} \leftarrow av \wedge Q' \equiv P$.

(iii) $P' \xrightarrow{\tau} Q' \;\Leftrightarrow\; P \xrightarrow{\tau} Q \wedge Q' \equiv (Q, \leftarrow av)$.   ∎

These facts show that the possible transitions of a term after receiving a message whose target receptor is not active, is exactly as before (except a trivial case of the output of that very message). This observation leads us to the following result, which gives us another characterization of the bisimilarity.

Proposition 3.21   We say $P_1 \approx_a^\star Q_1$ when $(P_1, Q_1) \in \mathcal{R}$ with

(i)   For any $(P, Q) \in \mathcal{R}$, whenever $P \xrightarrow{l} P'$ where l is sound with respect to Q and, if l is $\downarrow av$, $a \in \mathcal{FI}(P)$, then there exists Q' such that $Q \xRightarrow{l} Q'$ and $(P', Q') \in \mathcal{R}$.

(ii) $\mathcal{R}$ is symmetric.

Then $P_1 \approx_a Q_1$ if and only if $P_1 \approx_a^* Q_1$. ∎

Proof
($\Rightarrow$) By showing that $\approx_a$ is a relation satisfying the conditions.
($\Leftarrow$) We construct a relation $\mathcal{R} \stackrel{\text{def}}{=} \{((P, M), (Q, M))\}$ where $P \approx_a^* Q$ and, with $n > 0$ and $a_i \notin \mathcal{FI}(P) \cap \mathcal{FI}(Q)$, $M \equiv (\leftarrow a_1 v_1, .., a_n v_n)$, to show that it is a bisimulation. But Proposition 3.20 tells us that all the one-step transitions from $(P, \leftarrow a_1 v_1, .., a_n v_n)$ where $n \geq 1$ and $a_i \notin \mathcal{FI}(P)$, can be inferred from transitions starting from P except the trivial case of the output of one of $\leftarrow a_i v_i$'s. This establishes the closure property of $\mathcal{R}$. Alternatively, we can do without the construction by proving the analogue of Proposition 3.11 for $\approx_a^*$, from which the result is immediate. ∎

A minor variant of the above proposition is:

Corollary 3.22 If we change "$\mathcal{FI}(P)$" in Proposition 3.21 to "some $\mathcal{F} \supset \mathcal{FI}(P)$", the same holds. ∎

Proof The argument of Proposition 3.20 is still valid. ∎

Finally we note that, though these results may seem to suggest that a more restricted kind of IN rule will suffice, we still need the full generality of IN rule for sound formulation of the asynchronous interaction semantics. Interested readers may consult Appendix C.

Bisimilarity as a Weak Theory

It is well-known that the weak bisimulation in general can be characterised by weak transitions, i.e. transitions which ignore τ's. Not only the same holds for the asynchronous bisimilarity (which is not a surprise), but it enables us to position the theory among other (asynchronous) weak theories.

Definitions 3.23 *Weak asynchronous transitions.* A multi-step transition $P \stackrel{l_1 l_2 \ldots l_n}{\Longrightarrow} Q$ ($n \geq 0$) with $l_1, .., l_n \in L \backslash \{\tau\}$ is defined when

$$P \stackrel{\tau}{\longrightarrow}^* \stackrel{l_1}{\longrightarrow} \stackrel{\tau}{\longrightarrow}^* P_1 \stackrel{\tau}{\longrightarrow}^* \stackrel{l_2}{\longrightarrow} \stackrel{\tau}{\longrightarrow}^* P_2 \cdots \stackrel{\tau}{\longrightarrow}^* \stackrel{l_n}{\longrightarrow} \stackrel{\tau}{\longrightarrow}^* P_n \stackrel{\text{def}}{=} Q$$

for some $P_1..P_n$. Specifically, $P \Longrightarrow Q$ denotes $P \stackrel{\tau}{\longrightarrow}^* Q$ for some Q. ∎

Conventions 3.24

(i) $t, t', ..$ range over $(L \backslash \{\tau\})^*$.
(ii) $\mathcal{N}(t)$ is the set of names occurring in t. ∎

Definitions 3.25 A label t of P is sound with respect to Q if and only if, for each label $l_i = \uparrow av$ in t, either $v \in \mathcal{FN}(P)$ or $v \notin \mathcal{FN}(P) \cup \mathcal{FN}(Q)$. ∎

Proposition 3.26 *Characterization of asynchronous bisimilarity by weak transitions.*
$P_1 \approx_a Q_1$ if and only if $(P_1, Q_1) \in \mathcal{R}$ where

(i) For any $(P, Q) \in \mathcal{R}$, whenever $P \overset{t}{\Longrightarrow} P'$ where t is sound with respect to Q, there exists Q' such that $Q \overset{t}{\Longrightarrow} Q'$ and $(P', Q') \in \mathcal{R}$.

(ii) $\mathcal{R}$ is symmetric. ∎

Weak (asynchronous) *theories* are those which can be characterized by the weak asynchronous transitions (possibly with the soundness condition) and abstract nature of the relation. We will show two such examples, i.e. asynchronous trace equivalence and asynchronous failure equivalence. Let $P \overset{t}{\Longrightarrow}$ denote $P \overset{t}{\Longrightarrow} P'$ for some P'.

Definitions 3.27 *Asynchronous trace equivalence.* We say P and Q are (asynchronously) trace equivalent, denoted by $P \approx_{ta} Q$, if and only if

(i) $P \overset{t}{\Longrightarrow} \;\; \Rightarrow \;\; Q \overset{t}{\Longrightarrow}$ (for any t of P sound for Q).

(ii) $Q \overset{t}{\Longrightarrow} \;\; \Rightarrow \;\; P \overset{t}{\Longrightarrow}$ (for any t of Q sound for P). ∎

Definitions 3.28 *Asynchronous failure equivalence.* Let us first formulate the notion of failures as follows. Given a pair P and Q, we say P has a failure $(t, \mathcal{L})$, where $\mathcal{L} \subset \mathbf{L} \backslash \{\tau\}$ if and only if, for some P',

(1) $P \overset{t}{\Longrightarrow} P'$.

(2) For all $l \in \mathcal{L}$, we have $\neg P' \overset{l}{\Longrightarrow}$.

Then P and Q are failure equivalent, written $P \approx_{fa} Q$, if and only if they possess the identical failures, where the equality of the failure set is relativised by the soundness condition in Definition 3.25 [7]. ∎

The failure equivalence is more generous than the usual one, in that it does not care about the divergence. We can of course give a more strict version[8], but here we will be content with the fact that this way of formulation allows us easier comparison with other theories.

Proposition 3.29

(i) $P \approx_a Q \;\; \Rightarrow \;\; P \approx_{fa} Q$

(ii) $P \approx_{fa} Q \;\; \Rightarrow \;\; P \approx_{ta} Q$. ∎

Proof

(i) Suppose that $P \approx_a Q$ and that P owns a failure $(t, \mathcal{L})$ with $P \overset{t}{\Longrightarrow} P'$ where t is sound with respect to Q. Clearly there is Q' such that $Q \overset{t}{\Longrightarrow} Q'$ and $P' \approx_a Q'$. But if $Q' \overset{l}{\Longrightarrow}$ with $l \in \mathcal{L}$ then $P' \overset{l}{\Longrightarrow}$ (assuming w.l.o.g. l is sound with respect to P'), which contradicts the assumption. Thus Q owns the same failure as P relative to the soundness condition. Similarly for the symmetric case.

---

[7]E.g. even if $l \in \mathcal{L}$ and $Q \overset{t}{\Longrightarrow} Q' \overset{l}{\Longrightarrow}$ above, we neglect the difference if l of Q' is not sound with respect to P'.

[8]However, our current stipulation is that this weak failure equivalence is more natural in the asynchronous setting.

(ii) Immediate from the definitions. ∎

What is more interesting is that these inclusions are indeed *strict*.

Proposition 3.30

(i) $\approx_{fa} \not\supset \approx_{ta}$.

(ii) $\approx_a \not\supset \approx_{fa}$. ∎

Proof

(i) By (ii) of Example 3.8 which has a family of differentiating failures $(\uparrow av, \mathcal{L})$, where $\mathcal{L}$ includes $\uparrow bw$.

(ii) By (iii) of Example 3.8. ∎

Thus the asynchronous bisimulation is positioned as strictly stronger than the failure equivalence, and the latter is again strictly stronger than the trace equivalence.

In the setting of synchronous interaction, the notion of *deadlocks* is essential in the operational understanding of failure equivalence and bisimilarity. Interestingly, the notion is still significant in the asynchronous setting, if seen in the (abstract) framework of distributed computing. A simple example is enough to understand the situation.

$$P \stackrel{\text{def}}{=} \leftarrow av \oplus \leftarrow bw \oplus (\leftarrow av, \leftarrow bw) \quad Q \stackrel{\text{def}}{=} \leftarrow av, \leftarrow bw.$$

A failure $(\varepsilon, \mathcal{L})$ belongs to P, but not to Q, with $\mathcal{L} \not\supset \{\uparrow av, \uparrow bw\}$. Or, alternatively, if P's summand is non-deterministically selected, bisimulation cannot hold after $\uparrow av$.

Now, interpreted in the synchronous setting, the property of P means that the environment should offer *both* the a-input and the b-input, to ensure that P can proceed computation. However, in the context of asynchronous interaction, they embody the fact that, if the environment waits with both ports ready, it will surely get *either* $\leftarrow av$ or $\leftarrow bw$. If not, however, it may possibly get nothing. But we should notice that this *is* the basic element of deadlocks in the real distributed computing environment! Thus reinterpretation from a different perspective recovers the operational significance of the original notion developed in an apparently dissimilar setting.

The above discussions connote the soundness of applying the new semantic framework to problems in the real-world distributed computing environments. Such applications of the asynchronous interaction semantics should be important and challenging research topics in coming days.

4 Asynchronous Theories through Synchronous Theories

This section studies the proper characteristics of the asynchronous bisimilarity in terms of the difference from its synchronous counterpart, referring to the related results in other weak theories.

The Synchronous Theory

To understand the proper characteristics of $\approx_a$, comparison with its synchronous counterpart is helpful. The synchronous theory is, though restricted to our syntactic construction, embodiment of classic behavioural equivalence for processes, hence to know the difference between two theories should be instructive to appreciate the uniqueness of our asynchronous theory.

The synchronous theory is defined with a different transition relation with another IN rule, which is more in the spirit of the foregoing synchronous experiments framework and indeed has almost the same functionality as the one found in [22], except ours uses the so-called *early instantiation* rather than the late one[9].

Definitions 4.1 *Synchronous interaction of terms*, denoted by $\xrightarrow{l}_s$, is the smallest relation inferred by the same rules as Definition 2.15, with $\xrightarrow{l}$ replaced by $\xrightarrow{l}_s$, except IN rule which is reformulated as

$$\text{IN}_s: \quad |\tilde{w}|(\Gamma, ax.P, \Delta) \xrightarrow{\downarrow av}_s |\tilde{w}|(\Gamma, P[x/v], \Delta) \quad (a, v \notin \{\tilde{w}\}) \quad \blacksquare$$

Thus the synchronous "input" experiments can only proceed when some receptors are ready to receive them, in other words (cf. Proposition 2.16):

Proposition 4.2 Let us write $P \xrightarrow{l}_s$ when $P \xrightarrow{l}_s P'$ for some P'. Then

$$P \xrightarrow{\downarrow av}_s \quad \Leftrightarrow \quad a \in \mathcal{FI}(P). \quad \blacksquare$$

As an elementary comparison between $\xrightarrow{l}_s$ and $\xrightarrow{l}$, it is easy to see the following.

Proposition 4.3 For a specific l, we let $\xrightarrow{l}$ represent all (P, Q) such that (P, l, Q) is in the transition relation. Then, for any α, we have

$$\begin{aligned} \xrightarrow{\uparrow \alpha} &= \xrightarrow{\uparrow \alpha}_s \\ \xrightarrow{\tau} &= \xrightarrow{\tau}_s \\ \xrightarrow{\downarrow \alpha} \xrightarrow{\tau} &\supset \xrightarrow{\downarrow \alpha}_s . \quad \blacksquare \end{aligned}$$

Proof Direct from the definition. For the last subset relation, we have a transition

$$|\tilde{w}|(\Gamma, ax.P, \Delta) \xrightarrow{\downarrow av} \xrightarrow{\tau} |\tilde{w}|(\Gamma, P[v/x], \Delta)$$

which effectively captures $\xrightarrow{\downarrow av}_s$. $\blacksquare$

To define the synchronous bisimulation, derived transition is introduced as in the case of the asynchronous one (the soundness condition is the same as in Definition 3.5).

---

[9]The consistency of early instantiation scheme with reduction relation ($\xrightarrow{\tau}$) which we regard more fundamental than transition relation is basis of our choice, though we do not present the argument here. In passing, however, let us note that "instantiation" only occurs in COM rule in $\xrightarrow{l}$ (hence no dispute on instantiation schemes), and that the synchronous transition using early instantiation is the only natural candidate for comparison with this $\xrightarrow{l}$ (cf. Proposition 4.3).

Definitions 4.4 $P \overset{l}{\Longrightarrow}_s Q$ is defined as $P\overset{\tau}{\longrightarrow}_s{}^* \overset{l}{\longrightarrow}_s \overset{\tau}{\longrightarrow}_s{}^* Q$ with $l \neq \tau$ and $P\overset{\tau}{\longrightarrow}_s{}^* Q$ with $l = \tau$. ∎

We now define another equivalence relation for our system, this time based on $\overset{l}{\longrightarrow}_s$. The new equivalence is called *synchronous bisimulation* and is given as follows.

Definitions 4.5 *Synchronous bisimulation.* P_1 and Q_1 are synchronously bisimilar, denoted by $P_1 \approx_s Q_1$ if and only if $(P_1, Q_1) \in \mathcal{R}$ with

(i) For any $(P, Q) \in \mathcal{R}$, whenever $P \overset{l}{\longrightarrow}_s P'$ which is sound with respect to Q, there is Q' such that $Q \overset{l}{\Longrightarrow}_s Q'$ and $(P', Q') \in \mathcal{R}$.

(ii) $\mathcal{R}$ is symmetric. ∎

The following holds for $\approx_s$ in our formal system. We can prove that the same is also true in the fragment of the π-calculus presented in [22] (consult [14] for the proof). In the full calculus, we have a counter example in [19] [10].

Proposition 4.6 $\approx_s$ is a congruence relation. ∎

Proof Proofs for restriction and composition are more straightforward than those for $\approx_a$. For substitution, it is along the same line of $\approx_a$ except in the case of input, where we use a slightly different argument. The cases for prefix and recursion can be handled in the same way as in $\approx_a$. ∎

Later it becomes meaningful to understand this bisimilarity as a weak theory, i.e. as a theory based on the weak synchronous transition.

Definitions 4.7 *Weak synchronous transitions.* A multi-step transition $P \overset{l_1 l_2 \dots l_n}{\Longrightarrow}_s Q$ $(n \geq 0)$ with $l_1, .., l_n \in L \backslash \{\tau\}$ is defined when

$$P\overset{\tau}{\longrightarrow}_s{}^* \overset{l_1}{\longrightarrow}_s \overset{\tau}{\longrightarrow}_s{}^* P_1 \overset{\tau}{\longrightarrow}_s{}^* \overset{l_2}{\longrightarrow}_s \overset{\tau}{\longrightarrow}_s{}^* P_2 \cdots \overset{\tau}{\longrightarrow}_s{}^* \overset{l_n}{\longrightarrow}_s \overset{\tau}{\longrightarrow}_s{}^* P_n \overset{\text{def}}{=} Q$$

for some $P_1..P_n$. Specifically, $P \Longrightarrow_s Q$ denotes $P\overset{\tau}{\longrightarrow}_s{}^* Q$ for some Q. ∎

Then, with the same soundness condition as defined in 3.25, we have a characterization result for synchronous bisimilarity, corresponding to Proposition 3.26.

Proposition 4.8 *Characterization of synchronous bisimilarity by weak transitions.* $P_1 \approx_s Q_1$ if and only if $(P_1, Q_1) \in \mathcal{R}$ where

(i) For any $(P, Q) \in \mathcal{R}$, whenever $P \overset{l}{\Longrightarrow}_s P'$ which is sound with respect to Q, there exists Q' such that $Q \overset{l}{\Longrightarrow}_s Q'$ and $(P', Q') \in \mathcal{R}$.

(ii) $\mathcal{R}$ is symmetric. ∎

---

[10] The counterexample is: $x\bar{y} + \bar{y}x \approx x|\bar{y}$ but $(x\bar{y} + \bar{y}x)[y/x] \not\approx (x|\bar{y})[y/x]$ with $x \neq y$. We can find another example which uses matching, as in: $[x = y]P \approx [x = z]P$ but $([x = y]P)[x/y] \not\approx ([x = z]P)[x/y]$ where x, y, z are all distinct and $P \not\approx \Lambda$.

Other weak theories can be defined just as in the asynchronous case.

Definitions 4.9 *Synchronous trace equivalence.* We say P and Q are synchronously trace equivalent, denoted by $P \approx_{ts} Q$, if and only if, for any t,

(i) $P \overset{t}{\Longrightarrow}_s \quad \Rightarrow \quad Q \overset{t}{\Longrightarrow}_s$ (with t sound for Q).

(ii) $Q \overset{t}{\Longrightarrow}_s \quad \Rightarrow \quad P \overset{t}{\Longrightarrow}_s$ (with t sound for P). ∎

Definitions 4.10 *Synchronous failure equivalence.* Given a pair P and Q, we say P has a synchronous failure $(t, \mathcal{L})$, with respect to Q, where $\mathcal{L} \subset \mathbf{L} \backslash \{\tau\}$ if and only if

(1) $P \overset{t}{\Longrightarrow}_s P'$.

(2) For all $l \in L$, we have $\neg P' \overset{l}{\Longrightarrow}_s$.

Then P and Q are synchronously failure equivalent, written $P \approx_{fs} Q$, if and only if they possess the identical failures, where the equality of the failure set is relativised by the soundness condition in Definition 3.25. ∎

As the following proposition shows, here again bisimilarity is the most strict among three theories (cf. Propositions 3.29 and 3.30). We omit the proof, but only note that the *same* examples as used in Proposition 3.30 are effective for proving the strictness.

Proposition 4.11

(i) $\approx_{fs} \subset \approx_{ts}$ but $\approx_{fs} \not\supset \approx_{ts}$.

(ii) $\approx_s \subset \approx_{fs}$ but $\approx_s \not\supset \approx_{fs}$. ∎

Inclusion

The first result concerning the relationship between $\approx_a$ and $\approx_s$ shows that $\approx_a$ at least includes $\approx_s$, that is, the asynchronous theory is no less generous than the synchronous one. The result is almost immediate from the preceding propositions.

Proposition 4.12 For any P and Q, $P \approx_s Q \quad \Rightarrow \quad P \approx_a Q$. ∎

Proof We show that, when $P \approx_s Q$ holds,

$$P \overset{l}{\longrightarrow} P' \quad \Rightarrow \quad \exists Q' \text{ s.t. } (Q \overset{l}{\Longrightarrow} Q' \wedge P' \approx_s Q')$$

holds (note that the transition relation is *not* the synchronous transition relation but the asynchronous one). This tells us that $\approx_s$ is an asynchronous bisimulation, hence $\approx_s \subset \approx_a$.

When $l = \uparrow \alpha$ or $l = \tau$, the result is immediate because of Proposition 4.3.

In the case $l = \downarrow av$, we have $P \overset{\downarrow av}{\longrightarrow} (P, \leftarrow av) \wedge Q \overset{\downarrow av}{\longrightarrow} (Q, \leftarrow av)$. But because $\approx_s$ is a congruence relation, we have $(P, \leftarrow av) \approx_s (Q, \leftarrow av)$ and the proof is done. ∎

Thus we have shown that $\approx_a$ equates no less terms than $\approx_s$ does. The next question is whether it equates the same class of terms as $\approx_s$ or it equates strictly more than the synchronous theory. For the purpose, we should find out if there are any pair of expressions which are equivalent in $\approx_a$ but not so in $\approx_s$. The following shows that such a pair does exist.

Definitions 4.13 $\mathcal{I}(a)$ *which does nothing.* We define a family of *identity receptors* as

$$\mathcal{I}(a) \stackrel{\text{def}}{=} \{X(x) = xy.(\leftarrow xy, X(x))\}(a)$$

for an arbitrary port name a. ∎

Immediately we have

$$\mathcal{I}(a) \equiv ay.(\leftarrow ay, \mathcal{I}(a))$$

and also, for any $n \geq 0$,

$$\leftarrow av, \mathcal{I}(a) \; (\stackrel{\tau}{\longrightarrow})^n \; \leftarrow av, \mathcal{I}(a) \,.$$

Thus the expression $\mathcal{I}(a)$ behaves as if it were nothing. And this nothingness of $\mathcal{I}(a)$ turns out to be important for our study of the difference between two equational theories.

Proposition 4.14 $\approx_s \subset \approx_a$ but $\approx_a \not\subset \approx_s$.

Proof The first half is Proposition 4.12.

For the second half, let us take the pair $(\mathcal{I}(a), \Lambda)$ (a can be arbitrary) and show that these two are not equivalent as far as $\approx_s$ goes, but *are* in the theory of $\approx_a$, so that it becomes a counterexample to $\approx_a \subset \approx_s$.

First, as $\mathcal{I}(a) \stackrel{\downarrow av}{\longrightarrow}_s$ but $\Lambda \stackrel{\downarrow av}{\not\longrightarrow}_s$ (of course Λ has no derivation whatsoever!), we know immediately $\mathcal{I}(a) \not\approx_s \Lambda$.

Second, take a relation $\mathcal{R} = (\,(\mathcal{I}(a), P), \, P\,)$, where P is any term in **C**.

(1) In case $(\mathcal{I}(a), P) \stackrel{\downarrow av}{\longrightarrow} (\mathcal{I}(a), P, \leftarrow av)$. Then clearly $P \stackrel{\downarrow av}{\longrightarrow} (P, \leftarrow av)$ where $(\,(\mathcal{I}(a), P, \leftarrow av), (P, \leftarrow av)\,) \in \mathcal{R}$. We can similarly verify when $(\mathcal{I}(a), P) \stackrel{\downarrow av}{\longrightarrow} (\mathcal{I}(a), P')$.

(2) In case $(\mathcal{I}(a), P) \stackrel{\tau}{\longrightarrow} Q$. The case $Q \equiv (\mathcal{I}(a), P') \wedge P \stackrel{\tau}{\longrightarrow} P'$ is trivial. The only remaining possibility is $P \equiv (P', \leftarrow av)$ for some P'. Then

$$(\mathcal{I}(a), \leftarrow av, P') \stackrel{\tau}{\longrightarrow} (\mathcal{I}(a), \leftarrow av, P') \equiv (\mathcal{I}(a), P)$$

As obviously $P \stackrel{\varepsilon}{\Longrightarrow} P$, this case holds.

(3) Because the symmetric case can be proved trivially, the relation $\mathcal{R} \cup \mathcal{R}^{-1}$ is a bisimulation. To know $\mathcal{I}(a) \approx_a \Lambda$, take $P \stackrel{\text{def}}{=} \Lambda$. ∎

Some remarks are due in terms of this inclusion result.

(1) Proposition 4.14 shows that the theory of $\approx_a$ thinks the term $\mathcal{I}(a)$ is nothing, while the theory of $\approx_s$ treats it as something different from nothing. This is semantic discussion. But then we should think about *computational* behaviour of this expression $\mathcal{I}(a)$, to find out that (while it may consume computational resources somehow) $\mathcal{I}(a)$ behaves as nothing in any computational context whatsoever. In other words, $\mathcal{I}(a)$ (for any a) *may never give any influence to its environment,* situated anywhere[11]. Thus, albeit intuitively, the computational meaning of $\mathcal{I}(a)$ is better captured in the theory of $\approx_a$.

(2) We have similar strict inclusion results between other pairs of weak theories, i.e. $\approx_{ts} \subset \approx_{ta}$ but $\approx_{ta} \not\subset \approx_{ts}$ and $\approx_{fs} \subset \approx_{fa}$ but $\approx_{fa} \not\subset \approx_{fs}$. It is easy to see that we can use the same pair of terms as in the proof of Proposition 4.14 for strictness. Thus the position of the pair of agents as that which tells difference between synchronous and asynchronous theories, seems somewhat universal. In fact we can verify two terms have the identical weak asynchronous transition graph; and any sound synchronous theory may not equate two terms whose traces are different.

We conclude this subsection by presenting two additional kinds of identity receptors. They are examples of those receptors which behave as nothing asynchronously but as something synchronously (i.e. which are asynchronously bisimilar to Λ but are not synchronously). There are infinite kinds of such receptors; it is known, however, that one can construct any such receptors by a certain syntactic formation rules from three basic ones, one of which is $\mathcal{I}(x)$ and the other two are as defined below. Of the two kinds, "eager" one will play an essential role in the $\mathcal{I}$ completion we will discuss soon.

Definitions 4.15 *Variants of Identity Receptors.*

(1) *A degenerated variant.* $\mathcal{I}_0(x) \overset{\text{def}}{=} xy. \leftarrow xy.$

(2) *An eager variant.* $\mathcal{I}_2(a) \overset{\text{def}}{=} \{X(x) = xy.(\leftarrow xy, X(y), X(x))\}(a).$

Let $\mathcal{I}_1(a) \overset{\text{def}}{=} \mathcal{I}(a)$ to conform to the above notations. ∎

Proposition 4.16 We have $\mathcal{I}_0(a) \approx_a \mathcal{I}_1(a) \approx_a \mathcal{I}_2(a) \approx_a \Lambda$, but any pair of these are *not* synchronously bisimilar. ∎

$\mathcal{I}$ Completion

We already know that the relation $\approx_a$ is strictly wider than $\approx_s$, and that at least the identity receptors of various forms constitute the difference. As we noted the same holds for other weak theories. The exact difference between these two bisimilarities, however, is not clear yet. To study this, a method called $\mathcal{I}$ completion is suggestive.

The $\mathcal{I}$ completion is a method which syntactically transforms $\approx_a$ into $\approx_s$ by filling concerned configurations with enough identity receptors. It uses $\mathcal{I}_2(a)$ just defined, instead of $\mathcal{I}(a)$ in order to cope with a certain invariant condition[12], namely, covering of

---

[11] When fairness is to be considered, the statement needs some modification.

[12] We know that an important subclass of **C** where we can have the same effect by an operation using $\mathcal{I}(a)$. but the discussion on this subclass is beyond the scope of the present exposition.

the free input ports of the configuration by identity receptors. More exactly, it transforms the set of terms which are asynchronously bisimilar and whose free names are bounded by some finite set, into synchronously bisimilar. The basic idea is to enable a term to emulate all the (essential) asynchronous transitions by synchronous transitions with the help of identity receptors. But then all the original synchronous transitions are emulated by the corresponding asynchronous transitions from the beginning (cf. Proposition 4.3), hence the desired result. The emulation is done at the level of the *weak* transitions, so that the operation transforms weak asynchronous theories in general into their synchronous counterparts.

Definitions 4.17 *The $\mathcal{I}$ Completion.* With $P \in \mathbf{C}$, let $\mathcal{F}$ be a finite set of port names. We define the function $\psi : \mathbf{C} \to \mathbf{C}$ as follows.

$$\psi(\Lambda) \stackrel{\text{def}}{=} \Lambda$$
$$\psi(\leftarrow av) \stackrel{\text{def}}{=} \leftarrow av$$
$$\psi(X(\tilde{a})) \stackrel{\text{def}}{=} X(\tilde{a})$$
$$\psi(ax.P) \stackrel{\text{def}}{=} ax.(\mathcal{I}_2(x), \psi(P))$$
$$\psi(|x|P) \stackrel{\text{def}}{=} |x|(\mathcal{I}_2(x), \psi(P))$$
$$\psi(P, Q) \stackrel{\text{def}}{=} \psi(P), \psi(Q)$$
$$\psi(\{X(\tilde{x}) = yz.Q\}(\tilde{a})) \stackrel{\text{def}}{=} \{X(\tilde{x}) = yz.(\mathcal{I}_2(z), \psi(Q))\}(\tilde{a})$$

Then the $\mathcal{I}$ *Completion* of P for $\mathcal{F}$, denoted by $\Phi_{\mathcal{F}}(P)$, is given as

$$\Phi_{\mathcal{F}}(P) \stackrel{\text{def}}{=} \mathcal{I}_2(\mathcal{F}), \psi(P)$$

where, with $\mathcal{A} = \{a_1, a_2, .., a_n\}$, $\mathcal{I}_2(\mathcal{A})$ stands for $\mathcal{I}_2(a_1), .., \mathcal{I}_2(a_n)$. ∎

It is easy to see that the function ψ is computable and total, hence the whole procedure is. Now we establish the emulation results, starting from the level of non-weak one-step transitions. First we give a preliminary definition.

Definitions 4.18 $\Phi_{\mathcal{F}}^*(P)$ is the smallest set constructed by the rule:

(i) $\Phi_{\mathcal{F}}(P) \in \Phi_{\mathcal{F}}^*(P)$.

(ii) $P \in \Phi_{\mathcal{F}}^*(P) \wedge a \in \mathcal{F} \quad \Rightarrow \quad P, \mathcal{I}_2(a) \in \Phi_{\mathcal{F}}^*(P)$. ∎

Now we show how the asynchronous one-step transitions in the original term are transformed into the synchronous ones, with a possible increase of an active identity receptor.

Proposition 4.19 With $P \in \Phi_{\mathcal{F}}^*(P_0)$ for any P_0 and $\mathcal{F} \supset \mathcal{FN}(P_0)$,

(i) $P_0 \stackrel{\downarrow av}{\longrightarrow} P_0' \wedge a \in \mathcal{F} \quad \Rightarrow \quad P \stackrel{\downarrow av}{\longrightarrow}_s P'$ with $P' \in \Phi_{\mathcal{F} \cup \{v\}}^*(P_0')$.

(ii) $P_0 \stackrel{\uparrow av}{\longrightarrow} P_0' \quad \Rightarrow \quad P \stackrel{\uparrow av}{\longrightarrow}_s P'$ with $P' \in \Phi_{\mathcal{F} \cup \{v\}}^*(P_0')$.

(iii) $P_0 \stackrel{\tau}{\longrightarrow} P_0' \quad \Rightarrow \quad P \stackrel{\tau}{\longrightarrow}_s P'$ with $P' \in \Phi_{\mathcal{F}}^*(P_0')$. ∎

Proof Use the normal form representation and check transitions. ∎

The second shows the reverse side, which states that all the synchronous one-step transitions in the terms after the completion are really covered (somehow) by the original asynchronous transitions.

Proposition 4.20 With $P \in \Phi^*_{\mathcal{F}}(P_0)$ and $\mathcal{F} \supset \mathcal{FN}(P_0)$,

    (i) $P \xrightarrow{\downarrow av}_s P' \Rightarrow (P_0 \xrightarrow{\downarrow av} \xrightarrow{\tau} P'_0 \vee P_0 \xrightarrow{\downarrow av} P'_0)$ with $P' \in \Phi^*_{\mathcal{F} \cup \{v\}}(P'_0)$.

    (ii) $P \xrightarrow{\uparrow av}_s P' \Rightarrow P_0 \xrightarrow{\uparrow av} P'_0$ with $P' \in \Phi^*_{\mathcal{F} \cup \{v\}}(P'_0)$.

    (iii) $P \xrightarrow{\tau}_s P' \Rightarrow (P_0 \xrightarrow{\tau} P'_0 \vee P'_0 \equiv P_0)$ with $P' \in \Phi^*_{\mathcal{F}}(P'_0)$. ∎

Proof

    (i) By noticing P may receive a message by P_0's original receptor or by identity receptor.

    (ii) Trivial.

    (iii) By noticing there can be a void τ transition between a message and an identity receptor. ∎

A small but essential corollary follows.

Corollary 4.21 Let us have $P \in \Phi^*_{\mathcal{F}}(P_0)$ with $\mathcal{F} \supset \mathcal{FN}(P_0)$. Then

    (i) $\mathcal{FI}(P) = \mathcal{FN}(P) = \mathcal{F}$

    (ii) $P \xrightarrow{l} P' \Rightarrow P' \in \Phi^*_{\mathcal{F} \cup \mathcal{N}(l)}(P'_0)$ for some P'_0 with $\mathcal{F} \cup \mathcal{N}(l) \supset \mathcal{FN}(P'_0)$. ∎

Proof (i) trivially holds by the form of P. (ii) is direct from Proposition 4.20 and Lemma 2.17. ∎

Based on preceding results we gain the emulation result at the level of weak transitions.

Proposition 4.22 With $P \in \Phi^*_{\mathcal{F}}(P_0)$ for $\mathcal{F} \supset \mathcal{FN}(P_0)$, we have

    (i) $P \xRightarrow{t}_s P' \Rightarrow P_0 \xRightarrow{t} P'_0$ for some P'_0 with $P' \in \Phi^*_{\mathcal{F} \cup \mathcal{N}(t)}(P'_0)$.

    (ii) $P_0 \xRightarrow{t} P'_0 \Rightarrow P \xRightarrow{t}_s P'$ for some P' with $P' \in \Phi^*_{\mathcal{F} \cup \mathcal{N}(t)}(P'_0)$, if t of P_0 is sound with respect to P. ∎

Proof

    (i) Using induction on the length of t, we check each transition by Proposition 4.20. The repeated applications of the proposition are possible because of the invariant conditions in Corollary 4.21.

    (ii) Similarly, using Proposition 4.19. ∎

Thus, relative to the parameterized set of names and neglecting inessential restriction (due to collision of names), we have clean correspondence between two weak transitions, including the closure property of derivatives. The main result in this subsection follows.

Proposition 4.23 For some finite set of names $\mathcal{F}$ let us have $\mathbf{C}_{\mathcal{F}} = \{P \mid \mathcal{FN}(P) \subset \mathcal{F}\}$. Suppose $P_0, Q_0 \in \mathbf{C}_{\mathcal{F}}$. Then the following holds.

(i) $P \in \Phi_{\mathcal{F}}^*(P_0) \quad \Rightarrow \quad P \approx_a P_0 \wedge P \in \mathbf{C}_{\mathcal{F}}$.

(ii) $P_0 \approx_a Q_0 \quad \Leftrightarrow \quad \Phi_{\mathcal{F}}(P_0) \approx_s \Phi_{\mathcal{F}}(Q_0)$.

(iii) $\Phi_{\mathcal{F}}(\Phi_{\mathcal{F}}(P_0)) \approx_s \Phi_{\mathcal{F}}(P_0)$.   ∎

Proof

(i) By Corollary 4.16.

(ii) ($\Rightarrow$) For some finite set of names $\mathcal{F}$, let us have:

$$\mathbf{R}_{\mathcal{F}} = \{(P,\ Q) \mid P \in \Phi_{\mathcal{F}}^*(P_0),\ Q \in \Phi_{\mathcal{F}}^*(Q_0) \text{ for } P_0, Q_0 \in \mathbf{C}_{\mathcal{F}} \text{ and } P_0 \approx_a Q_0.\}$$

Then we show that the union of all such relations, $\bigcup_{\mathcal{F} \subset_f N} \mathbf{R}_{\mathcal{F}}$, where "$\subset_f$" stands for "is a finite subset of", is a synchronous bisimulation. Assuming $(P,\ Q) \in \mathbf{R}_{\mathcal{F}}$ for some $\mathcal{F}$, we have a following sequence of inferences.

$$
\begin{aligned}
P \xRightarrow{t}{}_s P' \quad &\Rightarrow \quad P_0 \xRightarrow{t} P_0' \text{ with } P' \in \Phi_{\mathcal{FUN}(t)}^*(P_0') && \text{(by Proposition4.22 (i))} \\
&\Rightarrow \quad Q_0 \xRightarrow{t} Q_0' \text{ with } P_0' \approx_a Q_0' && \text{(by } P_0 \approx_a Q_0) \\
&\Rightarrow \quad Q \xRightarrow{t}{}_s Q' \text{ with } Q' \in \Phi_{\mathcal{FUN}(t)}^*(Q_0') && \text{(by Proposition4.22 (ii))}
\end{aligned}
$$

Note that for each of these inference steps, the soundness condition is automatically satisfied, specifically because of $\mathcal{F} \supset \mathcal{FN}(P_0) \cup \mathcal{FN}(Q_0)$. Finally, since we easily get $(P',\ Q') \in \mathbf{R}_{\mathcal{FUN}(t)} \subset \bigcup_{\mathcal{F} \subset_f N} \mathbf{R}_{\mathcal{F}}$, and as symmetricity is obvious, using the characterization of $\approx_a$ in Proposition 4.8, the proof is done.

($\Leftarrow$) Using Proposition 4.12. i.e. the fact $P \approx_s Q$ implies $P \approx_a Q$, in combination with (i) above.

(iii) By (i) and (ii) above.   ∎

Let us give some remarks on the result above.

(1) The clause (ii), which can be seen as another characterization result of $\approx_a$, tells us that the exact difference in two bisimilarities, induced by two IN rules, can be captured by some collection of identity receptors.

(2) As is easily guessed, the exact image of the above result holds for asynchronous and synchronous trace equivalences and failure equivalences. This suggests the universality of the effect of the completion for weak theories. Indeed the core of the completion method lies in that it makes synchronous weak transitions proceed much like weak asynchronous transitions, while asynchronous behaviour of the concerned term remains unchanged (cf. (i) above). This means that, in the light of the discernibility of terms' behaviour, what the completion does is to let the synchronous theory forget insignificant details (i.e. the capability to

consume a message and immediately process it). Note that, intuitively, when we send messages asynchronously, one may not know when they will arrive at the target, in which order, or whether they ever will or not. In this regard one may say that the obscuration is done rightly.

(3) (i) of Proposition 4.19 tells us that the completion *maximizes* the synchronous input transitions of the concerned term as far as the parameterized set of names allow, to have the synchronous input rule mimic the extravagance of the asynchronous IN rule. Also (iii) shows that the operation sends a term to some kind of the *saturated* state (in terms of the synchronous theory). These observations motivate us to understand the effect of the operation on a certain synchronous ordering. Assume given the *synchronous simulation preorder* denoted by $\sqsubseteq_s$ (which is the synchronous bisimulation minus symmetry). Then with $\mathbf{A}$ being any equivalence class of $\approx_a$ *within* some $\mathbf{C}_{\mathcal{F}}$, we have:

- $P, Q \in \mathbf{A} \quad \Rightarrow \quad \Phi_{\mathcal{F}}(P) \approx_s \Phi_{\mathcal{F}}(Q)$.
- $P \in \mathbf{A}, \ Q \in \Phi_{\mathcal{F}}(\mathbf{A})(\subset \mathbf{A}) \quad \Rightarrow \quad P \sqsubseteq_s Q$.

Thus the operation sends all these terms to the top element in the equivalence class ordered by $\sqsubseteq_s$. Seen conversely, it means that the top element can be characterized syntactically by the completion. This suggests that we can capture the difference between synchronous bisimilarity and asynchronous bisimilarity in a more precise way than the completion method.

In regard of (3), detailed study reveals that not only the top elements but also *all* the points in the ordering relation can be characterized in a syntactic fashion. This result has non-trivial semantic consequences, one of which is the existence of a "downward" (but not necessarily finitary) synonym of the $\mathcal{I}$ completion, that is, the *erasure* of $\mathcal{I}$'s. Unfortunately we should leave the presentation of these and other results concerning the inequational theories for the calculus, to another occasion.

5 Conclusion

Our development so far shows that the general semantic framework of concurrent computation can be constructed based on the notion of pure asynchronous interaction, with non-trivial difference from the foregoing semantic framework for synchronous interaction. At the same time, many semantic concepts developed in terms of the synchronous interaction can find their respective positions in the new framework after suitable reconstruction. As our study has just begun, however, intense investigation is necessary for the asynchronous interaction semantics itself, as well as for the calculus itself. Before concluding, we pinpoint two further issues.

- While the results about the asynchronous interaction semantics in the present exposition, can be applied to other formalisms, such as CCS and CSP (after suitable syntactic contraction) or Boudol's γ-calculus [6], various evidences strongly suggest that the capability to create new ports and pass them should be indispensable ingredients for constructing the general computation in the setting of pure asynchrony. Computationally we already gained some results [12, 13, 14] but what is intriguing is whether we can find the significance of these properties in the semantic context. Logical characterization will play an important role here.

- There is a notable work by de Boer, Paramidessi, and his colleagues [4, 5], which tries to capture asynchronous communication using the notion of the common black board which serves as a kind of global mail delivery system, with the assumption that a system does not hold generated messages in it, but emit them immediately. In this context, notice that Proposition 3.12 shows that the pending messages are the indispensable elements in the setting of asynchronous interaction. Thus the framework by de Boer and others can be regarded as a special case where one neglects pending messages (or assumes they will get consumed immediately by the environment). Yet it is probable that the restricted theory may form an important subclass of the asynchronous interaction semantics, where reasoning etc. is more tractable than in the general case. The point deserves further investigation.

We finally note that the way to express pending messages by syntactic terms in process calculi-related formalisms, which plays a crucial role in our semantic construction, was concurrently discovered by us (early 1990), by Meseguer [16], and by Nierstrasz [25].[13] We can even trace back the idea to the representation of asynchronous messages in the actor event diagram [7] in the context of the actor model by Hewitt and others [9, 2]. But semantic significance of asynchronous communication in the general theoretical setting in contrast to synchronous communication, seems not to have been studied so much, in spite of the early work such as [3]. Our work develops the theory of asynchronous interaction based on the clean semantic and computational construction of process calculi, especially upon Milner's work on π-calculus, to acquire the general theoretical framework of concurrent computation interesting in its own right.

Acknowledgements

We would like to thank Professor Robin Milner for active and beneficial discussions in the Geneva workshop. We heartily thank Professor Peter Wegner who read the first version of the paper and gave us valuable suggestions. Our thanks also go to Makoto Kubo for many discussions, especially in terms of the new formulation of transition rules in Definition 2.15. Vasco Vasconcelos pointed out several typographical errors and ambiguities in the final version, to which the authors are grateful.

References

[1] Abramsky, S., Observational Equivalence as a Testing Equivalence, *Theoretical Computer Science*, 53, 1987.

[2] Agha, G.: *Actors: A Model of Concurrent Computation in Distributed Systems.* MIT Press, 1986.

[3] Bergstra, J., Klop, J., and Tucker, J., Process Algebra with Asynchronous Communication Mechanisms, In *Seminar on Concurrency*, LNCS 197, 1984, Springer Verlag.

---

[13]Nierstrasz further developed the work in [26].

[4] de Boer, F., and Palamidessi, C., On the asynchronous nature of communication in concurrent logic languages: a fully abstract model based on sequences, In *CONCUR '90*, LNCS 458, Springer-Verlag, 1990.

[5] de Boer, F., Kok, J., Palamidessi, C., and J.J.M.M. Rutten. The Failure of failures in a paradigm for asynchronous communication. In *CONCUR '91*, LNCS, Springer-Verlag, 1991.

[6] Boudol, Towards the Lambda Calculus for Concurrent Computation. In *Proc. TAP-SOFT 1989*, LNCS 351, Springer Verlag, 1989.

[7] Clinger, W. *Foundations of Actor Semantics*. AI-TR-633, MIT Artificial Intelligence Laboratory.

[8] Goguen, J., *Sheaf semantics for concurrent interacting objects*. To appear in Proc. REX School on Foundations of Object-Oriented Programming, Noorwijkerhout, The Netherlands, May 28-June1, 1990.

[9] Hewitt, C., *Viewing Control Structures as Patterns of Passing Messages*. Artificial Intelligence, 1977.

[10] Hindley,J.R., and Seldin, J.P., *Introduction to Combinators and λ-calculus*. Campbridhe university Press, 1986.

[11] Hoare, C.A.R., *Communicating Sequential Processes*. Prentice Hall, 1985.

[12] Honda, K. and Tokoro, M., An Object Calculus for Asynchronous Communication, In: *Proc. of European Conference on Object-Oriented Programming*, LNCS, Springer-Verlag, July 1991. Extended version to appear as a Keio CS report, Novemver 1992.

[13] Honda, K., *Functions and Functionals in Interaction*. A Manuscript, November 1991.

[14] Honda, K., *A Semantically Sound Mapping Between Two Calculi*. A Manuscript, November 1991.

[15] Lampson, B.W., Paul, M., and Siegert, H.J., *Distributed Systems – Architecture and Implementation An Advanced Course*. LNCS 105, Springer-Verlag, 1981.

[16] Meseguer J., *Conditional Rewriting Logic as a Unified Model of Concurrency*. SRI-CSL-91-05, Computer Science Laboratory, SRI International, 1991. Also to appear in *Theoretical Computer Science*.

[17] Milner, R., *Calculus of Communicating Systems*. LNCS 92, Springer-Verlag, 1980.

[18] Milner, R., *Calculi for Synchrony and Asynchrony*. TCS, 1983.

[19] Milner, R., Parrow, J.G. and Walker, D.J., *A Calculus of Mobile Processes. Part I*. ECS-LFCS-89-85, Edinburgh University, 1989

[20] Milner, R., Parrow, J.G. and Walker, D.J., *A Calculus of Mobile Processes. Part II*. ECS-LFCS-89-86, Edinburgh University, 1989

[21] Milner, R., *Communication and Concurrency*. Prentice Hall, 1989.

[22] Milner, R., Functions as Processes. In *Automata, Language and Programming*, LNCS 443, 1990. The extended version under the same title as *Rapports de Recherche No.1154*, INRIA-Sophia Antipolis, February 1990.

[23] de Nicola, E., and Hennessy, M., Testing Equivalence for Processes. *Theoretical Computer Science*, 34, 1983.

[24] Nielson and Engberg, *A Calculus of Communicating Systems with Label Passing*. Research Report DAIMI PB-208, Computer Science Department, University of Aarhus, 1986.

[25] Nierstrasz, O., *A Guide to Specifying Concurrent Behaviour with Abacus.* in [29].

[26] Nierstrasz, O., Towards an Object Calculus, in this volume, 1992.

[27] Park, D., *Concurrency and Automata on Infinite Sequences*. LNCS 104, Springer-Verlag, 1980.

[28] Tokoro, M., Toward Computing Systems in the 2000's. *Operating Systems of the 90s and Beyond,* LNCS 563, Springer Verlag, 1992.

[29] Tsichritzis, D., ed. *Object Management*. Centre Universitaire D'informatique, Universite de Geneve, July 1990.

Appendix A: Consistency with the Original $\xrightarrow{l}$

The reasoning below shows that $\xrightarrow{l}$ of Definition 2.15 faithfully captures the original $\xrightarrow{l}$ in [12] up to the difference in the strength of $\equiv$, in spite of the novel way of presentation and the lack of bound outputs. Let $\equiv_{org}$ and $\xrightarrow{l}_{org}$ denote the relations defined in Definition 3 and 8 of [12], respectively[14] We will use the extended set of labels which adds the labels of the forms $\uparrow a|v|$ to the labels in **L**.

Definitions 6.1 We construct the relation $\cdot\!\xrightarrow{l}$ from $\xrightarrow{l}$ as follows.

$$P \xrightarrow{\uparrow av} P' \quad \Rightarrow \quad P \cdot\!\xrightarrow{\uparrow a|v|} P' \text{ with } v \notin \mathcal{FN}(P).$$
$$P \xrightarrow{l} P' \quad \Rightarrow \quad P \cdot\!\xrightarrow{l} P' \quad \text{(otherwise)} \quad \blacksquare$$

As $\equiv_{org}$ is stronger than $\equiv$, we cannot immediately say $\xrightarrow{l}_{org} = \cdot\!\xrightarrow{l}$. But the following proposition shows that, if we add $\equiv_{org}$, we faithfully recover the original relation.

Proposition 6.2 $P \xrightarrow{l}_{org} P'$ if and only if $P \cdot\!\xrightarrow{l} \equiv_{org} P'$. $\qquad\qquad\blacksquare$

---

[14] Minor typograpghical errors in Definition 8 there should be corrected; τ has to be added as a label of the transition in COM rule, and the side condition for STRUCT rule is unnecessary (though harmless).

Proof By checking that each rule of one system is inferred in the other system. The fact that if $P \xrightarrow{\uparrow a|v|}_{org} P'$ then $v \notin \mathcal{FN}(P)$ while $P \xrightarrow{\uparrow av}_{org} P'$ then $v \in \mathcal{FN}(P)$, is crucial in the case of bound output. ∎

Finally we note that the above result does not imply that bound labels are useless: on the contrary, the introduction of bound labels becomes indispensable when one should deal with transition relation at a higher level of abstraction, e.g. in treating the transition graph *per se*, or in discussing multi-step transition relation. We leave the details to another occasion.

Appendix B: Proof of Lemma 3.14

The Lemma. For any P, Q, v and x, $P \approx_a Q \Rightarrow P[v/x] \approx_a Q[v/x]$. ∎

Proof We take the relation

$$\mathcal{R} \stackrel{\text{def}}{=} \bigcup_{i \geq 0} \mathcal{R}_i$$

where

$$
\begin{aligned}
\mathcal{R}_0 : \quad & \approx_a \\
\mathcal{R}_1 : \quad & P \, \mathcal{R}_0 \, Q \quad \Rightarrow \quad P[v/x] \, \mathcal{R}_1 \, Q[v/x] \\
& \vdots \\
\mathcal{R}_{n+1} : \quad & P \, \mathcal{R}_n \, Q \quad \Rightarrow \quad P[v/x] \, \mathcal{R}_{n+1} \, Q[v/x] \, .
\end{aligned}
$$

and prove that this is a bisimulation. As $(P, Q) \in \mathcal{R}_1 \subset \mathcal{R}$, this shows that $(P, Q) \in \mathcal{R}_1$ implies $P \approx_a Q$ (in fact, $\mathcal{R}_1 = \approx_a$). We show this by proving that, for any $n \geq 0$, if $(P, Q) \in \mathcal{R}_n$,

$$P \xrightarrow{l} P' \quad \Rightarrow \quad \exists Q' \text{ s.t. } (Q \stackrel{\hat{l}}{\Longrightarrow} Q')$$

with

(1) $l = \uparrow av$ or $l = \tau$ then $(P', Q') \in \mathcal{R}_n$, and

(2) $l = \downarrow av$ then $(P', Q') \in \mathcal{R}_{n+2}$.

W.l.o.g. we can omit the symmetric case.

Our proof is not based on induction on n, but uses the following construction. For $(P, Q) \in \mathcal{R}_n$, let P_0 and Q_0 denote two expressions such that

$$(P_0, Q_0) \in \mathcal{R}_0(=\approx_a) \ \wedge \ P \stackrel{\text{def}}{=} P_0[v_1/x_1]..[v_n/x_n] \ \wedge \ Q \stackrel{\text{def}}{=} Q_0[v_1/x_1]..[v_n/x_n] \ .$$

This pair of P_0 and Q_0 will be used when we check that each transition of one party can somulate that of the other. Note also for any n we have $\mathcal{R}_{n+1} \supset \mathcal{R}_n$.

Case $P \xrightarrow{\downarrow av} P'$. Immediately $P' \equiv (P, \leftarrow av)$. Similarly $Q \xrightarrow{\downarrow av} (Q, \leftarrow av)$. Using (iv) and (vi) of Lemma 2.6 repeatedly, we have

$$
\begin{aligned}
(P, \leftarrow av) & \stackrel{\text{def}}{=} (P_0[v_1/x_1]..[v_n/x_n], \leftarrow av) \\
& \stackrel{\text{def}}{=} (P_0, \leftarrow av[z_1/x_i][z_2/x_j])[v_1/x_1]..[v_n/x_n][x_1/z_1][x_2/z_2]
\end{aligned}
$$

where $z_1, z_2 \notin \mathcal{FN}(P) \cup \mathcal{FN}(Q) \cup \{x_1, .., x_n\}$ and that for any x_k with $1 \leq k \leq n$ and $k \neq i, j$, $x_k \notin \{a, v\}$, and similarly for Q (note we have $n+2$ substitutions outside the parenthesis above). But by Proposition 3.13 we have

$$(P_0, \leftarrow av[z_1/x_i][z_2/x_j]) \approx_a (Q_0, \leftarrow av[z_1/x_i][z_2/x_j])$$

which shows $((P, \leftarrow av), (Q, \leftarrow av))$ is in $\mathcal{R}_{n+2}$.

Case $P \xrightarrow{\uparrow av} P'$. Using the normal form representation, we have $P \equiv |\tilde{w}|(\Gamma, \leftarrow av, \Delta)$ with $a \notin \{\tilde{w}\}$. Hence $P_0 \equiv P_0' \overset{\text{def}}{=} |\tilde{w}|(\Gamma', \leftarrow a'v', \Delta')$ where $a' \notin \{\tilde{w}\}$ and $|\tilde{w}|(\Gamma', \leftarrow a'v', \Delta')[v_1/x_1]..[v_n/x_n] \overset{\text{def}}{=} P_0'$. The rest is easy reasoning using the property of $\approx_a$ and Substitution lemma for transition (Lemma 2.18).

Case $P \xrightarrow{\tau} P'$. Again using the normal form representation, we have

$$P \equiv |\tilde{w}|(\Gamma, \leftarrow av, ay.P, \Delta) \xrightarrow{\tau} |\tilde{w}|(\Gamma, P[v/y], \Delta) \equiv P'$$

hence $P_0 \equiv |\tilde{w}|(\Gamma', \leftarrow a_1 v', a_2 y.P', \Delta')$. Now it is easy to see that a_1 and a_2 should be either both free or both bound by $|\tilde{w}|$. If both are bound, we can use the property of $\approx_a$ and (iii) of Lemma 2.18. If both are free, we have transitions

$$|\tilde{w}|(\Gamma', \leftarrow a_1 v', a_2 y.P', \Delta') \xrightarrow{\uparrow a_1 v'} \xrightarrow{\downarrow a_2 v'} \xrightarrow{\tau} |\tilde{w} - v'|(\Gamma', P[v'/y], \Delta')$$

with $(\Gamma', P[v'/y], \Delta')[v_1/x_1]..[v_n/x_n] \equiv P'$. Using the property of $\approx_a$ and repeatedly applying Lemma 2.18, we can show that there exists Q' such that $Q \overset{\tau}{\Longrightarrow} Q'$ and $(P', Q') \in \mathcal{R}_n$. ∎

Appendix C: Consequences of Restricted IN Rule.

Some results are presented below concerning a transition system which restricts the IN Rule of $\xrightarrow{l}$, and bisimulation induced by it. They suggest that the full generality of IN rule is necssary for sound formulation of the asynchronous interaction semantics.

Definitions 6.3 We define a restricted asynchronous interaction, denoted $\xrightarrow{l}_r$, as the smallest relation inferred by the same rules as Definition 2.15, with $\xrightarrow{l}$ replaced by $\xrightarrow{l}_r$ except IN rule which is reformulated as

$$\text{IN}_r : \quad Q \overset{\text{def}}{=} |\tilde{w}|(\Gamma, ax.P, \Delta) \xrightarrow{\downarrow av}_r |\tilde{w}|(\Gamma, P[x/v], \Delta) \quad (v \notin \{\tilde{w}\} \wedge a \in \mathcal{FI}(Q)) \quad \blacksquare$$

The induced bisimulation is:

Definitions 6.4 $P_1 \approx_r Q_1$ if and only if $(P_1, Q_1) \in \mathcal{R}$ with

(i) For any $(P, Q) \in \mathcal{R}$, whenever $P \xrightarrow{l}_r P'$ which is sound with respect to Q, and, if l is $\downarrow av$, $a \in \mathcal{FI}(P)$, there is Q' such that $Q \overset{l}{\Longrightarrow}_r Q'$ and $(P', Q') \in \mathcal{R}$.

(ii) $\mathcal{R}$ is symmetric. ∎

What we show below is that this relation lies strictly between the synchronous bisimilarity defined in Definition 4.5 and the asynchronous bisimilarity. First, it is easy to see that:

Proposition 6.5 $P \approx_r Q \;\; \Rightarrow \;\; P \approx_a Q.$ ∎

Proof To prove $P \approx_r Q \;\; \Rightarrow \;\; P \approx_a^* Q$ is easy. Then we use Proposition 3.21. ∎

But the converse is not true.

Proposition 6.6 $P \approx_a Q$ does not imply $P \approx_r Q.$ ∎

Proof By the pair in Proposition 4.14. ∎

Thus $\approx_r$ is more strict than $\approx_a$. This shows that we cannot restrict the input label at the transition level if we want to get the generality of $\approx_a$. Finally we show that $\approx_r$ is not $\approx_s$ (cf. Definition 4.5), which is known to be more strict than $\approx_a$ in a meaningful way. The reasoning to establish this negative result uses an example where the synchronous bisimulation fails not by the lack of input ports but by the *forced* input transition whose result is disastrous, and is interesting in its own right.

Proposition 6.7 $P \approx_r Q$ does not imply $P \approx_s Q$. ∎

Proof By a pair $ax.(\leftarrow ax, \mathcal{I}(a), \mathcal{I}(b))$ and $ax.(\leftarrow ax, \mathcal{I}(b)), \mathcal{I}(a).$ ∎

In the pair which constitutes the counterexample, whenever one party has an asynchronous transition, the other has a simulating transition which satisfies the condition in Definition 6.4, hence they are in $\approx_r$. However, the synchronous transition of the second expression:

$$ax.(\leftarrow ax, \mathcal{I}(b)), \mathcal{I}(a) \xrightarrow{\;\downarrow av\;}_s ax.(\leftarrow ax, \mathcal{I}(b)), \mathcal{I}(a), \leftarrow av$$

cannot be simulated *synchronously* by the first one. Note that the corresponding transitions in the asynchronous setting,

$$ax.(\leftarrow ax, \mathcal{I}(b)), \mathcal{I}(a) \xrightarrow{\;\downarrow av\;}\xrightarrow{\;\tau\;} ax.(\leftarrow ax, \mathcal{I}(b)), \mathcal{I}(a), \leftarrow av$$

can be easily simulated trivially by

$$ax.(\leftarrow ax, \mathcal{I}(a), \mathcal{I}(b)) \xrightarrow{\;\downarrow av\;} ax.(\leftarrow ax, \mathcal{I}(a), \mathcal{I}(b)), \leftarrow av$$

satisfying the condition of Definition 6.4.

A Unifying Framework for Process Calculus Semantics of Concurrent Object-Oriented Languages

Michael Papathomas[1]
University of Geneva

Abstract

A framework for the semantic description of concurrent object-oriented languages based on CCS is outlined. We discuss how the essential object-oriented features, such as encapsulation, object identity, classes, inheritance and concurrency are captured. Then, the proposed framework is used for defining the semantics of significantly different versions of a toy language which supports the above features. The ease with which the different versions of this language are accommodated provides some evidence for the applicability of the framework for a wide range of languages, as well as its usefulness for comparing different language designs and examining the interaction of a rich set of object-oriented features.

1. Introduction

A variety of approaches has been followed for the design of Concurrent Object-Oriented Languages (COOPLs). The various language design approaches, however, are not equally successful in integrating concurrency with the other OO features mainly because of the interference between features. Such "design flaws" are generally uncovered only after the languages have been fully designed and, possibly, implemented, by appropriate examples illustrating the interference of features[13][5][15]. We believe that a more rigorous approach for describing the semantics of features, examining their interactions and comparing the various design choices would be more effective for a satisfactory integration of the features.

An approach for the semantic definition of a concurrent programming language is by translation of the language constructs to a process calculus. This approach has been used in [7] for the definition of a simple concurrent programming language by translation to CCS and also in [11][17][18], using CCS or other process calculi for defining the semantics of concurrent object-based languages. There are, however, different ways to translate the constructs of a language to a process calculus. These may vary in the amount of operational detail or may use completely different approaches for the translation of language features. This makes it hard to compare different language designs and draw useful conclusions about the interaction of a language's features.

In order to use the "semantics by translation" approach for examining the interaction of language features and for comparing language designs we propose a framework for the semantic

---

1. Author's address: Centre Universitaire d'Informatique, 12 rue du Lac, CH-1207 Geneva, Switzerland. E-mail: michael@cui.unige.ch. Tel: +41 (22) 787.65.80. Fax: +41 (22) 735.39.05.

definition of concurrent object-based languages by translation to CCS. This framework may be used for the definition of the semantics of concurrent object-based languages that follow very different approaches for object-based concurrency. For example, both languages that view objects as passive abstract data types and languages where objects are considered as single threaded message-passing processes can be accommodated. The proposed framework also supports class inheritance for which, to our knowledge, no process-calculus semantic definition has been given before.

The framework consists of the definition of a common base structure for the representation of COOPL features, such as objects, messages, classes, methods and their synchronization, in CCS. This structure is captured by the definition of a number of agents with agent parameters that act as derived operators. These derived operators define a derived calculus on top of CCS that more directly supports the description of the semantics of COOPLs. The differences on language design choices may be understood by variation of the definition of some of these operators. The underlying process calculus framework may be used for the analysis of the properties of the operators that correspond to different language design choices.

Apart from supporting the rigorous description of the semantics of COOPL features this approach has the benefit that the meaning of individual objects is given as a CCS agent. This provides us with a formal definition of object behavior and a notion of behavior equivalence induced from the equivalence defined on CCS terms. It also makes it possible to use the underlying formal, process calculus, framework for asserting and verifying properties of objects.

In section 2, we discuss our approach for capturing basic object-based features such as object identifiers, messages, classes and instances in CCS. We assume knowledge of CCS and the value-passing calculus used in [7]. We also use "functions" over agents which are expressed as definitions of agents with agent parameters as discussed in [7] chapter 9.

In section 3, we discuss how to map objects defined in object-oriented languages to CCS agents in a way that essentially different approaches for combining objects and concurrency are easily accommodated. We define a simple concurrent object based language named SCOOL and give its semantics. In section 4, as an illustration of the suitability of the framework for languages following significantly different approaches, we present the semantics of a different version of SCOOL.

In section 5 we extend the approach presented in the section 2 to include class inheritance by defining object classes as agents which take as parameters other agents, extend the syntax of SCOOL to include inheritance and give the semantics of the extensions.

In section 6 we discuss alternative approaches for developing such a semantic framework. Our choice of using CCS is compared to what could be done by using a process calculus such as the π-calculus[8] which supports label-passing or a higher order process calculus such as CHOCS[16].

2. Basic Framework: objects, classes and messages

The meaning of a program is given as the parallel composition of agents representing the classes defined in the program, agents representing predefined classes such as integers and Booleans, and a "start-up" agent which represents the "main program."

Classes are represented by agents that receive at the port $requestNew_c$, where c is the class's name, requests for creating a new instance and supply at the port $newid_c$ a value representing the object identifier of the new instance. Some values may also be supplied at the $requestNew$ port that are used for initializing the new instance.

Object identifiers belong to the set $Oid = \aleph \times Class$ where $Class$ is the set of class names in the program. Objects interact at $request_{id,m}$ and $reply_k$ ports. A $request$ port, indexed by id which belongs to the set of object identifiers and m which belongs to the set of method names, is used to send a message to the object identified by id requesting it to execute its m method. A sequence of the identifiers of the argument objects as well as a value k used to identify the invocation are transmitted as values along a request port.

The reply ports are used for communicating the object identifier of an object representing the reply to a request. The reply ports are indexed by invocation identifiers k. These are values supplied by the "caller" to allow different invocations to be distinguished. The port $reply_k$ is used by a caller to receive the reply to the request identified by k.

The use of reply identifiers may vary largely depending on the interaction primitives provided by the language. For modelling one-way message passing where the notion of reply is not supported, reply ports and thus reply identifiers would not be used. For modelling single threaded objects communicating by RPC the invoker's object identifier would do. However, for languages that support multi-threaded objects or asynchronous invocations the invoker's object identifier would not be sufficient to identify the invocation. To cope with all these cases we assume that reply identifiers are integers generated at each invocation by a global reply identifier agent. This provides a means to uniquely identify each invocation in the system.

The only object interaction mechanism discussed in this paper is remote procedure call. However, the approach for identifying requests discussed above is adequate for modelling various ways of receiving replies to requests such as *future variables* in ABCL/1[20] and CBoxes in ConcurrentSmalltalk[19].

2.1 The Structure of Class Agents

Agents representing classes will have a different structure depending on whether they correspond to predefined object classes or program-defined classes which are expressed in an object-oriented language.

2.1.1 Program-Defined Classes

The behavior of program-defined classes is described by the agent $Class\,(name, ClassBeh)$ defined below which is parameterized by the class's name and an agent $ClassBeh$ that represents the behavior of the class's instances. The latter agent is obtained from the class definition expressed in a programming language and is parameterized by two value parameters. These are bound at the creation of a new instance to a value representing the object identifier and sequence of values used for initializing the instance. The way that agents that correspond to the behavior of instances are obtained from a class definition is fully described in 3.2 for the example language SCOOL.

$$Class\,(name, ClassBeh)\ =\ Cl_0\,(name, ClassBeh)\ \text{where}$$

$$Cl_n\,(name, ClassBeh)\ =\ requestNew_{name}\,(p)\,.\overline{newid}_{name}\,(n, name)\,.$$

$$(ClassBeh\,(\,(n, name)\,,p)\,|Cl_{n+1}\,(name, ClassBeh))$$

The definition of the agent *Class* is based on a family of agents Cl_k. Each of these agents accepts at the port, $requestNew_{name}$, a request for creating a new instance of the class, identified by the *name* subscript, and receives in p a, possibly empty, sequence of values for initializing the new instance. It outputs at the port $newId_{name}$ the value *(k,name)* which corresponds to the object identifier of a new instance and then creates two new agents. The first of these agents represents the new instance and the second is the next agent, Cl_{k+1}, in the family of agents that will handle the next instance creation request. The name subscript of the ports $requestNew_{name}$ and $newId_{name}$ is the class name and is used to distinguish among requests directed to other classes in a program.

Note the use of "=" in defining equations. Also, for the definition of recursive agents we will use either the recursion operator, *fix*, or recursive defining equations, choosing in each particular case whichever is more convenient and produces a more readable result.

2.1.2 Predefined Classes

Generally object-oriented languages support a number of predefined object classes such as integers and Booleans. These are expressed in our framework by agents representing predefined classes which are composed with the user-defined ones in a program. In contrast to program-defined classes that are expressed in the syntax of a programming language, agents for predefined classes are directly expressed as CCS agents. However, predefined classes and their instances conform to the protocol for agents representing classes and instances described above. In section 3 we define agents corresponding to predefined classes for semaphores, Booleans and integers that are used for the semantic definition of our example language.

2.2 Remarks

The approach for modelling object interactions at fixed ports indexed by object identifiers is sufficient to model dynamic interconnections among objects which take place in object-oriented languages by the communication of object identifiers among objects. At the CCS level all possible interconnections between agents representing objects are set up beforehand and object identifiers act as switches in this huge interconnection network. We found this approach satisfactory, so far, for modelling object-oriented languages. In section 5 we discuss using the π-calculus[8] which directly supports dynamic interconnections among agents.

2.3 The Structure of Program Defined Objects

In this section we describe the structure of agents that represent objects whose behaviors are expressed in an object-based language. The mapping from class definitions to such agents is fully described in section 3.2 for an example language. The motivation for taking this approach for representing objects is to easily accommodate different object models and features. This will become clearer as we elaborate on these issues in later sections.

Agents representing objects are structured as an assembly of agents. Some of these agents are obtained by the object's class definition while others are proper to the language's object model. Objects from languages that take substantially different approaches for their object models are accommodated by the appropriate definition of the language dependent components. For instance, depending on the definition of the method scheduler component discussed below it is possible to capture the behavior of objects considered as passive abstract data types or as active single thread objects. The structure of objects is given in figure 1 and the purpose of the different kinds of components is explained below.

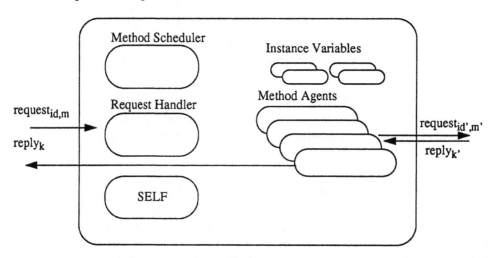

Figure 1

The Request Handler

This agent, defined below as *RH*, accepts requests, $request_{id,m}(r,<v_1,..,v_n>)$, for the execution of one of the object's methods identified by m. It creates an *Activate* agent, representing a pending request, which will interact with the appropriate method agent for the execution of the method. The *Activate* agent has to wait for an $\overline{activate_m}$ signal from the method scheduler before it interacts through a $call_m$ event with the method agent for executing the method.

$$RH\,(id,Meth) \;=\; fix\,(X= \sum_{m\,\in\,Meth} request_{id,\,m}(r,\,v).\,(Activate_m(r,\,v)|X)\,)$$

$$Activate_m(r,\,v) \;=\; (activate_m).\,\overline{call_m}(r,\,v)$$

This agent is very important for modelling inheritance in section 5.

Instance Variables

There is one such agent per instance variable. These agents are very similar to the agents used for modelling variables in [7]. The main difference is that instead of storing integer and Boolean values our variable agents store object identifiers. Also, our variable agents are defined in a way that they may be initialized at their creation.

$$Var_V\,(val) \;=\; set_V\,(val').\,Var_V\,(val') + \overline{get_V}val.\,Var_V\,(val)$$

The value *(0,nil)* standing for the identifier of the undefined object will be used to initialize all non explicitly initialized variables. This object accepts any request sent to it and generates an event indicating an error. This event could be used to model an exception handling mechanism, however, exception handling will not be discussed any further in this paper.

In order to restrict access to a variable and thus model local variables and encapsulation we define the *access sort* ACC_V of a variable V in way analogous to that in [7] as $ACC_v = \{get_v,set_v\}$. Restriction by ACC_V renders the variable V local to the scope of the restriction.

Method Agents

There is one such agent for each object method. These agents accept activation requests containing values for the method's arguments, they create an agent representing the method's body in an environment where "local" variable agents hold the arguments of the method activation. This way several activations of a method may take place concurrently.

$$Method\,(m,\,Mbody) \;=\; fix(X= call_m(r,\,a).\,MBody\,(r,\,a)\,|X)$$

This agent is parameterized by the method name m and an agent *MBody*. It repeatedly accepts invocations at the port $call_m$ where invokers supply a sequence of values $v_1,...,v_n$ representing object identifiers, denoted here as a, for the method's arguments and a value r which is used to identify where to send the reply. *MBody* is the agent that is obtained from the definition of the method in the modelled programming language in the way shown in section 3.

The Method Scheduler

The purpose of this agent is to control the concurrent execution of methods. It interacts with the Activate agents created by the request handler, imposing synchronization constraints on the activation of methods. By varying the nature of synchronization constraints imposed by this agent on the concurrent activation of methods we can accommodate significantly different object models. This agent will also interact with the execution of certain method statements. For example, consider a scheduler that does not allow method executions to take place concurrently. Before generating an $\overline{activate_m}$ to enable the execution of a method it has to be informed that the execution of the previous method is terminated. This may be done by a $\overline{terminate}$ event that is generated by the last statement of the executing method or by a "return" statement.

For modelling the synchronization of method execution that takes place in some languages more information needs to be exchanged between the method scheduler and the execution of method statements. For instance, to model languages with synchronization mechanisms derived from path expressions[7] it is necessary to know which method has terminated. This would require that the terminate events would carry information about the method name. As such information is not required by the scheduler of the languages discussed in this paper we have not included such information to simplify the presentation.

The agent *Orth* defined below, is used for modelling languages with an *orthogonal* [12] object model[12] where objects are considered as passive abstract data types. Synchronization of method execution in such languages is achieved within methods by the invocation of special objects as, for example, semaphores in Smalltalk-80 [4] or locks in Trellis/Owl[9]. So, the scheduler *Orth* used to model objects in these languages does not impose any synchronization constraints on the activation of an object's methods.

$$Orth = \sum_{m \in Meth} \overline{activate_m}.Orth + terminate.Orth$$

This scheduler agent is used in section 3 for defining the semantics of the language SCOOL. In section 4 we discuss an alternative approach for method scheduling corresponding to a different version of SCOOL.

Self

This agent operates as a "read-only variable" bound at object creation to the object's identifier. It is used by the object to find out about its own identity and class. This agent is used in the semantics of languages where the pseudo variable self may be used for designating the object itself. Its definition is:

$$Self(id) = \overline{get_{Self}id}.Self(id)$$

Objects

Finally, an object is modelled by an agent defined as the concurrent composition of the above agents and parameterized by its object identifier, which is used by the request handler for accepting requests. Restriction is used to hide the events used for the interaction between the above agents and eliminate the potential for interference with the events occurring in other objects.

3. Defining *SCOOL*, a Simple Concurrent Object-Oriented Language

In this section we define a very simple object-oriented language for illustrating how the semantics of various object-oriented features can be expressed in our framework. In later sections we will extend the language by including more features and discuss how to accommodate them in the basic framework.

3.1 Syntax and Informal Description of *SCOOL*

The version of SCOOL discussed in this section does not support inheritance and takes an orthogonal approach for concurrency. The operations of objects are invoked in a remote procedure call fashion by concurrent threads. The synchronization of operation execution has to be achieved by the judicious programming of the object's methods.

A program consists of a sequence of class declarations, variable declarations and a statement representing the "main" program.

The creation of a new concurrent thread is expressed by the fork expression. This expression is parameterized by a statement which will be executed by a new concurrent thread. The value of the fork expression is the object identifier of an instance of the predefined class *process*. Process objects allow threads to be synchronized. By invoking the wait operation of a process object the invoking thread is suspended until the thread corresponding to the process object terminates. Another means for thread synchronization is provided by invoking the P and V operations of semaphore objects which are instances of the predefined class *sema*.

We assume that the language is statically typed. This simplifies the semantics since we do not have to consider the eventuality that a requested operation is not supported by the invoked object.

Apart from the predefined classes *process* and *sema* mentioned above, SCOOL also supports predefined classes for integers and Booleans with the operations that are commonly attributed to these object types in programming languages. We also assume the existence of a single predefined instance representing the undefined object. This object, denoted by nil, accepts requests for any method and generates an event representing an error.

The syntax for SCOOL's expression and statements is listed below, where E and S, possibly indexed, stand for expressions and statements respectively.

Expressions

X	where X is a variable
self	the value of the executing object's identifier
n	where $n = 0,1,2...$
b	where $b =$ true, false
nil	denotes the undefined object

new $C(E_1,..,E_n)$	create an object of class C
$E.m(E_1,..,E_n)$	rpc invocation where m is a method name
$E_1 = E_2$	comparison of the object identifiers
fork S	Create a new thread for executing S

Statements

$X := E$	assignment
if E then S_1 else S_2	conditional
while E do S	iteration
$\{S\}$	compound statement
$S_1; S_2$	sequential composition
skip	no action
$E.$	turn the expression E into a statement by discarding the result
return E	return the value of E to the caller

Declarations

A declaration may be a variable declaration, a method declaration, a class declaration or a program declaration

$Decl ::= VarDecl + MethodDecl + ClassDecl + ProgramDecl$

$VarDecl ::= \text{var } X_1:C,...X_n:C;$

$MethodDecl ::= \text{method m } (a_1,..,a_n) \{ VarDecl\ S \}$

$ClassDecl ::= \text{Class C } \{ VarDecl\ MethodDecl_1...MethodDecl_n\}$

$ProgramDecl ::= ClassDecl_1 .... ClassDecl_n \{ VarDecl\ S \}$

3.2 Semantics

$[ProgramDecl] = [ClassDecl_1] | ... | [ClassDecl_n] | [VarDecl] |$

$RequestIdGen(0) | [S] | ProcClass | SemaClass | IntClass | BoolClass$

RequestIdGen is the agent used to generate identifiers for invocation requests. It is defined as:

$RequestIdGen(n) = \overline{requestId}\ n.RequestIdGen(n+1)$

ProcClass, *SemaClass*, *IntClass* and *BoolClass* are the agents representing SCOOL's predefined object classes. These agents are defined in section 3.2.2.

Class Declarations

$[\text{class } C \{ VarDecl\ MDecl_1...MDecl_n \}] = Class(C, ClassBehavior_c)$

where

$ClassBehavior_c(id, p) = Object(id, ms(C), [VarDecl] | MethDecl)$

with

$$MethDecl = [MDecl_1] | ... | [MDecl_n]$$

and

$$Object(id, \mathcal{M}, X) = (RH(id, \mathcal{M}) | Orth(\mathcal{M}) | Self(id) | X)$$
$$\setminus L(Orth(\mathcal{M})) \setminus L(Self(id))) \setminus L(X)$$

Where L is a function defined in [7] that gives the sort of an agent. ms is a function that gives the set of method names of a class.

The agents *Class*, the request handler agent *RH*, *Self* and the method scheduler *Orth* were discussed in section 2.

ClassBehavior is parameterized by two value parameters the second of which is not used in the SCOOL example. This second parameter p is needed in general is to supply values for initializing new instances of a class. However, as in SCOOL we provide no way for initializing instances at their creation this parameter is ignored. Also, the expression list $E_1,...,E_n$ in an expression "new $C(E_1,...,E_n)$", used for creating an instance of C, will be typically empty except in the case of some of the predefined classes discussed in 3.2.2.

Variable Declarations

$$[var\ V_1:C_1,...,V_n:C_k] = Var_{v_1}(0, nil) | ... | Var_{v_n}(0, nil)$$

Method Declarations

$$[method\ m(a_1,...,a_n)\ \{VarDecl\ S\}] = Method(m, MethodBody)$$

where

$$MethodBody(r, <v_1,...,v_n>) =$$
$$(Var_{a_1}(v_1) | ... | Var_{a_n}(v_n) | Var_{v_1}(nil) | ... | Var_{v_k}(nil) | ([S](r)\ Before\ Terminate))$$

$$\setminus ACC_{v_1} ... ACC_{v_k} \setminus ACC_{a_1} ... ACC_{a_n}$$

if

$$VarDecl = var\ V_1:C_1,...,V_k:C_k$$

and with $nil = (0, nil)$

The *Method* agent was defined in section 3. The "*Before Terminate*" expression is used to intercept the $\overline{done}$ event generated by the last statement in the method body and inform the method scheduler with a $\overline{terminate}$ event that the execution of the method is completed. The *Terminate* agent is defined as $Terminate = \overline{terminate}.0$ and *Before* is a binary operator over agents, defined in 3.2.1, that activates its right operand after the left one has generated a $\overline{done}$ event.

The $\overline{terminate}$ event may also be generated directly by the return statement discussed in the next section.

3.2.1 Expressions and Statements

The semantic description of SCOOL's statements and expressions builds on the semantic description of the language $\mathcal{M}_0$ given in [7]. However, apart from the fact that more statements and expressions are introduced a slightly different approach has been taken for predefined objects and for the semantics of statements.

Objects such as integers and Booleans are handled in [7] by the semantics given to expressions. Here, we represent integers and Booleans as predefined objects. This allows us to give the semantics of expressions independently of whether they evaluate to objects of predefined or user defined classes.

Another difference is that statements are mapped to parameterized agents. This is needed because of the way that we define the semantics of the return statement and is further discussed below.

Agents Representing Expressions

Expressions are mapped to agents that yield up the value of the expression at the port $\overline{res}$. The combinator *Into* defined below is used to allow an agent to refer to the value computed by another agent representing an expression.

$$P \ Into \ (x) \ Q = (P \, [b/res] \ | \ b(x) \, . Q) \backslash b$$

If Q is an agent expression where the variable x occurs free then *Into* binds this variable to the value computed by P.

The definition of this combinator is not exactly the same as that in [7]. There it is assumed that *res* is not in the sort of Q, so the relabelling *res* is unnecessary. Here, as we do not make this assumption, we have to relabel *res* to a label b which we assume does not occur free in either P or Q.

Statements and Sequential Composition

Agents that represent statements indicate their termination at the distinguished label $\overline{done}$. Sequential composition of two statements representing agents is expressed by the combinator *Before* defined as:

$$P \ Before \ Q = (P \, [b/done] \, | \, b.Q) \backslash b$$

We also define the agent *Done*, which will be useful in the definition of the semantics of statements, as

$$Done = \overline{done}.0$$

Semantics of Expressions

$$[\![X]\!] = get_X(x).\overline{res} \ x$$
$$[\![\,self\,]\!] = get_{Self}(x).\overline{res} \ x$$

$$[\![n]\!] = \overline{res} \ (n, int)$$

$$[\![true]\!] = \overline{res} \ (1, bool), \ [\![false]\!] = \overline{res} \ (0, bool)$$

$$[\![nil]\!] = \overline{res} \ (0, nil)$$

$$[\![new \ C\,(E_1, ..., E_n)]\!] = [\![E_1]\!] \ Into\,(x_1) ... \ [\![E_n]\!] \ Into\,(x_n)$$
$$\overline{newRequest_C} \ (x_1, ..., x_n) . newId_C \, (x) . \overline{res} \ x$$

$$[\![E.m \, (E_1, ..., E_n)]\!] = [\![E]\!] \ Into \ (t) \ [\![E_1]\!] \ Into\,(x_1) ... \ [\![E_n]\!] \ Into\,(x_n)$$
$$requestId\,(k) . \overline{request}_{t,m} \, (k, (x_1, ..., x_n)) . reply_k \, (x) . \overline{res} \ x$$

$$[\![E_1=E_2]\!] = [\![E_1]\!] \ Into\,(x_1) \ [\![E_2]\!] \ Into\,(x_2) \ Comp\,(x_1, x_2)$$

where

$$Comp\,((i_1, c_1), (i_2, c_2)) =$$
$$\text{if } c_1=c_2 \text{ then } \text{ if } i_1=i_2 \text{ then } \overline{res} \, (1, bool) + \text{if } i_1 \neq i_2 \text{ then } \overline{res} \, (0, bool) +$$
$$\text{if } c_1 \neq c_2 \text{ then } \overline{res} \, (0, bool)$$

$$[\![fork \ S]\!] = \overline{newRequest}_{proc} . newid_{proc} \, (x) . \overline{res} \ x . (\ [\![S]\!] \mid done.\overline{term}_x) \backslash done$$

The semantics of the fork expression whose informal semantics was discussed in section 3 merits some explanation. The execution of this expression creates an instance of the predefined class *process*, defined in 3.2.2, and yields its id as the result of the expression. This id may be used for invoking the wait operation of the process object which allows the invoker to be suspended until the execution of the associated statement terminates. Then it creates an agent for executing the forked statement as well as an agent that monitors the termination of this statement and informs the associated process object. The termination of the "forked" statement is signaled by $\overline{done}$ and the process that monitors its termination uses the $\overline{term}_x$ event to inform the process object with id x that the execution of its associated statement has terminated.

Semantics of Statements

Apart from "*E.*", the return statement and the fact that statements are mapped to parameterized agents, statements and their semantics are the same as those defined in[7] for the language $\mathcal{M}_0$. "*E.*" provides a way to turn expressions into statements by discarding the result yielded by the expression and by generating the $\overline{done}$ event as required by statements representing agents. It is useful when a method is invoked for its side effects rather than for its return value. Its semantics, given below, is straightforward and merits no further discussion.

The return statement deserves some more explanation. Actually it is because of this statement that we have to map statements to parameterized agents. In order to reply to the right caller the agent representing the return statement has to be parameterized by a value to be used as the subscript of the reply label. This value is made available in the agent representing method declaration and is passed down to the return statement of a method activation by syntactically enclosing statements. In fact agents representing the semantics of statements other than the return statement have no use for this parameter which is either ignored or passed on to the agents corresponding to component statements if there are any. The return statement also differs from other statements in that it does not pass control to the next statement through *done*. Thus, the execution of a method stops when it encounters a return statement. Instead it generates a *terminate* event, directed to the method scheduler, to indicate that the execution of the method has terminated. In case there is no return statement in the method the terminate event is generated by the *MethodBody* agent defined in section 3.

$$[X:=E] \ (k) \ = \ [E] \ Into \ (x) \ (\overline{set_X}x.\overline{done})$$

$$[E.] \ (k) \ = \ [E] \ Into \ (x) \ Done$$

$$[\{S\}] \ (k) \ = \ [S] \ (k)$$

$$[\text{if } E \text{ then } S_1 \text{ else } S_2] \ (k) \ =$$
$$\qquad\qquad [E] \ Into \ (x) \ (\text{if } x= (1, bool) \text{ then } \ [S_1] (k) \ \text{else} \ [S_2] (k) \ )$$

$$[\text{while } E \text{ do } S] \ (k) \ = W \ (k)$$
where

$$W \ (k) \ = \ fix(X= [E] \ Into \ (x) \ (\text{if } x= (1, bool) \text{ then } [S] \ Before \ X \ \text{else } Done)$$

$$[S_1;S_2] \ (k) \ = \ [S_1] (k) \ Before \ [S_2] (k)$$

$$[\text{skip}] \ (k) \ = Done$$

$$[\text{return } E] \ (k) \ = \ [E] \ Into \ (x) \ (\overline{reply_k}x.\overline{terminate})$$

3.2.2 Predefined Object Classes

The structure of the process and semaphore predefined classes is the same as the one for user defined classes so that the *Class* agent defined in section 2 is used for their definition. The only difference from program-defined classes is that the agents that represent the behavior of instances are directly encoded in CCS. A quite different approach is illustrated by the agents representing the Boolean and integer predefined classes.

Process Objects

The purpose of process objects is to delay the invokers of their *wait* operation until the thread to which they are associated terminates. Termination of the thread is signaled to process objects by a *term$_{id}$* event where *id* is the object's identifier, after which the object accepts wait requests, thus allowing to its callers to proceed.

$$ProcBeh \ (id) \ = \ term_{id}.fix \ (X \ = \ request_{id, wait} \ (k, ()) . \overline{reply_k}.X)$$

$$ProcClass \ = \ Class \ (process, ProcBeh)$$

Semaphores

The agent *SemaClass*, defined below, represents a predefined semaphore class used to create semaphore instances which are modelled as instances of the *SemBehavior* agent with the parameters bound to the corresponding object identifier. For simplicity we have ignored issues concerning the order in which suspended callers are woken up.

$$SemaClass = Class\,(sema, SemBehavior)$$

where

$$SemBehavior\,(id, p) = Sem_1\,(id)\,,$$

$$Sem_n\,(id) = request_{id,\,v}\,(k)\,.\overline{reply}_k.Sem_{n+1}\,(id)\,+$$

$$request_{id,\,p}\,(k)\,.\overline{reply}_k.Sem_{n-1}\,(id)$$

for $n \geq 1$ and

$$Sem_0\,(id) = request_{id,\,v}\,(k)\,.\overline{reply}_k.Sem_1\,(id)$$

Booleans

To represent integers and Booleans we take a slightly different approach from the one used above for semaphores. Here the agents corresponding to the predefined classes directly provide the behavior of their instances.

The predefined class for Booleans is given below by the agent *BoolClass*. This agent is defined as the parallel composition of two agents: *InstBeh* and *ClassBeh*. The *InstBeh* agent realizes the behavior of the instances of the class which are identified by *(0,bool)* and *(1,bool)* for the objects corresponding to the truth values true and false respectively. For encoding the operations on Booleans we have made the assumption that Boolean values and the usual Boolean operations are subsumed by the process calculus and we use the symbols 0 and 1 to denote the values true and false respectively. This assumption, which was not strictly necessary, as we could have encoded these operations by operations on integers, was made for convenience and increased readability. Also, note that the execution of operations on different Booleans takes place concurrently as the "product" symbol is used in the definition of *InstBeh* to denote parallel composition.

Apart from providing the operations of Boolean instances the agent *BoolClass* also supports the behavior of agents representing classes, that is the protocol for the creation of the class's instances. This behavior, which is provided by the agent *ClassBeh*, is supported so that all agents representing classes exhibit uniform behavior. In fact, the object identifier value returned by the Boolean class at the port $\overline{newid}_{bool}$ is the same as the value received along the *requestNew*$_{bool}$ port. This value is generated by the agent corresponding to the semantics of the expression true used, for example, as argument in the expression new Boolean(true) that may be used for explicitly creating a new instance of an object corresponding to the Boolean value true. Also, note that *ClassBeh* handles requests for the creation of instances serially so that no interference may occur among concurrent requests.

$$BoolClass = ClassBeh \mid InstBeh$$

$$ClassBeh = fix(\,X = requestNew_{bool}\,(n)\,.\overline{newid}_{bool}n.X\,)$$

$$InstBeh = \prod_{n \in \{0,1\}} [request_{(n, bool), not} (r) . \overline{reply_r} (not\ n, bool) . InstBeh\ |$$

$$request_{(n, bool), and} (r, (k, bool)) . \overline{reply_r} (k\ and\ n, bool) . InstBeh\ ]$$

Integers

The predefined class of integers, *IntClass* is defined below in a way analogous to Booleans. In order to shorten the presentation just some of the operations typically provided for integers in programming languages are shown.

$$IntClass = IntClassBeh\ |\ IntInstBeh$$

$$IntClassBeh = requestNew_{int} (n) . \overline{new_{int}} (n) . IntClassBeh$$

$$IntInstBeh = \prod_{n \in \aleph} request_{n, int, plus} (r, k, int) . \overline{reply_r} (n + k, int) . IntInstBeh\ |$$

$$request_{(n, int), minus} (r, (k, int)) . \overline{reply_r} (n - k, int) . IntInstBeh\ |$$

$$request_{(n, int), equal} (r, (k, int)) .$$

$$(if\ (n = k)\ then\ \overline{reply_r} (1, bool) . IntInstBeh\ +$$

$$if\ (n \neq k)\ then\ \overline{reply_r} (1, bool) . IntInstBeh)$$

4. Accommodating Other Object Models

In this section we define a different version of SCOOL inspired by the language POOL-T[1] and give its semantics. The facility with which this significantly different version of SCOOL is accommodated provides some evidence concerning the suitability of the proposed framework for a wide range of concurrent object-based languages.

In this version of SCOOL objects are single threaded active entities that explicitly accept requests to execute their methods. Method invocation takes place by remote procedure calls. The caller is suspended until the receiver answers the request and sends back a reply.

A statement, called the object's body, is associated with each object and starts executing when the object is created. An answer statement may be used in the object's body to accept requests for executing a method in a specified set. If there are no pending requests for any of the specified methods the execution of the objects body is suspended until such a request is made. After the execution of a method the execution of the object's body proceeds at the next statement.

It is also possible that a class does not define an object body. In this case a default one is assumed which repeatedly answers requests for any of the object's methods.

We also introduce a reply statement which is like return in that it sends a reply to the caller but, unlike return, passes control to the next statement. This statement is used to achieve an effect similar to POOL-T's post actions.

4.1 Modifying the Syntax

The syntax of this version of SCOOL differs from the one in section 3.1 as follows.

Declarations

Class declaration is modified as follows to include the object's body.

> $ClassDecl$ ::= class C { $VarDecl\ MethodDecl_1...MethodDecl_n\ BodyDecl$}
>
> class C { $VarDecl\ MethodDecl_1...MethodDecl_n$ }
>
> $BodyDecl$ ::= body S

Statements

We extend the definition of statements to include the answer and reply statements whose syntax is defined as:

> answer $(M_1,..,M_n)$ where $M_1,..,M_n$ are method names.
>
> reply E

Expressions

We exclude the fork expression since in this version of SCOOL objects are single threaded.

4.2 Semantics

Class Declaration

In order to take into account the object's body we modify the definition of the agent $ClassBehavior_c$ given in section 3.2 as follows.

> $ClassBehavior_c\ (id, p)\ =\ Object\ (id, meth\ (c),\ [VarDecl]\ |MethDecl|Body)$

where

> $Body\ =\ [S]\ Before\ 0$

if body S is the body declaration for the class C and

> $Body\ =\ [$while true answer $(m_1, ..., m_n)]$

if no body declaration is given in the declaration of C.

Method Scheduling

The scheduling of method execution is now done directly by the body so the scheduler in the definition of $Object$ is 0.

Semantics of Statements

$$[\text{answer } (m_1, ..., m_n)]\ =\ \sum_{m\,\in\,\{m_1,...,\,m_n\}} \overline{activate}_m.terminate.Done$$

$$[\text{reply } E]\ (k)\ =\ [E]\ Into\ (x)\ (\overline{reply}_k x.Done)$$

5. Class Inheritance

In this section we discuss how to extend the basic framework of section 2 to support class inheritance.

First, we include a new agent component, called *Super*, in the assembly of agents that we used for constructing an object. The purpose of this agent as we will see shortly, is to allow methods defined in a class to invoke methods defined in a superclass despite the fact that they have been overridden in the class.

Next, we modify the definition of agents representing the behavior of program-defined object classes to be parameterized by an agent parameter rather than by a value representing an object identifier. The resulting structure of agents is illustrated in figure 2(a). It is obtained from figure 1 by the addition of SUPER and the introduction of a place holder for an agent in place of the agent components of figure 1.

The hole in figure 2 can be filled in either by an agent equal to the composition of the components that were removed from figure 1 as illustrated by figure 2.(b) or by another agent with a hole as in figure 2(c). The first way to "fill the hole" is used to produce the behavior of instances. The second represents class inheritance where two classes are composed to yield a new class.

5.1 Extending SCOOL to Support Inheritance

In order to include inheritance in SCOOL we modify the class declarations as follows:

ClassDecl ::= class C *BasicDecl*

class C superclass C' *BasicDecl*

BasicDecl ::= { *VarDecl MethodDecl$_1$...MethodDecl$_n$*}

A class declaration may optionally specify, by using the keyword superclass as indicated above, that the newly defined class C inherits an already defined class C'.

The semantics of inheritance used for this version of SCOOL is inspired by Smalltalk-80. A subclass may define methods with the same names as its superclass's, in which case the subclass method definition overrides the inherited one. The pseudo variable super may be used by an object to invoke a method of the superclass despite the fact that it has been overridden by the subclass.

Instance variables defined in a class are accessible in methods of its subclasses and it is not allowed to redefine them in a subclass.

The pseudo variable self may be used by the object to invoke one of its methods. Invocations through self will always cause the execution of the most specialized version of the invoked method.

Method overriding and the super and self features are further discussed in section 5.3.

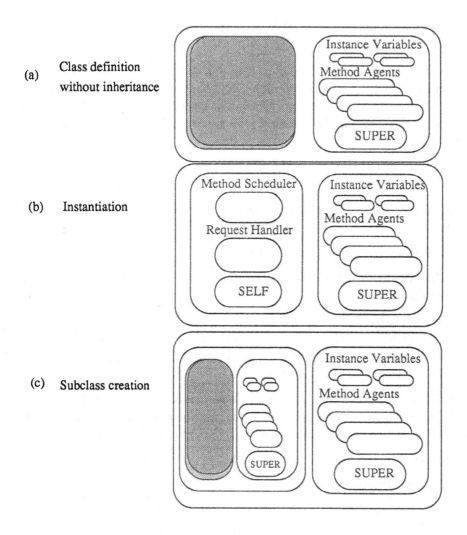

(a) Class definition without inheritance

(b) Instantiation

(c) Subclass creation

Figure 2

5.2 Agent Definitions for Modelling Class Inheritance

The agent *ObjectBehavior*$_c$, defined below, represents the behavior of C's instances, and is parameterized by their object identifiers.

$$ObjectBehavior_c(id) = Object(id, ms(c), ClassBehavior_c)$$

Where $ms(c)$ is the set of method names of the class, including the method names of all methods applicable to the class's instances, i.e. the new methods defined by c and all the inherited methods.

ObjectBehavior$_c$ is defined in terms of the agents *ClassBehavior*$_c$ and *Object*. The former is an agent with an agent parameter that represents the class C. It has the structure of the agents with a hole shown in figure 2(c) and (a) depending on whether or not inheritance is used in C's declaration.

The agent *Object* fills in the hole of its agent parameter as illustrated in figure 2(b), with the object agent components defined in section 2, yielding an agent representing the behavior of instances of the class. It also restricts the scope of events used for communication between object components. The way that restriction is used allows us to capture method overriding as it will be explained in section 5.3

$$Object\,(id, m, Cl)\ =\ (Cl\,(RH\,(id, m)\,)\,|\,Sch\,(m)\,|\,Self\,(id)\,)$$
$$\backslash L(Sch\,(m)\,)\,\backslash L(Self\,(id)\,)$$

where *Sch* is some method scheduler agent and *Cl* corresponds to the *ClassBehavior$_c$* agent for some class C.

ClassBehavior$_c$ for a class C is defined as follows:

1. *ClassBehavior$_c$(X)* = *BasicBehavior$_c$* *(X)* if C is defined without making use of inheritance.

2. *ClassBehavior$_c$* *(X)* =
   ClassBehavior$_{c'}$ ((*BasicBehavior$_c$* *(X)* | *Super* (*bm* (c)))\⟨*super$_m$*|m ∈ *bm* (c)⟩)
   where *bm*(c) is the set of method names defined in *Basic Decl$_c$*, if an already defined class C' is specified as C's superclass.

The restriction of *super* events in the second case above is necessary to ensure that interaction will take place with the "right" *Super* agent. In the case where inheritance was used in the definition of C' the definition of *ClassBehavior* for C' also includes a *Super* agent.

BasicBehavior$_c$ is obtained from the *BasicDecl* part of a class C as:

$$BasicBehavior_c\,(X)\ =$$
$$(X\,|\,[VarDecl]\,|\,[MethDecl_1]\,|...|\,[MethDecl_n]\,)$$
$$\backslash ACC_{V_1}...\backslash ACC_{V_k}\backslash\langle call_m|m \in bm(c)\rangle$$

if *BasicDecl$_c$* = { *VarDecl MethodDecl$_1$* ... *MethodDecl$_n$* }, is the *BasicDecl* part of class's C's declaration, the variables $V_1,..,V_n$ are declared in *VarDecl*.

The *Super* agent operates as an event transducer generating a $\overline{call_m}$ for each *super$_m$* event it consumes, with *m* in the set of the object's methods.

$$Super\,(meth)\ =\ fix\,(X = \sum_{m \in meth} super_m\,(k, a).\overline{call_m}\,(k, a).X)$$

Semantics of Class Declarations

Finally the semantics mapping for class declarations is given as:

$$[class\ C\ BasicDecl]\ =\ Class\,(C, ObjectBehavior_c)$$

⟦class C superclass C' $BasicDecl$⟧ = $Class$ (C, $ObjectBehavior_c$)

Where the agent $Class$ is that defined in section 2, and the use of inheritance in the definition of the class C is taken into account as discussed above in the definition of $ClassBehavior_c$ which is in turn used to define $ObjectBehavior_c$.

5.3 Overriding Superclass Methods, Self and Super

Overriding of methods is accomplished by the interplay of the restriction of the access sort for method agents in the definition of $BasicBehavior_c$ and the operation of the request handler agent.

When a class is instantiated the request handler agent is instantiated within the scope of $BasicBehavior_c$ where C is the most specialized class in a chain C1,..,Cn of classes. Because of the restriction of the access sort of method agents in the definition of $BasicBehavior_c$ the $call_m$ events generated by the request handler for executing method m will only be visible to the method agent for m of the most specialized class that defines m. This is illustrated in figure 3.

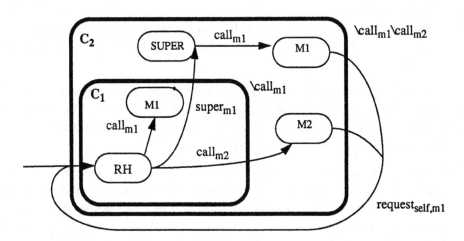

Figure 3

In some languages as for instance Smalltalk-80[4] the pseudo-variable super is used, in an expression like super m1: x, to indicate that the search for a method matching the method selector m should start at the object's superclass method dictionary. We capture the semantics of super as follows:

First the semantics for an expression involving super is given as:

$$⟦ super.m\ (E_1, ..., E_n) ⟧ = ⟦E_1⟧\ Into\ (x_1) ... ⟦E_n⟧\ Into\ (x_n)$$
$$\overline{super_m\ (k, (x_1, ..., x_n))}.reply_k\ (x).\overline{res}\ x$$

This way the event will be able to get out of the restriction of the access sorts for methods of the class. In the enclosing scope this event will be intercepted by the $Super$ agent and transduced to a $\overline{call}_m v$ event which is released outside of the class scope of restriction. Thus, the "search" for a matching method starts at the superclass level.

A method invocation through the pseudo-variable self appearing in any of the methods of inherited classes should cause the invocation of the most specialized version of that method. This is achieved by using the agent Self to retrieve the object's id and then using this id for the call. As self is bound in the most restricted scope it will necessarily cause the invocation of the most specialized method.

Figure 5.3 illustrates the above for a class C_1 which inherits a class C_2, having methods m_1 and m_2, and which redefines method m_1.

6. Considering Two Other Process Calculi

For developing the framework we have considered two alternative calculi. Although these are derived from CCS they incorporate features that substantially enhance its expressive power in ways that are important for modelling some object-oriented concepts. In this section we will discuss the issues related to the use of these calculi as alternatives for the development of the semantic framework as well as for modeling other object-oriented programming language features.

The first of these is the *Calculus of Higher Order Communicating Systems*, CHOCS, [16] which extends CCS by allowing processes to be sent and received as values. The second is the π-calculus [8] where ports or labels may be communicated as values so that systems with dynamic communication links between their components may be modelled.

The ability to express systems with dynamic communication topology is essential for modelling object-based systems where objects are created dynamically and object identifiers may be transmitted in messages. Although we have considered using the π-calculus for the semantic framework we finally preferred using CCS. The main reason which is further discussed below was that the semantic description of some language features was not as direct as one would expect.

The higher order approach of CHOCS could also be used to model systems with dynamic communication topology since, as suggested in [16], it is equivalent in expressive power to ECCS[3], the basis of the π-calculus. However, in order to go from ECCS to CHOCS a translation using a kind of continuation semantics is needed. We did not consider taking this approach for modelling dynamic interconnection since it appears to be less direct for modelling COOPLs than the approach we used in section 2.

Apart from modelling systems with dynamic communication topology, the higher order approach would be useful for modelling features found in some object-based systems that we did not want to consider in the present framework. These include systems where classes are first class objects as well as systems based on *prototypes* and *delegation*[6].

For instance, with CHOCS, an object class may be modelled as an agent that stores the description of the agents corresponding to the class's methods. Objects of the class receive the description of the method agents and execute them within a scope that restricts access to the object's instance variables. In this scope references to instance variables in the method agents are dynamically bound to the instance variables of the instance that executes them. Dynamic changes to classes and to the class inheritance hierarchy can be modelled by changing the description of method agents held by the agent representing the class or by changing in instances the value used to identify the agent acting as its class.

6.1 Modelling COOPL Features in the π-Calculus

The ability of the π-calculus to express the dynamic creation of ports and their communication among agents is very attractive for modelling object-oriented languages. These features have been used by Walker to model the semantics of some simple languages[18] in the π-calculus. We will first present how the π-calculus may be used to model COOPLs in a way, basically the one presented in [18], that takes advantage of the dynamic creation and communication of ports. Next, we discuss some shortcomings of the π-calculus and of the approach followed in [18] for expressing some object-oriented features. Although the main ideas for modelling COOPL features in the π-calculus that we present below are as in [18] we take a simpler approach for the semantics of invocation of object operations. This is possible because of the different way, discussed at length below, in which we model primitive objects, which simplifies the semantics of expressions.

Using π-Calculus Ports to Represent Object Identifiers

Object identifiers are modelled by the π-calculus ports that are used for interacting with the agents representing the corresponding objects. These ports may be stored in variables and used to communicate with the corresponding objects.

Variables can be modelled in a way similar to the one described in 2.3. The only difference is that now the values stored are ports used to represent object identifiers. The semantics of the invocation of an object's operation is to retrieve the port by communication with the variable agent and then use the received port to communicate with the object.

A class C may be modelled as an agent, *Class*, that accepts requests for the creation of a new instance at a port c, where c is a constant name. For each request it creates a new port: *id* which is communicated through c to the caller. The new port is used for representing the object identifier of the new instance and is bound to the parameter of an agent, here *Object*, that is created to represent the new instance.

$$Class\,(c) \; = \; \bar{c}\,(id)\,.\,(Object\,(id) \mid Class\,(c)\,)$$

The following protocol which avoids interference between concurrent requests is used to model operation invocation. For each request received along the port representing its object identifier the corresponding agent receives a "private" port that is used for receiving the information associated to a request such as a name identifying the requested operation, the operation's arguments and sending back the reply.

The agent *Object* defined below illustrates this approach. First, a private port associated with a particular request is received along the port *id*. Next, a name identifying the requested operation is received from the private port. According to this name the agent behaves as one of the agents *Method₁,...,Methodₙ*. These agents are parameterized by the request port which they use to receive the operation's arguments and return the result.

$$Object\,(id)\ =\ id\,(r)\,.\,(HandleRequest\,(r)\,|\,Object\,(id)\,)$$

$$HandleRequest\,(r)\ =\ r{:}\,[\,m_1 \Rightarrow Method_1\,(r)\,,...,m_n \Rightarrow Method_n\,(r)\,]$$

The agent *Call(id,m,a,result)* given below illustrates the sequence of actions that are executed at the caller for invoking the operation identified by *m* of the object associated to *id* with a single argument: *a* and receiving a port identifying the result which is sent along the port *result*.

$$Call\,(id, m, a, result)\ =\ \overline{id}\,(r)\,.\,\overline{r}\ m.\overline{r}\ a.r\,(v)\,.\overline{result}\ v$$

Comparing Object Identifiers

An issue that is not addressed by the languages modelled in [18] is the possibility to compare the identity of two objects. In most object-oriented languages an expression like x = y where x and y are program variables may be used to compare the equality of the object identifiers stored in these variables.

The only support offered by the π-calculus [8] for the comparison of labels is provided by the "match" operator $[x{=}y]$ defined as follows. The agent $[x{=}y]\,P$ behaves as P if the names x and y are identical otherwise it behaves as 0, the inactive agent. If object identifiers are modelled as π-calculus ports, the match operator is not sufficient for describing the semantics of an expression like $x{=}y$, since no action is possible if the compared labels are not identical.

In order to be able to use ports to represent object identifiers the π-calculus should be extended with an operator that would better supports the comparison of two names. For instance a "non-match" or an "if-then-else" operator defined in a way analogous to the match operator.

It would also be possible to use a less direct way for representing object identifiers. For instance, object identifiers could be modelled as pairs of ports consisting of the port used to communicate with the agent representing the object and the port of an agent representing an integer value. The comparison of object identifiers would take place by comparing the associated integer values which could be encoded in the calculus in the way presented in [18]. Such an approach however does not take advantage of the features of the calculus that made it in the first place attractive for modelling object-oriented systems.

Primitive Objects and the Semantics of Expressions

Practically every object-oriented language supports a number of primitive object classes such as integers and Booleans that are used as the starting point for defining other application specific classes. With the CCS-based approach we followed in 3.2 we represented primitive objects and their classes as agents that observe exactly the same protocol as the agents representing the semantics of program defined classes. With this approach the semantics of expressions, except the ones that specifically concern primitive objects such as expressions consisting of integer or Boolean constants, was defined uniformly independently of whether or not they involve primitive objects.

A different approach was followed in [18] for modelling primitive objects using the π-calculus. With this approach objects of primitive classes such as integer and Boolean values are encoded as agents which do not observe the same protocol as the agents representing instances of program defined classes. The semantics of expressions takes into account the type of the objects involved and in the case of primitive objects it depends on the structure of the agents that represent the objects of a particular primitive type.

With respect to the approach that we followed in section 3.2 the above approach has the disadvantage that the semantics of expressions is not defined uniformly independently of the type of the involved objects. Several cases have to be considered, one for each of the primitive types that are supported by a particular language. We have considered two alternative approaches for modelling primitive objects in the π-calculus that overcome the shortcomings of the above approach.

The first approach is to reserve a fixed set of constant names to represent the object identifiers of primitive objects and make use of these names in the encoding of the agents representing the objects of the type. For example, the fixed constant ports *true* and *false* and the agents *True* and *False* defined below illustrate this approach for the type Boolean.

$$True = \overline{true}\,(r)\,.r\,(op)\,.\,(TrueMethods\,(r)\;\mid\;True)$$

$$TrueMethods\,(r) = r:[not \Rightarrow \bar{r}\;false,\;or \Rightarrow r\,(x)\,.\bar{r}\;true,\;and \Rightarrow r\,(x)\,.\bar{r}\;x]$$

$$False = \overline{false}\,(r)\,.r\,(op)\,.\,(FalseMethods\,(r)\;\mid\;False)$$

$$FalseMethods\,(r) = r:[not \Rightarrow \bar{r}\;true,\;or \Rightarrow r\,(x)\,.\bar{r}\;x,\;and \Rightarrow r\,(x)\,.\bar{r}\;false]$$

The agent *True* encodes the behavior of the object corresponding to the Boolean value true. It accepts requests at the fixed port *true* over which it communicates the name of a new private port that is used for getting more information and for replying to each request. The agent *TrueMethods* which is parameterized by the port that is used for an individual request encodes the operations *not*, *or* and *and* for this object. *Not* has no argument and returns as a result the constant port *false* that is used by the agent that represents the object "false". *Or* inputs from the request port a port corresponding to its argument. It ignores the argument's value and always replies by the port *true* that corresponds to the object identifier of the object "true." *And* inputs the port associated to its argument which is either *true* or *false* and replies by sending back this same port.

The behavior of the agent *False* is analogous to that of *True*. Integers and other primitive objects may be represented in a similar way.

Note that only a finite number of integer objects may be represented by following this approach. This, however, is not a severe shortcoming for the description of the semantics of COOPLs since we could assume an arbitrary though finite number of integer objects in the environment.

The second approach for representing primitive objects such as Booleans and integers is to maintain the representation of integer and Boolean values as given in [18] but provide an object interface to these representations so that the semantics of expressions may be defined in a uniform way for all objects. This may be accomplished by encoding objects of primitive types, say integers, as follows. The agent representing the integer object stores the port of an agent that encodes an integer value in the way presented in [18]. Integer operations are realized by operating on this representation and returning the port of an integer object associated with the resulting representation.

With this approach it is not necessary to fix a finite number of ports to be used as the object identifiers of agents that represent integers. Each time an integer is returned as the result of an operation on integers a new port could be created for the integer object associated with the integer value corresponding to the result of the operation. However, if a new port is used each time that an integer object is returned as the result of an operation on integers different integer objects would be used for representing the same integer value. The result of this would be that the semantics of = based on the ports used for representing object identifiers would not coincide with the equality of the integer values. A way to ensure that exactly one integer object is used for each integer value is to have an agent in the environment that based on the integer value, creates and returns the port of an integer object. This agent would remember the ports used by integer objects associated with each integer value so that at most one integer object would be created for an integer value. The main disadvantage of this approach is that it is heavily operational.

7. Concluding Remarks

We have presented a framework for describing the semantics of concurrent object-oriented languages and features. This framework captures the essential concepts found in COOPLs such as objects and object identifiers, concurrent execution, classes and class inheritance. It supports a high level description of the semantics of language features that makes it possible to compare the different language design approaches and investigate in a formal setting the interaction of features such as inheritance and synchronization.

The framework captures the common structure of object-oriented features by a set of definitions of agents with agent parameters. These parameterized agents may be viewed as the operators of a derived calculus that supports in a direct and easy to follow way the specification of the semantics of COOPLs. The different language design approaches may be represented either by varying the agent parameters or by modifying the definition of certain parameterized agents.

Although CCS does not directly support the representation of systems with dynamic interconnection structure it was possible to encode object-oriented languages by assuming a static interconnection network where any object may interact with any other object and where object identifiers act like switches for communicating with a particular object. This could be done in a more elegant and direct way by using the π-calculus which directly supports the dynamic creation and establishment of communication links. However, in order to take advantage of these features it is necessary to extend the calculus by an operator that better supports the comparison of ports. Also, some more work is needed for representing primitive object types.

There are some features found in object-oriented languages that are not taken into account by our framework. These include support for classes considered as first class objects as well as for languages based on prototypes and delegation. A higher order calculus such as CHOCS would be more appropriate for expressing the semantics of such features.

An important consequence of using a process calculus such as CCS as the target for the semantics is that the underlying calculus may be used to formally investigate, specify and verify properties of languages and systems.

The meaning of individual objects is given by process calculus terms. This provides us with a behavioral equivalence relation on objects induced by the equivalence on the corresponding process calculus terms. Furthermore, it is possible to use the calculus directly to specify the behavior of an object by a process calculus term and to examine whether the specification is, in some sense, equivalent to the term corresponding to the meaning of an object.

The properties of the derived operators that we have defined, as agents with agent parameters, for representing language features can be investigated by using the underlying process calculus. The analysis of these operators and their interaction can be used to infer useful information about the language design and the combination of a language's features.

Our future research goals include the use of the underlying process calculus framework for the development of formal notions of behavioral compatibility of objects motivated by substitutability, the abstract specification of behavioral constraints on objects and the further development of formal criteria for the comparison and evaluation of language and application designs.

References

[1]   P. America, "POOL-T: A Parallel Object-Oriented Language," in *Object-Oriented Concurrent Programming*, ed. A. Yonezawa, M. Tokoro, pp. 199-220, The MIT Press, Cambridge, Massachusetts, 1987.

[2]   R.H. Campbell and A.N. Habermann, "The Specification of Process Synchronization by Path Expressions," LNCS 16, pp. 89-102, Springer-Verlag, New York, 1974.

[3]   U. Engberg and M. Nielsen, "A Calculus of Communicating Systems with Label Passing," DAIMI PB-208, University of Aarhus, 1986.

[4] A. Goldberg and D. Robson, *Smalltalk-80: The Language and its Implementation*, Addison-Wesley, 1983.

[5] D. G. Kafura and K. H. Lee, "Inheritance in Actor Based Concurrent Object-Oriented Languages," in *Proceedings* ECOOP'89, ed. S. Cook, British Computer Society Workshop Series, Cambridge University Press, 1989.

[6] H. Lieberman, "Using Prototypical Objects to Implement Shared Behavior in Object Oriented Systems," ACM SIGPLAN Notices, Proceedings OOPSLA '86, vol. 21, no. 11, pp. 214-223, Nov 1986.

[7] R. Milner, *Communication and Concurrency*, Prentice Hall International Series in Computer Science, 1989.

[8] R. Milner, J. Parrow and D. Walker, "A Calculus of Mobile Processes, Part I and II," Report ECS-LFCS-89-85 and -86, Laboratory for Foundations of Computer Science, Computer Science Department, University of Edinburgh, 1989.

[9] J.E.B. Moss and W.H. Kohler, "Concurrency Features for the Trellis/Owl Language,"*in Proc. of ECOOP'87*, BIGRE, no. 54, pp. 223-232, June 1987.

[10] O.M. Nierstrasz and M. Papathomas, "Viewing Objects as Patterns of Communicating Agents.," OOPSLA'90 Proceedings, SIGPLAN Notices, vol. 25, no. 10, ACM Press, October 1990.

[11] O.M. Nierstrasz, "A Guide to Specifying Concurrent Behavior with Abacus," in *Object Management*, ed. D.C. Tsichritzis, pp. 267-293, Centre Universitaire d'Informatique, University of Geneva, July 1990.

[12] M. Papathomas, "Concurrency Issues in Object-Oriented Languages," in *Object Oriented Development* , Centre Universitaire d'Informatique, University of Geneva, ed. D. Tsichritzis, pp. 207-245, 1989.

[13] M. Papathomas and D. Konstantas, "Integrating Concurrency and Object-Oriented Programming: An Evaluation of Hybrid," in *Object Management*, Centre Universitaire d'Informatique, University of Geneva, ed. D. Tsichritzis, pp. 229-244, 1990.

[14] A. Snyder, "Encapsulation and Inheritance in Object-Oriented Programming Languages," Proc. OOPSLA'86, ACM SIGPLAN Notices, vol. 21, no. 11, pp. 38-45, Nov 1986.

[15] C. Tomlinson and V. Singh, "Inheritance and Synchronization with Enabled Sets," ACM SIGPLAN Notices, Proceedings OOPSLA '89, vol. 24, no. 10, pp. 103-112, Oct 1989.

[16] B. Thomsen, "A Calculus of Higher Order Communicating Systems," Proc. 16th POPL, pp. 143-154, Austin, Texas, Jan 11-13, 1989.

[17] F.W. Vaandrager, "Process algebra semantics of POOL," in *Applications of Process Algebra*, ed. J.C. Baeten, Cambridge Tracts in Theoretical Computer Science 17, pp. 173-236, Cambridge University Press, 1990.

[18] D. Walker, "π-calculus Semantics of Object-Oriented Programming Languages," Report ECS-LFCS-90-122, Laboratory for Foundations of Computer Science, Computer Science Department, University of Edinburgh, Oct. 1990.

[19] Y. Yokote and M. Tokoro, "Concurrent Programming in ConcurrentSmalltalk," in *Object-Oriented Concurrent Programming*, ed. M. Tokoro, pp. 129-158, The MIT press, Cambridge, Massachusetts, 1987.

[20] A. Yonezawa, J-P Briot and E. Shibayama, "Object-Oriented Concurrent Programming in ABCL/1," ACM SIGPLAN Notices, Proceedings OOPSLA '86 , vol. 21, no. 11, pp. 258-268, Nov 1986.

A Sheaf Semantics for FOOPS Expressions (Extended Abstract) *

D.A. Wolfram

Programming Research Group, University of Oxford,
11 Keble Road, Oxford OX1 3QD, United Kingdom.

Joseph A. Goguen

Programming Research Group, University of Oxford,
11 Keble Road, Oxford OX1 3QD, United Kingdom,
and SRI International, 333 Ravenswood Avenue,
Menlo Park, CA 94025–3493, USA.

Abstract

We present a sheaf semantics for concurrent method expression evaluation in FOOPS. Evaluations of functions, methods, and attributes are treated in a uniform way. General E-strategies for functions, methods, attributes, and method combiners are assumed.

1 A Sketch of Sheaf Models of Concurrency

Sheaf theory, not really being a subject, cannot properly be said to have a history. Rather, it is an octopus spreading itself through everyone else's history. J.W. Gray

Gray [14] identifies the origins of sheaf theory in algebraic topology in the works of Alexander [1] in 1938, and Leray [15] in 1945. Apart from algebraic topology, Gray also describes its grasp on complex analysis, algebraic geometry, differential equations, and category theory.

Sheaves have more recently been used as models for concurrency. Perhaps the earliest models were those of Goguen from 1971 on a categorical formulation of General Systems Theory [5, 9, 10, 13]. This work led to formulating 'objects as sheaves' [5, 11]. In 1986, Monteiro and Pereira [16] gave a sheaf-theoretic model of concurrency which uses sheaves of monoids. Benson [2] (1991) gave conditions for a sheaf to contain 'realistic local histories' in the absence of a global clock, and a sheaf-theoretic view of 'process-channel systems' [3]. Dubey [4] (1991) considered a sheaf-theoretic definition of safety and liveness properties.

*This research was supported by the Fujitsu Corporation, Japan, and Christ Church, Oxford.

The formulation of sheaf semantics we use is based on that by Goguen [12], which is sufficiently general for a sheaf-theoretic semantics of concurrency in the programming language called FOOPS [8, 18].

2 Sheaves, Diagrams, and Behaviour

For the purposes of this paper, we make the following definitions.

Definition 2.1 A *sheaf* is a functor $\mathcal{O} : \mathcal{T}^{op} \to$ Set such that all of the following conditions hold:

- $\mathcal{T}$ is a *base category* whose set of objects $\mathcal{T}$ is a topological space, such that for all $U, V \in \mathcal{T}$, there is an arrow $U \to V$ if and only if there is an inclusion $i : U \hookrightarrow V$.

- If $i : U \hookrightarrow V$ is in $\mathcal{T}$, then $\mathcal{O}(i) : \mathcal{O}(V) \to \mathcal{O}(U)$ maps $f : V \to A$ to its restriction f filter U.

- For all $U, U' \in \mathcal{T}$ such that $f \in \mathcal{O}(U)$ and $g \in \mathcal{O}(U')$ and f filter $(U \cap U') = g$ filter $(U \cap U')$, then $f \cup g \in \mathcal{O}(U \cup U')$. The notation $f \cup g$ means the least upper bound of f and g, or the function represented by the union of their representations as sets of ordered pairs.

The last condition in Definition 2.1 is sometimes called the *finite pasting condition*. If this condition is omitted, the functor defined may be called a *pre-sheaf*. The target of $\mathcal{O}$ is called its *structure category*. In Definition 2.1, it is the category Set, but this can be generalized by allowing different structure categories. The finite pasting condition then becomes that

$$\mathcal{O}(U \cup V) \to \mathcal{O}(U) \times \mathcal{O}(V) \rightrightarrows \mathcal{O}(U \cap V)$$

is a limit diagram for all $U, V \in \mathcal{T}$, where the first arrow is the tupling of the restrictions to U and V, and the next two are π_1; filter $(U \cap V)$ and π_2; filter $(U \cap V)$.

Definition 2.2 A *sheaf morphism* is a natural transformation between two sheaves over the same base and structure categories.

2.1 Diagrams and Limits

Definition 2.3 A *diagram* is a directed graph with set of nodes N, where each node $n \in N$ is labelled by a sheaf $\mathcal{O}_n$, and each edge of the form $e : n \to n'$ is labelled by a sheaf morphism over a base category $\mathcal{T}$ and with structure category Set, $\varphi_e : \mathcal{O}_n \to \mathcal{O}_{n'}$. We may also call such a diagram a *system*.

Definition 2.4 Given a diagram whose nodes are labelled by sheaves $\mathcal{O}_n$ for $n \in N$, the *behaviour object* $\mathcal{L}$ of the diagram has for each $U \in \mathcal{T}$

$$\mathcal{L}(U) = \{\{f_n \mid n \in N\} \mid f_n \in \mathcal{O}_n(U) \wedge (\varphi_e : \mathcal{O}_n \to \mathcal{O}_{n'} \Rightarrow \varphi_e(f_n) = f_{n'})\}$$

Theorem 2.5 *If the structure category $\mathcal{C}$ for the sheaves that label the nodes of a diagram has limits, then the diagrams have limits. When $\mathcal{C}$ is Set, this limit is the behaviour object of the diagram.*

Remark 2.6 In Definitions 2.2, 2.3, 2.4 and Theorem 2.5, 'sheaf' and 'sheaves' can uniformly be replaced by 'pre-sheaf' and 'pre-sheaves', respectively.

3 Concurrency in FOOPS

FOOPS [8] (*F*unctional and *O*bject *O*riented *P*rogramming *S*ystem) is an object oriented extension of the OBJ functional programming language [6].

3.1 Method Expressions

Evaluable FOOPS expressions include only four kinds of operations: functions, attributes, methods, and method combiners. An evaluable expression in FOOPS is a well-sorted, well-formed first-order term, each of whose symbols is either a variable, constant, method combiner, function symbol, attribute symbol, or method symbol. In these expressions, attribute symbols are monadic and an argument of such a symbol evaluates to an object identifier. Function symbols, method symbols, and method combiners can be polyadic. A *method expression* is a FOOPS expression which contains a method symbol.

An evaluable FOOPS expression is evaluated either by conditional term rewriting, or by one of two forms of conditional assignment. A rule for an operation which is not built-in is specified by a conditional rule which is called an *axiom*. It has the form

$$\texttt{lhs = rhs if condition .}$$

where

- `lhs`, `rhs`, and `condition` are FOOPS expressions, `lhs` can contain *patterns* [6], but `rhs` and `condition` do not contain them or method symbols, but they can contain variables which occur in the patterns in `lhs`.

- `lhs` takes one of the two following forms:

  - A FOOPS expression which does not contain method symbols and attribute symbols.
  - A FOOPS expression of the form `attr(meth(O, arglist))`, or of the form `attr(O1 / meth(O, arglist))`, where `attr` is an attribute symbol, `meth` is a method symbol, `O1` is an object identifier, and `O` is a variable which matches individual object identifiers, and `arglist` is a finite sequence of patterns. All objects whose identifiers match `O` must be in the same class as the object whose identifier is `O1`, and none of them can be that object.

- The set of variables in `rhs` and in `condition` is not a superset of those in `lhs`.

- The least sorts of `lhs` and `rhs` are in the same component in the sort hierarchy [7].

- `condition` has boolean sort and does not contain method symbols [17]. Stipulating `condition` is optional. If it is not required, then `if` is also omitted.

Operationally, when lhs has the first form mentioned above, the axiom is used as a conditional order-sorted rewrite rule.

If the expression meth(0', arglist') is being evaluated, then each lhs of the form

$$attr(meth(0, arglist))$$

where attr(meth(0, arglist)) matches meth(0', arglist') has its condition and rhs instantiated using the matching substitution. If the instantiated form of condition evaluates to the constant representing true, the evaluation of rhs replaces the value of attr(0'). For each attribute name attr of 0', there is no more than one axiom whose lhs of the form above has attr as its principal operation symbol.

Every lhs of the form attr(01 / meth(0, arglist)) where meth(0', arglist') matches meth(0, arglist) has its instantiated condition evaluated as above. If it evaluates to the constant representing true, the instantiated form of rhs replaces the value of attr(01). For each attribute name attr of 0', there is no more than one axiom whose lhs of the form above has attr as its principal operation symbol and 01 as its first argument.

If the instantiated form of condition does not evaluate to the constant which represents true, then no action occurs. If condition is not present in an axiom, evaluation occurs using that axiom as though there were a condition which evaluated to the constant representing true. The order in which condition's and rhs's are evaluated, and in which replacements of values occur, is not specified.

The restrictions above on the principal operation symbols of lhs's of axioms for method expressions, and the restrictions on expressions which a lhs of the form attr(01 / meth(0, arglist)) matches ensure that at most one change in the value of an attribute can occur from the evaluation of a method expression of the form meth(0', arglist') when arglist' does not contain any method expressions.

3.2 Evaluation Strategies

In general, the result of evaluating a method expression depends on the order of evaluating its arguments. The order of evaluation of functions, attributes, method combiners, and methods can be stipulated and described by optional annotations called *E-strategies* [6, 17].

Every FOOPS expression $f(t_1, \ldots, t_n)$ has an E-strategy

$$[I_1|\cdots|I_m||I_{m+1}]$$

which is either provided by the programmer, or else is a default E-strategy supplied by the compiler. In such an E-strategy:

1. Each I_i is a subset of $\{1, \ldots, n\}$ where $1 \leq i \leq m+1$.

2. $|| I_{m+1}$ and $I_1|\ldots|I_m$ are both optional.

3. The default E-strategy is $[\{1\}|\ldots|\{n\}]$.

4. For every $i, j : 1 \leq i, j \leq m$, if $i \neq j$ then $I_i \cap I_j = \emptyset$.

5. If f is not a method combiner and if a subterm t_i could be a method expression, then $i \in \cup_{1 \leq j \leq m} I_j$.

6. $(\cup_{1 \leq j \leq m} I_j) \cap I_{m+1} = \emptyset$.

7. $\{1, \ldots, n\} - (\cup_{1 \leq j \leq m} I_j) - I_{m+1} = \emptyset$.

None of these assumptions restricts the generality of the definition of E-strategy in the design of FOOPS [8]. Assumption 4 is equivalent to the E-strategy definition there, because we can assume that the I_j are disjoint sets from the outset.

Assumption 5 ensures that method expressions are evaluated bottom-up in the method expression parse tree of a FOOPS expression; it is never left unevaluated. This is not necessary for method combiners. For example, _or_ does not evaluate its arguments.

Assumption 6 prevents the possible inconsistency of stating that an argument should be evaluated, and also left unevaluated. In practice, such an inconsistency could be solved by ensuring the argument is evaluated, or unevaluated if it is never a method expression, or by reporting an error.

Assumption 7 is implied by the design of FOOPS [8] which states that the set

$$\{1, \ldots, n\} - (\cup_{1 \leq j \leq m} I_j) - I_{m+1} = I_0$$

need not be the empty set. In this case, the arguments of $f(t_1, \ldots, t_n)$ whose indices occur in I_0 are evaluated, but the method of their evaluation is left unspecified. There is no loss of generality if we assume that $I_0 \subseteq (\cup_{1 \leq j \leq m} I_j)$ because their evaluation method can be regarded as fixed, and can be specified in the E-strategy for f.

Informally, the effect of this annotation is that all of the arguments of f whose place indices are in I_1 are evaluated concurrently until no further evaluations of them are possible. This is repeated for I_2, and so on until I_m. Finally, evaluation takes place at the top level. Arguments in I_{m+1} are not evaluated, and they do not occur in $\cup_{1 \leq i \leq m} I_i$. The order of evaluation of arguments not in $\cup_{1 \leq i \leq m+1} I_i$ is unspecified.

For example, evaluating the function _+_ with E-strategy $[\{1\}|\{2\}]$ would cause its first argument to be evaluated, and then its second argument, and then their sum would be evaluated. However, evaluating the function _+||_ with E-strategy $[\{1, 2\}]$ would result in the concurrent evaluation of its arguments before their sum is evaluated.

3.3 Method Combiners

FOOPS has four main built-in *method combiners*. Others can be defined by the user. They are listed below with their default E-strategies [17]. All of them have the rank AnyClass AnyClass -> AnyClass.

Sequential composition	_;_	$[\{1\}	\{2\}]$
Return	_return_	$[\{1\}	\{2\}]$
Non-deterministic choice	_or_	$[||\{1, 2\}]$
Concurrent execution	_||_	$[\{1, 2\}]$

The method combiner _return_ has the same effect as _;_.

3.4 Built-in Methods

FOOPS has two main built-in methods: `remove` and `new` for deleting and creating objects, respectively. Evaluating the method expression `remove(O)` deletes the object whose object identifier is O.

Evaluating the method expression `new.C(O)` creates an object of class C whose identifier is O. The object identifier O should be unique with repect to all previous object identifiers.

Objects usually contain attributes, which can either be non-object-valued attributes, or else objects. The initial value of an attribute can be specified by the user when an object is created. This is done using a method expression `new.C(O, eqs)` where eqs is a finite sequence of equations of the form `attr_name = attr_value`, `attr_name` is the identifier of an attribute which occurs in each object of the class C, and `attr_value` is an expression whose evaluation has the same sort as `attr_name`. In the sequence eqs, no two equations have the same left side, and equations are evaluated from left to right.

It is not necessary to specify the initial value of all attributes in a newly created object. Those attributes not specified are given default values. The default value of a non-object-valued attribute is given by the *principal constant* of its sort, which by convention is the first mentioned constant of that sort or supersort. A default value of a non-object-valued attribute may lie outside an expected range of values for a particular interpretation.

When it exists, the default value of an object-valued attribute of an object is the *principal constant* of its class. This is an object whose attributes have default values. Otherwise, a default object is created.

The object identifier `O.attr` of a newly created default object is formed from its attribute name `attr`, and the object identifier O of the object in which this attribute name occurs. This object identifier is unique.

Default objects are created by the breadth-first traversal of a graph which is called the *whole/part graph*. This is a finite directed graph computable from a method expression of the form `new.C(I)` [8]. Its nodes are classes, and its edges are subclass inclusions from a subclass to a superclass, or edges labelled by the name of an object-valued attribute.

Traversing an unlabelled edge does not result in the creation of any default objects. Traversing an edge labelled by a from a node A to a node B causes `new.B(I.a)` to be evaluated, where I is the object identifier of the object containing the object-valued attribute name a. The whole/part graph can be cyclic. When a cycle is detected, creating default objects is suspended until they are required[1]. This is called *lazy evaluation of default objects* [17].

4 Evaluating Method Expressions

The 'official semantics' of FOOPS [8] states that a method expression is evaluated by bottom-up evaluation of elementary method expressions in its method expression parse tree. The method expression parse tree can be defined as follows.

Definition 4.1 A FOOPS expression whose principal operation symbol is a method symbol or an attribute symbol is an *elementary object expression*. An elementary object ex-

---

[1]More precise details of this algorithm are given by Goguen and Meseguer [8].

pression whose principal operation symbol is a method symbol is an *elementary method expression*.

Definition 4.2 Given a FOOPS method expression t, an *immediate elementary object expression* of t is an elementary object expression which is a proper subterm of t, and is not a proper subterm of an elementary object expression which is a proper subterm of t.

Definition 4.3 The *method expression parse tree* of a FOOPS expression t, has t as its root. Each of its other nodes is labelled by an elementary object expression.

The immediate descendants of a node in the tree are the immediate elementary object expressions of the node. They are placed in the tree following the same left to right ordering that they occur in their immediate parent node.

The root occurs at depth 0 in the method expression parse tree. If a node occurs at depth k in the tree, then its immediate descendants each occur at depth $k + 1$.

If `meth(0, arglist)` is an evaluable FOOPS expression, but there is no axiom it matches whose lhs has the principal operation symbol `attr`, then evaluating `meth(0, arglist)` has no effect on the value `attr(0)`.

We shall give a sheaf-theoretic semantics for method expression evaluations.

4.1 Representing Objects

In general, the evaluation of a FOOPS expression occurs in the presence of objects, each of which has a unique identifier, and some attributes. Axioms for methods are associated with the class of an object. We shall represent an object by a tuple of the form

$$(\text{Id}, (a_1, v_1), \ldots, (a_n, v_n))$$

where Id is the identifier of the object, the a_i are its attribute names, and the v_i are their respective values. If a_i is an object-valued attribute, then v_i is the object identifier of the value of a_i, where $1 \leq i \leq n$.

We shall make the following assumptions about FOOPS. Each object has a unique object identifier with respect to all of the other objects that have existed, and the a_i are pairwise distinct in the representation of an object.

4.2 The Functional and Method Levels

A FOOPS expression which is not a method expression is evaluated by order-sorted conditional term rewriting using a canonical term rewriting system whose rules are axioms as described in Section 3.1. The principal symbols of the left sides of these rules are either function symbols or attribute symbols, and no rule contains a method expression. The term rewriting system is assumed to be canonical to ensure that the semantics of rewriting is well-defined [6].

At this 'functional level', FOOPS uses syntax very closely related to that of OBJ [6]: parameterized modules, views, and three forms of module importation [8]. In effect, these features enable a user to specify a particular term rewriting system concisely.

4.2.1 Errors

Four erroneous conditions can arise in evaluating a FOOPS expression, which do not occur in OBJ:

In evaluating meth(O, arglist), it is erroneous if an object with object identifier O does not exist. Evaluating this expression results in the error constant $\perp$.

It is also erroneous if attr is applied to an object identifier O of a non-existent object, or if the object exists but does not contain an attribute whose name is attr. Evaluating such a subterm yields the error constant $\perp$ of a suitable error supersort [8].

A combination of methods does not always evaluate to $\perp$ if one of its arguments is $\perp$. A function symbol is either a *built-in* function symbol, or a *user-defined* function symbol. A *user-defined* function symbol is one whose effect in applications is specified by axioms in a FOOPS program. A built-in function symbol, such as + or cons, is one whose effect in applications is known, and is never specified by axioms in a FOOPS program.

We shall assume that the evaluation of any attribute application and built-in function is $\perp$ whenever any one of its arguments evaluates to $\perp$.

4.2.2 Referents

By design, the first argument of an elementary method expression is an object identifier. Usually evaluating such an expression causes changes to the values of the attributes of the object with that identifier, and the object identifier is the evaluation of the expression. This effect can be overridden so that another object identifier which occurs in the method expression can be returned as the evaluation of the expression. To do so, we define referents as follows[2].

If s is an elementary object expression which occurs at depth k in a method expression parse tree, then one of its immediate subterms which is an object identifier can be prefixed by $k - j$ arrows $\uparrow$ provided that s is a subterm of an elementary object expression r occurring at depth j, and the first argument of r and the annotated immediate subterm of s are identifiers of objects which belong to the same class. The term r is called the *referent* of the annotated immediate subterm of s, and r must be the referent of no more than one of its annotated subterms.

This has the effect that the evaluation of the elementary method expression r at depth j of which s is a subterm can cause changes to occur to the attributes of the object whose identifier is the annotated immediate subterm of s, rather than the object whose identifier is the first argument of r.

5 Sheaf Semantics

The definitions and theorem of Section 2 can be used to model concurrency in FOOPS [8]. Before doing so, we shall make some assumptions and introduce some notations.

---

[2]The discussion here allows multiple referents. This seems to be more general than the original design [8].

5.1   Assumptions and Notations

We assume that every function symbol, attribute symbol, method symbol, and method combiner has a fixed E-strategy.

We shall also use the following notations:

- The sets of function symbols, attribute symbols, method symbols, and method combiners are disjoint sets.

- All of these symbols are written using prefix notation.

- A symbol occurring in one of these sets occurs with its arity, sort, and E-strategy. Each symbol is unique in each set.

- FOOPS expressions are written without parentheses and commas.

- If a term t has been evaluated, it is written $\bar{t}$.

- If a term $f t_1 \cdots t_n$ is not being evaluated, it is written $f t_1 \cdots t_n$. If $f t_1 \cdots t_n$ is being evaluated, it is written $\underline{f} t_1 \cdots t_n$.

- Every axiom has the form lhs = rhs if condition .

It is easy to see that these notational remarks also do not restrict generality. The first three of them allow a FOOPS expression to be written without parentheses and commas, since we can determine uniquely the arity of a symbol, the sorts of its arguments, and its E-strategy. The next two notations will be used below in the definition of sheaf semantics for FOOPS expressions. If an axiom appears without if condition, then if true can be joined to it without changing its effects.

For simplicity, we assume that ↑ never appears in a FOOPS expression, that ;, ||, and or are the only method combiners, and that no method combiner is defined by a user. The method combiner || is not allowed to appear in an elementary method expression. The other combiners differ because the evaluation of their application is either an object identifier or ⊥.

We also assume that method expressions of the form C.new(O, eqs) do not occur, objects are created by C.new(O) with default attribute values, and the whole/part graph for every object is acyclic.

The expression attr(O) is assumed to be evaluated by a built-in function which returns the value of the attribute attr in the object whose identifier is O. If such an attribute or such an object does not exist, then the function returns an error constant ⊥ of a suitable sort. We disallow an axiom whose lhs is an expression of the form attr(O) where attr is the name of an attribute, and O is an object identifier.

If a built-in function is applied to its arguments, and at least one of them has not been fully evaluated and none of them is ⊥, then the same application is returned as the result. For example, g 1 f(a) evaluates to itself, where g has the E-strategy $[\{1\}\|\{2\}]$. If at least one argument to a built-in function is ⊥, then the function application evaluates to ⊥.

5.2 Sheaves for FOOPS

We now define a sheaf for each function symbol, attribute symbol, method symbol, and method combiner. The base category for each such sheaf is the set

$$\mathcal{I}_0(\omega) = \{\emptyset, \{0\}, \{0,1\}, \{0,1,2\}, \ldots\} \cup \{\omega\}$$

whose elements represent the ticks of a clock. Using this base category, it is easy to observe that all of the following definitions actually are definitions of sheaves (Definition 2.1).

We shall use the notation of transitions [12].

Definition 5.1 Let $\mathcal{O}$ be a sheaf, and I, I' be elements of its base category. If A is the attribute object of $\mathcal{O}$, then $a \mapsto a'$ for $a, a' \in A$ means that if $f(i) = a$ for some $f \in \mathcal{O}(I)$, then there are $I' \supseteq I$ and $f' \in \mathcal{O}(I')$ such that $i + k \in I'$ where $k > 0$, f'filter $I = f$, and $f'(i + k) = a'$.

The notation $\mapsto a$ means that if $f \in \mathcal{O}(I)$ is defined at 0, then $f(0) = a$.

The transitions below use patterns for elements of the attribute object. They are really schemata for transitions. Each transition has the form:

$$\langle v, E, \; w_l \, t_l \, w_r \rangle \mapsto \langle v', E', \; w'_l \, t_r \, w'_r \rangle$$

where

- v and v' are k-th elements of N-tuples, where $1 \leq k \leq N$.

- There is a special constant symbol $\odot$ which never occurs in FOOPS programs, but can occur in the first position on the left or right side of a transition.

- w_l and w_r are sequences of symbols such that $w_l \, t_l \, w_r$ and $w'_l \, t_r \, w'_r$ are evaluable FOOPS expressions annotated with underlining and possibly overlining.

- E and E' are sets of the representations of objects whose elements are written using the notation in Section 4.1.

5.2.1 The Initial Sheaf

For an evaluable FOOPS expression $ft_1 \cdots t_n$ to be evaluated with respect to an initial set of representations of objects E_0, and a N-tuple all of whose elements are $\odot$ where N is the total of the number of sheaves for function, attribute, and method symbols, method combiners, and the number of object classes, there is a sheaf $\mathcal{O}_0$ whose transition schema is:

$$\mapsto \langle \odot, E_0, \; \underline{f}t_1 \cdots t_n \rangle$$

5.2.2 Functions, Attributes, and Methods

For each n-ary function or method symbol f, or monadic attribute symbol f with E-strategy $[I_1 | \cdots | I_m | I_{m+1}]$ there are sheaves $\mathcal{O}_f^{F_{p_1}}$ where $p_1 \geq 1$, with three groups of three transition schemata.

In general, a superscript on a sheaf identifier, such as F_7 on $\mathcal{O}_f^{F_7}$, is the unique name of that sheaf. Such a superscript is a constant symbol with a particular sort, which never occurs in the FOOPS program.

The schemata of the first group for the sheaf $\mathcal{O}_f^{F_j}$ where $j \in \{1, \ldots, p_1\}$ are

$$\langle \odot, \ E, \ w_l \ \underline{f} t_1 \cdots t_n \ w_r \rangle \mapsto \langle \underline{f} s_1 \cdots s_n, \ E', \ w_l' \ F_j \ w_r' \rangle$$

where

- $n > 0$.

- f and F_j have the same sort, and F_j is a constant symbol which does not occur in the FOOPS program.

- For each $i \in \{1, \ldots, n\}$ if t_i has the form $\overline{r_i}$ then s_i is $\overline{r_i}$.

- $S = \cup_{1 \leq j \leq m} I_j - \{i \mid i \in \{1, \ldots n\} \wedge (t_i = \overline{r_i})\}$ is not the empty set.

- There is a least $j : 1 \leq j \leq m$ such that $I_j \cap S = I_j$ and for all $i \in I_j$, if t_i has the form $g u_1 \cdots u_k$ where $k \geq 0$, then s_i has the form $\underline{g} u_1 \cdots u_k$.

- For all $i \in S - I_j$, s_i is t_i.

The second transition is:

$$\langle s, \ E, \ w_l \ F_j \ w_r \rangle \mapsto \langle \odot, \ E, \ w_l' \ s \ w_r' \rangle$$

where the preceding conditions hold and s is not $\odot$. The third transition is:

$$\langle s, \ E, \ w \rangle \mapsto \langle s', \ E', \ w' \rangle$$

where w and w' are FOOPS expressions in which F_j does not occur.

The schemata of the second group of transitions are:

$$\langle \odot, \ E, \ w_l \ \underline{f} t_1 \cdots t_n \ w_r \rangle \mapsto \langle s, \ E', \ w_l' \ F_j \ w_r' \rangle$$

where

- $n \geq 0$

- $S = (\cup_{1 \leq j \leq m} I_j) - \{i \mid i \in \{1, \ldots n\} \wedge (t_i = \overline{r_i})\} = \emptyset$.

- If f is not a built-in function or attribute symbol, then t is a term formed by one rewriting of $f r_1 \cdots r_n$ at its top level, where for all $i \in \cup_{1 \leq j \leq m} I_j$, $\overline{r_i} = t_i$, and for all $i \in I_{m+1}$, $r_i = t_i$. If t is a term which cannot be rewritten, then s is $\overline{t}$. Otherwise, if t has the form $h u_1 \cdots u_k$ where $k \geq 0$, then s is $\underline{h} u_1 \cdots u_k$.

- If f is a built-in function or attribute symbol then s is $\overline{r}$ where r is the evaluation of $f r_1 \cdots r_n$, and for all $i \in \cup_{1 \leq j \leq m} I_j$, $\overline{r_i} = t_i$, and for all $i \in I_{m+1}$, $r_i = t_i$.

- If f is an attribute symbol, then $n = 1$, and r_1 has the form $\overline{O}$ where O is an object identifier. If there is an element of E' of the form $(O, (a_1, v_1) \ldots, (f, v) \ldots, (a_l, v_l))$, then r is v. If there is no such element in E', then r is $\perp$.

- If f is a method symbol and r_1 is O, then s has the form

$$\underline{\text{Ev}} \text{ ev}_1 \, O \, d_1^1 \cdots d_M^1 \text{ ev}_2 \, O_2 \, d_1^2 \cdots d_M^2 \cdots \text{ev}_k \, O_k \, d_1^k \cdots d_M^k$$

where the objects in the class c to which the object whose identifier is O belongs have attribute names $a_1, \ldots, a_M$, and that Ev and ev_i are built-in function symbols of sorts $c \; \ldots \; c \; \text{->} \; c$, and $\text{s\_1} \; \ldots \; \text{s\_M} \; \text{->} \; c$ respectively, where the s_j are the sorts of the attribute names a_j, $M \geq 0$, $1 \geq k$, and $1 \leq j \leq M$. These function symbols have E-strategies $[\{1, 2, \ldots, k\}]$ and $[\{2, 3, \ldots, M\}\|\{1\}]$, respectively. Each d_1^i where $1 \leq i \leq k$ has the form

```
ifte condition' rhs' attr(0)
```

corresponding to a method axiom

```
attr(meth(0', arglist')) = rhs if condition .
```

whose lhs matches $fr_1 \cdots r_n$, and where `condition'` and `rhs'` are the instantiated forms of `condition` and `rhs` respectively by the matching substitution, and `attr` is a_1. If there is no matching axiom whose lhs has that form, then d_1^i is `attr(0)`. The function symbol `ifte` has sort `bool s_1 s_1 -> s_1`, and E-strategy $[\{1, 2, 3\}]$. In evaluating `ifte c g h`, if `c` evaluates to the constant representing true, then the expression evaluates to the evaluation of `g`, and otherwise it evaluates to the evaluation of `h`.

The other $k - 1$ subterms of the form $\text{ev}_j \, O_j \, d_1^j \cdots d_M^j$ each correspond to the non-empty set of axioms of the form

```
attr(01 / meth(0', arglist')) = rhs if condition .
```

where `01` is O_j and `meth(0', arglist')` matches $fr_1 \cdots r_n$. The d_l^j where $2 \leq l \leq M$ are formed in the same way as the d_1^i above.

The second and third transition schemata for this group are the same as those in the first group above.

The transitions in the third group of transition schemata are:

$$\langle \odot, \; E, \; w_l \, \overline{\text{Ev} \, \text{ev}_1 \, O \, e_1^1 \cdots e_M^1 \, \text{ev}_2 \, O_2 \, e_1^2 \cdots e_M^2 \cdots \text{ev}_k \, O_k \, e_1^k \cdots e_M^k \, w_r} \rangle$$
$$\mapsto \langle s, \; E', \; w_l' \, F_j \, w_r' \rangle$$

where

- If E' contains the representations of objects whose identifiers are

$$O, O_2, \ldots, O_k$$

  then E' contains the elements

$$(O, \ (a_1, e_1^1), \ldots, (a_M, e_M^1))$$

  and

$$(O_i, \ (a_1, e_1^i), \ldots, (a_M, e_M^i))$$

  where $1 \le i \le k$, and s is $\overline{O}$.

- If E' does not contain one of the representations of objects whose identifiers are $O, O_2, \ldots, O_k$, then s is $\overline{\bot}$.

The second and third transitions in this group are the same as those in the first and second groups above.

The first transition above for $\mathcal{O}_f$ states that after the subterms whose indices are in $\bigcup_{1 \le l < j} I_l$ have been evaluated, concurrent evaluation of the subterms whose indices are in I_j can begin, as the E-strategy for f stipulates. It does not restrict the evaluation of subterms which do not occur in $\underline{f} t_1 \cdots t_n$.

The second transition states that after removing the overlining of symbols on subterms of $\underline{f} t_1 \cdots t_n$, it can be rewritten once at the top level, evaluated if f is a built-in function or attribute symbol, or its matching axioms can be evaluated if f is a method symbol. If the replacement term can be evaluated, it is marked for evaluation by underlining its principal operation symbol. This does not affect E-strategies at higher levels, because f was already so marked. If the replacement term cannot be evaluated further, it is marked by overlining it. Again, this transition does not restrict the evaluation of subterms which do not occur in $\underline{f} t_1 \cdots t_n$.

The third transition states that after all axioms matching a method expression have been evaluated, the attributes of objects are changed using the evaluations. In general, only by using E-strategies and method combiners can other method expressions be prevented from changing the values of attributes before the method expression in question has been evaluated.

5.2.3 Method Combiners

Non-deterministic Choice

There are also three sheaves for the method combiners. The sheaves for non-deterministic choice are written $\mathcal{O}_{\text{or}}^{\vee p_2}$ where $p_2 \ge 1$. The transition schemata for the sheaf $\mathcal{O}_{\text{or}}^{\vee j}$ where $j \in \{1, \ldots p_2\}$ are

$$\langle \odot, E, \ w_l \ \underline{\text{or}} \ m_1 t_1 \cdots t_{k_1} \ m_2 s_1 \cdots s_{k_2} \ w_r \rangle \mapsto \langle \underline{m_1} t_1 \cdots t_{k_1}, \ E', \ w_l' \ \vee_j \ w_r' \rangle$$

and

$$\langle \odot, E, \ w_l \ \underline{\text{or}} \ m_1 t_1 \cdots t_k \ m_2 s_1 \cdots s_k \ w_r \rangle \mapsto \langle \underline{m_2} s_1 \cdots s_{k_2}, \ E', \ w_l' \ \vee_j \ w_r' \rangle$$

where

- or and V_j have the same sort, and V_j does not occur in the FOOPS program.

- $m_1 t_1 \cdots t_{k_1}$, and $m_2 s_1 \cdots s_{k_2}$ are method expressions and $0 \le k_1, k_2$.

The third transition is:

$$\langle s,\ E,\ w_l\ \mathsf{V}_j\ w_r \rangle \mapsto \langle \odot,\ E,\ w_l'\ s\ w_r' \rangle$$

where the preceding conditions hold and s is not $\odot$. The fourth transition is:

$$\langle s,\ E,\ w \rangle \mapsto \langle s',\ E',\ w' \rangle$$

where w and w' are FOOPS expressions in which V_j does not occur.

Sequential Composition

The sheaves for sequential composition are written $\mathcal{O}_;^{\circ p_3}$ where $p_3 \ge 1$. The transition schemata for the sheaf $\mathcal{O}_;^{\circ j}$ where $j \in \{1, \ldots p_3\}$ are:

$$\langle \odot,\ E,\ w_l\ ;\ m_1 t_1 \cdots t_{k_1}\ m_2 s_1 \cdots s_{k_2}\ w_r \rangle \mapsto$$
$$\langle \underline{;\ m_1 t_1 \cdots t_{k_1}}\ m_2 s_1 \cdots s_{k_2},\ E',\ w_l'\ \circ_j\ w_r' \rangle$$

$$\langle \odot,\ E,\ w_l\ ;\ \overline{n_1}\ m_2 s_1 \cdots s_k\ w_r \rangle \mapsto \langle \underline{;\ \overline{n_1}}\ m_2 s_1 \cdots s_{k_2},\ E',\ w_l'\ \circ_j\ w_r' \rangle$$

and

$$\langle \odot,\ E,\ w_l\ ;\overline{n_1}\ \overline{n_2}\ w_r \rangle \mapsto \langle \overline{;\ n_1 n_2},\ E',\ w_l'\ \circ_j\ w_r' \rangle$$

where

- ; and $\circ_j$ have the same sort, and $\circ_j$ is a constant symbol which does not occur in the FOOPS program.

- $m_1 t_1 \cdots t_{k_1}$, $m_2 s_1 \cdots s_{k_2}$, n_1, and n_2 are method expressions and $0 \le k_1, k_2$.

The fourth transition is:

$$\langle s,\ E,\ w_l\ \circ_j\ w_r \rangle \mapsto \langle \odot,\ E,\ w_l'\ s\ w_r' \rangle$$

where the preceding conditions hold and s is not $\odot$. The fifth transition is:

$$\langle s,\ E,\ w \rangle \mapsto \langle s',\ E',\ w' \rangle$$

where w and w' are FOOPS expressions in which $\circ_j$ does not occur.

Parallel Composition

The sheaves for parallel composition is written $\mathcal{O}_{||}^{\text{conc}_{p_4}}$ where $p_4 \geq 1$. The transition schemata for the sheaf $\mathcal{O}_{||}^{\text{conc}_j}$ where $j \in \{1, \ldots, p_4\}$ are

$$\langle \odot,\ E,\ w_l \ ||\ m_1 t_1 \cdots t_{k_1}\ m_2 s_1 \cdots s_{k_2}\ w_r \rangle \ \mapsto$$
$$\langle ||\underline{m_1 t_1 \cdots t_{k_1}}\ \underline{m_2 s_1 \cdots s_{k_2}},\ E',\ w'_l\ \text{conc}_j\ w'_r \rangle$$

and

$$\langle \odot,\ E,\ w_l \ ||\ \overline{n_1}\ \overline{n_2}\ w_r \rangle \mapsto \langle ||\overline{n_1 n_2},\ E',\ w'_l\ \text{conc}_j\ w'_r \rangle$$

where

- $||$ and conc_j have the same sort, and conc_j is a constant symbol which does not occur in the FOOPS program.

- $m_1 t_1 \cdots t_{k_1}$, and $m_2 s_1 \cdots s_{k_2}$, n_1, and n_2 are method expressions, and $0 \leq k_1, k_2$.

The third transition is:

$$\langle s,\ E,\ w_l\ \text{conc}_j\ w_r \rangle \mapsto \langle \odot,\ E,\ w'_l\ s\ w'_r \rangle$$

where the preceding conditions hold and s is not $\odot$. The fourth transition is:

$$\langle s,\ E,\ w \rangle \mapsto \langle s',\ E',\ w' \rangle$$

where w and w' are FOOPS expressions in which conc_j does not occur.

5.2.4   Built-In Methods

Unlike the sheaves for functions, attributes, and methods, and method combiners each of which corresponds to an element of the N-tuple in the first position in transitions, all of the sheaves for **remove** and **new** which are operations on objects of the same class correspond to one element of that N-tuple. This convention will be used in the transitions in this section. It enables the prevention of the concurrent creation and removal of objects in the same class.

The **remove** Method

The sheaves for the **remove** method are $\mathcal{O}_{\text{rem}}^{\mathcal{R}_{p_5}}$ where $p_5 \geq 1$. The transition schema for the sheaf $\mathcal{O}_{\text{rem}}^{\mathcal{R}_j}$ where $j \in \{1, \ldots, p_5\}$ are

$$\langle \odot,\ E,\ w_l\ \underline{\text{remove } O}\ w_r \rangle \mapsto \langle s,\ E',\ w'_l\ \mathcal{R}_j\ w'_r \rangle$$

where

- remove$O$ and $\mathcal{R}_j$ have the same sort, and $\mathcal{R}_j$ does not occur in the FOOPS program.

- If an object with identifier O does not exist in E, then s is $\overline{\perp}$.

- If an object with identifier O exists in E, then E' does not have this element, and s is $\overline{O}$.

The second transition is:

$$\langle s,\ E,\ w_l\, \mathcal{R}_j\, w_r \rangle \mapsto \langle \odot,\ E,\ w_l'\, s\, w_r' \rangle$$

where the preceding conditions hold and s is not $\odot$. The third transition is:

$$\langle s,\ E,\ w \rangle \mapsto \langle s',\ E',\ w' \rangle$$

where w and w' are FOOPS expressions in which $\mathcal{R}_j$ does not occur.

The new Method

The sheaves for the new method are $\mathcal{O}_{\text{new}}^{\mathcal{N}\,p_6}$ where $p_6 \geq 1$. The transition schemata for the sheaf $\mathcal{O}_{\text{new}}^{\mathcal{N}_j}$ where $j \in \{1, \dots, p_6\}$ are

$$\langle \odot,\ E,\ w_l\ \underline{\text{new.C}}\ O\ w_r \rangle \mapsto \langle \overline{O},\ E',\ w_l'\, \mathcal{N}_j\, w_r' \rangle$$

where

- new.CO and $\mathcal{N}_j$ have the same sort, and $\mathcal{N}_j$ does not occur in the FOOPS program.

- C and O have been defined in Section 3.4.

- E' contains the element $(O, (a_1, v_1), \dots, (a_n, v_n))$ where the a_i are attribute names of an object of class C.

- For each non object-valued attribute a_i, v_i is its default value.

- For each object-valued attribute a_i, v_i is the object identifer of its default value. The set E' also contains the representation of this default value, and recursively all representations of default values of object-valued attributes.

The third transition is:

$$\langle s,\ E,\ w_l\, \mathcal{N}_j\, w_r \rangle \mapsto \langle \odot,\ E,\ w_l'\, s\, w_r' \rangle$$

where the preceding conditions hold and s is not $\odot$. The fourth transition is:

$$\langle s,\ E,\ w \rangle \mapsto \langle s',\ E',\ w' \rangle$$

where w and w' are FOOPS expressions in which $\mathcal{N}_j$ does not occur.

5.2.5 The Event Sheaf and Diagram

The event sheaf is

$$\mathcal{E}(I) = \{f : I \to F \times \mathcal{A}\}$$

for every $I \in \mathcal{I}_0(\omega)$, where F is the set of all finite sets of representations of objects, and $\mathcal{A}$ is the set of all evaluable FOOPS expressions. This sheaf represents all event traces, where each event is an element of $F \times \mathcal{A}$.

We construct a diagram $\mathcal{L}$ (Definition 2.3) whose nodes are these sheaves, and whose edges have the form $\mathcal{O} \to \mathcal{E}$ only, where

$$\mathcal{O} \in \{\mathcal{O}_0, \mathcal{O}_f^{F_{p_1}}, \mathcal{O}_{\text{or}}^{\vee_{p_2}}, \mathcal{O}_;^{\circ_{p_3}}, \mathcal{O}_{\|}^{\text{conc}_{p_4}}, \mathcal{O}_{\text{rem}}^{\mathcal{R}_{p_5}}, \mathcal{O}_{\text{new}}^{\mathcal{N}_{p_6}}\}$$

where f ranges of the set of all function, attribute, and method symbols, $1 \leq j \leq 6$, and $p_j \geq 1$. The size of the N-tuple in transitions is $N = \Sigma_{1 \leq j \leq 6} \, p_j$.

6 Discussion

We have made several assumptions about FOOPS in defining the semantics of expression evaluation. Our assuming no user supplied values for attributes of newly created objects, no user-defined method combiners, acyclic whole/part graphs, and no expressions with $\uparrow$ affect the generality of our treatment of FOOPS's semantics, but only in a small way. We have also not discussed modularization and inheritance, because our principal aim was to define the semantics of concurrent evaluation of method expressions.

Cyclic whole/part graphs are the most complicated aspect not discussed. The semantics of FOOPS with these features will not differ greatly from that we have presented above.

References

[1] J.W. Alexander, A theory of connectivity in terms of gratings, *Ann. Math.* **39** (1938) 883–912.

[2] D.B. Benson, Global versus local enveloping behaviours of concurrent systems, Extended Abstract, Washington State University, Pullman, Washington, 1991.

[3] D.B. Benson, Sheaves of Process Histories, Draft #7, Washington State University, Pullman, Washington, 1991.

[4] R. Dubey, On a general definition of safety and liveness, M.Sc. thesis, Washington State University, Pullman, Washington, 1991.

[5] H.-D. Ehrich, J.A. Goguen, and A. Sernadas, A categorial theory of objects as observed processes, in: *Foundations of Object Oriented Languages, Proceedings of a REX/FOOL Workshop*, (Noordwijkerhout, the Netherlands, May/June 1990), J.W. de Bakker, W.P. de Roever and G. Rozenberg (Eds.), Lecture Notes in Computer Science, Springer, Berlin, **489** (1991) 203–228.

[6] K. Futatsugi, J.A. Goguen, J.-P. Jouannaud, and J. Meseguer, Principles of OBJ2, *Proceedings of the Twelfth Symposium on Principles of Programming Languages*, Association for Computing Machinery, New York, 1985, 52–66.

[7] J.A. Goguen and J. Meseguer, Order-sorted algebra solves the constructor-selector, multiple representation and coercion problems, in: *Proceedings of the Second IEEE Symposium on Logic in Computer Science*, IEEE Computer Society, Washington, D.C., 1987, 18–29.

[8] J.A. Goguen and J. Meseguer, Unifying functional, object-oriented and relational programming with logical semantics, Research Report SRI–CSL–87–7, SRI International, Menlo Park, California, 1987.

[9] J.A. Goguen, Mathematical representations of hierarchically organized systems, *Global Systems Dynamics*, S. Karger, 1971, 112–128.

[10] J.A. Goguen, Categorical foundations for general systems theory, in: *Advances in Cybernetics and Systems Research*, Transcripta Books, 1973, 121–130.

[11] J.A. Goguen, Objects, *International Journal of General Systems* 1 (1975) 237–243.

[12] J.A. Goguen, Sheaf semantics for concurrent interacting objects, *Mathematical Structures in Computer Science*, 1991, (to appear).

[13] J.A. Goguen and S. Ginali, A categorical approach to general systems theory, in: *Applied General Systems Research*, G. Klir, (Ed.), Plenum, 1978, 257–270.

[14] J.W. Gray, Fragments of the history of sheaf theory, in: *Applications of Sheaves: Proceedings of the Research Symposium on Applications of Sheaf Theory to Logic, Algebra, and Analysis*, M.P. Fourman, C.J. Mulvey, and D.S. Scott, (Eds.), Lecture Notes in Mathematics **753**, Springer, Berlin, 1979, 1–79.

[15] J. Leray, Sur la forme des espaces topologiques et sur les points fixes des représentations, *Journal de Math.* Ser. 9, **24** (1945) 95–167.

[16] L.F. Monteiro and F.C.N. Pereira, A sheaf-theoretic model of concurrency, *Proceedings of the Symposium on Logic in Computer Science*, IEEE Computer Society, Washington D.C., 1986, 66–76.

[17] E. Munthe-Kaas, J.A. Goguen, and J. Meseguer, Method expressions and default values for object-valued attributes, Research Report, SRI International, Menlo Park, California, 1987.

[18] J.A. Goguen and D.A. Wolfram, On types and FOOPS, *Proceedings of the IFIP Working Group 2.6 Working Conference on Database Semantics: Object Oriented Databases: Analysis, Design & Construction*, 1990, International Federation for Information Processing, (To appear).

Semantic Layers of Object-Based Concurrent Computing

Etsuya Shibayama

Department of Applied Mathematics and Informatics
Ryukoku University
Seta, Ootsu, Japan, 520-21

etsuya@ryukoku.ac.jp

Abstract

A layered semantics model of an object-based concurrent programming language is proposed, which provides a support for reasoning of object compositions. Upon construction and verification of a concurrent program, a mechanism which supports compositions of object descriptions and a technique which supports compositional reasoning are desirable. However, compositional semantics of a sufficiently rich concurrent language tends to be complicated so as to cope with rare anomalies.

In order to overcome this difficulty, a layered scheme is introduced: the bottom layer is based on a transition system and the top layer is based on the notion of program transformation, which supports compositional reasoning at least in some degree. Since more abstract descriptions rely on more concrete descriptions, all layers are not necessarily self-contained. By this scheme, information necessary for composition can be hidden away in abstract layers. Based on the layered semantics, each proof and reasoning should be performed in an appropriate level of abstraction.

1 Introduction

In this paper, we introduce a simple object-based concurrent language and present its formal model. In general, semantics or a formal model of a programming language should:

1. be simple and clear for better understanding of the language, and

2. support rigorous reasoning on the language or programs written in the language.

In a usual case, *operational* and *denotational* semantics of a programming language is defined. The operational semantics precisely defines *computations* in the target language in terms of *reductions*, *derivations*, or *transitions*. In contrast, the denotational semantics defines the results of computations in terms of mathematical equations. For instance, operational semantics of a program in (pure) Prolog can be defined in terms of SLD-derivations and its denotation can be represented by the least fixed point in a Herbrand base[Lloyd 84].

Upon proving some properties of a language or programs written in the language, we usually rely on *induction techniques*. Operational semantics provides a support for induction on the lengths of computations, whereas denotational semantics provides a support for *fixed point* and *structural induction* techniques. It is a significant point that denotational semantics is defined in a compositional manner, that is, supposing that for two program segments A and B and their denotations $S[\![A]\!]$ and $S[\![B]\!]$, the denotation of the combination of A and B, say $A+B$, is defined as:

$$S[\![A+B]\!] \;=\; S[\![A]\!] \oplus S[\![B]\!]$$

where $\oplus$ is some function which composes $S[\![A]\!]$ and $S[\![B]\!]$.

In case of a concurrent language, however, the definition of a (parallel) composition operator "$\oplus$" usually becomes complicated so as to cope with rare anomalies, e.g., the *Brock-Ackerman anomaly*[Brock and Ackerman 81]. By this reason, induction steps of proofs based on such a composition operator also becomes complicated. In order to get around of this complication, we give up using a compositional semantics as a rigorous basis of formal proofs on concurrent systems. Instead, we design a semantic description scheme consisting of multiple layers, in which a more abstract layer relies on a more concrete one. This means that all layers are not necessarily self-contained. In abstract layers, some pieces of information necessary for object compositions can be hidden away. We design the most abstract layer so that complicated information for object compositions is hidden away while easily utilized one is shown.

Currently our approach provides the following layers:

1. an operational model

2. a more abstract semantic model based on object diagrams, and

3. program transformation.

The first one provides a way to describe operational semantics of a program, where internal computations of objects are described in a denotational manner and inter-object interactions are described using a transition system. Since in our model internal actions can be performed sequentially, there are no essential difficulties on the former half. Our concern in this layer is descriptions of inter-object concurrent behaviors. We employ a transition system to describe operational information of concurrent computations. The design of this layer is influenced by the formalization of the Actor model by G. Agha[Agha 87].

At the second layer, a more abstract description scheme is presented. Each description, called an *object diagram*, consists of a set of events which occur in a computation and a partial order causality relation among the events. An object diagram is a similar device to an event diagram[Agha 87], which was introduced to formalize the Actor model. An object diagram does not include any higher order function values but *events* which consist of sole first order values (e.g., numbers and boolean values). Therefore, the complexity to reason about the equivalence of two descriptions is much reduced at this layer. Unfortunately, this layer does not support any compositional reasoning since no compositional style definitions are presented in this layer. Instead, a description of a program in this layer is defined in terms of the corresponding description of the lower layer.

At the third layer, we present several program transformation rules which were also proposed in [Shibayama 88] and which fuse and split object definitions and obtain the equivalent definitions. In this respect, these transformation rules provide a support for compositional reasoning. The transformation system presented in this paper is *not complete*, i.e., two semantically equivalent programs are not necessarily derived by each other by this system, but still useful in some application domains. Such an example is presented in [Shibayama 88].

As a result, our system consists of

1. concrete operational semantics,

2. more abstract semantics, and

3. supports for compositional reasoning.

We want to note that the third layer is the most important part for most people. This layer is designed to formalize programmers' intuitions that programs are composed of *parts* (i.e., objects and/or object groups). If compositions of programs are always so difficult as in a typical compositional semantics of concurrent languages, it is impossible for most people to construct programs from parts. In reality, a programmer can construct a concurrent program from parts and s/he can estimate the behavior of the program from the knowledge of its parts. That is, s/he performs compositional reasoning at least in an informal manner. From this observation, we assume that there are several or more patterns of object compositions whose effects can be easily estimated by a human programmer. The third layer is our attempts to enumerate such patterns of compositions, which are formally described in terms of program transformation rules. To be formal, such enumerated transformation rules are verified in terms of lower layers.

Our computing model can be considered as an extension of the Actor model in the sense that our model is based on more structured communication mechanisms (such as a one similar to the remote procedure call mechanism). The most important difference of our model and models of process calculus/algebra (e.g., [Milner 89]) is that our model provides (unbounded) buffered communications. Therefore, the state of an ongoing computation cannot be described sole in terms of the states of the objects. It also includes the information about the *not-yet-delivered* messages. Also, our model includes the notion of first-class object names, that is, an object name (or an object identity) can be transmitted via message passing. CCS[Milner 80] does not include this notion, which is introduced recently in the process calculus world by π-calculus[Milner et al. 89a], [Milner et al. 89b].

2   The Computing Model and Programming Language

In this section, we describe our object-based concurrent computing model and language. Each object in the model has its state and script (which the reader may consider instance variables and methods), which are described in the following syntax:

[object *object-name*
  ([*state-variable$_1$* := *initial-value$_1$*]
      $\vdots$
    [*state-variable$_k$* := *initial-value$_k$*])

```
(=> message @ reply form)]
```

The *state-variables* of an object are the variables which represent the internal persistent state of the object. Upon acceptance of a message by this object, two variables *message* and *reply* are bound to the contents and the *reply destination* (i.e., the destination to which the reply to the message will be sent) of the message, respectively. After accepting a message, the object will perform a sequence of actions described in *form*. During execution of the action sequence, *message* and *reply* can be read but cannot be updated. In contrast, *state-variables* can be both read and updated.

In order to specify an object as the destination of a message, a *unique name* of the object is required. Though each name is attached to exactly one object, an object may have more than one name in our model. More precisely, each object must have a *unique persistent* name called its *primary name* and may have a *temporary* name called its *reply name*. One who knows the primary name of an object can send a message to it by specifying the name as the destination of the message. Similarly, one who knows a reply name of an object can send back a reply to it. Upon each transmission of a message which requires a reply, an object dynamically creates a fresh reply name and attaches it to the message so that the receiver can know the reply destination of this message.

Messages arriving at an object will be *accepted* and then processed one at a time in a sequential manner. The execution of a message by an object may include the following sorts of actions:

- inquiries and updates of its *state*;

- creations of new objects;

- transmissions of messages and receptions of replies; and

- transmission of a value as a reply to a received message.

For describing these actions, our language provides the syntax for assignments, object creations, and message passing. An assignment form is in the following syntax:

```
[state-variable := expression]
```

where *expression* denotes some value. We will use lisp-like syntax to represent such values as integers, Boolean values, and lists.

An object creation form always occur in the right hand side of an assignment form:

```
[state-variable :=
  [object
    state-declaration-part
    script-description-part]]
```

The syntax of object creation forms is similar to the syntax of object definition forms. The only difference is that any object creation form does not include *object-name* part. An object creation form may be evaluated more than once during execution and thus a new name must be created at each evaluation time. In contrast, since an object definition form just defines a single object, the programmer can specify its name. Upon each evaluation, an object creation form returns the primary name of a fresh object which satisfies the definition specified by this form.

There are three types of message passing, *now*, *past*, and *actor*. They are described in the following syntax:

$$[object\text{-}name <== message] \quad (not)$$
$$[object\text{-}name <= message] \quad (past)$$
$$[object\text{-}name <- message] \quad (actor)$$

Just after an object transmits a message in now type, the execution of this object is *blocked* until the reply to the message arrives. In contrast, just after an object sends a message in either past or actor type, its execution continues, *not blocked*. Concurrently, if the receiver is not busy at that time, it can accept the message and execute the appropriate action sequence. The sender object does not expect any reply to the message in the past or actor case. In our model, a reply is just a message whose destination is a reply name. Therefore, no special syntax/primitive for returning replies are provided in our language/model.

Among messages in now and past types, the *transmission ordering law* is satisfied:

Transmission Ordering Law:
> Suppose that two messages μ_1 and μ_2 are transmitted by the same sender object; if μ_1 and μ_2 have the same destination, they arrive in the transmitted order.

Actor type is almost the same as past type but the messages transmitted in type of actor do not necessarily obey the *transmission ordering law*.

In this paper, for simplicity, we assume only three (sequential) control structures, if, while, and progn to describe conditional branches, loops, and sequential compositions, respectively. The full version of our language[Shibayama 91] has another control structure let, which creates local temporary bindings within an object.

3 An Operational Model

In this section we present a formal model of objects and message passing. In our model, an object is represented by a tuple:

$$\langle \nu, \nu^a, s, p \rangle$$

where ν is its primary name and ν^a is either its primary name, a reply name, or •. If ν^a is the primary name (or a reply name), the object is waiting for a message (or a reply, respectively) whose destination is represented by the name. We call this ν^a the current *active name* of the object. The object does not accept any message whose destination is not ν^a. While this object is executing its script and is not ready for accepting either a message or a reply, ν^a is a void name, In the tuple, s and p represent the internal state and the current procedure, respectively.

In contrast, a message is represented as a triple:

$$\langle c, \nu^r, \nu \rangle$$

in our model, where c, ν^r, and ν represent the message contents (i.e., the value passed by the message), the name of the reply destination, and the message name, respectively. The destination of this message will be represented in the state of *message buffers*. Triples representing different messages must have different names.

For a tuple $\langle \nu, \nu^a, s, p \rangle$ where $\nu^a \neq \bullet$ and which represents an object, suppose that the object receives a message or a reply represented as a triple μ whose destination is ν^a. During processing this message, this object may create objects and send messages. The number of the created objects and the transmitted messages may possibly be *infinite*.

Assume that:

1. the set of the created objects is $\{\pi_0, \ldots, \pi_i, \ldots\}$,

2. the set of the messages transmitted in actor type message passing to the destination represented by ν_i is $\{\mu_{i,0}, \ldots, \mu_{i,j}, \ldots\}$, and

3. the sequence of the messages transmitted in past and now type message passing to the destination represented by ν_i is $\langle \mu'_{i,0}, \ldots, \mu'_{i,j}, \ldots \rangle$.

The procedure p and the state s models the behavior of the object so that

$$p(\mu)(s) = \langle \nu', s', p', \{\pi_0, \ldots, \pi_i, \ldots\}, B \rangle$$

where B is a mapping satisfying:

$$B(\nu_i) = \langle \{\mu_{i,0}, \ldots, \mu_{i,j}, \ldots\}, \langle \mu'_{i,0}, \ldots, \mu'_{i,j}, \ldots \rangle \rangle$$

and this object enters the state which is represented by a tuple $\langle \nu, \nu', s', p' \rangle$.

Because of the transmission ordering law, for those messages transmitted in past and now type message passing, their transmission order is significant. Therefore, these messages are represented by a *sequences* (i.e., structures which can represent their element orders). In contrast, *sets* represent those messages transmitted in actor type message passing since their transmission order is not significant.

3.1 Domains

The following are the domain equations of our model.

$$Name = Id \cup Name.\{1, 2\} \tag{1}$$

$$Value = Int \cup Bool \cup Name \cup Value * \cup \{\bullet\} \tag{2}$$

$$State = Id \to Value \tag{3}$$

$$Mess = Value \times (Name \cup \{\bullet\}) \times Name \tag{4}$$

$$Buf = Name \to \mathcal{P}(Mess) \times Mess * \tag{5}$$

$$Obj = \bigcup_{i=0}^{\infty} Obj_i \tag{6}$$

$$Obj_0 = Name \times (Name \cup \{\bullet\}) \times State \times Proc_0 \tag{7}$$

$$Obj_{i+1} = Obj_i \cup (Name \times (Name \cup \{\bullet\}) \times State \times Proc_{i+1}) \tag{8}$$

$$Proc = \bigcup_{i=0}^{\infty} Proc_i \tag{9}$$

$$Proc_0 = (Mess \cup \{\bullet\}) \to State \to$$

$$(Name \cup \{\bullet\}) \times State \times Proc_0 \times \{\emptyset\} \times Buf \qquad (10)$$

$$Proc_{i+1} = (Mess \cup \{\bullet\}) \rightarrow State \rightarrow$$
$$(Name \cup \{\bullet\}) \times State \times Proc_i \times \mathcal{P}(Obj_i) \times Buf \qquad (11)$$

where *Int*, *Bool*, and *Id* are the domains of integers, Boolean values, and identifiers, respectively. Since their definitions are obvious, we do not define them in this paper.

Equation 1 defines the domain of names which includes every identifier. Furthermore, if ν is a name, $\nu.1$ and $\nu.2$ (where "." is a constructor for compound terms) are also names. In order to create unique names during computation, an object uses the name t of lastly received message as a *seed* and creates fresh names $t.1$ and $t.2$,

In equation 2, *Value* is the domain of the first class values in our computation model. $\bullet$ is a void value. In equation 3, *State* is the domain of the internal states of objects. Equation 4 describes the domain of triples representing messages. $\bullet$ represents the void reply destination and will occur in a triple representing a message which does not require any reply. In equation 5, *Buf* is the domain of message buffers, each of whose elements is a mapping from a destination name ν to the transmitted messages whose destinations are ν. $\mathcal{P}(X)$ denotes the power set of X.

Equations 6–11 define the domains of objects and procedures. *Obj* is made stratified and defined in a non-recursive way. It is defined as the union of Obj_is $(0 \leq i)$, where an element in Obj_0 represents an object which never creates new objects during execution and one in $Obj_i (1 \leq i)$ represents an object which may create objects represented by elements of Obj_j such that j is at most $i - 1$. Since in our language, infinite nesting of object creation forms cannot occur, these equations well models our objects.

The reader may consider that the following two equations:

$$Obj = Obj \cup (Name \times (Name \cup \{\bullet\}) \times State \times Proc) \qquad (12)$$

$$Proc = (Mess \cup \{\bullet\}) \rightarrow State \rightarrow$$
$$(Name \cup \{\bullet\}) \times State \times Proc \times \mathcal{P}(Obj) \times Buf \qquad (13)$$

describe the semantic domains of objects and procedures in a more concise manner. Furthermore, these equations may allow unbounded nesting of object creation forms. Still, however, compared with Equations 12 and 13, our equations can be solved more easily without using the power domain construction technique. Notice that our aim is not to define semantics of a program but to prove properties of a program based on our semantics. Therefore, for our purposes, equations which are solved easily are better than those which are defined concisely.

3.2 Global Computation States and Transitions

An operational semantics of a concurrent system in our model is described as the set of possible *computations*, which is defined by the transition rules among *global computation states*[1]. A pair:

$$\langle O, M \rangle$$

represents a global computation state, where O consists of the *objects* in the state and M consists of the *messages* which have already been transmitted but not yet been accepted by any object in the state. The transition rules presented in this section are in the form of:

$$\langle O, M \rangle \xrightarrow{\pi, \mu} \langle O', M' \rangle$$

which means that a transition from $\langle O, M \rangle$ to $\langle O', M' \rangle$ can occur during a computation and that at this stage the object π consumes the message μ. A global computation state is a similar device to a *configuration* introduced in [Agha 87].

The following are domain equations which define the domain S of global computation states.

$$\begin{aligned}
S &= \mathcal{O} \times \mathcal{M} & (14)\\
\mathcal{O} &= \mathcal{P}(Obj) & (15)\\
\mathcal{M} &= Name \rightarrow Buf & (16)
\end{aligned}$$

Equation 15 says that $O \in \mathcal{O}$ is a subset of Obj, i.e., a set of objects. Intuitively speaking, equation 16 says that, for $M \in \mathcal{M}$ and a primary name ν, $M(\nu)$ represents the *not-yet-delivered* messages sent by the object whose primary name is ν. $\mathcal{M}$ is defined in this way in order to maintain the transmission order of messages. In this respect, the Actor model is more elegant, that is, the state of the *not-yet-delivered* messages is represented simply as the set of such messages. Though the reader may consider that the introduction of the transmission ordering law complicates our operational model, we prefer this law since owing to it we can have good and natural program transformation rules. We want to emphasize that the most important part of our goals is to develop a good program transformation system which meets intuitions of programmers. Therefore, we may make the bottom layer more complicated if we can make the top layer more elegant.

Definition 3.1 *Let X and X' be sequences $\langle x_i \rangle_{0 \leq i < \alpha}$ and $\langle x_i \rangle_{\alpha \leq i < \alpha'}$ for some ordinal numbers α and α' ($\alpha \leq \alpha'$).*

$$\begin{aligned}
fst(X) &\overset{def}{=} x_0 & \text{if } 0 < \alpha\\
snd() &\overset{def}{=} x_1 & \text{if } 1 < \alpha\\
rest(X) &\overset{def}{=} \langle x_i \rangle_{1 \leq i < \alpha} & \text{if } 0 < \alpha\\
X @ X' &\overset{def}{=} \langle x_i \rangle_{0 \leq i < \alpha'}
\end{aligned}$$

Definition 3.2 *Suppose that M and B belong to $\mathcal{M}$ and Buf, respectively. Let ν be the primary name of an object and $\nu^a (\neq \bullet)$ be the active name of an object.*

---

[1]Since our model does not assume any global clock, it is strange to employ such global notions. However, even in a distributed system where objects interact with one another via asynchronous message passing, we can obtain distributed snapshots[Chandy and Lamport 85], which are consistent collections of the processes' (or objects') states. A global computation state is such a logically consistent collection of objects and messages. It does not necessarily depend on a particular global clock.

1. $(\dagger M)\nu\nu^a$ represents the messages ready to be accepted which are transmitted by the object of primary name ν and whose destinations are ν^a. It is defined as follows:

$$(\dagger M)\nu\nu^a = \begin{array}{ll} fst(M\nu\nu^a) & \text{if } snd(M\nu\nu^a) = \emptyset \\ fst(M\nu\nu^a) \cup \{fst(snd(M\nu\nu^a))\} & \text{otherwise} \end{array}$$

2. Assume that M' and B' are elements of $\mathcal{M}$ and Buf, respectively. $M + M'$ and $B + B'$ are also elements of $\mathcal{M}$ and Buf, respectively, which are defined by:

$$\begin{array}{rll} B + B' & = \lambda\nu^a.\langle fst(B\nu^a) \cup fst(B'\nu^a), snd(B\nu^a)@snd(B'\nu^a)\rangle & \text{if } B' \neq \bot \\ & = B & \text{otherwise} \\ M + M' & = \lambda\nu.(M(\nu) + M'(\nu)) & \end{array}$$

3. Let μ be an element of $(\dagger M)\nu\nu^a$. $retrieve(M, \mu)$ is an element of $\mathcal{M}$ so that:

$$\begin{array}{rll} retrieve(M, \mu)\nu\nu^a & = \langle fst(M\nu\nu^a) - \{\mu\}, snd(M\nu\nu^a)\rangle & \text{if } \mu \in fst(M\nu\nu^a) \\ & = \langle fst(M\nu\nu^a), rest(snd(M\nu\nu^a))\rangle & \text{if } \mu = fst(snd(M\nu\nu^a)) \\ retrieve(M, \mu)\nu'\nu'' & = M\nu'\nu'' & \text{if } \nu' \neq \nu \vee \nu'' \neq \nu^a \end{array}$$

4. $\lambda[\nu].B$ is an element of $\mathcal{M}$ which satisfies:

$$\begin{array}{rl} (\lambda[\nu].B)\nu & = B \\ (\lambda[\nu].B)\nu' & = \lambda\nu.\langle\emptyset, \langle\rangle\rangle \quad \text{if } \nu' \neq \nu \end{array}$$

Suppose that X belong to $\mathcal{P}(Mess) \times Mess*$, $\lambda[\nu].X$ is an element of Buf which satisfies:

$$\begin{array}{rl} (\lambda[\nu].X)\nu & = X \\ (\lambda[\nu].X)\nu' & = \langle\emptyset, \langle\rangle\rangle \quad \text{if } \nu' \neq \nu \end{array}$$

The following are the transition rules for our computation model introduced in this section.

Rule 3.3 Suppose that $\langle O_0, M_0\rangle$ and $\langle O_1, M_1\rangle$ are global computation states. Let $\pi = \langle \nu, \nu^a, s, p\rangle$ and μ belong to O_0 and $Mess$, respectively.

$$\langle O_0, M_0\rangle \xrightarrow{\pi, \mu} \langle O_1, M_1\rangle$$

is satisfied if and only if for some $\nu^s \in Name$,

$$\begin{array}{rl} \mu & \in (\dagger M_0)\nu^s\nu^a \\ p\mu s & = \langle\nu', s', p', o, B\rangle \\ O_1 & = (O_0 - \{\pi\}) \cup o \cup \{\langle\nu, \nu', s', p'\rangle\} \\ M_1 & = retrieve(M_0, \mu) + \lambda[\nu].B \end{array}$$

are satisfied.

Rule 3.4 *Suppose that* $\langle O_0, M_0 \rangle$ *and* $\langle O_1, M_1 \rangle$ *are global computation states. Let* π *belong to* O_0.

$$\langle O_0, M_0 \rangle \xrightarrow{\pi, \bullet} \langle O_1, M_1 \rangle$$

is satisfied if and only if $\pi = \langle \nu, \bullet, s, p \rangle$ *and:*

$$
\begin{aligned}
p \bullet s &= \langle \nu', s', p', o, B \rangle \\
O_1 &= (O_0 - \{\pi\}) \cup o \cup \{\langle \nu, \nu', s', p' \rangle\} \\
M_1 &= M_0 + \lambda[\nu].B
\end{aligned}
$$

are satisfied.

Note that Rule 3.3 is introduced to represent a serializable action which occurs just after an object receives a message or reply, whereas Rule 3.4 is introduced to represent a serializable action without any receptions of messages/replies. In the formalization of the Actor model by Gul Agha[Agha 87], the latter kind of transition does not appear since in the Actor model the action in response to a single message is always a serializable action. In case of our language, the action in response to a single message does not seem a serializable action because the **while** construct, which can describe an infinite iteration, is incorporated. Therefore, we introduce Rule 3.4. Currently, however, we do not discuss what are the serializable actions in our computing model. We just assume that, if only we divide the action sequence in response to a message/reply into small pieces, we can get a sequence of serializable actions, which is semantically equivalent to the original action sequence. Later, we will show that even with the **while** construct Rule 3.4 is not necessary. In other words, the action in response to a single message or reply can be represented as a single transition even if the action does not terminate in finite time. Notice that since we use a denotational technique to describe an internal sequential action within an object, the computation result of even an infinite action can be denoted by some mathematical object.

Our operational semantics is defined in terms of the *possible transitions*, that is, the semantics of a concurrent system whose initial configuration is represented by a global computation state $\langle O_0, M_0 \rangle$ is defined as the set of the possible transition sequences which begin with $\langle O_0, M_0 \rangle$[2]

The following lemma shows a sufficient condition for two consecutive transitions to be commutative. In the sequel, we may write:

$$\langle O_0, M_0 \rangle \xrightarrow{\pi_0, \mu_0} \cdots \xrightarrow{\pi_i, \mu_i} \cdots \xrightarrow{\pi_{k-1}, \mu_{k-1}} \langle O_k, M_k \rangle$$

if there exist global computation states $\langle O_1, M_1 \rangle, \langle O_2, M_2 \rangle, \ldots, \langle O_{k-1}, M_{k-1} \rangle$ such that:

$$
\begin{aligned}
\langle O_0, M_0 \rangle &\xrightarrow{\pi_0, \mu_0} \langle O_1, M_1 \rangle \\
\langle O_1, M_1 \rangle &\xrightarrow{\pi_1, \mu_1} \langle O_2, M_2 \rangle \\
&\;\;\vdots \\
\langle O_{k-1}, M_{k-1} \rangle &\xrightarrow{\pi_{k-1}, \mu_{k-1}} \langle O_k, M_k \rangle
\end{aligned}
$$

are satisfied.

---

[2]In case of infinite computations, we have to take *fairness* of computations into account. In this paper, however, we omit the details, which can be seen in [Shibayama 91].

Lemma 3.5 *Suppose that:*

$$\langle O_0, M_0 \rangle \xrightarrow{\pi_0, \mu_0} \langle O_1, M_1 \rangle \xrightarrow{\pi_1, \mu_1} \langle O_2, M_2 \rangle$$

is a possible transition sequence, where $\pi_0 \in O_0, \pi_1 \in O_1, \mu_0, \mu_1 \in Mess \cup \{\bullet\}$ (i.e., μ_0 and μ_1 can be $\bullet$). Let π_0 and π_1 be $\langle \nu_0, \nu_0^a, s_0, p_0 \rangle$ and $\langle \nu_1, \nu_1^a, s_1, p_1 \rangle$, respectively. If the following conditions:

1. *$\nu_0 \neq \nu_1$,*

2. *π_1 belongs not only to O_1 but also to O_0, and*

3. *μ_1 is either $\bullet$ or an element of $(\dagger M_0)\nu_1^a\nu_1^a$ for some ν_1^a*

are satisfied,

$$\langle O_0, M_0 \rangle \xrightarrow{\pi_1, \mu_1 \ \pi_0, \mu_0} \langle O_2, M_2 \rangle$$

is also a possible transition sequence.

Intuitively, commutative transitions may be performed in parallel and there are no causality relations among them.

Theorem 3.6 *For each finite possible transition sequence:*

$$\langle O_0, M_0 \rangle \xrightarrow{\pi_0, \mu_0} \cdots \xrightarrow{\pi_i, \mu_i} \cdots \xrightarrow{\pi_{k-1}, \mu_{k-1}} \langle O_k, M_k \rangle$$

where the active name of any object in O_0 is not $\bullet$, there exists a permutation σ on $\{0, 1, \ldots, i, \ldots, k-1\}$ such that:

$$\langle O_0, M_0 \rangle \xrightarrow{\pi_{\sigma(0)}, \mu_{\sigma(0)}} \cdots \xrightarrow{\pi_{\sigma(i)}, \mu_{\sigma(i)}} \cdots \xrightarrow{\pi_{\sigma(k-1)}, \mu_{\sigma(k-1)}} \langle O_k, M_k \rangle$$

is a possible transition sequence in which if $\mu_{\sigma(i)} = \bullet$ is satisfied, the primary names of $\pi_{\sigma(i)}$ and $\pi_{\sigma(i-1)}$ are the same.

This means that in case of finite transition sequence, the behavior of an object in response to a single message (including a reply) is always a *serializable* action in our model. We can also prove that the behavior of an object in response to a single message (including a reply) is always a *serializable* action even in an infinite computation.

Theorem 3.7 *Suppose that:*

$$\langle O_0, M_0 \rangle \xrightarrow{\pi_0, \mu_0} \cdots \xrightarrow{\pi_{i-1}, \mu_{i-1}} \langle O_i, M_i \rangle \xrightarrow{\pi_i, \mu_i} \cdots$$

is a possible transition sequence, which is infinite. For all i, let π_i be $\langle \nu_i, \nu_i^a, s_i, p_i \rangle$ and $p_i(\mu_i)(s_i)$ be $\langle \nu_i', s_i', p_i', o_i, B_i \rangle$. We assume that, there are infinitely many i such that $\nu_i = \nu_0$ and $\mu^i = \bullet$ and only $i = 0$ satisfies both $\nu_i = \nu_0$ and $\mu^i \neq \bullet$. Also let σ and $\overline{\sigma}$ be two functions which satisfy:

- $\sigma(0) = 0$

- $\sigma(1) < \sigma(2) < \ldots < \sigma(j) < \ldots$ and $\bigcup_{j=0}^{\infty}\{\sigma(j)\} = \{i | i > 0, \nu_i = \nu_0\}$, and

- $\overline{\sigma}(1) < \overline{\sigma}(2) < \ldots < \overline{\sigma}(j) < \ldots$ and $\bigcup_{j=0}^{\infty}\{\overline{\sigma}(j)\} = \{i | i > 0, \nu_i \neq \nu_0\}$.

Both:

$$\langle O_0, M_0 \rangle \xrightarrow{\pi_0, \mu_0} \xrightarrow{\pi_{\sigma(1)}, \bullet} \ldots \xrightarrow{\pi_{\sigma(i)}, \bullet} \ldots$$

and

$$\langle O_0 - \{\pi_0\} \cup (\bigcup_{i=0}^{\infty} o_{\sigma(i)}), retrieve(M_0, \mu_0) + \sum_{i=1}^{\infty} \lambda[\nu].B_{\sigma(i)} \rangle \xrightarrow{\pi_{\overline{\sigma}}(1), \mu_{\overline{\sigma}}(1)} \ldots \xrightarrow{\pi_{\overline{\sigma}}(i), \mu_{\overline{\sigma}}(i)} \ldots$$

are possible transition sequences, where $\sum_{i=1}^{\infty} \lambda[\nu].B_{\sigma(i)}$ *is an abbreviation of*

$$\lambda[\nu].B_{\sigma(1)} + \lambda[\nu].B_{\sigma(2)} + \ldots + \lambda[\nu].B_{\sigma(i)} + \ldots$$

Furthermore, if we define $\langle O_i', M_i' \rangle$ $(1 \leq i)$ *so that:*

$$\langle O_0, M_0 \rangle \xrightarrow{\pi_0, \mu_0} \xrightarrow{\pi_{\sigma(1)}, \bullet} \ldots \xrightarrow{\pi_{\sigma(i-1)}, \bullet} \langle O_i', M_i' \rangle$$

the following is satisfied:

$$\langle \lim_{i \to \infty} O_i', \lim_{i \to \infty} M_i' \rangle = \langle O_0 - \{\pi_0\} \cup (\bigcup_{i=0}^{\infty} o_{\sigma(i)}), retrieve(M_0, \mu_0) + \sum_{i=0}^{\infty} \lambda[\nu].B_{\sigma(i)} \rangle$$

This theorem suggests that by introducing a new transition rule:

$$\langle O_0, M_0 \rangle \xrightarrow{\pi_0, \mu_0} \langle O_0 - \{\pi_0\} \cup (\bigcup_{i=0}^{\infty} o_{\sigma(i)}), retrieve(M_0, \mu_0) + \sum_{i=0}^{\infty} \lambda[\nu].B_{\sigma(i)} \rangle$$

an infinite computation within an object can be described in a single step. The similar effect can be obtained by replacing π_0 by $\langle \nu_0, \nu_0^a, s_0, p' \rangle$ such that

$$p'(\mu_0)(s_0) = \langle \bot, \bot, \bot, \bigcup_{i=0}^{\infty} o_{\sigma(i)}, \sum_{i=0}^{\infty} \lambda[\nu].B_{\sigma(i)} \rangle$$

4 Object Diagrams

Though possible transitions well represent the semantics of a program, they are too *concrete* in two respects. First, it meets our intuition that possible transition sequences which are mutually derived from one another by applications of Lemma 3.5 are equivalent. Our semantic model should reflect this equivalence relation. The other point is that possible transitions contain higher order function values, which represent internal structures of objects (i.e., states and procedures). This means that a semantics description using possible transitions would necessarily depend on details of internal structures. Without questions, our semantic descriptions should not depend on internal details of objects and only depend on first order values.

For a more abstract formalization, we introduce the notion of *object diagrams* in this section.

Definition 4.1 *Suppose that:*

$$\langle O_0, M_0 \rangle \xrightarrow{\pi_0, \mu_0} \cdots \langle O_i, M_i \rangle \xrightarrow{\pi_i, \mu_i} \cdots$$

is a possible transition sequence, where $\pi_i = \langle \nu_i, \nu_i^a, s_i, p_i \rangle$ *and* $p_i(\mu^i)(s_i) = \langle \nu_i', s_i', p_i', o_i, B_i \rangle$.

1. *The* linear object diagram *corresponding to this transition sequence is a pair* $\langle E, \Rightarrow \rangle$ *where* E *is a multiset*[3] *of* $\langle \nu_0, \mu_0 \rangle$, $\langle \nu_1, \mu_1 \rangle$, $\ldots$, $\langle \nu_i, \mu_i \rangle$, $\ldots$ *and*

$$\Rightarrow = \{ \langle \langle \nu_i, \mu_i \rangle, \langle \nu_j, \mu_j \rangle \rangle | i < j \}$$

   When $\langle \langle \nu_i, \mu_i \rangle, \langle \nu_j, \mu_j \rangle \rangle$ *belongs to* $\Rightarrow$, *we may write* $\langle \nu_i, \mu_i \rangle \Rightarrow \langle \nu_j, \mu_j \rangle$. *We call each element* $\langle \nu_i, \mu_i \rangle$ *in* E *an event.*

2. *The* object diagram *corresponding to this transition sequence is a pair* $\langle E, \Rightarrow \rangle$ *where* E *is a multiset of* $\langle \nu_0, \mu_0 \rangle$, $\langle \nu_1, \mu_1 \rangle$, $\ldots$, $\langle \nu_i, \mu_i \rangle$, $\ldots$ *and* $\Rightarrow$ *is the transitive closure of:*

$$\left\{ \langle \langle \nu_i, \mu_i \rangle, \langle \nu_j, \mu_j \rangle \rangle \; \middle| \; \begin{array}{l} \nu_i = \nu_j, i < j \text{ or} \\ \langle \nu_j, \nu_j^a, s_j, p_j \rangle \in o_i \text{ or} \\ \mu_j \text{ belongs to } B_i(\nu_j^a) \end{array} \right\}$$

A linear object diagram is just a linear order set of pairs. The i-th pair $\langle \nu_i, \mu_i \rangle$ represents the primary name ν_i of an object and the message μ_i in the way that the object accepts the message at the i-th stage. In contrast, an object diagram is a partial order set of the similar pairs. In terms of linear object diagrams and object diagrams, we can define both linear and partial order semantics.

The notions of object diagrams and linear object diagrams are more *abstract* than the notion of possible transition in the sense that they do not depend on the internal world of objects (e.g., *state* and *procedure*). They only depend on the names of objects and messages, which are externally observable. Furthermore, they have a nice property, i.e., names and messages are not *functions* but first order *values*.

Definition 4.2 *A linearization of an object diagram* $\langle E, \Rightarrow \rangle$ *is a linear object diagram* $\langle E, \Rightarrow' \rangle$ *where* $\Rightarrow'$ *is a linear order on* E *which satisfies* $\langle \nu_i, \mu_i \rangle \Rightarrow \langle \nu_j, \mu_j \rangle \supset \langle \nu_i, \mu_i \rangle \Rightarrow' \langle \nu_j, \mu_j \rangle$

In general, a single object diagram have more than one linearization. Notice that a linearization can be obtained by *topological sorting*.

Theorem 4.3 *Suppose that an object diagram* $\langle E, \Rightarrow \rangle$ *corresponds to a possible transition sequence:*

$$\langle O_0, M_0 \rangle \xrightarrow{\pi_0, \mu_0} \langle O_1, M_1 \rangle \cdots \xrightarrow{\pi_k, \mu_k} \langle O_{k+1}, M_{k+1} \rangle$$

and that there exists a permutation σ *on the set* $\{0, 1, \ldots, k\}$ *such that:*

$$\langle \nu_{\sigma(0)}, \mu_{\sigma(0)} \rangle \Rightarrow' \langle \nu_{\sigma(1)}, \mu_{\sigma(1)} \rangle \Rightarrow' \cdots \Rightarrow' \langle \nu_{\sigma(k)}, \mu_{\sigma(k)} \rangle$$

---

[3] $\langle \nu_i, \mu_i \rangle = \langle \nu_j, \mu_j \rangle$ is satisfied if $\nu_i = \nu_j$ and $\mu_i = \mu_j = \bullet$ since different occurrences of $\bullet$ do not have unique names. In this paper, when we need to specify some particular occurrence of $\bullet$, we describe it so that it can be distinguished from other occurrences from the context, for instance, μ_i.

is a linearization of the object diagram $\langle E, \Rightarrow \rangle$. *There exists a possible transition sequence:*

$$\langle O_0, M_0 \rangle \xrightarrow{\pi_{\sigma(0)},\mu_{\sigma(0)}} \cdots \xrightarrow{\pi_{\sigma(i-1)},\mu_{\sigma(i-1)}\pi_{\sigma(i)},\mu_{\sigma(i)}} \cdots \xrightarrow{\pi_{\sigma(k)},\mu_{\sigma(k)}} \langle O_{k+1}, M_{k+1} \rangle$$

such that $\langle E, \Rightarrow' \rangle$ *and* $\langle E, \Rightarrow \rangle$ *are the linear object diagram and object diagram, respectively, corresponding to this transition sequence.*

This theorem shows that a finite object diagram represents a bunch of finite possible transition sequences which are essentially equivalent. We have a similar result in the infinite cases under the condition that the length of the linearization is no greater than ω. However, we omit the details.

5 Translating Programs

In this section we translate an object definition form into a tuple which represents the object defined by the form. For the purposes, later on, we define a function Θ:

$$\Theta \in Def \rightarrow State \rightarrow Obj$$

where Def is the syntactic domain for object definition forms and $State$ represents the domain of the global name environments. Global names may occur in an object definition form to designate objects defined by some object definition forms. Θ maps an object definition form to an appropriate element of Obj.

Definition 5.1 *Let c be a Boolean expression.* $c \rightarrow v; v'$ *denotes the value of v if c denotes* true *and the value of v' if c denotes* false.

$$c_1 \rightarrow v_1; c_2 \rightarrow v_2; \ldots; c_n \rightarrow v_n; v_{n+1}$$

is an abbreviation of

$$c_1 \rightarrow v_1; (c_2 \rightarrow v_2; (\ldots; (c_n \rightarrow v_n; v_{n+1}) \ldots))$$

Definition 5.2 *Let s be an element of $Id \rightarrow Value$.*

$$
\begin{aligned}
s[I_1/v_1, I_2/v_2, \ldots, I_n/v_n] \;=\; \lambda I.I &= I_0 &&\rightarrow v_0; \\
I &= I_1 &&\rightarrow v_1; \\
&\cdots && ; \\
I &= I_n &&\rightarrow v_n; \; sI
\end{aligned}
$$

A program is a finite set U of object definitions, say d_1, d_2, ..., and d_n, whose first arguments (i.e., the object name part) are I_1, I_2, ..., and I_n. Let O_0 be the solutions of the following equations:

$$
\begin{aligned}
s_U &= (\lambda I.\bot)[I_1/I_1, I_2/I_2, \ldots, I_n/I_n] \\
O_0 &= \{\Theta d_1 s_U, \Theta d_2 s_U, \ldots, \Theta d_n s_U\}
\end{aligned}
$$

We use two other semantic functions $\mathcal{C}$ and $\mathcal{E}$ which translate statements and expressions, respectively, of our language.

$$\mathcal{E} \in Exp \to State \to Value$$
$$\mathcal{C} \in St \to State \to Cont \to Name \to (Name \cup \{\bullet\}) \times State \times Proc \times \mathcal{O} \times Buf$$

where

$$Cont = State \to Name \to (Name \cup \{\bullet\}) \times State \times Proc \times \mathcal{O} \times Buf$$

and St and Exp are syntactic domains of statements and expressions. We omit the details of $\mathcal{E}$ since it is obvious.

Definition 5.3
Suppose that $\nu \in Name \cup \{\bullet\}$, $s \in State$, $p \in Proc$, $o, o' \subset OBj$, *and* $B, B' \in Buf$.
1.

$$o \uplus o' \stackrel{def}{\equiv} o \cup o' \quad if\ o' \neq \bot$$
$$\stackrel{def}{\equiv} o \quad\quad\ if\ o' = \bot$$

2.

$$\langle o', B' \rangle + \langle \nu, s, p, o, B \rangle \stackrel{def}{\equiv} \langle \nu, s, p, o' \uplus o, B' + B \rangle$$

Notice that for message buffers, $+$ *is already defined such that* $B + \bot = B$.

Using $\mathcal{E}$ and $\mathcal{C}$, Θ is defined as follows:
Definition 5.4

$$\Theta[\![\text{object}\ \nu\ ([I_1 := E_1]\ \ldots [I_n := E_n])\ (\Rightarrow M \otimes R\ F)]\!]s_U = \langle \nu, \nu, s, p \rangle$$

where

$$s = s_U[I_1/\mathcal{E}[\![E_1]\!]s_U, \ldots, I_n/\mathcal{E}[\![E_n]\!]s_U]$$
$$p = Y\lambda p.\lambda\langle c, r, t\rangle s.\mathcal{C}[\![F]\!]s[M/c, R/r](\lambda st.\langle \nu, s, p, \emptyset, \lambda\nu.\langle\emptyset, \langle\rangle\rangle\rangle)t$$
$$Y\ \text{is}\ \text{Curry's Y-operator}$$

Definition 5.5 *We define* $\mathcal{C}$ *as follows:*

$\mathcal{C}[\![(\text{progn}\ F_1 \ldots F_m)]\!] = \mathcal{C}[\![F_1 \ldots F_m]\!]$

$\mathcal{C}[\![F_1 \ldots F_m]\!] = \mathcal{C}[\![F_1]\!] \star \mathcal{C}[\![F_2 \ldots F_m]\!]$

$(\mathcal{C}[\![F_1]\!] \star \mathcal{C}[\![F_2]\!])sk = \mathcal{C}[\![F_1]\!]s(\lambda s't'.\mathcal{C}[\![F_2]\!]s'kt')$

$\mathcal{C}[\![(\text{if}\ E\ F_1\ F_2)]\!]s = \mathcal{E}[\![E]\!]s \to \mathcal{C}[\![F_1]\!]s; \mathcal{C}[\![F_2]\!]s$

$\mathcal{C}[\![(\text{while}\ E\ F_1 \ldots F_m)]\!] = Y(\lambda c.\lambda sk.(\mathcal{E}[\![E]\!]s \to ks; (\mathcal{C}[\![F_1 \ldots F_m]\!] \star c)sk))$

$\mathcal{C}[\![I := E]\!]sk = ks[I/\mathcal{E}[\![E]\!]s]$

       where E *is neither now type message passing form nor object creation form*

$\mathcal{C}[\![E_1 \text{ <- } E_2]\!]skt = \langle \emptyset, \lambda[\mathcal{E}[\![E_1]\!]s].\langle\{\langle\mathcal{E}[\![E_2]\!]s, \bullet, t.1\rangle\}, \langle\rangle\rangle\rangle + ks(t.2)$

$\mathcal{C}[\![E_1 \text{ <= } E_2]\!]skt = \langle \emptyset, \lambda[\mathcal{E}[\![E_1]\!]s].\langle\emptyset, \langle\langle\mathcal{E}[\![E_2]\!]s, \bullet, t.1\rangle\rangle\rangle\rangle + ks(t.2)$

$\mathcal{C}[\![I := [E_1 \text{ <== } E_2]]\!]skt = \langle t.2, s, \lambda\langle c, r, t'\rangle s.ks[I/c]t', \emptyset, \lambda[\mathcal{E}[\![E_1]\!]s].\langle\emptyset, \langle\langle\mathcal{E}[\![E_2]\!]s, t.2, t.1\rangle\rangle\rangle$

$\mathcal{C}[\![I := [\text{object}\ ([I_1 := E_1]\ \ldots [I_n := E_n])\ (\Rightarrow M \otimes R\ F)]]\!]skt$

$\quad = \langle\{\langle t.1, t.1, s_U[I_1/\mathcal{E}[\![E_1]\!]s_U, \ldots, I_n/\mathcal{E}[\![E_n]\!]s_U], p'\rangle\}, \lambda\nu.\langle\emptyset, \langle\rangle\rangle\rangle + ks[I/t.1]t.2 \quad where$

$\quad p' = Y\lambda p.\lambda\langle c, r, t'\rangle s.\mathcal{C}[\![F]\!](s[M/c, R/r])(\lambda st'.\langle t.1, p, s, \emptyset, \lambda\nu.\langle\emptyset, \langle\rangle\rangle\rangle)t'$

With this definition of C, we do not have to use Rule 3.4. That is, for any possible transition sequence whose initial configuration contains only such objects that are translation results of Θ, the second element of any tuple representing an object that appears in a transition cannot be •.

6   Program Transformation

We have already proposed several program transformation rules in [Shibayama 88], which fuse and split concurrent objects. In this section, we only show a typical rule. We assume that two objects π_a and π_b, whose primary names are ν_a and ν_b, respectively, are defined by:

```
[object νₐ                    [object ν_b
   ([I_{a,1} := e_{a,1}]          ([I_{b,1} := e_{b,1}]
       ⋮                              ⋮
    [I_{a,n_a} := e_{a,n_a}])       [I_{b,n_b} := e_{b,n_b}])
   (=> Mₐ @ Rₐ Fₐ)]              (=> M_b @ R_b F_b)]
```

In the following, we assume that the following are pairwise disjoint:

1. the set of the identifiers that occur in the global environment,

2. the set of the identifiers that represent the local variables in π_a, and

3. the set of the identifiers that represent the local variables in π_b

We can assume these without loss of generality since α-conversions (i.e., renaming of local variables) of objects do not change their semantics.

Rule 6.1 *Pipeline Composition Rule: Supposing that two objects π_a and π_b satisfy the following conditions:*

1. *The only object who knows the primary name ν_b is π_a, which does not send any message containing this name. That is, all the messages whose destination is ν_b are transmitted by π_a, if they exist.*

2. *Each message passing form in S_a is either past or now type (i.e., the transmission ordering law is satisfied among these messages), and the destinations of the form are always ν_b.*

3. *In response to each now type message, π_b sends back a single reply before it completes the action sequence.*

The pipeline composition rule transforms the objects π_a and π_b into a single object $\pi_a + \pi_b$ which is defined as:

```
[object νₐ
   ([I_{a,1} := e_{a,1}] ... [I_{a,n_a} := e_{a,n_a}]
    [I_{b,1} := e_{b,1}] ... [I_{b,n_b} := e_{b,n_b}]
    [M_b := nil] [R_b := nil])
   (=> Mₐ @ Rₐ Fₐθₐ)]
```

```
[object generator                [object filter
  ([n := 1])                       ()
  (=> any @ r                      (=> number
     (while t                         (if (evenp number)
        [filter <= n]                    [output <= number])))]
        [n := (+ n 1)])))]
```

Program 6.1: Two Objects generator and filter

where θ_a is a substitution defined in the following.

θ_a is defined in terms of another substitution $\theta_b(I)$ and a new primitive (gensym) so that θ_a substitutes each occurrence of a message passing form $[E_1$ <= $E_2]$ or $[I$:= $[E_1$ <== $E_2]]$ of F_a by:

(progn $[M_b$:= $E_2]$ $[R_b$:= •] F_b), or
(progn $[M_b$:= $E_2]$ $[R_b$:= (gensym)] $F_b\theta_b(I)$),

respectively. (gensym) is an expression to produce a unique name upon each evaluation. Roughly speaking, $[M_b$:= $E_2]$ and $[R_b$:= ...] simulate the effect of binding variables upon message acceptance by π_b. In case of past type message passing, F_b does not have to be modified but in case of past type message passing, F_b does have to be modified so that returning a reply by π_b is replaced by an assignment to I. For the purposes, $\theta_b(I)$ substitutes each occurrence of a message passing form $[E_1$ <= $E_2]$, $[E_1$ <- $E_2]$, or $[E_1$ <== $E_2]$ by:

(if (eq E_1 R_b) $[I$:= $E_2]$ $[E_1$ <= $E_2]$)
(if (eq E_1 R_b) $[I$:= $E_2]$ $[E_1$ <- $E_2]$)
(if (eq E_1 R_b) (stop) $[E_1$ <== $E_2]$)

where stop is a new construct defined as:

$$C[\![(\texttt{stop})]\!]skt \; = \; \langle t.2, s, \bot, \emptyset, \lambda\nu.\langle\emptyset, \langle\rangle\rangle\rangle$$

For instance, by this rule, two objects in Program 6.1 are fused into the one in Program 6.2. With a program transformation technique for sequential programs, it could be simplified.

The correctness proof of transformation rules are long and boring. We omit the details in this paper. Those who are interested in the details should see [Shibayama 91].

7   Summary

We introduce in this paper a layered semantic model of object-based concurrent computing which consists of:

1. an operational model

```
[object generator
  ([n := 1] [number := nil])
  (=> any @ r
     (while t
      (progn
        [number := n]
        (if (evenp number) [output <= number]))
      [n := (+ n 1)]))]
```

Program 6.2: The Fusion of **generator** and **filter**

2. a more abstract semantic model based on object diagrams, and

3. program transformation.

The third layer, which is the most important for most people, provides a support for composing/decomposing object descriptions and thus it also provides a support for compositional reasoning at least in some degree.

We give up using a fully compositional semantics since it tends to be complicated. Instead, we employ a partially compositional approach, that is, by introducing a program transformation system, some collections of objects can be composed but the others could not. We assume that there are several or more patterns of object compositions which human programmers use intensively to (informally) reason about their concurrent programs. The design of the third layer is our attempts to enumerate such patterns. Though this layer cannot provide a complete system, it is useful in many situations. We presented the verification methodology based on such a transformation system in [Shibayama 88].

Acknowledgments

The author would like to thank Professor A. Yonezawa for his help and suggestions. Also he would like to thank the anonymous referees for their useful comments to improve this paper.

References

[Agha 87] G. Agha. *Actors : A Model of Concurrent Computation in Distributed Systems.* The MIT Press, 1987.

[1] P. America. Denotational semantics of a parallel object-oriented language. *Information and Computation*, Vol. 83, pp. 152–205, 1989.

[Brock and Ackerman 81] J. D. Brock and W. B. Ackerman. *Scenarios: A Model of Nondeterminate Computation,* volume 107 of *Lecture Notes in Computer Science,* pages 252–259. Springer-Verlag, 1981.

[Burstall and Darlington 77] R. M. Burstall and J. Darlington. A transformation system for developing recursive programs. *Journal of the ACM*, 24(1):44–67, 1977.

[Chandy and Lamport 85] K. M. Chandy and L. Lamport. Distributed snapshots: Determining global states of distributed systems. *ACM Transactions on Computer Systems*, 3(1):63–75, 1985.

[Lloyd 84] J. W. Lloyd. *Foundations of Logic Programming*. Springer-Verlag, 1984.

[Milner 80] R. Milner. *A Calculus of Communicating Systems*, volume 92 of *Lecture Notes in Computer Science*. Springer-Verlag, 1980.

[Milner 89] R. Milner. *Communication and Concurrency*. Prentice-Hall, 1989.

[Milner et al. 89a] R. Milner, J. Parrow, and J. Walker. A calculus of mobile processes part I. Technical Report ECS-LFCS-89-85, Lab. for Foundations of Computer Science, Univ. of Edinburgh, 1989.

[Milner et al. 89b] R. Milner, J. Parrow, and J. Walker. A calculus of mobile processes part II. Technical Report ECS-LFCS-89-86, Lab. for Foundations of Computer Science, Univ. of Edinburgh, 1989.

[Pratt 82] V. Pratt. On the composition of processes. In *Proceedings of ACM Symposium on Principles of Programming Languages (POPL)*, pages 213–223, 1982.

[Pratt 86] V. Pratt. Modeling concurrency with partial orders. *International Journal of Parallel Programming*, 15(1):33–71, 1986.

[Shibayama 88] E. Shibayama. How to invent distributed implementation schemes of an object-oriented concurrent language — a transformational approach. In *Proceedings of ACM Conference on Object-Oriented Programming Systems, Languages, and Applications, San Diego CA.*, pages 297–305. ACM, September 1988. A revised version in [Yonezawa 90]

[Shibayama 91] E. Shibayama. An object-based approach to modeling concurrent systems. Doctor Thesis, Dept. of Information Science, Univ. of Tokyo, 1991.

[Yonezawa 90] A. Yonezawa, editor. *ABCL: An Object-Oriented Concurrent System — Theory, Language, Programming, Implementation and Application*. The MIT Press, 1990.

Formal Techniques for
Parallel Object-Oriented Languages

Pierre America

Philips Research

P.O. Box 80.000

5600 JA Eindhoven

The Netherlands

Abstract

This paper is intended to give an overview of the formal techniques that have been developed to deal with the parallel object-oriented language POOL and several related languages. We sketch a number of semantic descriptions, using several formalism: operational semantics, denotational semantics, and a new approach to semantics, which we call *layered semantics*. Then we summarize the progress that has been made in formal proof systems to verify the correctness of parallel object-oriented programs. Finally we survey the techniques that we are currently developing to describe the behaviour of objects independently of their implementation, leading to linguistic support for behavioural subtyping.

1 Introduction

Over the last few years, object-oriented programming has gained widespread use and considerable popularity. Until now, the use of object-oriented techniques for parallel programming is mainly restricted to research environments, but nevertheless it holds considerable promises to contribute to the solutions of many problems associated with the programming of parallel computers.

At the Philips Research Laboratories in Eindhoven, the Netherlands, several research projects in this area have been carried out. The DOOM project (Decentralized Object-Oriented Machine) was a subproject of ESPRIT project 415: 'Parallel Architectures and Languages for Advanced Information Processing: a VLSI-directed Approach' [AHO+90]. This ESPRIT project aimed at improving the performance of computers in the area of symbolic applications by the use of large-scale parallelism. Several approaches were explored in different subprojects, which were tied together at a disciplinary level by working groups [Bak89, Tre90]. The DOOM subproject had chosen an object-oriented

This paper was written in the context of ESPRIT Basic Research Action 3020: *Integration*.
It is a slightly revised version of an invited paper for the *Concur 91* conference, published in LNCS 527.

approach [AH90]. This subproject developed a parallel object-oriented programming language POOL in which applications can be written, together with a parallel machine architecture suitable to execute programs in this language. A number of example applications have been developed as well.

Another project, PRISMA (PaRallel Inference and Storage MAchine), built on the same object-oriented principles as the DOOM project. It aimed at developing a system that is able to handle very large amounts of knowledge and data, again using parallelism to reach a high performance. One of the concrete results of this project is a prototype relational database machine which can automatically exploit parallelism in evaluating the users' queries [AHH+90]. Together with the DOOM project, a prototype computer, POOMA (Parallel Object-Oriented Machine Architecture), has been built, on which the software developed in these projects is running. It comprises 100 processor nodes, each with its own local memory, and connected by a high-speed packet switching network.

The language POOL (Parallel Object-Oriented Language) used in these projects has been the subject of extensive theoretical studies. In the present paper, we give a survey of the results of these studies, and we shall try to assess their influence on the design and the use of the language. In fact, the name POOL stands for a family of languages, developed over a period of seven years. The most important one is POOL2 [Ame88], the language that was implemented on the POOMA machine. Whenever the exact member of the POOL family does not matter, we shall just use the name POOL.

Section 2 gives an introduction to the language POOL itself. Section 3 gives an overview of the techniques that have been used to describe the semantics of POOL in a formal way. Then Section 4 sketches the research that has been done in the area of formal verification of POOL programs. Finally, in Section 5 we describe the typically object-oriented phenomena of inheritance and subtyping, and show how formal techniques can help to clarify many of the issues involved.

2 An overview of the language POOL

This section gives a summary of the most important ingredients of the POOL language. For more details, we refer the reader to [Ame89b], or to the official language definition [Ame88].

In POOL, a system is described as a collection of *objects*. An object can be thought of as a kind of box, containing some data and having the ability to perform some actions on these data. An object uses *variables* to store its data. This data always takes the form of a *reference* to an object. The object's ability to perform operations on its internal data lies in two mechanisms: First, an object can have a set of *methods*, a kind of procedures, which can access and change the values of the variables. (Up to this point, the mechanisms that we have described are generally present in object-oriented languages.) Second, an object has a so-called *body*, a local process that can execute in parallel with the bodies of all the other objects in the system. This is specific for POOL; it constitutes the main source of parallelism in POOL programs.

A very important principle in object-oriented programming is *encapsulation*: The variables of one object are not directly accessible to other objects. In fact, the only way for objects to interact is by sending *messages*. A message is a request to the receiving object to execute one of its methods. The sending object explicitly mentions the receiver and the method name. It can also pass some parameters (again references to objects) to the method. The sender blocks until the receiver has answered its message. The receiver also explicitly states when it is prepared to answer a message. However, it does not specify the sender but only lists a set of possible method names. As soon as synchronization between sender and receiver takes place, the receiver executes the required method, using the parameters that the sender gave. The method returns a *result* (once again, a reference to an object), which is then passed back to the sender. After that, sender and receiver both continue their own processing in parallel.

Because of the above mechanisms, the only parallelism in the system is caused by the parallel execution of the bodies of the different objects. Inside each object everything happens sequentially and deterministically, so that the object is protected from the parallel and nondeterministic (and therefore 'dangerous') outside world. The interesting thing in POOL is that, like in other object-oriented languages, new objects can be *created dynamically* in arbitrary high numbers. In POOL, where as soon as an object is created, its body starts executing, this means that also the degree of parallelism can be increased dynamically. (Objects are never destroyed explicitly; rather, useless objects are removed by a garbage collector working behind the screens).

In order to describe these dynamically evolving systems of objects in a static program, the objects are grouped into *classes*. All the objects in one class (the *instances* of the class) have the same names and types for their variables (of course, each has its own private set of variables) and they execute the same methods and body. In a program, a *class definition* is used to describe this internal structure of the objects. Whenever a new object is to be created, a class is named which serves as a blueprint.

3 Semantics

A number of different techniques have been used to describe the semantics of POOL in a formal way. The following subsections sketch several of these approaches. In all of these descriptions, a syntactically simplified version of POOL is used. This is more convenient in the semantic definition but not very well readable in concrete programs. There is a straightforward translation from POOL2 or POOL-T (an older version) to this simplified notation.

3.1 Operational Semantics

The simplest semantic technique is the use of *transition systems* to define an *operational* semantics. This technique has been introduced by Hennessy and Plotkin [HP79, Plo81, Plo83]. It describes the behaviour of a system in terms of sequences of *transitions* between *configurations*. A configuration describes the system at one particular moment during the execution. Apart from a component describing the values of the variables, it typically contains as a component that part of the program that is still to be executed. The possible transitions are described by a *transition relation*, a binary relation between configurations (by having a relation instead of a function, it is possible to model nondeterminism). This transition relation is defined by a number of *axioms* and *rules*. Because of the presence of (the rest of) the program itself in the configurations, it is possible to describe the transition relation in a way that is closely related to the syntactic structure of the language.

The term 'operational' can now be understood as follows: The set of configurations defines a (very abstract) model of a machine, and the transition relation describes how this machine operates: each transition corresponds to an action that the machine can perform. The fact that the semantic description follows the syntactic structure of the language so closely (as we shall see below) is a definite advantage of the transition system approach to operational semantics.

In the operational semantics of POOL [ABKR86] uses configurations having four components:

$$Conf = \mathcal{P}_{fin}(LStat) \times \Sigma \times Type \times Unit$$

The first component is a finite set of *labelled statements*:

$$\{\langle \alpha_1, s_1 \rangle, \ldots, \langle \alpha_n, s_n \rangle\}$$

Here each α_i is an object name and the corresponding s_i is the statement (or sequence of statements) that the object is about to execute. This models the fact that the objects $\alpha_1, \ldots, \alpha_n$ are executing in parallel. The second component is a *state* $\sigma \in \Sigma$, which records the values of the instance variables and temporary variables of all the objects in the system. The third component is a typing function $\tau \in Type$, assigning to each object name the class of which the object is an instance. Finally, the last component is the complete POOL program or *unit*, which is used for looking up the declarations of methods (whenever a message is sent) and bodies (when new objects are created).

The transition relation $\rightarrow$ between configurations is defined by axioms and rules. In general, an axiom describes the essential operation of a certain kind of statement or expression in the language. For example, the axiom describing the assignment statement looks as follows:

$$\left\langle X \cup \{\langle \alpha, x := \beta \rangle\}, \sigma, \tau, U \right\rangle \rightarrow \left\langle X \cup \{\langle \alpha, \beta \rangle\}, \sigma\{\beta/\alpha, x\}, \tau, U \right\rangle$$

Here, X is a set of labelled statements which are not active in this transition, β is another object name, a special case of the expression that can in general appear at the right-hand side of an assignment, and $\sigma\{\beta/\alpha, x\}$ denotes the state that results from changing in the state σ the value of the variable x of the object α into the object name β.

Rules are generally used to describe how to evaluate the components of a composite statement or expression. For example, the following rule describes how the (general) expression at the right-hand side of an assignment is to be evaluated:

$$\frac{\left\langle X \cup \{\langle \alpha, e \rangle\}, \sigma, \tau, U \right\rangle \rightarrow \left\langle X' \cup \{\langle \alpha, e' \rangle\}, \sigma', \tau', U \right\rangle}{\left\langle X \cup \{\langle \alpha, x := e \rangle\}, \sigma, \tau, U \right\rangle \rightarrow \left\langle X' \cup \{\langle \alpha, x := e' \rangle\}, \sigma', \tau', U \right\rangle}$$

According to this rule, *if* the transition above the line is a member of the transition relation, *then* so is the transition below the line. In this way the rule reduces the problem of evaluating the expression in an assignment to evaluating the expression on its own. The latter is described by specific axioms and rules dealing with the several kinds of expressions in the language. Note that as soon as the right-hand side expression has been evaluated completely, so that an concrete object name β results, the assignment axiom above applies and the assignment proper can be performed.

The semantics of a whole program can now be defined as the set of all maximal (finite or infinite) sequences of configurations $\langle c_1, c_2, c_3, \ldots \rangle$ that satisfy $c_i \rightarrow c_{i+1}$. Each of these sequences represents a possible execution of the program.

3.2   Denotational semantics

The second form of semantic description that has been used to describe POOL is *denotational* semantics. Whereas operational semantics uses an abstract machine that can perform certain actions, denotational semantics assigns a mathematical value, a 'meaning', to each individual language construct. Here, the most important issue is compositionality: the meaning of a composite construct can be described in terms of only the *meanings* of its syntactic constituents without considering their form.

For sequential languages, it is very natural that the value associated with a statement is a function from states to states: when applied to the state before the execution of the statement, this function delivers the state after the execution. However, for parallel languages this is no longer appropriate: Not only does the presence of nondeterminism lead to a *set* of possible final states, in addition, information on the intermediate states is required to be able to compose a statement in parallel with other statements. This leads us to the concept of *resumptions* (introduced by Plotkin [Plo76]). Instead of delivering the final state after the execution of the statement has completed, we divide the execution of the statement into its atomic (indivisible) parts, and we deliver a pair $\langle \sigma', r \rangle$, where σ' is the state after the execution of the first atomic action and r is the resumption, which describes the execution from this point on. In this way, it is possible to put another statement in parallel with this one: the execution of the second statement can be interleaved with the original one in such a way that between each pair of subsequent atomic actions of the first statement an arbitrary number of atomic actions of the second one can be executed. Each atomic action can inspect the state at the beginning of its execution and possibly modify it.

For a very simple language (not yet having the power of POOL) we get the following equation for the set (the *domain*) in which the values reside that we want to assign to our statements:

$$P \cong \{p_0\} \cup \big(\Sigma \rightarrow \mathcal{P}(\Sigma \times P)\big). \tag{1}$$

The intended interpretation of this equation is the following: Let us call the elements of the set P *processes* and denote them with letters p, q, and r. Then a process p can either be the terminated process p_0, which cannot perform any action, or it is a function which, when provided with an input state σ, delivers a set X of possible actions. Each element of this set X is a pair $\langle \sigma', q \rangle$, where σ' is the state after this action, and q is a process that describes the rest of the execution after this first step.

It is clear that equation (1) cannot be solved in the framework of *sets*, because the cardinality of the right-hand side would always be larger than that of the left-hand side. In contrast to many other workers in the field of denotational semantics of parallelism, who use the framework of complete partial orders (cpo's) to solve this kind of equations (see, e.g., [Plo76]), we have chosen to use the framework of *complete metric spaces*. (Readers unfamiliar with this part of mathematics are referred to standard topology texts like

[Dug66, Eng89] or to [BZ82].) The most important reason for this choice is the possibility to uses Banach's fixed point theorem:

> Let M be a complete metric space with distance function d and let $f :$ $M \to M$ be a function that is *contracting*, i.e., there is a real number ϵ with $0 < \epsilon < 1$ such that for all $x, y \in M$ we have $d(f(x), f(y)) < \epsilon.d(x, y)$. Then f has a unique fixed point.

This ensures that whenever we can establish the contractivity of a function we have a *unique* fixed point, whereas in cpo theory mostly we can only guarantee the existence of a *least* fixed point.

Another reason for using complete metric spaces is the naturalness of the power domain construction. Whereas in cpo theory there are several competing definitions (see, e.g., [Plo76, Smy78]) all of which are somewhat hard to understand, in complete metric spaces there is a very natural definition:

> If M is a metric space with distance d, then we define $\mathcal{P}(M)$ to be the set of all *closed* subsets of M, provided with the so-called *Hausdorff distance* d_H, which is defined as follows:
>
> $$d_H(X, Y) = \max\Big\{\sup_{x \in X}\{d(x, Y)\}, \sup_{y \in Y}\{d(y, X)\}\Big\}$$
>
> where $d(x, Z) = \inf_{z \in Z}\{d(x, z)\}$ with the convention that $\sup \emptyset = 0$ and $\inf \emptyset = 1$ (we only use metric spaces where the maximum distance is 1).

(Minor variations on this definition are sometimes useful, such as taking only the non-empty subsets of M or only the compact ones. The metric is the same in all cases. Note that $d(x, Z)$ can be interpreted as the distance between the point x and the set Z.)

The domain equation that we use for the denotational semantics of POOL [ABKR89] is somewhat more complicated than equation (1), because it also has to accommodate for communication among objects. For POOL, the domain P of processes is defined as follows:

$$P \cong \{p_0\} \cup \big(\Sigma \to \mathcal{P}(Step_P)\big)$$

where the set $Step_P$ of *steps* is given by

$$Step_P = (\Sigma \times P) \cup Send_P \cup Answer_P,$$

with

$$Send_P = Obj \times MName \times Obj^* \times (Obj \to P) \times P$$

and

$$Answer_P = Obj \times MName \times \big(Obj^* \to (Obj \to P) \to^1 P\big).$$

The interpretation of these equations (actually, they can be merged into one large equation) is as follows: As in the first example, a process can either terminate directly, or it can take one out of a set of steps, where this set depends on the state. But in addition to internal steps, which are represented by giving the new state plus a resumption, we now also have communication steps. A *send step* gives the destination object, the method name, a sequence of parameters, and *two* resumptions. The first one, the *dependent* resumption, is a function from object names to processes. It describes what should happen after the message has been answered and the result has been returned to the sender. To do that, this function should be applied to the name of the result object, so that it delivers a process that describes the processing of that result in the sending object. The other resumption, also called the *independent* resumption, describes the actions that can take place in parallel with the sending and the processing of the message. These actions do not have to wait until the message has been answered by the destination object. (Note that for a single object the independent resumption will always be p_0, because a sending object cannot do anything before the result has arrived. However, for the correct parallel composition of more objects, the independent resumption is necessary to describe the actions of the objects that are not sending messages.) Finally we have an *answer step*: This consists of the name of the destination object and the method name, plus an even more complicated resumption. This resumption takes as input the sequence of parameters in the message plus the dependent resumption of the sender. Then it returns a process describing the further execution of the receiver and the sender *together*.

Equations like (1) can be solved by a technique explained in [BZ82]: An increasing sequence of metric spaces is constructed, its union is taken and then the metric completion of the union space satisfies the equation. The equation for POOL processes cannot be solved in this way, because the domain variable P occurs at the left-hand side of the arrow in the definition of answer steps. A more general, category-theoretic technique for solving this kind of domain equations has been developed to solve this problem. It is described in [AR89]. Let us only remark here that it is necessary to restrict ourselves to the set of *non-distance-increasing* functions (satisfying $d(f(x), f(y)) \leq d(x, y)$), which is denoted by $\rightarrow^1$ in the above equation. Intuitively, having a non-distance-increasing function from processes to processes means that the result process can run the argument process and possibly delay it, but it can not observe the future behaviour of the argument process.

Let us now give more details about the semantics of statements and expressions. These are described by the following two functions:

$$[\ldots]_S : Stat \rightarrow Env \rightarrow AObj \rightarrow Cont_S \rightarrow^1 P$$

$$[\ldots]_E : Exp \rightarrow Env \rightarrow AObj \rightarrow Cont_E \rightarrow^1 P.$$

The first argument of each of these function is a statement (from the set *Stat*) or an expression (from *Exp*), respectively. The second argument is an *environment*, which contains the necessary semantic information about the declarations of methods and bodies in the program (for more details, see [ABKR89]). The third argument is the name of the (active) object executing the statement/expression. The last argument is a *continuation*. This is explained in more detail below. Continuations are necessary to describe the sequential composition of statements that can create processes and for dealing with expressions that can have arbitrary side-effects (such as sending messages).

Continuations work as follows: The semantic function for statements is provided with a continuation, which is just a process ($Cont_S = P$), describing the execution of all the statements following the current one. The semantic function then delivers a process that describes the execution of the current statement plus the following ones. Analogously, the semantic function for expressions is fed with a continuation, which in this case is a function which maps object names to processes ($Cont_E = Obj \rightarrow P$). This function, when applied to the object name that is the result of the expression, gives a process describing everything that should happen in the current object after the expression evaluation. Again, the semantic function delivers a process describing the expression evaluation plus the following actions.

Let us illustrate this by giving some examples of clauses that appear in the definition of the semantic functions $[\![\ldots]\!]_S$ and $[\![\ldots]\!]_E$. Let us start with a relatively simple example, the assignment statement:

$$[\![x := e]\!]_S(\gamma)(\alpha)(p) = [\![e]\!]_E(\gamma)(\alpha)\Big(\lambda\beta.\lambda\sigma.\big\{\langle\sigma\{\beta/\alpha, x\}, p\rangle\big\}\Big).$$

This equation says that if the statement $x := e$ is to be executed in an environment γ (recording the effect of the declarations), by the object α, and with continuation p (describing the actions to be performed after this assignment), then first the expression e is to be evaluated, with the same environment γ and by the same object α, but its resulting object is to be fed into an expression continuation $\lambda\beta.\lambda\sigma\{\langle\sigma', p\rangle\}$ that delivers a process of which the first action is an internal one leading to the new state σ' and having the original continuation p as its resumption. Here, of course, the new state σ' is equal to $\sigma\{\beta/\alpha, x\}$.

The semantic definition of sequential composition is easy with continuations:

$$[\![s_1; s_2]\!]_S(\gamma)(\alpha)(p) = [\![s_1]\!]_S(\gamma)(\alpha)\Big([\![s_2]\!]_S(\gamma)(\alpha)(p)\Big).$$

Here the process describing the execution of the second statement s_2 just serves as the continuation for the first statement s_1.

As a simple example of a semantic definition of an expression let us take an instance variable:

$$[\![x]\!]_E(\gamma)(\alpha)(f) = \lambda\sigma.\big\{\langle\sigma, f(\sigma(\alpha)(x))\rangle\big\}.$$

Evaluating the expression x takes a single step, in which the value $\sigma(\alpha)(x)$ of the variable is looked up in the state σ. The resumption of this first step is obtained by feeding this value into the expression continuation f (which is a function that maps object names into processes).

As a final example of a semantic definition, let us take object creation: The expression $\mathsf{new}(C)$ creates a new object of class C and its value is the name of this object. Its semantics is defined as follows:

$$[\![\mathsf{new}(C)]\!]_E(\gamma)(\alpha)(f) = \lambda\sigma.\big\{\langle\sigma', \gamma(C)(\beta) \parallel f(\beta)\rangle\big\}.$$

Here β is a fresh object name, determined from σ in a way that does not really interest us here, and σ' differs from σ only in that the variables of the new object β are properly initialized. We see that execution of this new-expression takes a single step, of which the resumption consists of the parallel composition of the body $\gamma(C)(\beta)$ of the new object with the execution of the creator, where the latter is obtained by applying the expression continuation f to the name of the new object β (which is, after all, the value of the new-expression). The parallel composition operator $\parallel$ is a function in $P \times P \rightarrow P$, which can be defined as the unique fixed point of a suitable contracting higher-order function $\Phi_{PC} : (P \times P \rightarrow P) \rightarrow (P \times P \rightarrow P)$ (an application of Banach's fixed point theorem).

From the above few equations it can already be seen how the use of continuations provides an elegant solution to the problems that we have mentioned.

There are a number of further steps necessary before we arrive at the semantics of a complete program. One interesting detail is that in the denotational semantics, sending messages to standard objects is treated in exactly the same way as sending messages to programmer-defined objects. The standard objects themselves (note that there are infinitely many of them!) are represented by a (huge) process p_{ST}, which is able to answer all the messages sent to standard objects and immediately return the correct results. This process p_{ST} is composed in parallel with the process p_U, which describes the execution of the user-defined objects in order to give the process describing the execution of the whole system.

Despite the fact that the two forms of semantics described above, the operational and the denotational one, are formulated in widely different frameworks, it turns out that it is possible to establish an important relationship between them:

$$\mathcal{O} = abstr \circ \mathcal{D},$$

which in some sense says that the different forms of semantics of POOL are *equivalent*. Here $\mathcal{D}$ is the function that assigns a process to a POOL program according to the denotational semantics and $\mathcal{O}$ assigns to each program a set of (finite or infinite) sequences of states, which can be extracted from the sequences of configurations obtained from the operational semantics. Finally, *abstr* is an abstraction operator that takes a process and maps it into the set of sequences of states to which the process gives rise. The complete equivalence proof can be found in [Rut90].

3.3 Layered semantics

The denotational semantics described above has one significant disadvantage: it does not describe the behaviour of a single *object*. In order to get a better grip on this fundamental concept of object-oriented programming, a layered form of denotational semantics for POOL has been developed [AR90]. In this formalism, there are different semantic domains (again complete metric spaces) for the meanings of statements, objects, and systems.

The semantic domain *SProc* of *statement processes* is used for the semantic descriptions of POOL statements and expressions. It reflects precisely the different ways in which statements and expressions can interact with their environment:

$$
\begin{aligned}
SProc \cong \ & \{p_0\} \cup (\Sigma \times SProc) \\
& \cup (CName \times (Obj \to SProc)) \\
& \cup (Obj \times MName \times Obj^* \times (Obj \to SProc)) \\
& \cup (MName \xrightarrow{fin} (Obj^* \to SProc)) \\
& \cup (MName \xrightarrow{fin} (Obj^* \to SProc)) \times SProc \\
& \cup (Obj \times SProc)
\end{aligned}
$$

(With $A \xrightarrow{fin} B$ we denote the set of finite partial maps from A to B.)

A statement (or expression) can do nothing, it can do an internal step, it can create a new object, it can send a message, it can answer a message, it can conditionally answer a message, or it can return a result. In an internal step $\langle \sigma, p \rangle$, the first component σ

is the new state, and p is the resumption. In a creation step $\langle C, f \rangle$, a new object β of class C is created, after which execution is resumed with $f(\beta)$. A send step $\langle \beta, m, \bar{\beta}, f \rangle$ indicates that a message is sent to the destination β, with method name m and arguments $\bar{\beta}$. When a result r arrives, the object will resume with $f(r)$. In an answer step g, any message with method name $m \in \text{dom } g$ can be answered by executing $g(m)$ applied to the arguments. A conditional answer step $\langle g, p \rangle$ can answer a message with a method name in $\text{dom } g$, but if no message is present, it can continue by just executing p. Finally, in a result step $\langle \beta, p \rangle$, the result β is returned to the sender of the last message, and then the current object resumes with p.

In all these cases, the exact mechanism to perform the task (e.g., determining the name for a new object or synchronizing on communication) is not described here, but only the information necessary to perform it (e.g., the class of the new object). We should also note that a state $\sigma \in \Sigma$ only describes the variables of a single object. Semantic functions like the ones in section 3.2 deliver for each statement or expression the statement process that describes its meaning.

The domain $OProc$ of $object\ processes$ is very similar to $SProc$, but it does not include the internal steps:

$$
\begin{aligned}
OProc \cong \ & \{q_0\} \cup (CName \times (Obj \to OProc)) \\
& \cup (Obj \times MName \times Obj^* \times (Obj \to OProc)) \\
& \cup (MName \xrightarrow{fin} (Obj^* \to OProc)) \\
& \cup (MName \xrightarrow{fin} (Obj^* \to OProc)) \times OProc \\
& \cup (Obj \times OProc)
\end{aligned}
$$

The semantics of an object is obtained by applying an abstraction operator $abstr : SProc \to OProc$ to the meaning of the body of this object. This operator $abstr$ removes all the internal steps. It turns out that this operator is not continuous (in the classical metric/topological meaning), since it has to transform an arbitrarily long sequence of internal steps followed by a non-internal step into this non-internal step, but an infinite sequence of internal steps by q_0. For the mathematical treatment, this non-continuity presents no problem.

Finally, the domain $GProc$ of $global\ processes$ is determined by the following domain equation:

$$
\begin{aligned}
GProc \ = \ & \{r_0\} \cup \mathcal{P}(GStep) \\
GStep \ = \ & Obj \times MName \times Obj^* \times Obj \times GProc && \text{send message} \\
& \cup \ \ Obj \times (Obj \to GProc) && \text{receive result} \\
& \cup \ \ MName \times Obj \times (Obj \to Obj^* \to GProc) && \text{answer message} \\
& \cup \ \ Obj \times Obj \times Obj \times GProc && \text{return result} \\
& \cup \ \ Comm^+ \times GProc && \text{completed step}
\end{aligned}
$$

where

$$
\begin{aligned}
Comm^+ \ &= \ Comm \cup \{*\} \\
Comm \ &= \ Obj \times MName^+ \times Obj^* \times Obj \\
MName^+ \ &= \ MName \cup \{*\}
\end{aligned}
$$

Note that only at this global level we find nondeterminism, indicated by the power set operation $\mathcal{P}$. The possible steps in a global process are either one-sided communication attempts (sending or receiving a message or result) or completed actions, reflected by a communication record $c \in Comm$ in case of communications and by $*$ in case of other actions, such as object creations.

An object process in *OProc* is 'globalized', i.e., transformed into a global process, by an operator ω. This operator ω also takes care of the naming of new objects and it remembers to which object the result of a method should be returned. There is a parallel composition operator $\|$: *GProc* $\times$ *GProc* $\rightarrow$ *GProc*, which takes care of synchronization between sender and receiver of a message or result. The global process describing the whole execution of a program can be obtained by applying ω to the object process that belongs to the root object (the first object in the system).

If desired, the set of traces of all successful communications in program executions can be obtained from this global process. However, it is much more interesting to determine the real observable input/output behaviour of a program. This is done by distinguishing a special object *world* to which input and output messages can be sent. By concentrating on the interactions of the rest of the system with this object, one can view a program as a nondeterministic transformation from an input stream of standard objects (integers, booleans) to an output stream of standard objects.

The advantage of this layered approach to POOL semantics is not only that it really gives a semantic interpretation of a single object, but also that it develops a framework in which issues about *full abstractness* can be studied (a denotational semantics is called fully abstract if it does not give more information than necessary to determine the observable behaviour of a program construct in context). These issues are present on two levels: the statement/expression level and the object level. They are subject of ongoing research.

In addition to the different forms of semantics described above, POOL has been the subject of a number of other semantic studies. In [Vaa86], the semantics of POOL is defined by means of *process algebra* [BK84, BK85]. In [ELR90], a simplified version of POOL is used as an example to illustrate POTs (Parallel Object-based Transition systems), an extended version of Petri nets. Finally, in [DD86, DDH87] a description is given of an abstract POOL machine. In contrast to the 'abstract machine' employed in the operational semantics described above, this abstract POOL machine is intended to be the first step in a sequence of refinements which ultimately lead to an efficient implementation on real parallel hardware. This abstract POOL machine is described formally in AADL, an Axiomatic Architecture Description Language.

4 Verification

Developing a formal proof system for verifying the correctness of POOL programs is an even harder task than giving a formal semantics for this language. Therefore this work has been done in several stages. A moree detailed account of the research on verification of POOL programs is given in [Boe91].

4.1 A sequential version

First the proof theory of SPOOL, a sequential version of POOL, has been studied (see [Ame86]). This language is obtained by omitting the bodies (and the possibility to return a result before a method ends) from POOL, such that now at any moment there is only one active object and we have a sequential object-oriented language. For this language a Hoare-style [Apt81, Hoa69] proof system has been developed. The main contribution from the proof theory of SPOOL was a formalism to deal with dynamically evolving pointer structures. This reasoning should take place at an abstraction level that is at least as high as that of the programming language. More concretely, this means the following:

1. The only operations on 'pointers' (references to objects) are

   - testing for equality
   - dereferencing (determining the value of an instance variable of the referenced object)

2. In a given state of the system, it is only possible to reason about the objects that exist in that state, i.e., an object that does not exist (yet) cannot play a role.

Requirement 1 can be met by only admitting the indicated operations to the assertion language (however, this excludes the approach where pointers are explicitly modelled as indices in a large array that represents the 'heap'). In order to satisfy requirement 2, variables are forbidden to refer to nonexisting objects and the range of quantifiers is restricted to the existing objects. (The consequence is that the range of quantification depends on the state!)

In reasoning about pointer structures, first-order predicate logic is not enough to express interesting properties, and therefore several extensions have been explored. The first extension is the possibility to use recursively defined predicates. One variant of this formalism uses a so-called μ-notation to express these predicates. More precisely, the phrase

$$\mu X(z_1, \ldots, z_n)(P)$$

is used to denote the smallest predicate X satisfying

$$\forall z_1, \ldots, z_n \quad X(z_1, \ldots, z_n) \leftrightarrow P.$$

(In order to be sure that such a predicate exists, we require that X must not occur negatively in P.)

In this notation, the assertion

$$\mu X(y, z)\Big(y \doteq z \lor X(y.x, z)\Big)(v, w) \tag{2}$$

can be used to express the property that the object denoted by the variable w is a member of the linked list starting with v and linked by the variable x, or in other words, that starting from v one can get to w by following the reference stored in the variable x an arbitrary number of times.

Another notational variant for using recursively defined predicates is to name and declare them explicitly. The declaration

$$q(z_1, \ldots, z_n) \Leftarrow P$$

defines q to be the smallest predicate satisfying

$$\forall z_1, \ldots, z_n \quad q(z_1, \ldots, z_n) \leftrightarrow P.$$

The property expressed in equation (2) can now simply be written as $q(v, w)$, where the predicate q is declared by

$$q(y, z) \;\Leftarrow\; y \doteq z \vee q(y \cdot x, z).$$

The μ-notation is easier to deal with in reasoning about the proof system, but the version with declared predicates is more convenient in actual proofs.

Since an assertion language with recursively defined predicates does not admit the standard techniques for establishing the completeness of the proof system, we have also explored a different extension to first-order logic: quantification over finite sequences of objects. In this formalism, the property in equation (2) can be expressed as follows:

$$\exists z \left(z \cdot 1 \doteq v \wedge z \cdot |z| \doteq w \wedge \forall n \, (0 < n \wedge n < |z|) \rightarrow (z \cdot n).x \doteq z \cdot (n+1) \right)$$

where z ranges over finite sequences of objects, $z \cdot n$ denotes the nth element of the sequence z, and $|z|$ denotes its length.

It is somewhat surprising that even with the restrictions on pointer operations, mentioned above as items 1 and 2, it is possible to describe, e.g., the creation of a new object. This is done by an axiom that is similar in form to the traditional axiom of assignment:

$$\{P[\text{new}/u]\} \; u \leftarrow \text{new} \; \{P\}.$$

The trick is in the definition of the substitution operation $[\text{new}/u]$, which is not ordinary substitution, but fulfils the same goal: replacing any expression or assertion by another one that, when evaluated in the state before the assignment, has the same value as the original one in the state after the assignment. In the case of object creation, this is not possible for every expression, because the variable u will refer to the new object after the statement and this object cannot be denoted by any expression before the statement. However, this variable u can only occur in two contexts in an assertion: either it is compared for equality with another expression, or it is dereferenced. In both cases we know what the result will be. The precise definition of the substitution $[\text{new}/u]$ is somewhat complicated, so here we just give a few examples (see [Ame86] for full details):

$$u \doteq y.x[\text{new}/u] \;=\; \text{false}$$
$$u \doteq u[\text{new}/u] \;=\; \text{true}$$
$$u.x \doteq z[\text{new}/u] \;=\; \text{nil} \doteq z$$
$$u.x \doteq u[\text{new}/u] \;=\; \text{false}$$

In the case of quantification, the substituted assertion contains one component that ranges over the old objects and one component that talks about the new one, for example:

$$(\forall z \, P)[\text{new}/u] = \forall z \, (P[\text{new}/u]) \wedge P[u/z][\text{new}/u].$$

In the presence of recursively defined predicates or quantification over finite sequences, similar measures are taken to ensure correct functioning of the substitution operation, so that the axiom for object creation can be shown to be sound, i.e., everything that can be proved is actually true.

If the left-hand side of the assignment is an instance variable instead of a temporary variable, then certain other modifications to the substitution used in the assignment axiom are necessary to deal with *aliasing*, i.e., the possibility that two different expressions denote the same variable. For example, applying the substitution $[1/x]$ to the assertion

$$\forall z \, (z \not\doteq \textsf{self} \rightarrow z.x \doteq 0)$$

yields the assertion

$$\forall z \, (z \not\doteq \textsf{self} \rightarrow \textsf{if } z \doteq \textsf{self then } 1 \textsf{ else } z.x \textsf{ fi} \doteq 0),$$

which can be simplified to $\forall z \, (z \not\doteq \textsf{self} \rightarrow z.x \doteq 0)$.

Another contribution of the SPOOL proof system is a proof rule for message passing and method invocation (in a sequential setting). In this rule the context switching between sending and receiving object and the transmission of parameters and result are representing by appropriate substitution operations. For details, see [Ame86].

In the version with quantification over finite sequences, the SPOOL proof system has been proved to be not only sound but also complete [AB89], i.e., every correctness formula that is true can be proved in this system.

4.2 Dealing with parallelism

Along a different track a proof theory was developed to deal with parallelism, in particular with dynamic process creation. In [Boe86] a proof system was given for a language called P, which essentially only differs from POOL in that message passing only consists of transmitting a single value from the sender to the receiver (like in CSP [Hoa78]).

Whereas the proof system in [Boe86] uses an explicit coding of object references by numbers, an integration with the work on SPOOL has led to a more abstract proof system for the same language P [AB88, AB90].

To deal with parallelism, this proof system uses the concepts of *cooperation test*, *global invariant*, *bracketed section*, and *auxiliary variables*, which have been developed in the proof theory of CSP [AFR80]. Described very briefly, the proof system for the language P consists of the following elements:

- A *local* stage. This deals with all statements that do not involve communication or object creation. These statements are proved correct with respect to pre- and postconditions in the usual manner of sequential programs [Apt81, Hoa69]. At this stage, *assumptions* are used to describe the behaviour of the communication and creation statements. These will be verified in the next stage.

- An *intermediate* stage. In this stage the above assumptions about communication and creation statements are verified. For each creation statement and for each pair of possibly communicating send and receive statements it is verified that the specification used in the local proof system is consistent with the global behaviour.

- A *global* stage. Here some properties of the system as a whole can be derived from a kind of standard specification that arises from the intermediate stage.

In the local stage, a *local assertion language* is employed, which only talks about the current object in isolation. In this assertion language, the variables of the current object can be named directly, but the variables of other objects cannot be named at all. Likewise, quantification over integers (and booleans) is possible, but quantification over all (existing) objects is not available. In the intermediate and global stages, a *global assertion language* is used, which reasons about all the objects in the system. Here quantification over all existing objects and even over finite sequences of existing objects is possible. An assertion p in the local assertion language can be transformed to a global assertion $p \downarrow z$ by applying a syntactic substitution (denoted by $\downarrow z$, where z is a global expression that denotes the object that p should talk about). For example, if the local assertion p is

$$b \neq \text{nil} \rightarrow \forall i \, (i < m \rightarrow \exists j \, i \times j \doteq b)$$

then $p \downarrow z$ is

$$z \, . \, b \neq \text{nil} \rightarrow \forall i \, (i < z \, . \, m \rightarrow \exists j \, i \times j \doteq z \, . \, b).$$

Whereas in the local stage the axioms and rules are the same as in traditional Hoare logic, the axioms and rules of the intermediate stage make use of the same techniques as the ones developed for SPOOL to deal with object creation and aliasing.

The global proof system makes use of the fact that the initial state is precisely known: there is one single object and all its variables have the value nil. Therefore the precondition can have the form $(p \wedge x_1 \doteq \text{nil} \wedge \cdots \wedge x_n \doteq \text{nil}) \downarrow z$, where p is an assertion talking only about logical variables (variables that do not occur in the program).

Again this proof system has been proved to be sound and complete (for details see [AB88]). Moreover, using the same basic ingredients, but with the addition of an assumption/commitment mechanism, a sound and complete proof system has been developed for the full language POOL, with its rendezvous communication [Boe90, Boe91]. Nevertheless, this proof system also has its shortcomings. The most important problem is that it involves *global reasoning*: the invariant incorporates all the objects in the system. For even slightly complicated programs, this leads to an unmanageably complex proof. The only way out here seems to be the use of compositional proof techniques (see [HR87] for a survey). Unfortunately, since the configuration of objects in POOL is not static but dynamic, it is not so clear how the decomposition should work here.

5 Inheritance and subtyping

Inheritance is a mechanism that is tightly bound to the notion of object-oriented programming. Its basic idea is that in defining a new class it is often very convenient to start with all the ingredients (variables, methods) of an existing class and to add some more and possibly redefine some in order to get the desired new class. The new class is said to *inherit* the variables and methods of the old one. This can repeated several times and one can even allow a class to inherit from more than one class (multiple inheritance). In this way a complete *inheritance hierarchy* arises. By sharing code among classes in this way, the total amount of code in a system can sometimes be drastically reduced and its maintenance can be simplified.

This inheritance relationship between classes also suggests another relationship: If a class B inherits from a class A, each instance of B will have at least all the variables and methods that instances of A have. Therefore it seems that whenever we require an object of class A, an instance of class B would do equally well, or in other words, that we can regard the class B as a *specialized version* of A. Note, however, that inheritance is concerned with the *internal structure* of the objects (variables and methods), whereas this specialization phenomenon is about the possible use of the objects, characterized by their *externally observable behaviour*. For a long time the idea has prevailed in the object-oriented community that the inheritance hierarchy coincides completely with the specialization hierarchy. However, recently it is becoming clear that identifying these two hierarchies leads to several problems and that it is useful to separate them (see also [Ame87, Sny86]).

In order to get a clear conceptual view, we proposed the following definitions [Ame89a]: Whereas a class is a collection of objects that have (exactly) the same internal structure (variables, method code, body), a *type* is a collection of objects that share the same externally observable behaviour. In this context we can see that inheritance forms a relationship between classes, while subtyping is a relationship between types. A language called POOL-I has been designed that works according to these principles [AL90]. Now inheritance is adequately described by the syntax for writing code in the programming language under consideration (which does not mean that it is a simple task to design an inheritance mechanism that works well in practice), but in order to get a good formal grip on subtyping we need to do some more work.

Let us start with realizing that a type is in essence a specification of object behaviour. The important point here is that the specification should only consider those aspects of this behaviour that can be observed from outside the object, independently of its internal structure. Ideally, the specification should only talk about the messages that are received and sent by the object. Now specifying objects in terms of possible sequences of messages is certainly possible, but for most kinds of objects, this is not the best way to characterize them. For example, consider the following specification, which is written in English to avoid notational problems:

> The object will accept put and get messages, but it will accept a get message only if the number of put messages already received exceeds the number of get messages. A put message contains one integer as an argument and does not return a result. A get message contains no arguments and it returns as its result the integer that was the argument of the last put message that has preceded an equal number of put and get messages.

It is not immediately clear that this specification characterizes something as simple and well-known as a stack of integers. The most important reason for this difficulty is that the intuitive view most people have of such an object is that inside it stores a certain amount of information (a sequence of integers) and that the messages interact with this information. A more technical disadvantage is that reasoning in terms of sequences of message fails to make explicit that different sequences may lead to the same end result: a stack into which three elements have been inserted and subsequently removed is equivalent to an empty stack.

Therefore we propose to specify object behaviour in terms of an *abstract state*, which is an abstraction from the object's concrete internal state. For our stack, the abstract state would just be a sequence of integers. In a sequential setting, methods can now be described by pre- and postconditions formulated in terms of the abstract state. For example, the method **get** of the above stack is specified by

$$\{s \neq \langle\rangle\}\, \mathbf{get}()\, \{s_0 = s * \langle r \rangle\}.$$

Here s is the sequence representing the current state of the stack, s_0 in the postcondition stands for the value of s before the method execution, and r stands for the result of the **get** method. Furthermore, the operator $*$ denotes concatenation of sequences, $\langle\rangle$ is the empty sequence, and $\langle n \rangle$ is the sequence having n as its only element.

In general, a specification of a type σ consists of a domain Σ, representing the set of possible abstract states of objects of type σ, plus a set of method specifications of the form $\{P\}m(\bar{p})\{Q\}$, where the precondition $P = P(s, \bar{p})$ describes the state of affairs before the method execution and the postcondition $Q = Q(s, s_0, \bar{p}, r)$ describes the situation after its execution (s always stands for the current abstract state, s_0 for the abstract state before the method execution, $\bar{p}$ for the method parameters, and r for the result). The meaning of such a method specification is that each object of type σ should have a method with name m available such that if the method is executed in a state where the precondition P holds, then after the method execution Q holds.

The next important question is under what conditions the objects of a given class C are members of a type σ, in which case we say that the class C *implements* the type σ. We do this as follows: We require a *representation function* $f : C \rightarrow \Sigma$, where C is the set of possible concrete states of objects of class C, i.e., the set of possible values of the variables $\bar{v}$ of such an object, and Σ is the set of abstract states associated with the type σ. The representation function f maps the values $\bar{v}$ of the variables of an object of class C to an element s of the mathematical domain Σ that is used in the specification of the type σ. We also need a *representation invariant* I, which is a logical formula involving the values of the variables of the class C. This invariant will describe the set of values of these variables that can actually occur (in general this is a proper subset of the set C). The representation function f should at least be defined for all concrete states for which the invariant I holds.

For the class C to implement the type σ the following conditions are required to hold:

1. The invariant I holds initially, i.e., just after the creation and initialization of each new object.

2. Every method m of the class C (the ones that are mentioned in σ's specification as well as the ones that are not mentioned) should maintain the invariant.

3. For every method specification $\{P\}m(\bar{p})\{Q\}$ occurring in the specification of σ, the class C should also have a method m with parameters $\bar{p}$ of the right number and types. Furthermore this method should satisfy

$$\{P \circ f \wedge I\}\, m(\bar{p})\, \{Q \circ f \wedge I\}.$$

Here $P \circ f$ stands for the formula P where every occurrence of the abstract state s is replaced by the function f applied to the variables and analogously with s_0: $P \circ f = P[f(\bar{v})/s, f(\bar{v_0})/s_0]$.

Now we can say that a type σ is a subtype of a type τ if all objects belonging to σ also belong to τ (note that nontrivial subtyping relationships are indeed possible, because one can write specifications that leave some degree of freedom in behaviour so that other specifications can be more specific). Of course, we would like to be able to conclude such a subtyping relationship from the specifications of σ and τ. At a first glance, it seems sufficient to require that for every method specification $\{P\}m(\bar{p})\{Q\}$ occurring in τ's specification there should be a method specification $\{P'\}m(\bar{p})\{Q'\}$ in the specification of σ such that the latter implies the former, which can be expressed by $P \to P'$ and $Q' \to Q$. Under these circumstances we can indeed use any element of σ whenever an element of τ is expected: When we send such an object a message listing the method m, using it as an element of τ guarantees that initially the precondition P will hold. By the implication $P \to P'$ we can conclude that the precondition P' in σ's specification also holds. Then after the method execution the postcondition Q' from σ will hold and this again implies the postcondition Q that is required by τ.

However, in general we must assume that the type τ has been specified using a different mathematical domain T than the domain Σ used in σ's specification. Therefore in order to show that a type σ is a subtype of the type τ, we require the existence of a function $\phi : \Sigma \to T$, called *transfer function*, that maps the mathematical domain Σ associated with σ to T, the one associated with τ. This time we do not need an extra invariant, because we can assume that Σ has been chosen small enough to exclude all the values that cannot actually occur. We now require that for every method specification $\{P\}m(\bar{p})\{Q\}$ occurring in τ's specification there should be a method specification $\{P'\}m(\bar{p})\{Q'\}$ in the specification of σ such that

$$P \circ \phi \to P' \quad \text{and} \quad Q' \to Q \circ \phi.$$

Again $P \circ \phi$ can be obtained from P by replacing the abstract state of τ by ϕ applied to the abstract state of σ and analogously for the old values of the abstract states.

On the basis of the above definitions one can easily prove the desirable property that whenever a class C implements a type σ and σ is a subtype of τ, then C implements τ.

In order to make these ideas more formal, a language, called SPOOL-S, has been defined that allow the formal expression of the abovementioned ingredients: classes and types, connected by representation and transfer functions [DK91]. The abstract domains, in which the abstract states reside, can be specified in any formalism in which mathematical entities can be specified (in [DK91] the Larch Shared Language [GHM90] was chosen as an example). Method specifications can be written using a formalism that is slightly different from the one above. In addition to a pre- and a postcondition, a method specification also contains a so-called *modifies-list*, in which all the objects are mentioned that could be modified by the method. This is necessary to be able to describe an object on its own, because ordinary Hoare logic does not provide a mechanism to state that 'all the rest stays the same'.

The language also allows for the situation where one abstract object is implemented by a collection of concrete objects. For example, a stack can be implemented by a linked list of objects that each store a single item. This can be expressed in the representation function, which maps the concrete state of an object into its abstract state, possibly using the abstract states of other objects as well. In our example, if the modifies-list allows a method to change a stack object, then all the concrete objects implementing this stack could possibly be modified.

Up to now, a formal proof system for verifying SPOOL-S programs has not yet been developed, but it seems certainly possible with the techniques that have been used for SPOOL (see section 4.1). It is a much greater challenge, however, to generalize them to deal with parallelism. Here the techniques described in section 4.2 definitely fall short, because they involve global reasoning on an abstraction level that is as high as that of the programming language, but not higher. Probably a viable approach to this problem will still include the use of abstract internal states, but in the presence of parallelism it will be hard to avoid reasoning about sequences of messages. Perhaps a judicious combination of compositional proof techniques and the techniques describe above will lead to a satisfactory solution.

References

[AB88]   Pierre America and Frank de Boer. A proof system for a parallel language with dynamic process creation. ESPRIT Project 415 Document 445, Philips Research Laboratories, Eindhoven, the Netherlands, October 1988. Chapter 2 (pages 121–200) of [Boe91]. A slightly shortened version was published as [AB90].

[AB89]   Pierre America and Frank de Boer. A sound and complete proof system for a sequential version of POOL. ESPRIT Project 415 Document 499, Philips Research Laboratories, Eindhoven, the Netherlands, 1989. Chapter 2 (pages 15–119) of [Boe91].

[AB90]   Pierre America and Frank de Boer. A proof system for process creation. In *IFIP TC2 Working Conference on Programming Concepts and Methods*, Sea of Galilee, Israel, April 2–5, 1990, pages 303–332.

[ABKR86] Pierre America, Jaco de Bakker, Joost N. Kok, and Jan Rutten. Operational semantics of a parallel object-oriented language. In *Conference Record of the 13th Symposium on Principles of Programming Languages*, St. Petersburg, Florida, January 13–15, 1986, pages 194–208.

[ABKR89] Pierre America, Jaco de Bakker, Joost N. Kok, and Jan Rutten. Denotational semantics of a parallel object-oriented language. *Information and Computation*, 83(2):152–205, November 1989.

[AFR80]   Krzysztof R. Apt, Nissim Francez, and Willem Paul de Roever. A proof system for Communicating Sequential Processes. *ACM Transactions on Programming Languages and Systems*, 2(3):359–385, July 1980.

[AH90]   J. K. Annot and P. A. M. den Haan. POOL and DOOM: The object-oriented approach. In P. C. Treleaven, editor, *Parallel Computers: Object-Oriented, Functional, Logic*, Wiley, 1990, pages 47–79.

[AHH+90] Peter Apers, Bob Hertzberger, Ben Hulshof, Hans Oerlemans, and Martin Kersten. PRISMA, a platform for experiments with parallelism. In Pierre America, editor, *Parallel Database Systems: Proceedings of the PRISMA Workshop*, Noordwijk, The Netherlands, September 24–26, 1990, Springer Lecture Notes in Computer Science 503, pages 169–180.

[AHO+90]   Pierre America, Ben Hulshof, Eddy Odijk, Frans Sijstermans, Rob van Twist, and
           Rogier Wester. Parallel computers for advanced information processing. *IEEE Micro*,
           10(6):12–15, 61–75, December 1990.

[AL90]   Pierre America and Frank van der Linden. A parallel object-oriented language
           with inheritance and subtyping. In *Proceedings of OOPSLA/ECOOP '90*, Ottawa,
           Canada, October 21–25, 1990, pages 161–168.

[Ame86]   Pierre America. A proof theory for a sequential version of POOL. ESPRIT Project
           415 Document 188, Philips Research Laboratories, Eindhoven, the Netherlands, Oc-
           tober 1986.

[Ame87]   Pierre America. Inheritance and subtyping in a parallel object-oriented language. In
           ECOOP '87: European Conference on Object-Oriented Programming, Paris, France,
           June 15–17, 1987, Springer Lecture Notes in Computer Science 276, pages 234–242.

[Ame88]   Pierre America. Definition of POOL2, a parallel object-oriented language. ESPRIT
           Project 415 Document 364, Philips Research Laboratories, Eindhoven, the Nether-
           lands, April 1988.

[Ame89a]   Pierre America. A behavioural approach to subtyping in object-oriented program-
           ming languages. In M. Lenzerini, D. Nardi, and M. Simi, editors, *Workshop on
           Inheritance Hierarchies in Knowledge Representation and Programming Languages*,
           Viareggio, Italy, February 6–8, 1989, Wiley, 1991, pages 173–190. Also appeared in
           Philips Journal of Research, Vol. 44, No. 2/3, July 1989, pages 365–383.

[Ame89b]   Pierre America. Issues in the design of a parallel object-oriented language. *Formal
           Aspects of Computing*, 1(4):366–411, 1989.

[Apt81]   Krzysztof R. Apt. Ten years of Hoare logic: A survey — part I. *ACM Transactions
           on Programming Languages and Systems*, 3(4):431–483, October 1981.

[AR89]   Pierre America and Jan Rutten. Solving reflexive domain equations in a category of
           complete metric spaces. *Journal of Computer and System Sciences*, 39(3):343–375,
           December 1989.

[AR90]   Pierre America and Jan Rutten. A layered semantics for a parallel object-oriented
           language.   In *Foundations of Object-Oriented Languages: Proceedings of the
           REX School/Workshop*, Noordwijkerhout, The Netherlands, May 28–June 1, 1990,
           Springer Lecture Notes in Computer Science 489, pages 91–123. To appear in *Formal
           Aspects of Computing*.

[Bak89]   J. W. de Bakker, editor. *Languages for Parallel Architectures: Design, Semantics,
           Implementation Models*. John Wiley & Sons, 1989.

[BK84]   J. A. Bergstra and J. W. Klop. Process algebra for synchronous communication.
           Information and Control, 60:109–137, 1984.

[BK85]   J. A. Bergstra and J. W. Klop. Algebra of communicating processes with abstraction.
           Theoretical Computer Science, 37(1):77–121, May 1985.

[Boe86]   Frank S. de Boer. A proof rule for process creation. In Martin Wirsing, editor, *Formal Description of Programming Concepts III — Proceedings of the Third IFIP WG 2.2 Working Conference*, Gl. Avernæs, Ebberup, Denmark, August 25–28, 1986, North-Holland, pages 23–50.

[Boe90]   Frank S. de Boer. A proof system for the language POOL. In *Proceedings of the 17th International Colloquium on Automata, Languages, and Programming*, Warwick, England, July 16–20, 1990, Springer Lecture Notes in Computer Science 443.

[Boe91]   Frank S. de Boer. *Reasoning about Dynamically Evolving Process Structures: A Proof Theory for the Parallel Object-Oriented Language POOL*. PhD thesis, Free University of Amsterdam, April 15, 1991.

[BZ82]   J. W. de Bakker and J. I. Zucker. Processes and the denotational semantics of concurrency. *Information and Control*, 54:70–120, 1982.

[DD86]   W. Damm and G. Döhmen. The POOL-machine: A top level specification for a distributed object-oriented machine. ESPRIT Project 415 Document 1, Lehrstuhl für Informatik, RWTH Aachen, West Germany, October 3, 1986.

[DDH87]   W. Damm, G. Döhmen, and P. den Haan. Using AADL to specify distributed computer architectures: A case study. In J. W. de Bakker, editor, *Deliverable 3 of the Working Group on Semantics and Proof Techniques*, Chapter 1.4, ESPRIT Project 415, October 1987.

[DK91]   Hans Demmers and Pieter Kleingeld. SPOOL-S: An object-oriented language with behavioural subtyping. Master's thesis, University of Utrecht, Department of Computer Science, Utrecht, the Netherlands, May 1991.

[Dug66]   J. Dugundji. *Topology*. Allyn and Bacon, Boston, Massachusetts, 1966.

[ELR90]   Joost Engelfriet, George Leih, and Grzegorz Rozenberg. Net-based description of parallel object-based systems, or POTs and POPs. In *Foundations of Object-Oriented Languages: Proceedings of the REX School/Workshop*, Noordwijkerhout, The Netherlands, May 28–June 1, 1990, Springer Lecture Notes in Computer Science 489, pages 229–273.

[Eng89]   R. Engelking. *General Topology*, volume 6 of *Sigma Series in Pure Mathematics*. Heldermann, Berlin, 1989.

[GHM90]   John V. Guttag, James J. Horning, and Andrés Modet. Report on the Larch shared language, version 2.3. Report 58, DEC Systems Research Center, Palo Alto California, April 1990.

[Hoa69]   C. A. R. Hoare. An axiomatic basis for computer programming. *Communications of the ACM*, 12(10):576–580,583, October 1969.

[Hoa78]   C. A. R. Hoare. Communicating sequential processes. *Communications of the ACM*, 21(8):666–677, August 1978.

[HP79]   Matthew Hennessy and Gordon Plotkin. Full abstraction for a simple parallel programming language. In J. Bečvář, editor, *Proceedings of the 8th Symposium on Mathematical Foundations of Computer Science*, Springer Lecture Notes in Computer Science 74, 1979, pages 108–120.

[HR87]   Jozef Hooman and Willem-P. de Roever. The quest goes on: A survey of proof systems for partial correctness of CSP. In J. W. de Bakker, W. P. de Roever, and G. Rozenberg, editors, *Current Trends in Concurrency*, Springer Lecture Notes in Computer Science 224, 1987, pages 343–395.

[Plo76]   Gordon D. Plotkin. A powerdomain construction. *SIAM Journal on Computing*, 5(3):452–487, September 1976.

[Plo81]   Gordon D. Plotkin. A structural approach to operational semantics. Report DAIMI FN-19, Aarhus University, Computer Science Department, Aarhus, Denmark, September 1981.

[Plo83]   Gordon D. Plotkin. An operational semantics for CSP. In D. Bjørner, editor, *Formal Description of Programming Concepts II*, North-Holland, 1983, pages 199–223.

[Rut90]   Jan Rutten. Semantic correctness for a parallel object-oriented language. *SIAM Journal on Computing*, 19(3):341–383, 1990.

[Smy78]   Michael B. Smyth. Power domains. *Journal of Computer and System Sciences*, 16:23–36, 1978.

[Sny86]   Alan Snyder. Encapsulation and inheritance in object-oriented programming languages. In *Proceedings of the ACM Conference on Object-Oriented Programming, Systems, Languages and Applications*, Portland, Oregon, September 1986, pages 38–45.

[Tre90]   P. C. Treleaven, editor. *Parallel Computers: Object-Oriented, Functional, Logic.* Wiley, 1990.

[Vaa86]   Frits W. Vaandrager. Process algebra semantics for POOL. Report CS-R8629, Centre for Mathematics and Computer Science, Amsterdam, the Netherlands, August 1986.

Trace semantics for actor systems

Vasco Vasconcelos and Mario Tokoro *
Keio University
Department of Computer Science
3-14-1 Hiyoshi Kohoku-ku Yokohama 223
Japan
vasco@mt.cs.keio.ac.jp   mario@mt.cs.keio.ac.jp

Abstract

The theory of traces is used to describe the behavior of actor systems. The semantics is built from two simple concepts: a set of events representing the reception of messages by objects, and a binary symmetric and irreflexive relation on events—independence—representing permissible concurrency. Causality, the dual notion of concurrency, is expressed by the dependence relation—the complement of independence. A particular execution of a system is described by a trace: a labeled acyclic graph where nodes are labeled with events and the only edges are between nodes labeled with dependent events. The behavior of a system is viewed as the set of traces representing all possible executions. Finally, a composition operation on systems and a synchronization operation on behaviors are presented: they allow to derive the behavior of complex systems from the behavior of its components.

1 Introduction

Although widely acknowledged as a powerful tool describe and develop complex systems, concurrent objects have not received enough attention on what respects semantics that closely describe the phenomena of concurrency involved in computations. We present some ideas towards concurrent semantics for systems of objects. In this particular exposition we concentrate on the actor model of computation; an extended and somewhat more general version being [16].

Concurrent or non-interleaving models take the notion of concurrency—or its dual notion of causality—as fundamental. On the other hand, interleaving models simulate concurrency with arbitrary interleaving of events, thus reducing the notion of concurrency to those of sequentiality and nondeterminism. As a result, interleaving models have fewer primitive notions and are easier to deal with. Also, they naturally inherit results

---

*Also with Sony Computer Science Laboratory Inc. 3-14-13 Higashi-Gotanda Shinagawa-ku, Tokyo 141, Japan.

from models of sequentiality, and this is why research on semantics of concurrency has concentrated primarily on interleaving models.

Interleaving semantics were developed for several models of objects, including actors [2], and particularly after the appearance of Plotkin's method of Structured Operational Semantics [14], have been mostly developed with respect to Milner's Calculus of Communicating Processes [11] and other similar algebraic process languages. On the other hand, true concurrent models (including Petri nets [13], Winskel's event structures [12, 17] and Mazurkiewicz's traces [1]) were primarily developed in relation to Petri nets. Meseguer's concurrent term rewriting logic [9] is another true concurrent model: it aims at describing a wide variety of concurrent systems. While there is some work done on concurrent semantics for process calculi such as CCS ([3] discusses and compares three of them) and for Petri nets (e.g., [1, 5, 7]), except for Meseguer's work [10], not much work on concurrent semantics for objects has been done.

We propose a concurrent semantics for actor systems, based on the theory of traces [1, 5, 7]. The theory of traces—introduced in computer science by Mazurkiewicz [8] to describe the behavior of safe Petri nets—views concurrent systems as a

1. a set of atomic actions X, together with

2. a relation $I \subseteq X \times X$ specifying which actions can be performed independently or concurrently.

This relation—independence—is assumed to be symmetric and irreflexive: both assumptions express specific axioms concerning the phenomenon of concurrency. Irreflexivity represents the assumption that no action in a system can occur concurrently with itself; symmetry represents the assumption that the concurrency of actions is always mutual. The dual notion of concurrency is *causality*, it is captured in the theory of traces by the dependence relation: the complement of the independence relation.

The structure of the paper is as follows. Next section introduces the notion of actor systems. Section 3 describes an interleaving semantics based on the set of all possible sequential transitions obtainable from the initial configuration of an actor system. We then develop the notion of dependence on events (section 4) and abstract from sequential transitions by using traces of events (section 5). Building the concurrent behavior of a complex system may not be an easy task: in section 6 we develop a notion of composition of systems that helps in building the concurrent behavior of a system from the behavior of its components. We then notice that there are situations where the defined semantics do not extract the full concurrency of a system; section 7 proposes an extension to the independence relation. Work done on semantics for actors as well as that on the application of the theory of traces to Petri nets is compared to our in section 8. The last section contains some concluding remarks.

2   Actor systems

A program in some actor based programming language is composed of a collection of behavior descriptions (scripts) together with a declaration of the initial actors and messages. These actors and messages constitute the initial configuration. Investigating the behavior of an actor program reduces to investigating the behavior of the initial configuration, constrained to the restrictions presented in the program. Semantics of actor based programming languages can be described in two stages. In the first, semantics of sequential programming languages is used to assign to each script a function representing the behavior of actors. This information, together with the initial configuration, constitute the actor system described by the program. The actor system is then used to define the possible evolutions or histories of the initial configuration. Clearly, the second stage is largely independent of the programming language: we assume the first step and concentrate on the second.

Actors communicate solely via message passing and messages convey all the information actors exchange. We will not elaborate on the form of this information; it suffices to assume that the communication a message carries is just a value from some domain K. Every message is sent by a single actor and has a single destination. Messages must then carry, not only a communication, but also the name of the target actor. Names (or identifiers) are taken from the set of names N. The set of all possible messages is $M = N \times K$. We use μ to range over finite subsets of messages and define an auxiliary function $target : M \to N$ that extracts the identifier in a message.

Every actor has a name and reacts to incoming messages by following a predetermined script. The script contains not only information on how to process a given message, but also a list of other known actors. The *behavior* is a function of incoming messages, and involves sending messages to specified targets, creating new actors, and specifying a replacement behavior. Behaviors are then taken from the set $B = M \to \mathcal{P}(M) \times \mathcal{P}(A) \times B$, where $\mathcal{P}(M)$ is the set of all finite subsets of messages and $\mathcal{P}(A)$ is the set of all finite subsets of actors. An actor is an association between a name and a behavior. We denote by $A = N \times B$ the set all of actors and use α to range over finite subsets of A.

Computations in actor systems happen inside configurations. Configurations provide the environment for computation: they contain actors and messages in transit and provide for rooting messages to their destinations. A *configuration* is then a collection of messages and actors. We represent it by an ordered tuple (μ, α), where no two actors in α have the same name. $C = \mathcal{P}(M) \times \mathcal{P}(A)$ is the set of all configurations and we define two auxiliary functions, $msgs : C \to \mathcal{P}(M)$ and $actors : C \to \mathcal{P}(A)$, that extract the first and second component of a configuration, respectively.

DEFINITION 1 (ACTOR SYSTEM) *An actor system is any ordered seven-tuple of the form*

$$S = (N, K, M, B, A, C, c_i)$$

where N is a set of names, K a set of communications, $M = N \times K$ the set of messages, $B = M \to \mathcal{P}(M) \times \mathcal{P}(A) \times B$ a set behaviors, $A = N \times B$ the set of actors, $C = \mathcal{P}(M) \times \mathcal{P}(A)$ the set of configurations, and $c_i \in C$ the initial configuration of S.

Since N is an arbitrary set, we are interested not on the configurations themselves, but on the equivalence class generated by isomorphisms on names. Thus, for the rest of the paper, when referring to a configuration, we will mean the equivalence class the configuration belongs to. We finish the section with an example of an actor system.

EXAMPLE 1 (THE FORWARDER OF TWO MESSAGES)   The 'forwarder of two messages' actor forwards the first two messages it receives and ignores subsequent ones. More precisely, the 'forwarder of two messages' behavior *forward2* forwards the message it receives to a fixed actor and becomes a 'forwarder of a single message' behavior. In turn, the 'forwarder of a single message' behavior *forward1* forwards to the same actor the message it receives and becomes a 'sink' behavior. Lastly, the 'sink' behavior "sinks" (or ignores) every message it receives; that is, upon reception of any message, it creates no messages or actors, nor it replaces its behavior.

To avoid proliferation of parenthesis and increase readability, we will write $k \triangleright n$ (read "k targeted to n") for a message (n, k), and $n{:}b$ (read "at n behavior b") for an actor (n, b). The behaviors are expressed by functions

$$forward2_n(k \triangleright f) \;=\; \langle\, \{k \triangleright n\},\; \emptyset,\; forward1_n \,\rangle$$
$$forward1_n(k \triangleright f) \;=\; \langle\, \{k \triangleright n\},\; \emptyset,\; sink \,\rangle$$
$$sink(k \triangleright f) \;=\; \langle\, \emptyset,\; \emptyset,\; sink \,\rangle$$

where k is any communication and f, n are names. We will be interested in an actor system with an initial configuration composed of a forwarder and a consumer (with a sink behavior) for the messages forwarded, together with three messages targeted to the forwarder; that is,

$$c_i = (\{x \triangleright f, y \triangleright f, z \triangleright f\}, \{f{:}forward2_u, u{:}sink\})$$

where x, y, z are communications and f, u are names.   □

3   Sequential behavior

This section presents a state-transition interleaving semantics for actor systems. It will be used as a stepping stone towards more abstract, concurrent semantics to be defined later. We develop the notion of single transition on configurations and, based on this, we define the reachability function. The domain of the reachability function contains all the possible sequential transitions an actor system may engage in; its codomain contains all the configurations reachable from the system's initial configuration. The sequential behavior of the system is just the set of all possible sequential transitions.

In an interleaving model, an actor system evolve by replacing a configuration by a new one that is the result of processing some message in the former. When there is more than one message in a configuration, there will be more than one possible transition. Even when more than one message can be physically processed at the same time, the model here presented records one single transition at a time, by non-deterministically ordering the transitions. The processing of a message by some actor triggers a transition; it involves consuming the message and the actor involved, and adding to the configuration the messages and the actors created, as well as the actor that replaces the one consumed. We capture the replacement of configurations by the transition function defined as follows.

DEFINITION 2 (TRANSITION FUNCTION)   Let $S = (N, K, M, B, A, C, c_i)$ be an actor system. The transition function δ_S of S is a partial function

$$\delta_S : C \times M \to C$$

such that $\delta_S(c_0, m) = c_1$ if and only if m is a message in c_0 targeted to some n, $n{:}b_0$ is an actor in c_0 and b_0 is defined at m. In this case, if $b_0(m) = \langle \mu, \alpha, b_1 \rangle$, then [1]

$$\begin{aligned}
msgs(c_0) - \{m\} &= msgs(c_1) - \mu \\
actors(c_0) - \{n{:}b_0\} &= actors(c_1) - (\{n{:}b_1\} \cup \alpha)
\end{aligned}$$

where the names of the actors created α do not occur in the actors of c_0.

The transition function expresses possible one-step transitions between configurations. If a message is responsible for a single transition, (finite) sequences of messages can be viewed as responsible for composed transitions, the effect of such composed transitions being the joint effect of the constituent single transitions executed in the order indicated. *Finite sequences* of messages are elements of M^*. The monoid of finite sequences (strings) over M is the ordered triple $(M^*, \circ, \varepsilon)$ where $\circ$ is the concatenation operation on sequences, and ε is the empty sequence (whenever possible we will omit the concatenation operator.)

Equipped with the notion of finite sequences of messages we are now ready to develop the notion of reachable configurations. *Reachable configurations* are those configurations obtainable from the initial one, by a (finite) sequence of transitions governed by a (finite) sequence of messages. The reachability function embodies this idea.

DEFINITION 3 (REACHABILITY FUNCTION) *Let $S = (N, K, M, B, A, C, c_i)$ be an actor system. The reachability function R_S of S is a partial function*

$$R_S : M^* \to C$$

such that

$$\begin{aligned}
R_S(\varepsilon) &= c_i \\
R_S(wm) &= \delta_S(R_S(w), m)
\end{aligned}$$

for all $m \in M$ and $w \in M^*$.

We denote by ST_S the domain of the reachability function and call the elements of ST_S (i.e., some sequence of events) *sequential transitions* of S. ST_S is then the set of all possible sequential transitions of system S; it forms a string language. Similarly, we define RC_S to be the codomain of the reachability function and call the elements of RC_S *reachable configurations* of S. If w is a sequential transition and $R_S(w) = c$, we say w *leads* S to c. Finally, we call the string system (M, ST_S) the *sequential behavior* of S, and denote it by SB_S. Clearly, SB_S is prefix closed and ordered into a tree by the prefix ordering. Let us illustrate this notions with the example of the forwarder of two messages.

EXAMPLE 2   The following configuration is a reachable configuration in the actor system defined in Ex. 1,

$$c = (\emptyset, \{f{:}sink, u{:}sink\})$$

To see why, notice that, e.g., (we write x for the event $x \triangleright f$, x' for $x \triangleright u$, and similarly for y and z) the sequence of events $w = xyzx'y'$ is a sequential transition of S and that $R_S(w) = c$. The sequential transition $w' = xyy'zx'$ also leads S to c. In fact, transitions w and w' are just two different sequential views of the same concurrent computation of system S, as will be seen soon. ☐

---

[1] '_' binds tighter than '∩' and this tighter than '∪'.

4 Independent events

The previous section defined the sequential behavior of an actor system. The ordering of events in SB_S reflects not only the causality relation between events, but also an observation ordering resulting from a specific sequential view of concurrent events. Therefore, the structure of the sequential behavior is not powerful enough to decide whether different orderings of events are caused by conflict resolution (order of message arrival at a particular actor) or by different observations of concurrency. In order to extract from the sequential behavior of S the causal ordering of events, we must equip SB_S with the information on dependence (or independence) of events.

The intuition behind *independent messages* is that they may be processed simultaneously or concurrently by their target actors. The simplest case of independent messages are those targeted to different actors. Since actors run in parallel, different actors may process different messages concurrently. Pairs of messages targeted to the same actor may also be included in the independence relation if we obtain the same configuration by processing the messages in any order.

DEFINITION 4 (INDEPENDENCE RELATION) *Let $S = (N, K, M, B, A, C, c_i)$ be an actor system. Independence in S, $I_S \subseteq M \times M$, is the least symmetric irreflexive relation such that $(x, y) \in I_S$ if and only if either*

1. *$target(x) \neq target(y)$ and there is at least a reachable configuration which contains x and y or*

2. *$target(x) = n = target(y)$ and for every configuration c which contains x and y, if $n{:}b$ is an actor in c such that*

$$b(x) = \langle \mu_0, \alpha_0, b_0 \rangle, \quad b_0(y) = \langle \mu_{01}, \alpha_{01}, b_{01} \rangle$$
$$b(y) = \langle \mu_1, \alpha_1, b_1 \rangle, \quad b_1(x) = \langle \mu_{10}, \alpha_{10}, b_{10} \rangle$$

the following equalities hold

$$\alpha_0 \cup \alpha_{01} = \alpha_1 \cup \alpha_{10}$$
$$\mu_0 \cup \mu_{01} = \mu_1 \cup \mu_{10}$$
$$b_{01} = b_{10}$$

The definition above implies that independent events can never affect the future of the computation, in the sense that any sequential ordering of independent events will always lead to the same configuration. The effect of independent events upon the computation of a configuration has the shape of a diamond as depicted in the following figure and captured in Lemma 1.

LEMMA 1 *Let c be a configuration in some actor system S and x, y two independent messages in c. Then, there exists a single configuration c' such that $c' = \delta_S(\delta_S(c, x), y) = \delta_S(\delta_S(c, y), x)$.*

PROOF: We distinguish two cases.

1. $target(x) \neq target(y)$. Let the behaviors b_0 and b_1 of the actors target of messages x and y, respectively, be such that $b_0(x) = \langle \mu_0, \alpha_0, b_0' \rangle$ and $b_1(y) = \langle \mu_1, \alpha_1, b_1' \rangle$. We then have

$$
\begin{aligned}
\delta_S(c, x) &= (msgs(c) - \{x\} \cup \mu_0, \ actors(c) - \{n_0{:}b_0\} \cup \alpha_0 \cup \{n_0{:}b_0'\}) \quad (= c_0)\\
\delta_S(c, y) &= (msgs(c) - \{y\} \cup \mu_1, \ actors(c) - \{n_1{:}b_1\} \cup \alpha_1 \cup \{n_1{:}b_1'\}) \quad (= c_1)
\end{aligned}
$$

That the above configurations are the only configurations obtained from c by messages x and y follows from the fact that behaviors are functions. From the above definition of c_0 it follows that, if $n_1{:}b_1$ is an actor in c then it is also an actor in c_0. Similarly, $n_0{:}b_0$ is an actor of c_1. We then have,

$$
\begin{aligned}
\delta_S(c_0, y) &= (msgs(c_0) - \{y\} \cup \mu_1, \ actors(c_0) - \{n_1{:}b_1\} \cup \alpha_1 \cup \{n_1{:}b_1'\})\\
\delta_S(c_1, x) &= (msgs(c_1) - \{x\} \cup \mu_0, \ actors(c_1) - \{n_0{:}b_0\} \cup \alpha_0 \cup \{n_0{:}b_0'\})
\end{aligned}
$$

By substituting the values of the messages and actors of c_0 and c_1 in the last two equations, it becomes clear that $\delta_S(c_0, y) = \delta_S(c_1, x)$.

2. $target(x) = target(y)$. The result follows directly from the definition of independent events. $\square$

Figure 1: Transitions obtained by independent events x and y lead to the same configuration (nodes represent configurations; arcs represent transitions.)

Sequential systems are those systems whose independence relation is empty. In fact, in a sequential system no two events can occur at the same time and, therefore, the independence relation cannot register any pair of concurrent events. Conversely, an empty independence relation reflects a sequential system. An empty independence relation means no two possible events can occur at the same time, and therefore (if events are to occur at all) they must occur one at a time; that is, sequentially.

An actor is called *unserialized* if it does not changes its behavior over time. Unserialized actors are capable of processing any number of messages at the same time, as shown in the proposition below.

PROPOSITION 2 *Two messages coexisting in some reachable configuration and targeted to the same unserialized actor are independent.*

PROOF: Let x and y be two messages targeted to an unserialized actor with behavior b. In any configuration which contains x and y, if $b(x) = \langle \mu_0, \alpha_0, b \rangle$, $b(y) = \langle \mu_1, \alpha_1, b \rangle$ then the last three equalities of the definition of the independence relation hold trivially. $\square$

We define *dependence* in S as the complement of I_S; that is, $D_S = M \times M - I_S$. Dependence is obviously a reflexive and symmetric relation. We call $\Sigma_S = (M, D_S)$ the *concurrent alphabet* associated with actor system S.

EXAMPLE 3   Let S be the actor system defined in Ex. 1. Independence in S, I_S, is the least symmetric relation obtained from the following pairs,

$$(x', y'), (y', z'), (z', x')$$
$$(x, y'), (x, z'), (y, x'), (y, z')(z, x'), (z, y')$$

To see why any pair of forwarded messages (first line above) is independent, notice that they are targeted to the same unserialized actor. By Prop. 2, each pair is independent if there exists a reachable configuration which contains both messages in the pair. For example, configuration $R_S(xy)$ contains messages x' and y'. As for the messages targeted to different actors (second line above), it can be easily seen that there exists a reachable configuration which contains each of the pairs and, therefore, they are independent. For example, configuration $R_S(y)$ contains the pair (x, y'). Notice that no two initial messages are independent. In fact, although, e.g., messages x and y verify the diagram of Fig. 1 for the initial configuration, they do not do so for configuration $R_S(z)$ and, therefore, they are not independent. Finally, the concurrent alphabet associated with S is $\Sigma_S = (M, D_S)$, where $D_S = M^2 - I_S$.   □

5   Concurrent behavior

Equipped with the notion of dependent events we can replace the total order on events imposed by sequential transitions, by a more faithful partial order where two events are related only if they are dependent. The dependence relation on events enables to abstract from particular orderings of sequences of events and leads to the notion of traces of events, called concurrent transitions. Traces may be viewed as dependence graphs or equivalence classes of sequential transitions: both views will be discussed in this section.

By *labeled acyclic graph* (over an alphabet A) we understand a triple (V, R, φ) where (V, R) is a finite directed acyclic graph with vertex set V, edge set $R \subseteq V \times V$ and where $\varphi : V \rightarrow A$ is a labeling function. We say a labeled acyclic graph (V, R, φ) is a *dependence graph* (over a concurrent alphabet $\Sigma = (A, D)$) if the only edges are between different vertices labeled with dependent symbols. If the concurrent alphabet Σ is fixed, then the whole information of a trace is contained in the Hasse diagram of the dependence graph of the trace. Thus we do not need to draw redundant edges.

The *composition of dependence graphs* γ_0 and γ_1, $\gamma_0 \circ \gamma_1$, is a graph arising from the disjoint union of γ_0 and γ_1 by adding new arcs leading from each node of γ_0 to each node of γ_1, provided that they are labeled with dependent symbols. Formally, if $\gamma_0 = (V_0, R_0, \varphi_0)$ and $\gamma_1 = (V_1, R_1, \varphi_1)$, then $\gamma_0 \circ \gamma_1$ is a graph (V, R, φ) such that

$$
\begin{aligned}
V &= V_0 \cup V_1 \quad (V_0 \cap V_1 = \emptyset) \\
R &= R_0 \cup R_1 \cup \{(x, y) \in V_0 \times V_1 \mid (\varphi_0(x), \varphi_1(y)) \in D\} \\
\varphi &= \varphi_0 \cup \varphi_1
\end{aligned}
$$

Two dependence graphs γ_0 and γ_1 are isomorphic, $\gamma_0 \cong \gamma_1$, if there exists a bijection between their nodes preserving labeling and edges. Let Γ_Σ denote the set of all isomorphism classes of dependence graphs and λ the empty graph $(\emptyset, \emptyset, \emptyset)$. Then Γ_Σ forms a monoid with multiplication $\circ$ and neutral element λ.

We now define a mapping from sequential transitions to dependence graphs that allows to extract the trace associated with a sequential transition. The mapping is defined as

$$\langle\rangle_\Sigma : M^* \to \Gamma_\Sigma$$

by setting for each u, v in M^* and e in M:

$$\langle \varepsilon \rangle_\Sigma \cong \lambda$$
$$\langle e \rangle_\Sigma \cong (\{e\}, \emptyset, \{(e, e)\})$$
$$\langle uv \rangle_\Sigma \cong \langle u \rangle_\Sigma \circ \langle v \rangle_\Sigma$$

From the mapping it follows that for any sequence of events w and event e, $\langle we \rangle_\Sigma$ is a graph arising from $\langle w \rangle_\Sigma$ by adding to $\langle w \rangle_\Sigma$ a new node labeled with e and new arcs leading from all nodes of $\langle w \rangle_\Sigma$ labeled with dependent events on e, to e. The following example illustrates the construction of a dependence graph from a sequential transition.

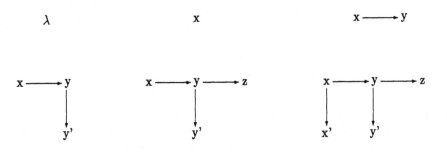

Figure 2: The various stages in the construction of the dependence graph associated with the sequential transition $xyy'zx'$ (left to right, top to bottom.)

EXAMPLE 4   The sequence of events $xyy'zx'$ is a sequential transition of the forwarder of two messages actor system. From this sequential transition and the information on dependent events (Ex. 3) we can built the dependence graph associated. Starting with the empty graph λ, we add to the graph nodes labelled with the events in the sequence, drawing arcs from all the already existing nodes to the new one if they are labeled with dependent events. Fig. 2 depicts the construction of the dependence graph associated with the sequential transition.   □

As we mentioned before traces can also be represented as equivalence classes of sequences of events. If two independent events occur next to each other in a sequential transition, the order of their occurrence is irrelevant. We can abstract from a particular ordering of independent events, by replacing sequential transitions by equivalence classes of strings of events. The *trace equivalence* relation $\equiv_S$ on M^* is the relation generated by all pairs of the form

$$(uxyv, uyxv) \text{ where } u, v \in M^* \text{ and } (x, y) \in I_S$$

The equivalence class $\equiv_S$ containing the sequence of events w is called the *trace* of w and denoted by $[w]_S$. An important theorem from the theory of traces—for each concurrent alphabet $\Sigma = (A, D)$, the monoid $([A]_\Sigma, \circ, [\varepsilon]_\Sigma)$ is isomorphic to the monoid $(\langle A \rangle_\Sigma, \circ, \lambda)$—ensures the equivalence of both representations.

EXAMPLE 5   The equivalence class generated by the sequential transition $xyy'zx'$ of the actor system defined in Ex. 1; that is, the trace of $xyy'zx'$ is

$$[xyy'zx']_S = \{xx'yy'z, \; xx'yzy', \; xyy'x'z, \; xyy'zx', \\ xyx'y'z, \; xyx'zy', \; xyzx'y', \; xyzy'x'\}$$

This is just another way of representing the trace depicted in the last dependence graph of Fig. 2. In fact, the elements of $[xyzx'y']_S$ are the linearizations of that graph.   □

From the above definition of $\equiv_S$ it follows that every sequential transition belongs to some trace. Conversely, the theorem below ensures that each representative of a trace is a sequential transition, and that all equivalent sequential transitions lead to the same configuration.

THEOREM 3   *The reachability function R_S is congruent with respect to trace equivalence $\equiv_S$; that is, for each two sequential transitions w_0, w_1 in M^*,*

$$w_0 \equiv_S w_1 \Rightarrow R_S(w_0) = R_S(w_1)$$

PROOF: Let $w_0 \equiv_S w_1$; prove $R_S(w_0) = R_S(w_1)$. Because of the definition of trace equivalence we have only to consider the case of $w_0 = uxyv$ and $w_1 = uyxv$ for independent events x and y. Because of the reachability function definition we have to prove only $\delta_S(\delta_S(c, x), y) = \delta_S(\delta_S(c, y), x)$ for a reachable configuration c which contains x and y, and that is the result of Lemma 1.   □

The set of all dependence graphs generated by an actor system S (more precisely, by the set of sequential transitions ST_S of S) is the trace language $\langle ST_S \rangle = \{\langle w \rangle_S \mid w \in ST_S\}$. We call the trace system $CB_S = (\Sigma_S, \langle ST_S \rangle)$ the *concurrent behavior* of S and call the elements of CB_S the *concurrent transitions* of S. Alternatively, if traces are viewed as equivalence classes of sequential transitions, and if the set of all traces generated by S is the trace language $[ST_S] = \{[w]_S \mid w \in ST_S\}$, then the concurrent behavior of S is $CB_S = (\Sigma_S, [ST_S])$.

Let σ and τ be traces over some concurrent alphabet Σ. *Trace composition* of σ and τ, denoted by $\sigma\tau$, is defined by $\sigma\tau = [uv]_\Sigma$, where $u, v \in M^*$ are elements of σ and τ, respectively. We say σ is a *prefix* of τ if there exists a trace δ (over Σ) such that $\tau = \sigma\delta$. The set of all prefixes of a trace τ will be denoted by $Pref(\tau)$. The prefix ordering of traces (over Σ) is the relation $\tau_1 \sqsubseteq \tau_2 \Leftrightarrow \tau_1 \in Pref(\tau_2)$. It can be easily seen that the set of all traces over Σ_S is partially ordered by $\sqsubseteq$. For each trace language T define $Pref(T) = \bigcup_{\tau \in T} Pref(\tau)$; the elements of $Pref(T)$ are called prefixes of T. A trace system is said to be prefix closed, if its trace language is prefix closed.

THEOREM 4 CB_S *is a prefix closed trace system.*

PROOF: Trace language of CB_S is the set of equivalence classes of the sequential transitions that compose the domain of the reachability function R_S. That this set is prefix closed follows directly from the recursive definition of R_S. □

A trace language T is *directed* if any two traces in T are prefixes of some trace in T; that is, T is directed if $\tau_1, \tau_2 \in T \Rightarrow \exists \tau \in T : \tau_1 \sqsubseteq \tau$ and $\tau_2 \sqsubseteq \tau$. A trace system is said to be directed, if its trace language is directed. A *subsystem* of $X = (\Sigma, T)$ is any trace system $X' = (\Sigma, T')$ such that T' is a subset of T. Directed subsystems of CB_S represent *histories of computations* of actor system S; each element of the subsystem describing a possible *state* of the computation; the whole subsystem describing all the possible states a particular computation may pass through. Maximal directed subsystems of CB_S represent *histories of completed computations*; the maximal element representing the *terminal* state of the computation. Directed subsystems with no maximal element represent nonterminating computations.

EXAMPLE 6 The concurrent behavior CB_S of the actor system S defined in Ex. 1 is given by the set of dependence graphs

$$\langle ST_S \rangle = Pref \begin{pmatrix} x \to y \to z \\ \downarrow \quad \downarrow \\ x' \quad y' \end{pmatrix} \bigcup Pref \begin{pmatrix} x \to z \to y \\ \downarrow \quad \downarrow \\ x' \quad z' \end{pmatrix} \bigcup Pref \begin{pmatrix} y \to z \to x \\ \downarrow \quad \downarrow \\ y' \quad z' \end{pmatrix} \bigcup$$

$$Pref \begin{pmatrix} y \to x \to z \\ \downarrow \quad \downarrow \\ y' \quad x' \end{pmatrix} \bigcup Pref \begin{pmatrix} z \to x \to y \\ \downarrow \quad \downarrow \\ z' \quad x' \end{pmatrix} \bigcup Pref \begin{pmatrix} z \to y \to x \\ \downarrow \quad \downarrow \\ z' \quad y' \end{pmatrix}$$

together with the concurrent alphabet Σ_S defined in Ex. 3. There are six possible different histories for the computation of the system, depending on the order of the two messages accepted first by the forwarder: they are precisely the six maximal directed subsystems depicted above.

Viewing traces as equivalence classes of sequential transitions, the concurrent behavior CB_S is given by the set of all possible concurrent transitions,

$$[ST_S] = Pref([xyzx'y']_S) \cup Pref([xzyz'x']_S) \cup Pref([yzxy'z']_S) \cup$$
$$Pref([yxzx'y']_S) \cup Pref([zxyz'x']_S) \cup Pref([zyxy'z']_S)$$

together with the concurrent alphabet Σ_S. □

Sometimes it is useful to think of a trace as a *pomset* [15] (the isomorphism class of a labeled partial order). In fact, the dependence graph $\gamma = (V, R, \varphi)$ over a concurrent alphabet $\Sigma = (A, D)$ is just a labeled partial order $(V, A, \leq, \varphi)$, where the partial order $\leq$ can be obtained as the transitive closure of the directed edges of γ.

6 Composition of actor systems

Deriving the behavior of complex actor systems may not be an easy task. Taking a modular approach often facilitates things: we could split a complex system into smaller components; then, developing the behavior of each component separately, we could in the end combine the partial results to obtain the behavior of the original system. In this section we describe a notion of actor systems suitable to be composed (extended actor systems) and then define a composition operation on actor systems. Behaviors, in turn, are combined through an operation on trace systems called synchronization; we prove that the behavior of the composed system is the synchronization of the behaviors of its components.

Actor systems, as defined in section 2 are *closed* in the sense that they may never send (or receive) messages to (from) the exterior. In order to compose actor systems we must equip actor systems with some notion of the "exterior". This can be accomplished by introducing *external names*—identifiers of actors external to the configuration. Messages supposed to leave a configuration are bound to some external actor; that is to say, their target is an external name. We then have two kinds of names: local (or internal) names and external names. Obviously, external names and local names must form two disjoint sets. The actors of this extended actor system are those whose identifier is a local name. Actors whose identifier is an external name are not part of the actor system, but their names are. Here is the definition of extended actor systems.

DEFINITION 5 (EXTENDED ACTOR SYSTEM)   *An extended actor system is any ordered ten-tuple of the form*

$$S = (L, E, K, LM, EM, M, B, A, C, c_i)$$

where L is a set of local names, E is a set of external names, K is a set of communications, L and E are disjoint ($L \cap E = \emptyset$), and

$$
\begin{aligned}
LM &\subseteq L \times K & &\text{local messages} \\
EM &\subseteq E \times K & &\text{external messages} \\
M &= LM \cup EM & &\text{messages} \\
B &= LM \to \mathcal{P}(M) \times \mathcal{P}(A) \times B & &\text{behaviors} \\
A &= L \times B & &\text{actors} \\
C &= \mathcal{P}(M) \times \mathcal{P}(A) & &\text{configurations} \\
c_i &\in C & &\text{initial configuration}
\end{aligned}
$$

From the above exposed, it is clear that external messages will never be "consumed" inside a configuration; that is, external messages will never create *events*. Since we cannot assume nothing about the behaviors of external actors, the dependence relation must not contain pairs of messages targeted to external actors. Dependence is now a relation $D \subseteq M \times LM \cup LM \times M$. For similar reasons, independence is also defined over $M \times LM \cup LM \times M$, and therefore D and I do not form a partition of $M \times M$ anymore.

When splitting an actor system in some components, we must anticipate all the messages each component may receive from other components: these messages are placed in the component's initial configuration. Then, with the tools developed in the previous sections, we build the trace behavior of each component. Finally, we obtain the behavior of the original system through trace synchronization on the behavior of the components.

We compose actor systems by identifying external names of one system with local names of another: these will become local names of the composed system. Because actors should still be unique after the composition, we require the sets of local names of the components to be disjoint. The same reasoning applies to messages; when we bring together two distinct systems, some external messages of one system will be local to another system. Again, these messages will be local messages of the composed system. To obtain the initial configuration of the composed system, we exclude from the union of the initial configurations of the components those messages that are local to one system and external to another. These messages are precisely the ones we "artificially" placed in the initial configurations of the components, and that are supposed to be produced by other components as computation proceeds.

DEFINITION 6 (COMPOSITION OF ACTOR SYSTEMS)
An actor system $S = (L, E, K, LM, EM, M, B, A, C, c_i)$ is composed of actor systems $S_k = (L_k, E_k, LM_k, EM_k, M_k, B_k, A_k, C_k, c_{ik}), k = 1, 2$, written

$$S = S_1 + S_2$$

if L_1 and L_2 are disjoint $(L_1 \cap L_2 = \emptyset)$, and

$$
\begin{aligned}
E &= E_1 - L_2 \cup E_2 - L_1 \\
EM &= EM_1 - LM_2 \cup EM_2 - LM_1 \\
C &= \mathcal{P}(M_1 \cup M_2) \times \mathcal{P}(A_1 \cup A_2) \\
msgs(c_i) &= (msgs(c_{i1}) \cup msgs(c_{i2})) - ((LM_1 \cup LM_2) \cap (EM_1 \cup EM_2)) \\
actors(c_i) &= actors(c_{i1}) \cup actors(c_{i2})
\end{aligned}
$$

Elements L, K, LM, M, B and A are obtained from the set union of the respective elements of S_k. S_1 and S_2 are called components *of S.*

It can be easily seen that the above definition is correct; that is, if S_1 and S_2 are actor systems, so is $S_1 + S_2$. Also, simple set manipulation is all we need to prove that '+' is associative and commutative, and thus we may omit parenthesis and disregard the order of terms in composition.

THEOREM 5 *Let S_1 and S_2 be two actor systems with concurrent alphabets Σ_1 and Σ_2, respectively. Then*

$$\Sigma_{S_1 + S_2} = \Sigma_1 \cup \Sigma_2$$

PROOF: Refer to [16]. $\square$

Before we go on to define the concurrent behavior of composed actor systems, we need some auxiliary notions on traces. The *trace projection* operation is the trace analog to string projection. Intuitively, the projection of a trace τ (over a concurrent alphabet $\Sigma_1 = (A_1, D_1)$) onto a concurrent alphabet $\Sigma_2 = (A_2, D_2)$, written τ/Σ_2, is a trace over $\Sigma_1 \cap \Sigma_2$ that keeps the symbols belonging to $A_1 \cap A_2$ and the dependencies belonging to $D_1 \cap D_2$. Formally, we say that the projection of τ (over Σ_1) onto Σ_2, is a trace over $\Sigma_1 \cap \Sigma_2$ such that if $\tau = [w]_{\Sigma_1}$ and $\Sigma = \Sigma_1 \cap \Sigma_2 = (A, D)$, then

$$\tau/\Sigma_2 = [w/A]_\Sigma$$

Synchronization on trace systems is the trace analog to the merge operation on string systems. It is a binary relation over the class of all trace systems, Π, defined in the following way: $X \parallel Y$ is a trace system whose concurrent alphabet is the union of the concurrent alphabets of X and Y, and whose trace language is the set of all possible traces over the union of X and Y such that when projected onto X yields a trace over X, and when projected onto Y yields a trace over Y. Formally, synchronization is a binary relation on Π,

$$\parallel \; : \Pi \times \Pi \to \Pi$$

such that, for trace systems $X_1 = (\Sigma_1, T_1)$ and $X_2 = (\Sigma_2, T_2)$, $X_1 \parallel X_2 = (\Sigma, T)$ is a trace system such that

$$\Sigma = \Sigma_1 \cup \Sigma_2$$
$$T = \{\tau \in \Theta(\Sigma_1 \cup \Sigma_2) \mid \tau/\Sigma_1 \in T_1, \tau/\Sigma_2 \in T_2\}$$

where $\Theta(\Sigma)$ represents the set of all traces over Σ.

We are now ready to define the concurrent behavior of a composed system. The main theorem of this section states that the concurrent behavior of an actor system is just the trace synchronization of the concurrent behaviors of its components.

THEOREM 6 *If $S_1, S_2, \ldots, S_n$ are pairwise L-disjoint actor systems,*

$$CB_{S_1+S_2+\cdots+S_n} = CB_{S_1} \parallel CB_{S_2} \parallel \cdots \parallel CB_{S_n}$$

PROOF: We sketch the proof; the full proof will appear in [16]. Let $CB_{S_1+S_2+\cdots+S_n} = (\Sigma, T)$ and $CB_{S_k} = (\Sigma_k, T_k)$, where Σ and Σ_k are concurrent alphabets and T and T_k are trace languages, and let R_S be the reachability of S and R_k that of S_k, $k = 1 \ldots n$. We have to prove that

$$\Sigma = \bigcup_{k=1}^{n} \Sigma_k$$
$$T = \{\tau \in \Theta(\bigcup \Sigma_k) \mid \forall k, \tau/\Sigma_k \in T_k\}$$

The first result is the object of theorem 5. As for the trace language, by making $\tau = [w]_\Sigma$, we have to prove that for all w

$$\exists c : R_S(w) = c \Leftrightarrow \forall k \exists c_k : R_k(w/LM_k) = c_k$$

Here is how to obtain c_k from c:

$$msgs(c_k) = msgs(c) \cap M_k \cup c_{ik} - Rng(w) \cap LM_k \cup (c_{ik} \cup Rng(w)) \cap EM_k$$
$$actors(c_k) = actors(c) \cap A_k$$

($Rng(w)$ represents the set of all symbols in string w.) The proof follows by induction on the length of w. □

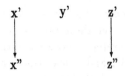

Figure 3: A trace representing the terminal state of the filter actor system.

EXAMPLE 7   We introduce a second actor system: the "filter of y messages". A filter of y messages actor forwards, to a fixed actor, all messages different from y. In the initial configuration, we place all those messages the filter may possibly receive, namely x', y', and z', together with a filter actor and a sink receptor for the non-y messages forwarded by the filter. The trace language of the extended actor system obtained is the set of all prefixes of the trace depicted in Fig. 3.

Revisiting our old forwarder of two messages actor system, we make the receptor of the forwarded messages an external actor. Because messages x', y' and z' are now targeted to an external actor, they do not constitute events of *this* system. Fig. 4 shows two traces belonging to the trace language of the extended actor system obtained.

$$x \longrightarrow y \longrightarrow z \qquad\qquad z \longrightarrow x \longrightarrow y$$

Figure 4: Two traces representing terminal states of the new forwarder system.

We may now compose the two systems. Since messages x', y' and z' are external to the forwarder system, the initial configuration of the composed system will only contain messages x, y and z. Two of the terminal states of the composed system are depicted in Fig. 5. Notice that the projections of these traces onto the concurrent alphabet of the forwarder are the traces depicted in Fig. 4, and that the projections onto the concurrent alphabet of the filter belong to the trace language of the filter (they are prefixes of the trace shown in Fig. 3.)   □

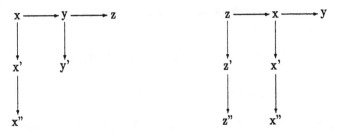

Figure 5: Two traces from the behavior of the composed system.

7 Extending independence

As we mentioned in the introduction, by extending or restricting the independence relation we may obtain more or less concurrency within the events of a system. The definition proposed in section 4 fails, in some cases, to extract the full concurrency of an actor system. In this section we show where more concurrency can be added to, and how it can be done by extending the independence relation.

Let us try to see through the forwarder example why the independence relation defined before unnecessarily sequentializes events that could otherwise happen concurrently. Remember the initial configuration c_i contains a forwarder actor together with three messages, x, y and z, targeted to it. According to our definition, no pair built from this messages is independent. Pick pair (x, y) for example. Then, it is not the case that in *every* reachable configuration which contains the pair, the diamond diagram (figure 1) holds. In fact, although events x and y may occur simultaneously in the initial configuration, they cannot occur concurrently in configuration c obtained from c_i by processing message z; and therefore events x and y are dependent.

But clearly, any pair of messages in the initial configuration may be processed concurrently; our definition of independence is describing them as sequential. What is the difference between c_i and c that makes events x and y potentially independent in c_i but not in c? Obviously, it is the behavior of the target actor; for in c_i it is ready to forward any two messages, whereas in c it is ready to forward a single message (because it has already forwarded z). In order to extend the dependence relation to cope with this kind of concurrency, we have to take into account behaviors (at least in the case of events with the same target). Thus, independence will be no more a relation on pairs of messages but will also encompass behaviors, and that will take us away from the theory of traces. Nevertheless, let us pursue this line a little further. We can define an extended independence relation

$$I'_S \subseteq (M \times B) \times (M \times B)$$

and say $((x, a), (y, b)) \in I'_S$ if and only if there exists *some* reachable configuration c which contains messages x, y, and actors $n_0{:}a$, $n_1{:}b$ (where $n_0 = target(x)$, $n_1 = target(y)$) and either

1. $n_0 \neq n_1$ or

2. $n_0 = n_1$ and if

$$b(x) = \langle \mu_0, \alpha_0, b_0 \rangle, \quad b_0(y) = \langle \mu_{01}, \alpha_{01}, b_{01} \rangle$$
$$b(y) = \langle \mu_1, \alpha_1, b_1 \rangle, \quad b_1(x) = \langle \mu_{10}, \alpha_{10}, b_{10} \rangle$$

then the following equalities hold

$$\alpha_0 \cup \alpha_{01} = \alpha_1 \cup \alpha_{10}$$
$$\mu_0 \cup \mu_{01} = \mu_1 \cup \mu_{10}$$
$$b_{01} = b_{10}$$

We can then define an equivalence relation $\equiv'_S$ on sequential transitions, generated by all pairs of the form $(uxyv, uyxv)$ where $u, v \in M^*$, $((x, a), (y, b)) \in I'_S$ and $(target(x), a)$,

($target(y), b$) are actors in configuration c reachable through sequential transition u; that is, $c = R_S(u)$. Clearly, this extended independence relation contains the one defined in section 4; that is $I_S \subseteq I'_S$. Let us see the concurrent transitions this extended definition of independence yields on the forwarder actor system.

Figure 6: A dependence graph associated with sequential transition $xyzx'y'$.

EXAMPLE 8   The extended independence relation $I'_S \subseteq (M \times B) \times (M \times B)$ of the actor system S defined in Ex. 1, contains the following pairs,

Targeted to the same actor f:$forward2$ $(x, y), (y, z), (z, x)$
Targeted to the same actor u:$sink$ $(x', y'), (y', z'), (z', x')$
Targeted to actors with different behaviors $(x, y'), (x, z'), (y, x'), (y, z')(z, x'), (z, y')$

Now we have the initial messages x, y and z independent when targeted to $forward2$, but dependent when targeted to $forward1$. The remaining pairs are just natural extensions to the ones described in Ex. 3. Notice that when messages are targeted to different actors, the behavior of the target is irrelevant. Extended independence allows for events x and y to occur concurrently in sequence $xyzx'y'$; the concurrent transition associated with $xyzx'y'$ is depicted in Fig. 6 (compare it to the last graph in figure 2.)

Because the first two messages accepted by the forwarder are concurrent, $xyzx'y'$ and $yxzx'y'$ belong to the same trace. Similarly, $xzyx'z'$ and $zxyx'z'$ belong to the same trace, and so does $yzxy'z'$ and $zyxy'z'$. Therefore, the concurrent behavior of S has only three different histories of completed computations: $Pref([xyzx'y']_S)$, $Pref([yzxy'z']_S)$ and $Pref([zxyz'x']_S)$ (c.f. with Ex. 6 where we had six.) Thus, we see that I'_S yields a more abstract behavior in the sense that it places more sequential transitions in the same trace, by allowing greater concurrency among events.   □

8   Related work

Hewitt and Baker's laws. The idea of using partial orders to describe actor systems is not new. Hewitt and Baker [6] made use of partial orders to represent concurrency in actors. Their work is based on the existence of a treelike activation order (e_1 *activates* e_2 if e_2 is the event associated with some message created by event e_1) and a set of linear arrival orders, one for each actor. Each linear order is enforced by an arbiter in front of the actor which allows a single message to be received at a time. Concurrency is represented by the history order: the transitive closure of the activation order and the arrival order. While physically appealing, total orders on events with the same target are too strong a restriction: they differentiate between too many similarly behaving computations. An example taken from [6] will suffice to illustrate the point.

"Fork-join synchronization" arises when an actor must delegate some tasks to other actors and needs to collect the results afterwards. Suppose an actor f receives a request to calculate $f(x) = h(g_1(x), g_2(x))$ and send the reply back to some actor u. Upon reception of such a message, f creates a continuation h and sends messages to g_1 and g_2 requesting the values of $g_1(x)$ and $g_2(x)$ respectively (together with the information that the replies must be sent to h). The continuation h, in turn, upon collecting the replies from g_1 and g_2, calculates $f(x) = h(g_1(x), g_2(x))$ and sends the result back to u. For the sake of brevity, let us call f to the event $[x \text{ reply-to: } u] \triangleright f$; g_1 to the event $[x \text{ reply-to: } h] \triangleright g_1$; g_2 to the event $[x \text{ reply-to: } h] \triangleright g_2$; h_1 to the event $[g_1(x)] \triangleright h$; h_2 to the event $[g_2(x)] \triangleright h$; and u to the event $[f(x)] \triangleright u$.

Figure 7: Two possible scenarios for the fork-join synchronization problem (Thin arrows indicate activation order; thick arrows represent arrival order.)

If messages h_1 and h_2 arrive simultaneously, the arbiter in front of actor h must decide upon one of the two orders $h_1 h_2$ or $h_2 h_1$. Therefore, depending on the arbiter's decision, we obtain two distinct precedes orders: they are illustrated in Fig. 7. Thinking in terms of traces, we can easily see that events h_1 and h_2 are independent. Notice that there is a unique reachable configuration—$R_S(fg_1g_2)$—that contains both messages, and that the configurations obtained from this configuration, by sequential transitions $h_1 h_2$ and $h_2 h_1$, are the same. The dependence graph representing the terminal state of the only history of the computation is depicted in Fig. 8.

Figure 8: The dependence graph of the fork-join synchronization problem.

The decisions an arbiter makes may or may not affect the course of the computation. For example, the decisions made by the arbiter in front of the join actor cannot affect in any way the future of the computation. On the other hand, decisions made by an arbiter in front of a bank account actor, affect the computation if the actor is to receive two withdraw messages and has not enough balance to satisfy both. We thus see that what is really important is to distinguish between decisions that affect the course of the computation and those that do not; and that is just what the ordering induced by traces accomplishes. Trace semantics does not take into account meaningless decisions of arbiters.

Notice that by restricting the independence relation to pairs of messages coexisting in the same configuration and targeted to different objects (i.e., by removing item 2 from the definition of independence relation in section 4) we obtain a relation that is weaker than the two previously defined and that induces Hewitt and Baker's precedes ordering.

Clinger's power domains. Based on Hewitt and Baker's work mentioned above, Clinger developed a power domain semantics for actor systems [4]. The domain used is made of event diagrams augmented by a set of pending messages, together with the "initial history" partial order. Event diagrams describe a stage of computation by recording the history of the computation since the the initial configuration. They are made up of the set of events that occurred in the course of computation, partially ordered by the precedes relation discussed above. Since elements of the domain are sets of events ordered by the precedes relation, the semantics obtained distinguishes between too many similarly computations. Also, the complexity of detail involved in event diagrams (together with pending events), distract from the fundamental issues.

Traces do not represent finite computations. Not having limit points, traces do not form domains. However, we can add limit points by taking a completion by ideals, as proposed in [17].

A most strikingly difference between [6, 4] and trace semantics concerns activation. In the former works activation forms an irreflexive partial order on events such that each event has *at most* one immediate predecessor. This means we have to single out one only event as the direct cause of any event (different from the least event.) Concurrent transitions do not respect single activation. There may be the case where we have multiple events as immediate predecessors of a given event. This happens when we can not point out a single event, but else some set of independent events as activators (c.f. activators of event u in the graph of Fig. 8).

Petri nets. The theory of traces is particularly adequate to describe the behavior of safe Petri nets. The structure of a Petri net may be represented as a directed bipartite graph. Once fixed, this graph will remain unchanged throughout computation. Dependence is a relation defined directly on the graph and is not influenced by the initial marking of the net. In contrast, the structure of an object configuration is intrinsically dynamic, and therefore, dependence in object systems is a dynamic concept: it depends not only on the initial configuration, but also on the dynamic behavior of the system.

Composing and decomposing Petri nets presents no difficulty. If the sets of places of the components are disjoint, the composed net is formed by the union of the graphs representing the components, and the initial marking is the union of the markings of the components. The most interesting feature of the approach is that there exists a standard set of very simple nets with known behaviors, such that an arbitrary net can be composed of nets taken from this set. In the case of actor systems, things are not that easy: a composed actor system cannot be formed simply by the "union" of its components, nor its initial configuration can be built from the union of the components' initial configurations.

9 Conclusions

From an operational model, based on the theory of traces we built a simple concurrent semantics for actor-based programs. The meaning of a program is the concurrent behavior of the object system induced by the program. In turn, the concurrent behavior of an object system is the set of all concurrent transitions the system's initial configuration may engage in. Each concurrent transition is a trace on the events of a particular computation of the system. The theory of traces provides us with two different (though isomorphic) ways of viewing concurrent transitions: dependence graphs where nodes represent events and edges link nodes labeled with causal related events, and equivalence classes of sequences of events up to commutation of concurrent events. We presented a notion of composition of object systems: it allows to decompose a complex system into some components, to develop the concurrent behavior of the simpler components separately and, in the end, to bring the concurrent behaviors of the components together to obtain the concurrent behavior of the original system.

Not much work on concurrent objects addresses the issue of composition of systems. Also, when compared to Hewitt and Baker's ordering laws for events in actor systems [6], our work yields a more abstract description of computations, in the sense that it distinguishes less similarly behaving computations. Nevertheless, the scenario is not that bright when compared to the application of the theory of traces to the description of the behavior of safe Petri nets. In particular, the dependence relation for actor systems, being a dynamic concept, may not be trivial to extract and, the composition of systems cannot be obtained simply by the union of their components. But that's expectable: it reflects an intrinsic difference between dynamic systems of objects and static nets.

The notion of objects from which we built our semantics synchronizes on a single message. There are times however when we would like to have objects synchronizing in more than one message. The join object of section 8 is such an object. The problem with expressing this kind of objects in actor-based programming languages is that not only the programmer must write a complex script to handle the reception of a message at a time (memorizing the number and the contents of the messages received), but also previous semantics attribute to such a simple object a different behavior depending on the order of message arrival. The semantics presented can be easily extended to objects that synchronize in more than one incoming message. All we have to do is to associate with events, not single messages, but else sets of messages. Most results achieved extend naturally to this notion of events. However, the semantics obtained are slightly more complicated and less intuitive and that is why we opted by a model of objects that synchronize on a single message.

An interesting feature of trace semantics is that the "degree of concurrency" of a system may be adjusted. By expanding or restricting the independence relation on events, more or less concurrency is permitted. In particular, an empty independence relation induces a sequential system. We presented three different such relations ordered by inclusion, the weakest of which corresponds to the precedes relation of [6].

Finally, the authors would like to thank Kohei Honda for its continuous support throughout all stages of development of this project; Prof. Peter Wegner for its constructive comments during his stay at Keio University; and Prof. Akinori Yonezawa for fruitful discussions.

References

[1] J. Aalbersg and G. Rozenberg. Theory of traces. *Theoretical Computer Science*, 60:1–82, 1988.

[2] Gul Agha. *Actors: A model of concurrent computation in distributed systems.* The MIT Press, Cambridge, MA, 1986.

[3] Gérard Boudol and Ilaria Castellani. Three equivalent semantics for CCS. In *Semantics of Systems of Concurrent Processes, Lecture Notes in Computer Science 469*, pages 96–141, Springer-Verlag, April 1990.

[4] William Clinger. *Foundations of actor semantics.* AI-TR 633, M.I.T. A.I. Laboratory, Cambridge, MA, May 1981.

[5] Volker Diekert. *Combinatorics on traces.* Volume 454 of *Lecture Notes in Computer Science*, Springer-Verlag, 1990.

[6] Carl Hewitt and Henry Baker. Laws for communicating parallel processes. In *IFIP*, pages 987–992, August 1977.

[7] Antoni Mazurkiewicz. Basic notions of trace theory. In *Linear time, Branching Time and Partial Orders in Logics and Models for Concurrency, Lecture Notes in Computer Science 354*, pages 285–363, Springer-Verlag, May 1988.

[8] Antoni Mazurkiewicz. *Concurrent program schemes and their interpretation.* DAIMI Rept. PB 78, Aarhus University, Aarhus, 1977.

[9] José Meseguer. *Conditional rewriting logic as a unified model of concurrency.* SRI-CSL 91-05, SRI-International, Menlo Park, CA, February 1991.

[10] José Meseguer. A logical theory of concurrent objects. In *OOPSLA/ECOOP*, pages 101–115, ACM Press, October 1990.

[11] Robin Milner. *Communication and concurrency. C.A.R. Hoare Series Editor,* Prentice-Hall Int., 1989.

[12] M. Nielsen, G. Plotkin, and G. Winskel. Petri nets, event structures and domains. *Theoretical Computer Science*, 13:85–108, 1981.

[13] C. A. Petri. *Non-sequential processes.* GMD-ISF 77-S, Gesselschaft Math., Datenverarb., St. Augustin, 1977.

[14] Gordon Plotkin. *A structural approach to operational semantics.* Daimi FN 91, Aarhus University, 1981.

[15] Vaughan Pratt. Modeling concurrency with partial orders. *International Journal of Parallel Programming*, 15(1):33–71, 1986.

[16] Vasco T. Vasconcelos. Trace semantics for concurrent objects. February 1992. To appear as a technical report, Dep. of Computer Science, Keio University.

[17] G. Winskel. An introduction to event structures. In *Linear time, Branching Time and Partial Orders in Logics and Models for Concurrency, Lecture Notes in Computer Science 354*, pages 364–397, Springer-Verlag, May 1988.

Dynamic Programming as Multiagent Programming

Jean-Marc Andreoli, Remo Pareschi and Marc Bourgois
European Computer-Industry Research Centre
Arabellastraße 17
D-8000 Munich 81, Germany
{jeanmarc,remo,marc} @ecrc.de

Abstract

We show that the search technique of dynamic programming models a form of multiagent computation characterized by the interaction of cooperating/competing agents. For this reason, dynamic programming algorithms can be easily implemented in an object-oriented concurrent language environment. We illustrate this by a simple example implemented in the object-oriented concurrent language *LO*, involving the finding of the best path from the initial to the final vertex in a network where the connecting edges are associated with cost weights.

1 Introduction

The problem of coordinating behavior among collections of (semi-)autonomous computational entities (agents) is currently attracting a great deal of interest. The growing discipline of distributed artificial intelligence is explicitly concerned with this problem area (see for instance [FJ90]). In this paper, we show that the operations research technique of *dynamic programming*, traditionally viewed as a way of partitioning the solution of a certain problem into successive stages (so that decisions at a certain stage can be based on decisions at earlier stages), can also be reinterpreted in a concurrent and truly dynamic manner as the sharing of common information among agents working towards different, possibly competing goals.

Although our approach is language-independent, we rely for its illustration on the object-oriented concurrent programming language *LO* [AP91a]. Indeed, there are specific features of *LO* which make it an ideal candidate for encoding problems involving independent, richly structured agents sharing a common environment [AP91a], like the fact that *interobject* communication through a shared communication medium (the *forum*) is a primitive of the language, and that there exists also a form of *intraobject* communication, locally pertaining to single objects, which accounts for inherited behavior and knowledge sharing. We shall therefore start by giving a quick characterization of *LO*'s operational semantics, and shall then illustrate our approach by a simple *LO* program capable of optimally solving a path-finding problem.

2   *LO*'s Operational Semantics

LO (for Linear Objects) is a concurrent object-oriented language which allows the programmer to declaratively specify, at an abstract level, the behavior of a system of concurrent, communicating, agents. But *LO* also provides a basic computational mechanism to execute such specifications. The behavior of each individual agent is characterized by a set of well-defined, observable states and a set of transitions over these states. Transitions can either be *transformations* (from one state to one new state), *creations* (from one state to two or more new states), or *terminations* (from one state to no state at all). Hence, the behavior of a system of agents can be represented as a tree structure, whose nodes are the states and whose branches are the transitions; when one (resp. several, resp. no) branch(es) stem(s) from a given node, the corresponding transition is a transformation (resp. a creation, resp. a termination) of the agent. By convention, trees are represented with their root at the bottom and growing upward.

2.1   The Declarative Aspect

LO specifications of agents' behavior are completely abstract, as they make no assumptions on the run-time chronological order in which these transitions are actually selected and triggered. Therefore, *LO* programs have a purely declarative reading, which we informally characterize in this section (for more formal characterizations see [And90, AP90, AP91b, AP91a], where we also describe the relationship between *LO* and Linear Logic [Gir87]).

In *LO*, the state of an agent is a multiset (i.e. an unordered list) of bounded computational resources. Syntactically, resources are represented by expressions from a class G of "goals", built from a given initial class A of "atoms" and three connectives $\otimes$ (called "par"), $\&$ (called "with") and $\top$ (called "top"), responsible, respectively, for transformations, creations and terminations.

$$G \;=\; A \mid G \otimes G \mid G \,\&\, G \mid \top$$

The state of an agent is encoded as a multiset of such goals, called a "context". The comma "," denotes the multiset constructor in contexts.

A first set of transitions is defined in terms of the following "transition schemata", which explicit the semantics of the connectives occuring in goals. In each schema, the context below the line represents the input state of the transition while the context(s) above (if any) are the output states (this convention is consistent with the bottom-up representation for trees). For convenience, states are prefixed with the symbol $\vdash$ and transitions are labeled with their corresponding connectives. By convention, the symbol $\mathcal{C}$ stands for any context, and G_1, G_2 for any goals.

$$[\otimes]\ \frac{\vdash \mathcal{C}, G_1, G_2}{\vdash \mathcal{C}, G_1 \otimes G_2} \qquad\qquad [\&]\ \frac{\vdash \mathcal{C}, G_1 \quad \vdash \mathcal{C}, G_2}{\vdash \mathcal{C}, G_1 \,\&\, G_2} \qquad\qquad [\top]\ \frac{}{\vdash \mathcal{C}, \top}$$

Thus, a context containing a goal of the form $G_1 \otimes G_2$ can trigger a transformation $[\otimes]$, where the goal $G_1 \otimes G_2$ is replaced by the two subgoals G_1 and G_2, with a consequent increase in the size of the context (since a formula has been split into two) and a decrease in its complexity (since an occurrence of a connective has been eliminated). Similarly, a context containing a goal of the form $G_1 \& G_2$ can trigger a creation [&], thus yielding two output contexts by replacing $G_1 \& G_2$ with, respectively, each of the subgoals G_1 and G_2. Notice how the remaining resources from the input context are duplicated, each output context receiving a separate copy, which means that the two output contexts are quasi-clones (they differ only by the goal G_1, resp. G_2). Finally, terminations are handled via the schema [⊤], which allows a context to terminate if it contains the distinguished element ⊤.

Given that the complexity of contexts (their total number of connectives) strictly decreases in all the transitions above, after several occurences of such transitions we end up with a "flat" context of null complexity, that is, containing only atoms.

We must therefore allow for the possibility of user-defined, application-specific transitions, operating on flat contexts and complementing the transition schemata [⅋], [&] and [⊤]. We shall refer to transitions of this second kind as "methods" and to sets of such transitions as "programs". Formally, the class M of methods is built from goals and atoms using the connective ⅋ as well as a new symbol ○–:

$$M = A \circ\!\!- G \mid A \,⅋\, M$$

Thus, a method of the form $A_1 \,⅋\, \cdots \,⅋\, A_n \circ\!\!- G$ (where $n \geq 1$) consists of a head (the multiset of atoms $A_1, \ldots, A_n$, connected by ⅋, on the left-hand side of the symbol ○–) and a body (the goal G on the right-hand side of the symbol ○–). Now, for any flat context C, we permit a method $A_1 \,⅋\, \cdots \,⅋\, A_n \circ\!\!- G$ to fire in terms of the following new transition schema, to which we refer as "propagation":

$$[\circ\!\!-] \quad \frac{\vdash C, G}{\vdash C, A_1, \ldots, A_n}$$

According to this new schema, any flat context can propagate if it contains the head of a method in the program; the output state of the transition is simply obtained by replacing in the input state the head with the body of the given method.

2.2 The Operational Aspect

An LO query is given by a program $\mathcal{P}$ and an initial goal G_o. Its execution consists of building a tree representing one of the possible behaviors (under program $\mathcal{P}$) of a system of agents initially reduced to one agent whose state *contains* G_o. Thus, the initial context is incompletely specified (it is only constrained to contain G_o). The basic execution mechanism consists then of incrementally building the tree, starting with the initial context and recursively selecting and triggering transitions at each created node. To be computationally viable, this approach must be supported by the following strategy for selecting the transition to trigger at each step.

- If the current context is not flat (i.e. contains at least one non-atomic goal), then one of the non-atomic goals must be selected and the transition corresponding to its topmost connective be applied. It can be shown that this choice can be solved deterministically, as any choice of a non-atomic goal can be commuted with any other choice.

- If the current context is flat, then the Propagation rule [o—] is the only possible choice left. It involves the non-deterministic choice of a method, which in practice is deterministically solved via a "committed choice" strategy and is anyway partially controlled by the fact that the head of the method must be included in the current context. However, as the initial context is not completely specified, neither is the current context; therefore, if no constraint is put on its unspecified part, then the head of any method can be assumed to be included in this part and thus any method could in principle be triggered. To alleviate this situation, LO supplies a control primitive, to which we refer as the *tell* marker, which allows the programmer to control assumptions on the unspecified part of the context.

We take the *tell* marker $^\wedge$ to be an operator which can prefix any atom in the head of a method. Let us take for example the following (marked) program and initial goal

$$\mathcal{P} = \begin{cases} p \,\wp\, {}^\wedge a \,o{-}\, r \\ q \,\wp\, a \,\wp\, {}^\wedge b \,o{-}\, \top \\ r \,\wp\, b \,o{-}\, \top \end{cases} \quad \text{and} \quad G_o = p \,\&\, q$$

The role of the marker can be described as follows: when the Propagation rule [o—] is applied using a particular method, say the first one in $\mathcal{P}$ above, the *non-marked* atoms in the head of the method (in this case the single item p) must be found in the *already specified* part of the context, while the *marked* atoms (in this case the single item a) are assumed in the *still unspecified* part of the context. Therefore, we can build a proof for the example above as follows. (We use the symbol $\mathcal{C}$ to refer to the initially unspecified part of the context.)

1. Since the initial context $\mathcal{C}, p \,\&\, q$ is not flat, the first step is necessarily

$$[\&] \; \frac{\vdash \mathcal{C}, p \quad \vdash \mathcal{C}, q}{\vdash \mathcal{C}, p \,\&\, q}$$

2. At this point no method can apply to the rightmost node: the second method of $\mathcal{P}$ is a candidate for application, since q is in the already specified part of the context, but the marking of this method also requires a to be in this part. This is not yet the case here and the execution at this node suspends. Meanwhile, the first method of $\mathcal{P}$ applies to the leftmost node, yielding the assumption $\mathcal{C} = \mathcal{C}', a$ (since a is marked). Therefore the leftmost node expands into

$$[o{-}] \; \frac{\vdash \mathcal{C}', r}{\vdash \mathcal{C}', a, p}$$

and then the execution suspends on the left branch.

3. The execution can instead be resumed on the right branch, as now the context is sufficiently specified. The second methods of $\mathcal{P}$ can in fact fire by making the assumption $\mathcal{C}' = \mathcal{C}'', b$ (since b is marked) and then expanding the rightmost node into

$$[o{-}] \; \frac{[\top] \; \dfrac{}{\vdash \mathcal{C}'', \top}}{\vdash \mathcal{C}'', b, a, q}$$

which leads to a termination.

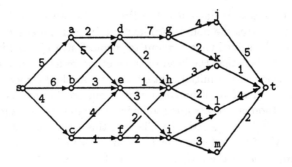

Figure 1: Network with weighted edges.

4. Now that b is available, the execution can resume on the left branch, where the third method can be applied; this leads to another termination.

We finally end up with the following tree (the transition labels refer to the chronological order in which transitions have been triggered):

$$[1]\frac{[2]\frac{[5]\frac{[6]\frac{}{\vdash C'',\top}}{\vdash C'',b,r}}{\vdash C'',b,a,p}\quad [3]\frac{[4]\frac{}{\vdash C'',\top}}{\vdash C'',b,a,q}}{\vdash C'',b,a,p\,\&\,q}$$

Thus, by using the tell marker we have enforced control on the execution by synchronizing the processes associated with the different branches of the tree. Synchronization of this kind is analogous to message passing (the atoms a and b, broadcast from one branch to the other, are acting as messages). Furthermore, activity within a single branch can now be viewed as a bundle of computation threads, where synchronization is achieved in terms of the Propagation rule [o—].

2.3 Typography for *LO* connectives

From now on, in the programming example that we shall illustrate, we replace the logical symbols for the *LO* connectives ⅋, &, ⊤ and o— with, respectively, keyboard typable symbols @, &, #t and <>-, which are those used in the actual implementation of *LO*.

3 A Simple Path-finding Problem

Consider a network, i.e. a directed acyclic graph, like the one in Fig. 1, where the edges connecting the vertices are associated with cost weights. Given one such network, we want to find the best path (i.e. the one with the lowest total weight) connecting any vertex with another vertex of the network. A naive solution for this problem consists of recomputing all possible paths until no further improvements can be achieved; this can be easily implemented within a concurrent programming environment, even if such an environment does not really support the notion of cooperating/competing agents. See [BCLM88] for one such solution.

But intelligent solutions in a concurrent context are instead more easily achieved if the programming environment has the capability to model the computation as the work of cooperating/competing agents.

3.1 An Intelligent Multiagent Solution

In this section, we illustrate a distributed version of the dynamic programming technique of saving intermediate results of the computation by two intelligent solutions for the shortest path problem.

The approach we follow in implementing both solutions is very different from the usual sequential implementations of dynamic programming algorithms, characterized as they are by a centralized scheduler which reproposes all the cached results at each different point in the search space; instead, we partition the search space into a set of points, each of which is associated with a decentralized agent with the task of finding the best result relatively to the given point. The cooperative/competitive work of all the agents will produce the final result.

We assume two different ways of representing nodes in a network: i.e. by associating them with either (*i*) the cost and the destination of their *outgoing* edges or (*ii*) the cost and the source of their *incoming* edges. As we shall see:

- One of the solutions described here implements *forward* search in the case of the "outgoing edges" representation, and implements *backward* search in the case of the "incoming edges" representation;

- Conversely, the other solution implements *backward* search in the case of the "outgoing edges" representation, and implements *forward* search in the case of the "incoming edges" representation.

Furthermore, the two solutions share a part of their behavioral definition. Thus, our approach is characterized by maximal reusability.

In the course of the computation, every agent offers some results coming from its own work to other agents; such results are used by the receiving agents to perform the task which is primarily assigned to them, i.e. finding their own "locally" best path; successful termination occurs once the locally best path has been found relatively to the target node (if we started working from the source node), or relatively to the source node (if we started working from the target node). Thus, interagent *cooperation* corresponds essentially to the fact that agents which are located at earlier stages in global search space of the problem communicate results to agents located at more advanced stages; as a result, the global computational work comes from the summation of the local computational work of all the agents.

However, there is also a complementary phenomenon of interagent *competition*: in fact, an agent may receive "offers" from different agents, and will have consequently to decide which one is the best. This ensures that the final solution is indeed the best one.

3.1.1 Encoding the Network

The network is encoded as a conjunction of *LO* agents, where every agent corresponds to a distinct node, and is characterized by 2 + n components, namely, the name of the node, a datum storing the number of outgoing/incoming edges, plus data corresponding to either the outgoing or the incoming edges (with their destination/origin vertex and associated cost weight). An encoding of the network where the representation of nodes uses outgoing edges is given in Fig. 2; the alternative representation, where nodes are associated with incoming edges, is displayed in Fig. 3.

3.1.2 The Basic Methods

Once a network is activated, and the agent nodes start computing their locally optimal paths, there are two kinds of data which are generated and consumed during the computation: data corresponding to candidates for best paths, and data corresponding to best paths. The first kind of data is encoded in terms of a predicate npath/3, and the other one in terms of a predicate bpath/3; the two predicates take exactly the same type of arguments, where

- The first argument corresponds to the name of the vertex where the path begins/ends;

- The second argument corresponds to the cost of the path (obtained as the summation of the costs of all the edges that are in it);

- The third argument corresponds to the sequence of vertices through which the path goes.

For instance,

$$bpath(h, 4, [h,k,t])$$

encodes the best path from vertex h to vertex t, while

$$bpath(e, 4, [s,c,e])$$

encodes the best path from vertex s to vertex e. As we shall see, the direction of the search (forward or backward) determines whether the first argument of a generated bpath or npath datum is the end or the start vertex of the associated path.

Depending on the chosen direction of search, the number of possible candidates that an agent node has to consider equals either the number of incoming edges or the number of outgoing edges. Such information can be stored in a counter, whose initial state corresponds to either one of the two arguments in the pair contained in the datum in_out.

The methods displayed in Fig. 4 for the selection of the best path have a straightforward interpretation: once the counter has been set to 1, then there is only one remaining npath, which becomes therefore the best path for the given node; otherwise, the agent node keeps carrying on the selection process by comparing candidates, eliminating those with higher costs, and decrementing the counter each time that a candidate is eliminated.

```
network @ outgoing <>-

    node(s) @ in_out(0,3) @ e(5,a) @ e(6,b) @ e(4,c) &

    node(a) @ in_out(1,2) @ e(2,d) @ e(5,e) &

    node(b) @ in_out(1,2) @ e(1,d) @ e(3,e) &

    node(c) @ in_out(1,2) @ e(4,e) @ e(1,f) &

    node(d) @ in_out(2,2) @ e(7,g) @ e(2,h) &

    node(e) @ in_out(3,2) @ e(1,h) @ e(3,i) &

    node(f) @ in_out(1,2) @ e(2,h) @ e(2,i) &

    node(g) @ in_out(1,2) @ e(4,j) @ e(2,k) &

    node(h) @ in_out(3,2) @ e(3,k) @ e(2,l) &

    node(i) @ in_out(2,2) @ e(4,l) @ e(3,m) &

    node(j) @ in_out(1,1) @ e(5,t) &

    node(k) @ in_out(2,1) @ e(1,t) &

    node(l) @ in_out(2,1) @ e(4,t) &

    node(m) @ in_out(1,1) @ e(2,t) &

    node(t) @ in_out(4,0).
```

Figure 2: Encoding of the network in Fig.1: nodes are associated with outgoing edges.

```
network @ incoming <>-

  node(s) @ in_out(3,0) &

  node(a) @ in_out(2,1) @ e(5,s) &

  node(b) @ in_out(2,1) @ e(6,s) &

  node(c) @ in_out(2,1) @ e(4,s) &

  node(d) @ in_out(2,2) @ e(1,b) @ e(2,a) &

  node(e) @ in_out(3,3) @ e(4,c) @ e(3,b) @ e(5,a) &

  node(f) @ in_out(2,1) @ e(1,c) &

  node(g) @ in_out(2,1) @ e(7,d) &

  node(h) @ in_out(2,3) @ e(2,f) @ e(1,e) @ e(2,d) &

  node(i) @ in_out(2,2) @ e(2,f) @ e(3,e) &

  node(j) @ in_out(1,1) @ e(4,g) &

  node(k) @ in_out(1,2) @ e(3,h) @ e(2,g) &

  node(l) @ in_out(1,2) @ e(4,i) @ e(2,h) &

  node(m) @ in_out(1,1) @ e(3,i) &

  node(t) @ in_out(0,4) @ e(2,m) @ e(4,l) @ e(1,k) @ e(5,j).
```

Figure 3: Encoding of the network in Fig.2: nodes are associated with incoming edges.

```
count(N) @ npath(V,C1,P1) @ npath(V,C2,P2) @ node(V) @

      {N > 1, DecrN is N-1, C1 =< C2}

            <>- count(DecrN) @ npath(V,C1,P1) @ node(V).


count(1) @ npath(V,C,P) @ node(V) <>- bpath(V,C,P) @ node(V).
```

Figure 4: The basic selection procedure

```
spread @ bpath(V,C,P) @ e(C1,V1) @

      {NewC is C+C1} @ ^npath(V1,NewC,P-V1)

      <>- spread @ bpath(V,C,P).
```

Figure 5: Spreading information

3.1.3 Spreading Information

The method displayed in Fig. 5 implements forward search if the encodings of the nodes are characterized by representations of the outgoing edges; symmetrically, it implements backward search if the encodings of the nodes are characterized by representations of the incoming edges. It is based on the following principle: a node which knows already about its local best path proposes a candidate path to a node to which it is connected via an edge, where the candidate's cost is obtained by summating the cost of the local best path with the cost of the connecting edge. Thus, information *spreads* from the node owning a link to the node at the other end of the link.

3.1.4 Collecting Information

The methods displayed in Sec. 6 work exactly in the opposite way, permitting backward search with node representations in terms of outgoing edges, and forward search with node representations in terms of incoming edges. They are based on the following principle: once an agent node has been able to determine its local best path, then it makes this information available to whoever can make use of it. The information will be indeed picked up, and exploited for further computations, by those agent nodes having a connecting edge to the offering node. Thus, an agent owning a link *collects* information coming from the node at the other end of the link.

```
collect @ node(V) @ bpath(V,C,P) @ ^bpath(V,C,P)

        <>- collect @ node(V).

collect @ bpath(V,C,P) @ e(C1,V) @ node(V1) @ {NewC is C+C1}

        <>- collect @ npath(V1,NewC,V1-P) @ node(V1).
```

Figure 6: Providing information to be collected by agents owning corresponding links

3.1.5 Getting Things Going

In order to get a network computing a path from one vertex to another, we must have a way to input the problem as an initialization of the activity of the network. Furthermore, we need to have a way of communicating an answer when one is found.

Now, consider the case of node representations in terms of outgoing edges. If information spreads from the source towards the target (forward search), the source node must be initialized to an empty optimal path of null length, while the target node must report the answer; things will go just the other way around if information is collected starting from the target while making progress towards the source (backward search). A symmetric situation characterizes the case of the representation in terms of incoming edges, with the role of target and source nodes inverted. The set of methods in Fig. 7 define the exact computational requirements for initialization and termination. Figure. 8 shows instead the set of bpath data generated in the course of finding the best path from vertex s to vertex t in the network displayed in the Fig .1, by doing backward search with the outgoing edges encoding of the network displayed in Fig. 2.

4 Summary

We have shown how dynamic programming solutions, which optimally solve search problems, can be easily implemented within a programming environment, like the one provided by the object-oriented concurrent language LO, where computation is naturally seen as the interaction coming from the cooperative/competitive work of multiple agents. This is not surprising, as the themes of cooperation and competition are intrinsic to dynamic programming itself, which admits sharing of optimal partial results among alternative search paths. By contrast, dynamic programming techniques are difficult to implement in traditional programming environments, which lack the adequate linguistic support for cooperative/competitive behavior.

For the sake of clarity, we have chosen a particularly simple example (finding the best path from one vertex to another in a network with weighted edges); however, other more complex problems have been tackled with the same methodology, like variations on the knapsack problem (a well-known problem from operations research), and the problem of optimally parsing context-free languages, which has been described in [AP91a].

```
spread(S,T,outgoing) <>-

        network @ outgoing @ source(S) @ target(T) @ spread.

collect(S,T,outgoing) <>-

        network @ outgoing @ source(S) @ target(T) @ collect.


spread(S,T,incoming) <>-

        network @ incoming @ source(T) @ target(S) @ collect.

collect(S,T,incoming) <>-

        network @ incoming @ source(T) @ target(S) @ spread.


collect @ in_out(_,N) <>- collect @ count(N).

spread @ in_out(N,_) <>- spread @ count(N).


collect @ target(T) @ node(T)

        <>- node(T) @ bpath(T,0,T) @ collect.

collect @ source(S) @ bpath(S,C,P) @ ^answer(C,P) <>- #t.


spread @ target(T) @ bpath(T,C,P) @ ^answer(C,P) <>- #t.

spread @ source(S) @ node(S)

        <>- node(S) @ bpath(S,0,S) @ spread.
```

Figure 7: Methods for initialization and termination

```
bpath(t,0,[t]), bpath(j,5,[j,t]), bpath(k,1,[k,t]),
bpath(l,4,[l,t]), bpath(m,2,[m,t]), bpath(g,3,[g,k,t]),
bpath(h,4,[m,t]), bpath(i,5,[i,m,t]), bpath(d,6,[d,h,k,t]),
bpath(e,5,[e,h,k,t]), bpath(f,6,[f,h,k,t]),
bpath(a,8,[a,d,h,k,t]), bpath(b,7,[b,d,h,k,t]),
bpath(c,7,[c,f,h,k,t]), bpath(s,11,[s,c,f,h,k,t]).
```

Figure 8: Generated path-encoding data

5 Future Work

In the immediate future, we plan to integrate all the different applications of distributed dynamic programming in a "dynamic programming" library, where basic search components are identified and then specialized towards specific tasks. We would like also to explore the possibility of different specializations interacting on complex tasks (i.e., tasks decomposable in simpler ones); for instance, the complex task of natural language understanding involves different subtasks (speech recognition, syntactic parsing, semantic disambiguation) where dynamic programming can be applied.

Another very promising line of research is that of exploiting object-oriented concurrent computing not just for natural implementations of optimal search techniques, but also for interfacing them with additional heuristics needed to cope with the challenge of the "real world" environments in which such techniques have to be used. Indeed, in an object-oriented concurrent/distributed context, an agent's behavior corresponding to the abstract view of a problem embodied in a dynamic programming algorithm can be modularly composed (via an adequate knowledge sharing mechanism) with behavior capable of dealing with initially unforeseen events arising in the context of the concrete environment where the given agent acts (e.g. interference on optimal production scheduling in the face of external events like unforecast shortage of the materials needed for the production); the agent should then opportunistically choose the most suitable behavior in the current state of affairs.

Acknowledgments

We thank the people of the Distributed Artificial Intelligence group at ECRC for helpful discussions on the subject of this paper. We are grateful to Gerard Comyn and Alexander Herold for their encouragement and support.

References

[And90]   J.M. Andreoli. Proposition pour une synthèse des paradigmes de la programmation logique et de la programmation par objets, 1990. Thèse d'Informatique de l'Université de Paris VI (Paris, France).

[AP90]   J.M. Andreoli and R. Pareschi. LO and behold! concurrent structured pro-
            cesses. In *Proc. of OOPSLA/ECOOP'90*, Ottawa, Canada, 1990.

[AP91a]   J.M. Andreoli and R. Pareschi. Communication as fair distribution of knowl-
            edge. In *Proc. of OOPSLA'91*, Phoenix, U.S.A., 1991.

[AP91b]   J.M. Andreoli and R. Pareschi. Linear objects: Logical processes with built-in
            inheritance. *New Generation Computing*, To appear, 1991. (Special issue,
            Selected papers from ICLP'90).

[BCLM88]   J.P. Banâtre, A. Coutant, and D. Le Metayer. A parallel machine for multi-
            set transformation and its programming style. *Future Generation Computer
            Systems*, 4, 1988.

[FJ90]   J. Ferber and E. Jacopin. The framework of eco problem solving. In *Proc. of
            MAAMAW'90*, 1990.

[Gir87]   J.Y. Girard. Linear logic. *Theoretical Computer Science*, 50, 1987.

Scheduling Predicates

Ciaran McHale[1], Bridget Walsh,
Seán Baker, Alexis Donnelly

Abstract

In this report, we present a powerful new synchronisation mechanism called *scheduling predicates*. These predicates—*there_are_no, there_exists* and *for_all*—allow the programmer to schedule the order of execution of operations based on relative arrival times, values of parameters, and built-in synchronisation counters.

Since many synchronisation problems are, in fact, scheduling problems, these facilitate much simpler and clearer solutions to such problems. We also show that this mechanism subsumes and unifies the existing declarative synchronisation mechanisms used in some object-oriented languages, and extends the number of problems for which a purely declarative approach is possible.

1 Introduction

There has been extensive research into developing powerful synchronisation mechanisms. The approaches taken generally fall into one of two categories.

Firstly are procedural mechanisms which combine synchronisation primitives with sequential flow control constructs and data structures, thus allowing the programmer to implement synchronisation policies by algorithmic means.

In contrast to these are declarative mechanisms in which the programmer simply specifies the synchronisation policy desired. An ideal declarative mechanism would have the desirable property that the specification of a synchronisation policy *is* its implementation. When the power of a declarative mechanism is sufficient for a particular policy, the solution is usually trivial.

However, declarative mechanisms are currently limited in their power in that they can only directly specify simple policies.

For more complex policies, the programmer must fall back to a procedural approach which, when implemented in the declarative notation, results in quite inelegant solutions. The use of *synchronisation procedures*[2] in Path Expressions [8] is a prime example of this; the Guide solution to the FIFO variant of the readers/writer problem [11] is another example of the need for synchronisation procedures when a declarative mechanism has insufficient power to express a synchronisation policy directly.

---

[1]Authors' address: Department of Computer Science, Trinity College, Dublin 2, Ireland.
Tel: +353-1-7021538   Email: {cjmchale,bwalsh,baker,donnelly}@cs.tcd.ie
[2]This term was coined by Bloom [6].

Our approach is to increase the power of declarative mechanisms so that they can easily solve a wider range of synchronisation policies: in particular, policies which *schedule* as well as *synchronise* requests. This report takes a step in this direction by presenting the concept of *scheduling predicates*. Rather than being just "yet another synchronisation mechanism" with its own strengths and weaknesses, *scheduling predicates* will be shown to unify several other synchronisation mechanisms. As such it is both an improvement on, and a generalisation of existing mechanisms.

1.1 Syntax Used in Report

The syntax used in this report (see Figure 1) should, for the most part, be self-explanatory. Comments are denoted by "//" and last until the end of the line. Macros are declared by use of the "#define" C preprocessor directive.

```
class <class_name> is
        <declaration of instance variables>
        <declaration of operations Op₁, Op₂, ... >
        entry guards
        Op₁: <a guard>;
        Op₂: <another guard>;
            ⋮
end <class_name>;
```

Figure 1: Syntax used in this report

The synchronisation constraints are expressed in the **entry guards** clause which appears after all of the class' operations. An **entry guard** is a boolean expression which must become true before a request to execute an operation on an object is permitted to continue. Several languages employ the concept of guards, in one form or another, in their synchronisation mechanisms: CSP [15], Synchronising Resources (SR) [4], Ada [1], Guide [10], Mediators [13] DRAGOON [12] and Predicate Path Expressions [2] are the best known examples. Scheduling predicates improve upon these previous mechanisms by having more expressively powerful guards.

1.2 Structure of Report

This report is structured as follows:

Section 2 presents a brief overview of the different object models which can be commonly found in concurrent object-oriented languages. Section 3 then discusses some existing declarative synchronisation mechanisms and their limitations. Section 4 introduces *scheduling predicates*, and an analysis of their power is presented in section 5. This analysis shows up a weakness of the mechanism which is discussed in section 6. Section 7 then shows how scheduling predicates subsume the mechanisms discussed in section 3. Section 8 discusses implementation and optimisation issues. Section 9 discusses the problem of synchronisation counter overflow. Finally, section 10 concludes the report and mentions some areas in which we intend to work in future.

2 Object Models

In some concurrent object-oriented languages (e.g., Guide [11]), objects are *passive* entities which reside in shared memory and may be accessed simultaneously by several processes. This model can support concurrency within an object.

In other systems, objects are deemed to be *active*: they have a thread of control which receives requests and schedules them for service. Some active object models (e.g., Hybrid [18] and Caromel [9]) have just a single thread within an object which both schedules and services requests. This object model does not support concurrency *within* objects, though usually some form of inter-object concurrency is supported.

Other active object models do support internal concurrency. For example, an object may have a thread of control which receives and schedules requests; and when a request may start execution, another thread is created to service it [17].

Most mechanisms have inherent limitations which makes then suitable for only one object model, and less suitable, or even totally unsuitable, for others. For example, Caromel's mechanism [9] provides good support for scheduling requests; however it provides no facilities to manage internal concurrency, thus limiting its usability to single-threaded, active objects. Conversely, the main strength of synchronisation counters [11, 12] is in managing internal concurrency rather than scheduling requests; so while they are suitable for passive object models, they would be of limited use in the single-threaded, active object model.

The mechanism presented in this paper does not have this limitation: since it provides good facilities to both manage internal concurrency and schedule pending requests, it is effective in both passive and active object models.[3] Being able to deal with synchronisation and scheduling in a uniform manner across different object models reduces the learning curve for programmers who must move between different environments, and it also promotes reuse of concurrent code.

3 Limitations of Existing Declarative Mechanisms

3.1 Synchronisation Counters

Synchronisation counters [3] feature heavily in declarative mechanisms such as the Guide and DRAGOON languages. These, automatically maintained, variables of an object count the total number of invocations for each operation of the object that have been *requested*, have *started* execution and have *terminated* execution etc. There are actually five counters for each operation on an object. These are:[4]

$req(Op)$: number of requests to execute operation Op.
$wait(Op)$: number of requests that are waiting to execute Op.
$start(Op)$: number of requests that have started executing Op.
$exec(Op)$: number of requests that are currently executing Op.

---

[3]The aspects of our mechanism which deal with internal concurrency of an object are, by definition, redundant in the single-threaded, active object model.

[4]These are the counter names used throughout this report. Unfortunately, there are no standard names for these counters; for example, both Guide and DRAGOON use different names.

$term(Op)$: number of requests that have terminated execution of Op.

Only three of these need to be stored since the following relationships hold:

$$wait(Op) = req(Op) - start(Op)$$
$$exec(Op) = start(Op) - term(Op)$$

Synchronisation counters may be used in guards. Although they have been used most extensively in languages which embody the passive object model, they could also be used in active object models. However, in the single-threaded, active object model the *exec* counter becomes redundant.

All of the synchronisation counters are initialised to zero and the compiler produces the necessary code to ensure that they are updated atomically. An example of their usage is given in Figure 2 which solves the bounded buffer problem. The reader is referred elsewhere [5, 10] for further examples illustrating the use of synchronisation counters.

> **entry guards**
> **#define** not_full = $term(\text{Put})$ - $term(\text{Get}) <$ size
> **#define** not_empty = $term(\text{Put})$ - $term(\text{Get}) > 0$
> Put: $exec(\text{Put}) = 0$ **and** not_full;
> Get: $exec(\text{Get}) = 0$ **and** not_empty;

Figure 2: Solution to the Bounded Buffer problem

Synchronisation counters have their limitations. In particular, they provide no way to *schedule* requests based on either request parameters or arrival time. Thus, though Guide and DRAGOON can easily solve the simpler variations of the readers/writer problem (such as readers' priority or writer's priority), synchronisation counters are of little assistance in solving the FIFO variant. The complexity of the Guide solution to this problem [11] clearly shows this limitation. Other scheduling problems, such as Shortest Job Next [7] and the Disk Head Scheduler [14] are probably impossible to solve with synchronisation counters alone.

3.2 Scheduling with the "By" Clause

A step towards providing scheduling support is the **by** clause as provided in Synchronising Resources (SR) [4]: this can be used to schedule requests based on one of their parameters. The **by** keyword is followed by an arithmetic expression whose value determines the order in which invocations are to be executed (minimum value first). Figure 3 shows (in the notation of this report) the **by** clause implementation of the Shortest Job Next Scheduler. The **by** clause is noteworthy in that it provides a declarative way to schedule requests based on their parameters. However, it has the following limitations:

1. Requests cannot be scheduled based on their relative arrival times.

2. Scheduling may only be easily performed based on a single parameter.[5]

---

[5]If scheduling based on two parameters is required then a **by** clause of the form

3. It may only be used to schedule requests for the same operation. Thus, for example, it could not be used to implement the FIFO variant of the readers/writer problem in which the scheduling of a *Write* request is dependent not only on other *Write* requests, but also on *Read* requests; and where scheduling of a *Read* request is dependent on *Write* requests.

The first limitation could be easily overcome by having the compiler implicitly associate an *arrival* time attribute with each request. If this were done then a FIFO scheduler could be implemented with "**by** *arrival*". The second limitation would be overcome if a list of expressions could follow the **by** keyword. For example, "**by** *len, arrival*" would implement a SJN scheduler with FIFO sub-ordering, i.e., if several requests have equal *len* parameters then they will be served in *arrival* order. However it is hard to imagine any variation of the **by** clause which could overcome the third limitation.

```
class Printer is
       Print(len: Integer, FileName: String ) is ...

       entry guards
       Print: exec(Print) = 0 by len;
End Printer;
```

Figure 3: Shortest Job Next

4   Scheduling Predicates

Consider the basic readers/writer problem. An English description of this synchronisation policy might be:

> *Read* may execute if there are currently no executions of *Write*.
>
> *Write* may execute if there are currently no executions of either *Read* or *Write*.

A solution to this using synchronisation counters is:

```
       entry guards
       Read: exec(Write) = 0;
       Write: exec(Read, Write) = 0;
```

Note that this solution closely mirrors the English description of the problem. This is an excellent example of the desirable "specification is the implementation" property of declarative mechanisms. Unfortunately, synchronisation counters provide little support to *schedule*, as opposed to just *synchronise*, requests. Thus, for many scheduling

---

by $param_1 * scale_1 + param_2$

where $scale_1$ is one higher than the maximum value of $param_2$. (This can obviously be extended to allow scheduling on any number of parameters.) Problems with this approach are (i) the meaning is not immediately obvious; and (ii) there must be a fixed upper bound on $param_2$.

problems, a solution using synchronisation counters bears little resemblance to the specification of the problem. As an example, consider the following English specification of the "Shortest Job Next" scheduler:

> *Print* may execute if (i) there are no current executions of *Print* and (ii) there are no requests waiting to execute *Print* which have a smaller *len* parameter.

Synchronisation counters can be used to implement part (i) of this policy but a more powerful mechanism is required to implement part (ii) directly. We now introduce the concept of *scheduling predicates* in which part (ii) is expressed as:

> *there_are_no*(p *waiting* Print: p.len < *my_req*.len)

In reading this notation, ":" denotes "such that". The variable p is used to iterate through all the requests waiting to execute *Print*, and *my_req* denotes the request for which the guard is being evaluated. Thus we can read the above as:

> There are no requests p waiting to execute *Print* such that the *len* parameter of p is less than my own *len* parameter.

Anding this scheduling predicate with "$exec(\text{Print}) = 0$" yields a complete entry guard for the SJN scheduler.

It is frequently desired to schedule access to an object based on the arrival time of requests rather than (or sometimes, as well as) request parameters. For example, one might wish to have a FIFO print queue. Scheduling predicates handle this by implicitly associating an *arrival* time attribute with each request. *Arrival* can be likened to a ticket machine in a tax office which gives a numbered ticket to each customer that arrives [19].

class Printer **is**
      Print(len: Integer; FileName: String) **is** ...

      entry guards
      Print: $exec(\text{Print}) = 0$ **and** *there_are_no*(p *waiting* Print:
                             p.len < *my_req*.len **or**
                             p.len = *my_req*.len **and** p.arrival < *my_req*.arrival);
end Printer;

Figure 4: Shortest Job Next with FIFO sub-ordering

Each customer has a different numbered ticket and this can be used to ensure that customers are served in order of their arrival.[6] To implement a FIFO printer queue, all that need be done is to replace *len* with *arrival* in the solution to the SJN scheduler discussed previously. Further changing of "<" to ">" would turn the FIFO scheduler

---

[6]The reader may be wondering if there is any relationship between *arrival* and the synchronisation counters. An implementation might maintain the relationship $arrival = \sum_{i=1}^{n} req(Op_i)$ where n is the number of synchronised operations of the object. However, an implementation is not *required* to maintain this relationship. For example, an implementation might use a high speed clock to note *arrival* times.

into a LIFO scheduler. The entry guard in Figure 4 specifies the SJN scheduler with FIFO sub-ordering.

So far, we have demonstrated two ways in which *there_are_no* is more powerful than SR's **by** clause: not only can requests be scheduled on several parameters, the relative *arrival* time of requests can also be taken into account.

Figure 5 (FIFO readers/writer) shows how interdependent scheduling of several operations may be handled just as easily. In this scheme a *Read* request may only be executed if there are no *Write* requests ahead of it. Similarly, a *Write* request may only start if there are no *Read* or *Write* requests ahead of it.

class ReadersWriter **is**
    Read: Element **is** ...
    Write(elem: Element) **is** ...

    entry guards
    Read: $exec(\text{Write}) = 0$ **and** *there_are_no*(w *waiting* Write:
                                    $w.arrival < my\_req.arrival$);
    Write: $exec(\text{Read}, \text{Write})^{7} = 0$ **and** *there_are_no*(rw *waiting* Read,Write:
                                    $rw.arrival < my\_req.arrival$);

end ReadersWriter;

Figure 5: Solution to the FIFO Readers/Writer problem

4.1 Other Scheduling Predicates

There_are_no is actually syntactic sugar for the more fundamental function *count*. *Count* returns an integer indicating how many outstanding requests satisfy *count*'s boolean condition. The following equality holds:

$$there\_are\_no(\text{var\_id } waiting \text{ operation\_id} : boolean \ expr)$$
$$\equiv count(\text{var\_id } waiting \text{ operation\_id} : boolean \ expr) = 0$$

The companion predicates *there_exists*, and *for_all* are also available to the programmer for which the following equalities hold:

$$there\_exists(\text{var\_id } waiting \text{ operation\_id} : boolean \ expr)$$
$$\equiv count(\text{var\_id } waiting \text{ operation\_id} : boolean \ expr) > 0$$

$$for\_all(\text{var\_id } waiting \text{ operation\_id} : boolean \ expr)$$
$$\equiv count(\text{var\_id } waiting \text{ operation\_id} : boolean \ expr) = wait(operation\_id)$$

As an example of the use of *for_all*, consider the following entry guard which implements the Shortest Job Next scheduling policy:

    Print: $exec(\text{Print}) = 0$ **and** *for_all*(p *waiting* Print: p.arrival $\geq my\_req$.arrival);

It is trivial to express the same scheduling policy using *there_are_no*: simply replace "$\geq$" with "$<$". This interchangeable nature of the scheduling predicates gives the programmer the freedom to express a desired scheduling policy with whichever predicate feels the most natural for the task.

---

[7]Note that the form $exec(A, B, \ldots, Z)$ is a shorthand for $exec(A) + exec(B) + \cdots + exec(Z)$.

4.2 Other Scheduling Verbs

All the examples of scheduling predicates so far have made use of the *waiting* "verb", which is related to the *wait* counter. The other counters also have related "verbs":[8] *requested*, *started*, *executing*[9] and *terminated*.

The *executing* verb can be shown to good effect in solving the Dining Philosophers problem. A philosopher may eat if there are no other philosophers eating with a fork which she herself needs. This condition can be restated as: a philosopher may *Eat* if there are no other philosophers already *Eat*ing to her left, to her right at or at the table position she wants to use. This is implemented directly, using the *executing* verb, in Figure 6. Note, however, that this solution does not guarantee against starvation of a philosopher by conspiracy on the part of the others to keep her blocked. The random eating and thinking times of philosphers would presumably rule this out, but if such a guarantee is required then this can be easily derived by employing the *waiting* verb and *arrival* in addition to *executing*.

```
class Table is
     Eat(pos: 0..4) is ...

     entry guards
     #define RightOf(k)      ((k + 1) mod 5)
     #define ShareForks(i, j)    ( RightOf(i) = j or i = j or RightOf(j) = i )
     Eat: there_are_no(p executing Eat: ShareForks(p.pos, my_req.pos));
end Table;
```

Figure 6: Solution to Dining Philosophers problem using the *executing* verb

4.2.1 Modification of Parameters in Operations

The introduction of scheduling verbs other than *waiting* raises an issue which needs to be resolved.

Many languages (e.g., C and Pascal) allow call-by-value parameters to be modified in the body of operations.[10] Consider the code in Figure 7; the entry guard references the i parameter of requests currently executing *Bar*. However, this parameter is modified in the body of *Bar* which raises the question of which value of i the entry guard should see: the *original* value of i (i.e., the value at the time the request was received), or its *current* value?

The semantics we have chosen is that entry guards always see the *original* value of parameters. This has several advantages over entry guards seeing the most up-to-date value:

- If entry guards saw the most up-to-date value of parameters then this would reduce the separation between the implementation of operations and the synchronisation over them, thus breaking one of Bloom's [6] modularity requirements.

---

[8]This relationship between synchronisation counters and scheduling predicate "verbs" is defined in Section 7.1.

[9]Like the *exec* counter, the *executing* verb is redundant in the single-threaded, active object model.

[10]Some other languages, such as Ada, do not allow this.

- Efficient implementation is likely to be easier since entry guards do not need to be continually re-evaluated if the body of an operation updates a parameter referenced in an entry guard.

```
class Foo is
     Bar(i: integer) is
     begin
          ...
          i := ... ;
          ...
     end Bar;

     entry guards
     Bar: there_are_no(p executing Bar: p.i = my_req.i);
end Foo;
```

Figure 7: Modification of parameters which appear in entry guards

4.2.2 Implementation Concerns of the Scheduling Verbs

It should be noted that, in general, it would be infeasible for an implementation to support the *requested*, *started* and *terminated* verbs since this would require maintaining information indefinitely and the amount of information to be maintained would grow indefinitely large. However, it is possible for an implementation to support the *waiting* and *executing* verbs, as we shall now discuss.

The "waiting" verb: In object models which provide only synchronous calls to objects, there is an upper limit on the number of pending requests (equal to the number of processes which the system supports). Similarly, in object models which support asynchronous calls, there are usually fixed size message buffers at either the client or server sides which limit the number of pending requests. Thus, in both synchronous and asynchronous systems, there is an upper limit on the number of pending requests and hence it is possible for an implementation to support the *waiting* verb.

The "executing" verb: An object operation may invoke itself recursively resulting in a single process *executing* the operation an unbounded number of times.[11] Thus there would appear to be no upper limit on the amount of information to store in order to support the *executing* verb. However, synchronised objects do not usually engage in deeply recursive invocations so, *in practice* there tends to be an upper limit on the amount of information which would need to be maintained.

---

[11]Subject, of course, to stack space limitations.

5 Evaluation of Power

Bloom [6] insists that an ideal synchronisation mechanism should exhibit several characteristics:

- A straightforward way to combine independent synchronisation constraints to construct more complex constraints. (Bloom calls this the *ease of use* requirement.)

- Separation of code to implement an object's operations from the code to provide synchronisation for the object. (This is a *modularity* requirement.)

The *ease of use* requirement is met by being able to combine constraints with the boolean operators **and, or, not** etc. This can be clearly seen in the solution to the Bounded Buffer (Figure 2) where the independent constraints "$exec(\text{Put}) = 0$" and "not_full" are combined without difficulty.

The **entry guards** clause separates synchronisation from the code implementing an object's operations; this meets the *modularity* requirement.

Bloom also lists six types of information which a synchronisation mechanism should have access to in order for it to have good expressive power. Most synchronisation mechanisms provide access to at least three of these types of information: (i) the operation requested, (ii) the synchronisation state of the object and (iii) history information. The power of scheduling predicates shows itself in not only providing access to the these types of information, but also in allowing the (iv) parameters and (v) relative *arrival* times of requests to be compared. Mediators [13] and Caromel [9] are two of the few other mechanisms which also provide this level of power.

Alas, scheduling predicates do not allow (vi) instance variables to be used *safely* in entry guards. This is a serious limitation since the solutions to many synchronisation and scheduling policies require access to these. The next section discusses this problem in more detail.

6 The Problem of Instance Variables

Synchronisation state (synchronisation counters and information about the set of pending requests etc.) is only updated under well defined circumstances: whenever an operation is *requested*, or has *started* or *terminated* execution. This makes it possible for the compiler to generate code which guarantees that:

1. Synchronisation state is updated atomically with respect to the evaluation of entry guards, i.e., guards may only be evaluated when synchronisation state is consistent

2. Entry guards will be re-evaluated whenever (relevant) synchronisation state has been modified

These two guarantees are necessary for a correct implementation.

The updating of instance variables is not as restrictive as that of synchronisation state. Instance variables may be updated by direct assignment, or indirectly through pointers or when passed as reference parameters. Thus, unlike synchronisation state, we can not easily predict when instance variables will be updated.

If instance variables are allowed to appear in entry guards then we need to provide the above two guarantees for instance variables as well as for synchronisation state, i.e., we need to guarantee that:

1. Entry guards may only be evaluated when instance variables, referenced in the guards, are in a consistent state

2. Entry guards will be re-evaluated whenever instance variables, referenced in the guards, have been modified

It is difficult to imagine how these guarantees could be met in an elegant manner. Although we have already done some research in this area, we have yet to find a construct which is totally suitable, and the problem remains open.

7 Unification of Concepts

This section discusses how scheduling predicates subsumes some other notable synchronisation mechanisms.

7.1 Synchronisation Counters

One can consider synchronisation counters to be a restricted form of scheduling predicates. The following equalities hold:

$$wait(Op) \equiv count(\text{var\_id } waiting\ Op : \textbf{True})$$
$$req(Op) \equiv count(\text{var\_id } requested\ Op : \textbf{True})$$
$$start(Op) \equiv count(\text{var\_id } started\ Op : \textbf{True})$$
$$exec(Op) \equiv count(\text{var\_id } executing\ Op : \textbf{True})$$
$$term(Op) \equiv count(\text{var\_id } terminated\ Op : \textbf{True})$$

The significance of this is that instead of having two complementary, but separate, mechanisms with which to solve synchronisation/scheduling problems, we now conceptually have a single generalised mechanism. Having a minimum of conceptual constructs makes it easier to reason about the behavior of a concurrent program.

7.2 The "By" Clause

Like synchronisation counters, the **by** clause is also a restricted form of scheduling predicates: "**by** *parameter*" is equivalent to:

$$there\_are\_no(\text{p } waiting\ Op: p.parameter < my\_req.parameter).$$

Expressions are just as easy to handle as single parameters. The more general form of the **by** clause is:

by $p_1, p_2, \ldots, p_n$

This maps into the following general scheduling predicate form:

$$there\_are\_no \left(\begin{array}{l} O \ waiting \ operation\_id : \\ \bigvee_{i=1}^{n} \left(\bigwedge_{j=1}^{i-1} O.p_j = my\_req.p_j \right) \ \textbf{and} \ O.p_i < my\_req.p_i \end{array} \right)$$

In the above formula $\bigvee$ denotes the combining of its terms with the boolean operator **or**; similarly $\bigwedge$ is used to denote **and**. In this generalised form, this formula looks unwieldy. For a concrete example of this with $n = 2$, the reader is referred back to the Shortest Job Next scheduler with FIFO sub-ordering, as shown in Figure 4.

7.3 Path Expressions

It has been shown elsewhere [16] that Predicate Path Expressions [2] can be implemented in terms of synchronisation counters. Since we have already shown in Section 7.1 that synchronisation counters are simply a restricted form of scheduling predicates, it follows that Predicate Path Expressions are also subsumed by scheduling predicates.

8 Efficient Implementation

This section deals with the efficient implementation of scheduling predicates. It is organised as follows:

Section 8.1 discusses some compiler optimisation techniques. These techniques are independent of any particular object model. Section 8.2 then gives a brief overview of some run-time optimisation techniques suitable for passive objects in shared memory.

8.1 Compile time Optimisation

8.1.1 Re-evaluation Matrices

One method to improve run-time efficiency is for the compiler to examine the entry guards and construct a re-evaluation matrix; this matrix informs the run-time when it is necessary to re-evaluate each guard. Without this, the run-time would have to re-evaluate all guards whenever an operation call is requested, started or terminated.[12] Recall the entry guards used in the solution of the Bounded Buffer problem:

> **entry guards**
> **#define** not_full = $term(\text{Put})$ - $term(\text{Get})$ < size
> **#define** not_empty = $term(\text{Put})$ - $term(\text{Get})$ > 0
> Put: $exec(\text{Put}) = 0$ **and** not_full;
> Get: $exec(\text{Get}) = 0$ **and** not_empty;

An initial re-evaluation matrix can be obtained by direct examination of these:[13]

---

[12]Guide, which uses synchronisation counters, only re-evaluates guards when an operation terminates. This can lead to process starvation [16] and deadlock [11].

[13]There is no need to have the counters *wait* and *exec* in the matrix since they are macros defined in terms of *req*, *start*, and *term*. Similarly, there is no need to have *arrival* in the matrix since this is updated whenever a *req* counter is incremented.

	$req(Put)$	start(Put)	$term(Put)$	req(Get)	start(Get)	$term$(Get)
Put		√	√			√
Get			√		√	√

Each operation has one row in the matrix, giving the set of synchronisation counters that, when changed, could make the operation's guard become true. Thus we note that if a call to the *Put* operation is blocked because its entry guard evaluates to false then the entry guard need only be re-evaluated when there is a change in one of the counters: $start(Put)$, $term(Put)$, or $term(Get)$.

An important optimisation is to remove some of the entries from the matrix, thereby avoiding more unnecessary re-evaluations. In the solution to the bounded buffer problem, the expression "$exec(Put) = 0$" leads to *Put*'s entry guard being re-evaluated when $start(Put)$ is updated. However, a pending *Put* request need not have its guard re-evaluated whenever $start(Put)$ is incremented since incrementing $start(Put)$ can only make $exec(Put)$ non-zero. Similarly, the entry guard of *Get* need not be re-evaluated when $start(Get)$ is updated. Taking this into account, the re-evaluation matrix can be reduced to:

	$req(Put)$	start(Put)	$term(Put)$	req(Get)	start(Get)	$term$(Get)
Put			√			√
Get			√			√

Three comments are in order about this optimisation on the matrix. Firstly, a similar optimisation can be applied to entry guards containing the expression "$wait(Put) = 0$". In this case, a request need not have its entry guard re-evaluated whenever $req(Put)$ is incremented, since this can only make $wait(Put)$ non-zero.

Secondly, this optimisation can only be applied where the constant 0 is used. For example, if the expression "$exec(Put) \leq 1$" was given then the entry guard *would* have to be re-evaluated when $start(Put)$ is incremented. Nevertheless, the optimisation is worthwhile because the constant 0 is so frequently used. In fact, all but one of the example programs in this report have expressions of the form "$exec(Op_i) = 0$" or "$wait(Op_i) = 0$".

Thirdly, this optimisation works on expressions of the more general form

$$exec(Op_1) + exec(Op_2) + \cdots + exec(Op_n) = 0$$

in which case $start(Op_{1..n})$ need not be marked in the re-evaluation matrix.

The re-evaluation matrix can also cater for entry guards containing scheduling predicates. An entry guard containing an expression of the form

there_are_no(p *waiting* Op_i: <boolean expression>)

needs to be re-evaluated whenever a change occurs to the set of pending Op_i requests, that is, whenever $req(Op_i)$ or $start(Op_i)$ are updated, indicating an addition to or removal from the set, respectively.

8.1.2 Transformations of Scheduling Predicates

Even allowing for these optimisations, it is likely that the evaluation of guards will
be expensive relative to the cost of using a less powerful synchronisation mechanism.
Therefore, an interesting research topic will be recognising that certain patterns of entry
guards specify particular synchronisation policies, and then generating code which will
implement these policies in a cheaper manner.[14]

For example, consider an object which has three synchronised operations: A, B and
C. The following entry guards specify that A and B execute in mutual exclusion of
each other, and that C executes in mutual exclusion of itself:

> **entry guards**
> A: *exec*(A, B) = 0;
> B: *exec*(A, B) = 0;
> C: *exec*(C) = 0;

If a compiler can recognise the semantics of these guards then it could transform them
into appropriate **P** and **V** operations on semaphores (one semaphore for A and B, and
another for C) surrounding the body of the operations.

Transformations may also be applied to guards with scheduling predicates. For
example, an intelligent compiler might recognise that the entry guard shown in Figure 4
(SJN with FIFO sub-ordering) queues requests based on the tuple (*len*, *arrival*) and
hence generate code to maintain an ordered linked list of requests.

If implemented, such transformations would offer the programmer the high-level
declarative power of scheduling predicates but with the efficiency of low-level procedural
mechanisms.

8.2 Optimisation for Passive Objects in Shared Memory

In a passive object model, objects are held in shared memory which may be accessed
by several processes simultaneously. In such a system there is a one-to-one mapping
between pending requests and blocked processes. It thus seems natural for each blocked
process to re-evaluate its own guard whenever a relevant (as determined by the re-
evaluation matrix) synchronisation counter has been updated.[15] However, this has the
disadvantage that if several processes need to re-evaluate their guards then many context
switches will take place.

A better approach would be for the process which updated the synchronisation
counter to re-evaluate the entry guards on behalf of the other blocked processes, and
only wake them up if they evaluate to true. This removes the possibility of a process
being woken up to re-evaluate its entry guard only to find that it is still false. Hence,
unnecessary context switches are avoided.

---

[14]Optimisation by transformation has been applied successfully in other contexts: e.g., tuple space
operations in Linda [20].

[15]In the current implementation of Guide, each process re-evaluates its own guard.

9 Synchronisation Counters Overflow

One problem with synchronisation counter based mechanisms is that, for long-lived objects, the counters will eventually overflow. A solution to this problem has yet to be found. This section briefly examines some ways in which the problem might be tackled.

Let us make the (unrealistic) assumption that in the next few years CPU speeds will increase dramatically but that their word size will remain at 32 bits. With this increase in speed, assume that we have a maximum invocation rate of 1 invocation on a given object every microsecond. At this rate, we can expect counter overflow in just over one hour.

One obvious way to alleviate the problem is to increase the size of the counters from 32 to, say, 64 bits. This results in counter overflow being postponed for approximately 500,000 years. If need be, 64 bit counters can be achieved on current machines, at a slight performance penalty, by performing multi-word arithmetic. When 64 bit CPUs appear in a few years, this extended lifetime will be gained for free.

Another obvious, but flawed, solution would be to reset all the synchronisation counters to 0 whenever the object is in a quiescent state. To see the flaw in this scheme, consider the bounded buffer (Figure 2). The number of elements currently in the buffer is given by the expression:

$$term(\text{Put}) - term(\text{Get})$$

This expression is used in the entry guards to determine if the buffer is empty or full. If the synchronisation counters were reset to zero then entry guards would lose count of the number of elements in the buffer and thus the buffer contents would be lost.

However, the idea of resetting counters does have potential. It might be possible to introduce a new language construct in which the programmer would specify conditions under which counters could be *safely* decremented. More ambitious would be for the compiler to determine these rules by itself, thus relieving the programmer of the responsibility.

Lastly, it is worth noting that if techniques are developed for optimisation by transformation (Section 8.1.2) then by eliminating synchronisation counters, the problem of their overflow disappears.

10 Conclusions and Future Work

This report has presented a new notation called *scheduling predicates*. Examples like the Shortest Job Next scheduler, Figure 4, and the FIFO readers/writer, Figure 5, exemplify their suitability as a *specification notation* for synchronisation/scheduling policies.

As well as being a specification notion, it is also feasible to implement scheduling predicates. The potential for optimisation, as discussed in Section 8, shows that their high expressive power need not result in slow execution speed.

An evaluation of power was given in Section 5; few other synchronisation mechanisms can claim a similar level of power, and of those that do, none are declarative. The main failing of scheduling predicates is that they cannot be used for policies which require access to the instance variables of an object.

We are currently investigating how scheduling predicates can be integrated with inheritance and also extended to allow instance variables. A prototype implementation is under way.

Acknowledgements

We would like to thank the other members of the research group whose constructive criticism has helped in the development of the synchronisation mechanism presented in this report. This research is partially funded by the ESPRIT Comandos project (numbers 834 and 2071).

References

[1] The Programming Language Ada Reference Manual. Published in: Lecture Notes in Computer Science, Vol 155, Springer-Verlag, 1983.

[2] Sten Andler. Predicate Path Expressions. In *Sixth Annual ACM Symposium on Principles of Programming Languages*, pages 226–236, San Antonio, Texas, 1979.

[3] Françoise André, Daniel Herman, and Jean-Pierre Verjus. *Synchronisation of Parallel Programs*. Studies in Computer Science. North Oxford Academic, 1985. Original French language edition (Synchronisation de Programmes Parallèles, Dunod) ©BORDAS 1983.

[4] Gregory R. Andrews. Synchronising Resources. *ACM Transactions on Programming Languages and Systems*, 3(4):405–430, October 1981.

[5] Colin Atkinson. *An Object-Oriented Language for Software Reuse and Distribution*. PhD thesis, Department of Computing, Imperial College of Science, Technology and Medicine, University of London, London SW7 2BZ, February 1990.

[6] Toby Bloom. Evaluating Synchronisation Mechanisms. In *Seventh International ACM Symposium on Operating System Principles*, pages 24–32, 1979.

[7] Per Brinch Hansen. Distributed Processes: A Concurrent Programming Concept. *Communications of the ACM*, 21(11):934–941, November 1978.

[8] R. H. Campbell and A. N. Habermann. The Specification Of Process Synchronisation by Path Expressions. In *Lecture Notes in Computer Science, No. 16*, pages 89–102. Springer Verlag, 1973.

[9] Denis Caromel. Concurrency: An Object-Oriented Approach. In Jean Bézivin, Bertrand Meyer, and Jean-Marc Nerson, editors, *TOOLS 2 (Technology of Object-Oriented Languages and Systems)*, pages 183–197. Angkor, 1990.

[10] D. Decouchant, S. Krakowiak, M. Meysembourg, M. Riveill, and X. Rousset de Pina. A Synchronisation Mechanism for Typed Objects in a Distributed System. Presented at the workshop on "Object-Based Concurrent Programming", OOPSLA '88, San Diego, September 1988. Abstract in *ACM Sigplan Notices*, 24(4):105–107, April 1989.

[11] D. Decouchant, P. le Dot, and M. Riveill. A Synchronisation Mechanism for an Object Oriented Distributed System. Bull-IMAG, Z. I. de Mayencin - 2, rue Vignate, 38610 Gières - France, February 1990.

[12] Stefano Genolini, Andrea Di Maio, Cinzia Cardigno, Stephen Goldsack, and Colin Atkinson. Specifying Synchronisation Constraints in a Concurrent Object-Oriented Language. In *Technology of O-O Languages and Systems (TOOLS '89)*.

[13] J. E. Grass and R. H. Campbell. Mediators: A Synchronisation Mechanism. In *Proceedings of the Conference on Distributed Computer Systems*, pages 468–477. IEEE, September 1986.

[14] C.A.R. Hoare. Monitors: An Operating System Structuring Concept. *Communications of the ACM*, 17(10):549–557, October 1974.

[15] C.A.R. Hoare. Communicating Sequential Processes. *Communications of the ACM*, 21(8):666–677, August 1978.

[16] Ciaran McHale. Pasm: A Language for Teaching Concurrency. B.A. project report, Department of Computer Science, Trinity College, Dublin 2, Ireland, April 1989.

[17] Christian Neusius. Synchronising Actions. In Pierre America, editor, *ECOOP '91*, pages 118–132, Geneva, Switzerland, July 1991. Springer-Verlag. Available as Volume 512 of *Lecture Notes in Computer Science*.

[18] O. M. Nierstrasz. Active Objects in Hybrid. In Norman Meyrowitz, editor, *OOPSLA '87 Proceedings*. ACM. Special issue of *ACM SIGPLAN Notices*, 22(12):243–253.

[19] David P. Reed and Rajendra K. Kanodia. Synchronisation with Eventcounts and Sequencers. *Communications of the ACM*, 22(2):115–123, February 1979.

[20] Steven Ericsson Zenith. Linda coordination language: subsystem kernel architecture (on transputers). Research Report YALEU/DCS/RR-794, Yale University, Departmemt of Computer Science, New Haven, Connecticut. USA., 29 May 1990.

A Concurrency Control Mechanism for C++ Objects*

Hayssam Saleh
Philippe Gautron

Rank Xerox France & Université Paris VI – LITP

4 place Jussieu, 75252 PARIS CEDEX 05, France

[saleh,gautron]@rxf.ibp.fr

Abstract

This paper discusses the integration of a concurrency control mechanism in class-based languages. First, activity control issues are isolated and different object-oriented languages supporting concurrency are studied. We observe that they generally fail to integrate concurrency without interference with other language behaviors. Then, we present a model of concurrency control for C++ objects, based on a concept called *conditional wait*. The support is split between an extension to the language and a code server. The language extension is discussed in regard to inheritance and component reusability. An implementation on a multiprocessor architecture is outlined.

1 Introduction

Object-oriented methodology claims that the object-oriented approach to application design closely matches our conception of concrete world entities. But real world entities often interact and thus will be better expressed with an object-oriented language providing programming support for concurrency.

This paper focuses on the integration of concurrency in class-based languages. A few object-oriented languages integrate concurrency but generally fail to provide a solution that does not interfere with other language behaviors. Our goal is to implement a concurrency control mechanism for C++ objects orthogonal to other language properties, such as encapsulation, inheritance and component reusability. More precisely, our motivation is to address the following specific issues:

- It should be possible to design parallel object oriented applications by reusing sequential components as such. As counter-example, ACT++ [Kafura and Lee 89] and Rosette [Tomlinson and Singh 89] supply a concurrency control mechanism requiring to re-write existing library components, thus restricting code reusability.

---

*This work is partially supported by the European Community under ECC "Parallel Computing Action".

- Concurrency control model should not have to interfere with other language mechanisms. As counter-example, Guide [Decouchant and *al* 89] synchronization constraints interfere with inheritance, thus restricting language support.

- It should be possible to parameterize the concurrency control mechanism with informations included in incoming messages. As counter-example, in an extension to Eiffel [Caromel 89] and in the family of the POOL languages [America 87][America 90], synchronization constraints can only be expressed according to the internal state of the object. Methods arguments cannot be parameters of constraints, thus restricting message acceptance policy.

This paper presents an extension of C++ to support concurrent executions of methods. In our model, synchronization constraints may be attached to each method of a class. The language extension concerns *delay declarations*, based on the concept of *conditional wait*. We show that in a standard object-oriented environment, with inheritance and parameterized types, asynchronous procedure calls and futures can be implemented as components of class library. Finally, an implementation on a multi-processor architecture is outlined.

The paper is organized as follows. The second section discusses activity control. The third section studies concurrency control in class-based languages. The fourth section presents our model. The fifth section introduces the library support. The sixth section outlines the implementation.

Our examples are presented with a C++ syntax or with the appropriate syntax when referred to a particular language.

2 Concurrency and Activity Control

A concurrent object interface can be interpreted as a set of corrolated operations with only a subset available for execution at a given time. In a sequential environment, the sequence of method[1] calls is under the programmer control. In a parallel environment, an object may be accessed by different concurrent activities, which may send arbitrary messages at arbitrary times. In this context, simple sequential control becomes inadequate. Should the object be not shared, asynchronous messages might be desenquenced. Thus, a realistic programming approach is, instead of relying on programmer control, to consider an object as a *code server* which will accept or delay execution of methods according to its internal state and different parameters.

On the one hand, [Andrews and Schneider 83] identifies two types of synchronization constraints in the context of shared objects: mutual exclusion of execution and synchronization conditions. Mutual exclusion ensures that a set of statements will execute as an indivisible operation. Synchronization conditions control the order in which operations are executed.

On the other hand, [Liskov and *al* 86] identifies two common situations where activity management must rely on a synchronization mechanism:

---

[1]A method is a member function in the C++ terminology and a routine in the Eiffel terminology.

- local delay: a server cannot spontaneously serve a client request because some *local* resource is not available. For example, a get request cannot be satisfied whilst a buffer is empty. The request must be delayed and a new request may be accepted.

  According to [Liskov and *al* 86], a synchonization mechanism has to satisfy the following points to cope with local delays:

  1. the code server must be able to (1) identify a request by the name of the method, and, (2) access to the arguments of methods.
  2. messages must be serialized.
  3. object internal state must be accessible.

- remote delay: a server cannot spontaneously serve a client request because some *remote* resource is not available. For example, consider the following situation:

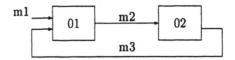

An object 01 processes a message m1 and sends a message m2 to an object 02. Then, the execution of m1 blocks, waiting for 02's reply while 02 sends a message m3 to 01, waiting for 01's reply. To avoid a deadlock, the execution of m1 must not prevent the execution of m3.

[Liskov and *al* 86] notices that most languages fail to cope with remote delays because (1) they only support synchronous communications, and, (2) they do not support arbitrary number of activities within an object. Solving remote delay issues requires to support asynchronous communications and, possibly, futures.

3   Concurrency Control in Class-Based Languages

This section examines four approaches to concurrency control through their solutions in different class-based languages. It also discusses the integration of concurrency with regard to object-oriented techniques, such as encapsulation, inheritance and code reusability. An exhaustive discussion on concurrency issues in object oriented languages may be found in [Papathomas 90].

The four approaches we study are:

- a delay queue attached to a method (Hybrid).

- counters managed by the compiler and attached to each method (Guide).

- instead of distributing concurrency control among methods, a unique method devoted to synchronization management (POOL and Eiffel).

- objects seen as sets of states. Each state accepts a subset of the object interface (ACT++).

Two standard examples, a queue with a fixed size and a vector of queues, will serve as test examples for our case studies. A possible C++ interface for these two classes looks like this:[2]

```
// Item is an arbitrary user-defined type

    class FixedQueue {
        public:
            FixedQueue();                  // class constructor
            virtual void putback (Item);   // inserts item
            virtual void getfront (Item&); // gets item (by reference)
            virtual bool empty();
            virtual bool full();
    };

    class VectorQueue {
        public:
            VectorQueue (int nbqueue);     // class constructor
            virtual void putback (int qnum, Item);
                                           // inserts item in queue qnum
            virtual void getfront (int qnum, Item&);
                                           // gets item from queue qnum
            virtual bool empty(int qnum);
            virtual bool full(int qnum);
    };
```

3.1 Delay Queues

Hybrid [Nierstraz 87] objects are active entities. A queue, handling delayed executions, is attached to a method. The queue may be in one of two states: open or close. Incoming messages are registered in the corresponding queues, according to the method name. Only methods associated with an opened queue may execute, opening or closing then other queues. The getfront and putback methods of the class FixedQueue can be outlined as follows:

```
    getfront: ->Item; uses notEmpty;
    {
      # first get an item
        ...

        if (empty) {      # refuse all subsequent getfront
            notEmpty.close;
        }
        notFull.open;     # an item has been extracted, a put may be accepted
```

---

[2]In a standard C++ *declaration*, such as void m (aType aVariable), the name of the variable behaves like a comment and is ignored by the parser.

```
}

putback: Item->; uses notFull;
{
# first insert an item
   ...

   if (full){        # refuse all subsequent putback
      notFull.close;
   }
   notEmpty.open;
}
```

One can reproach Hybrid with the following points:

- message acceptance cannot be based on the arguments of the called method.

- inheritance and queue management are not orthogonal. If a method of a base class needs to use a queue attached to a method of a derived class, the programmer may have to rewrite the base class method.

- sequential components cannot be reused as such since synchronization rules are described *within* the method body. Indeed, deriving a concurrent class from a sequential one leads at least to redefine the methods involved in the management of concurrent accesses.

3.2   Synchronization Counters

Guide [Decouchant and *al* 89] synchronization constraints are expressed with activation conditions. A boolean activation condition is associated to each method, and a method remains blocked until its activation condition be satisfied. Activation conditions can be expressed with instance variables of the receiver, arguments of the calling method, name of methods and a set of predefined methods. Each method owns a synchronization counter [Robert and Verjus 77] and the following informations are available from the counter interface:

- number of **started** invocations (already executed or under execution).

- number of **completed** executions.

- number of **current** executions.

- number of **pending** invocations.

The synchronization constraint for the **putback** method of the class **FixedQueue** might be expressed as follows:

```
completed(putback) - completed(getfront) < maxitems and current(putback) = 0;
```

This expression means that the difference between the number of inserted elements and the number of extracted elements must be inferior to the size of the queue and that no putback can execute.

This approach correctly fits local delay requirements. Remote delays may be partly handled separately since the language supports intra-object concurrency and concurrent execution of a set of statements (cobegin/coend sections).

However, this technique interferes with inheritance and restricts synchronization code reusability. Indeed, defining a method in a derived class may invalidate synchronization constraints defined in a base class. Similarly, adding a member in a base class may lead to re-write synchronization constraints in a derived class. Another flaw is that message acceptance cannot be based on arguments of an active method.

3.3 Centralized Concurrency Control

The two previous approaches support the definition of separated concurrency constraints for each method. Conversely, POOL-T [America 87], POOL-I [America 90] and a concurrent extension to Eiffel [Caromel 89] centralizes concurrency control around one method. For example, parallelizing the class FixedQueue in Eiffel requires to inherit from the library class Process and to override the Live method as follows:

```
Live is -- Process object script
    do
        until i_am_alone  -- declared in Process class
        loop
            if not full then Serve putback end;
            if not empty then Serve getfront end;
        end  -- loop
    end; -- Live
```

Sequential library components can be reused for the design of concurrent classes. However, this approach suffers from the following problems:

- synchronization constraints cannot be parameterized with methods arguments.

- only one method at once can be executed within an object (no intra-object concurrency).

- the Live method must be redefined whenever an additional synchronization constraint is declared in a derived class.

3.4 Behavior Abstraction

ACT++ [Kafura and Lee 89] is an extension to C++ where concurrent objects are designed as a set of states. An object can be only in one state at once and the execution of a method may change the state. Each state describes the set of methods that may execute under this state. A declaration of the class FixedQueue can be outlined as follows:

```
class FixedQueue : ACTOR {
    behavior:           // C++ extension
        empty_queue = { putback };
        full_queue  = { getfront };
        partial_queue = { putback, getfront };

    public:
        virtual void putback(Item& val);
        ...               // other methods
};
```

The putback method can be defined as follows:

```
void FixedQueue::putback (Item& value){
    ...                                    // insert value

    if (full()) become full_queue;    // C++ extension
    else become partial_queue;
}
```

States are inherited and, states may be redefined in a derived class without a method needing a redefinition.

Drawbacks of this approach are: (1) non-reusability of sequential components, (2) become expressions do not allow usual call/return synchronous sequences of C++, and, (3) synchronization states cannot be parameterized with methods arguments.

3.5 Summary

Different techniques to integrate a concurrency control mechanism in class-based object oriented languages have been studied: synchronization counters, boolean conditions similar to the technique pioneered by [Per Brinch Hansen 78] and sets of enabled operations.

On one side, when the synchronization mechanism fits well with concurrency requirements, its implementation interferes with the usual object-oriented techniques. On the other hand, when the object-oriented behaviors are respected, the proposed synchronization mechanism does not allow to deal with concurrency issues raised by local and/or remote delays. In the following section, we present a synchronization mechanism, based on boolean conditions and orthogonal to the object-oriented techniques as supported by C++.

4 Our Model

This section describes a concurrency control mechanism for C++ objects.

The following points were of particular concern during the development of our model:

- reuse of sequential components
- orthogonality between concurrency and inheritance

- intra-object concurrency

- simple priority mechanism

A *conditional wait* associated to a method conditions its execution. Conditional waits are boolean C++ expressions evaluated when the method is called. Execution is *delayed,* and another request processed, when the conditional expression evaluates to true, that is to say when its evaluation returns a value different from zero.

The keyword `delay` has been added to the C++ grammar, both as access specifier and to declare conditions of synchronization. The following example might be a concurrent version of the class `FixedQueue` described in section 3:

```
class ConQueue : public FixedQueue {
    delay:                              // access specifier
        full()  delay putback (Item);   // declaration
        empty() delay getfront (Item&); // declaration
};
```

By default, methods are *mutually exclusive*: their execution obeys a sequential scheme. In the example above, `putback` and `getfront` will *not* simultaneously execute on the same object, even if both are ready to execute.

The next paragraphs discuss our grammar extension in relation to (1) C++ semantics, and, (2) its ability to support concurrency. Other extensions are introduced when appropriate.

4.1 An Extension to C++

A `delay` access specifier specifies the synchronization rules for `delay` declarations following it until another C++ access specifier (`private`, `public`, `protected`, or `delay`) is encountered. In accordance with C++ semantics, any number of `delay` specifiers is allowed and no particular specifier order is required.

A simple `delay` declaration has the form:

```
wait () delay m();
```

and must be read: "the execution of the method m will be delayed if the conditional wait expression `wait` is evaluated to true".

Both `wait` and `m` must be declared otherwise as standard methods of the current class or of a base class. Access rules are ignored under a `delay` specifier. They are checked by the compiler, according to their original declaration.

In a `delay` declaration, methods are named with their signature. Signatures must be strictly identical to their original declarations. The `const` qualifier is part of the signature,[3] the return type is not.

---

[3]The following declarations:
```
int f();
int f() const;
```
are considered two different declarations.

C++ `const` methods may apply to `const` and non-`const` objects, whereas non-`const` methods may only apply to non-`const` objects.

4.2 Concurrency and Inheritance

Like declarations of methods, delay declarations are inherited or may be overridden.

In the following declarations, the class AfirstConQueue derives from the class ConQueue described in section 4:

```
class AfirstConQueue : public ConQueue {
    public:
            void putfront(Item);
            void getback(Item&);
};
```

In this example, putfront and getback are overriden. The delay declarations are inherited and will apply to these methods. Overriden methods with a same name but different signatures are considered different methods.

In the following declaration, a class AnotherConQueue derives from the same class ConQueue:

```
class AnotherConQueue : public ConQueue {
    public:
            bool full();              // overrides the base class function
    delay:
            full() delay putback(Item);  // optional
};
```

In this example, the full method, previously defined in ConQueue, is overriden in AnotherConQueue and will be the conditional wait associated to putback when this method is applied to objects of this latter class. In this particular case, the delay declaration is optional since it already appears in the base class.

Additional conditional waits may be added to previous declarations. For example:

```
class YetAnotherConQueue : public ConQueue {
    private:
            bool notReady ();
    delay:
            notReady() delay putback(Item);
};
```

In this example, the execution of putback will be delayed as long as *one* of these conditional waits (full *or* notReady) is true. In that sense, delay declarations behave like pre-conditions as defined, for example, in Eiffel (see section 4.6).

These different examples demonstrate that concurrency and inheritance can be orthogonal properties. The rules for synchronization are attuned to the C++ rules for access and inheritance. Method and synchronization redefinitions are limited to their respective strict need since there is a clear separation between the delay declarations and the method definitions.

4.3   Parameterizing Synchronization

In some occasions, a conditional wait as such may be a too strong condition, delaying execution needlessly. For example, when considering a vector of queues, a conditional wait full does not concern the queues as a whole, but can address only one queue. In our model, the synchronization rules may be parameterized with the arguments of the invoked method.

The class ConVectorQueue below might be the concurrent version of the class VectorQueue defined in section 3:

```
class ConVectorQueue : public VectorQueue {
    delay:
        empty (int num) delay getfront (num, Item&);
        full (int num)  delay putback (num, Item&);
};
```

In this example, empty and full are conditional waits associated to the queue of index num. Getback or putfront may execute if their conditional wait applied to the corresponding queue allows it.

Type-checking is a necessary support to distinguish between a variable name and a type name. Typing with an exact match is required: for example, the first argument in getfront's signature must be of type int.

Support for parameterized delay declaration allows a better approach to local delay issues, particularly when accessing to a local resource is parameterized by the arguments of a method.

4.4   Intra-Object Concurrency

Mutual exclusion of execution is the default. Remote delay issues may require intra-object concurrency to avoid potential deadlocks.

The declaration of constant methods is a first way to permit safe concurrent execution within a same object. For example, the consultation of the first element of a queue is a non-destructible access, and might be declared as follows:

```
class ConQueue : public Queue {
    public:
        void consult (Item&) const;    // does not modify object data
    delay:
        empty() delay consult (Item&) const;
};
```

In this example, the consult method can execute simultaneously with other const methods applied to the same object.

In addition, our model supports a particular syntax for concurrent execution of non-constant methods. For example:

```
class ConVectorQueue : public VectorQueue {
    private:
        sameBuffer (int buf1, int buf2) { return buf1 == buf2; }
    delay:
        sameBuffer (int b1, int b2) delay putfront(b1,Item&),
                                          putfront(b2, Item&);
};
```

In this example, the `delay` declaration means that two `putfront` methods can execute concurrently when called for the same object if they do not apply to the same buffer.

4.5 Controlling Activity Priorities

When concurrent execution occurs, the scheduling is based on the following strategy: FIFO mode, priorities. Priorities are static declarations to arrange the activities of a same object.

In the example of a producer and a consumer sharing a same queue, one can favour the producer activity. In our model, such a declaration looks like this:

```
class SharedQueue : public Queue {
    delay:
        putback > getfront;
};
```

In the current version, the priority mechanism is fairly simple. Priorities obey a partial order. A method priority may merely be inferior, superior or equivalent (the default) to another method priority. Equivalent C++ symbols are used. The number of queues can be known at compile-time, and the scheduler only needs to manage the appropriate number of queues. Any ambiguity entails a compiler error. Priorities are inherited.

Should experience show this model insufficient then a more complex mechanism could be implemented.

4.6 Conclusion

The concurrency control mechanism we have presented is based on the concept of conditional waits. C++ inheritance and strong type-checking are suitable supports to express a clean and safe interface to concurrency, although an extension to the language is needed to break its sequential nature.

Conditional waits look like pre-conditions. Whereas pre-conditions check object integrity, conditional waits organize object activity from arbitrary access. Moreover, conditional waits are dynamic attributes (they are functions which may be overridden) while pre-conditions (as defined in Eiffel) are static attributes.

5 Library Support

Library support must be distinguished from language support. A library relies on language support to offer safe but optional components through an interface. A language support is required when compile-time information is needed or when duplication of error-prone code can be avoided. C++ does not generate run-time information[4]

The concurrency model we have presented in section 4 relies on compile-time parsing and type-checking and, thus, justifies to extend the language.

This section introduces additional programming supports, asynchronous procedure calls and futures, implemented as generic components of class library.

5.1   Asynchronous Procedure Call

In C++ as in standard object-oriented languages, objects are passive and activated by synchronous procedure calls. Our language extension supports active objects and asynchronous calls. We supply a library class to interface asynchronous calls. Genericity is achieved by the use of parameterized types, *templates* in the C++ terminology.[5]

Public declaration of the class AsynchronousCall looks like this:

```
template <class T> class AsynchronousCall {
    public:
        AsynchronousCall (T*);        // class constructor
        T* operator -> ();            // overloads access operator
};
```

Overloading the class member access operator allows a procedure call to appear like a synchronous call but to behave like an asynchronous call. For example:

```
ConQueue *aConQueue = new ConQueue; // instantiates a concurrent queue

AsynchronousCall<ConQueue> asyncQueue(aConQueue);
    // (1) instantiates a new class type: AsynchronousCall<ConQueue>
    // (2) instantiates this class:  asyncQueue
    // (3) initializes the instance with aConQueue

Item item;                        // arbitrary item
aConQueue->putback(item);         // synchronous call
asyncQueue->putback(item);        // asynchronous call
```

5.2   Future

A support for asynchronous calls is necessary to cope with remote delay issues. The result of an asynchronous call is not generally immediately available after the call. Results must be encapsulated in *futures*, sometimes called *early replies*. In our library, futures are implemented as parameterized types, declared as follows:

```
template <class T>  class Future {
    public:
```

---

[4]Introduction of run-type information in C++ is discussed in [Lenkov and al 91] and [Interrante and Linton 90].

[5]Templates are standard C++ although any compiler implementation is not yet available. Nevertheless, different macro preprocessing simulations[Fontana and al 90], including ours, are available.

```
    Future ();                      // class constructor

    void operator = (T&);           // to assign a value to the future
    operator T();                   // to coerce the result

    bool ready();                   // true if value ready
    bool waiting();                 // true if value not assigned

delay:
    waiting() delay operator T();   // delay until result available
};
```

Futures may be combined with the management of a concurrent queue to handle the result of an asynchronous call. For example:

```
class AsynchronousQueue : public ConQueue {
    public:
        getfront (Future<Item>&);   // result of asynchronous call
    delay:
        empty() delay getfront (Future<Item>&);
};
```

The getfront method is there overriden and will automatically handle the result of an asynchronous call in a future:

```
// allocation of resources
    AsynchronousQueue *aQueue = new AsynchronousQueue;
    AsynchronousCall<AsynchronousQueue> asyncQueue(aQueue);
    Future<Item> result;

// asynchronous call
    asyncQueue->getfront (result);

// boolean tests on result are here possible
    ...

// blocking call of the coercion operator to wait for the result
    Item it = result;
```

Call of the coercion operator entails a "wait by necessity". As expressed in the delay declaration of the class Future, the underlying activity will be delayed until the result be available.

6   Outline of the Implementation

A first version of our model has been implemented on a distributed memory multiprocessor machine with 16 transputers. The target machine is a T.Node running the Helios[6] [Perihelion 89] operating system. Our design is not specific to Helios but we rely on the

---

[6]Helios is a trademark of Perihelion Software Ltd.

underlying system to guarantee reliable inter-processor communications. Helios is of particular interest for our implementation because it supplies a C library to efficiently deal with message passing. The machine architecture was designed to support efficient management of concurrent processes (single sequential flows of control in Occam terminology) on each transputer. Our implementation of intra-object concurrency relies naturally on this facility.

Our implementation is split into two parts: extra code generated by the compiler when `delay` declarations are parsed and a run-time library for transputer process management. Parsing convert passive objects into active objects behaving like code servers. User's methods are renamed and the procedure calls redirected to the code server. The code server is then responsible for execution or delay of the original calls. Inline and virtual methods are generated when possible and appropriate.

Porting our implementation should require to interface the generated code to an underlying task system.

7 Conclusion

This paper discusses concurrency control issues. Different existing concurrent object-oriented languages are analyzed. A model for C++ concurrent objects is presented. An additional library supplying generic components, such as asynchronous calls and early replies, is introduced. This model allows to reuse sequential classes, to parameterize and inherit synchronization conditions, to specify intra-object concurrency and to arrange activity priorities. Although implemented as extension to C++, it is our belief that this model could be suitable to any class-based typed language.

We believe our model suitable for applications with a high degree of parallelism. For example, transputer-based architectures were designed to support process creation and scheduling in a same way than it is usually done with procedure calling. Resource availability is the (current) limitation. But we conjecture that the next generation of parallel architecture will make large memory available and that they will include virtual memory management.

A distributed memory multi-processor architecture requires a support for *both* concurrent and distributed programming. In a complementary work, we have implemented a distributed object model [Saleh and Gautron 91] to cope with issues relative to remote pointers, object migration and persistence [Shapiro 89a]. Our ultimate goal is to provide a system platform suitable for programming active objects on parallel machines. [Gautron and *al* 92] summarizes our first experience under the European Community PCA project.

Acknowledgments

The authors thank Mamoun Filali and the anonymous referees for their helpful comments on earlier drafts of this paper.

References

[America 87] Pierre America, Inheritance and Subtyping in a Parallel Object-Oriented Language. In *ECOOP'87*, Paris (France), June 1987.

[America 90] Pierre America, A Parallel Object-Oriented Language with Inheritance and Subtyping. In *OOPSLA'90*, Ottawa (Canada), October 1990.

[Andrews and Schneider 83] Gregory R. Andrews and Fred B. Schneider. Concepts and Notations for Concurrent Programming. In *ACM Computing Surveys*, Volume 15, Number 1, March 1983.

[Caromel 89] Denis Caromel. A General Model for Concurrent and Distributed Object Oriented Programming. In *Proceedings of the ACM SIGPLAN Workshop on Object-Based Concurrent Programming*, Volume 24, number 4, April 1989, San Diego (USA).

[Decouchant and al 89] D. Decouchant, S. Krakowiak, M. Meysembourg, M. Riveill, X. Rousset de Pina, A Synchronization Mechanism for Typed Objects in a Distributed System. In *Proceedings of the ACM SIGPLAN Workshop on Object-Based Concurrent Programming*, Volume 24, number 4, April 1989, San Diego (USA).

[Ellis and Stroustrup 90] Margaret A.Ellis and Bjarne Stroustrup. The Annotated C++ Reference Manual. *Addison Wesley*, 1990.

[Fontana and al 90] Mary Fontana, LaMott Oren, Martin Neath. A Portable Implementation of Parameterized Templates Using A Sophisticated C++ Macro Facility, *EARLY DRAFT*, Texas Instruments Incorporated, Dallas (USA), 1990.

[Gautron and al 92] P. Gautron. J.P. Briot, H. Saleh, L. Lescaudron, S. Lemarié. Development of an Environment for Specification and Execution of Active Objects on Parallel Machines. Submitted to *European Workshop on Parallel Computing (EWPC'92)*, Barcelone (Spain), March 1992.

[Interrante and Linton 90] John A. Interrante, Marc A. Linton. Runtime Access to Type Information in C++. In *Usenix C++'90*, San Francisco (USA), April 1990.

[Kafura and Lee 89] Dennis G.Kafura and Keung Hae Lee. Inheritance in Actor Based Concurrent Object Oriented Languages. In *ECOOP'89*, Nottingham (GB), July 1989.

[Lenkov and al 91] Dmitry Lenkov, Michey Metha, Shankar Unni. Type Identification in C++. In *Usenix C++'91*, Washington (USA), April 1991.

[Liskov and al 86] Barbara Liskov, Maurice Herlihy, Lucy Gilbert. Limitations of Synchronous Communication with Static Process Structure in Languages for Distributed Computing. In *Proceedings of the 13th Annual ACMSymposium on Principles of Programming Languages*. St Petersburg Beach (Florida), January 1986.

[Nierstraz 87] Oscar Nierstraz. Active Objects in Hybrid. In *OOPSLA'87*, Orlando (Florida), October 1987.

[Papathomas 90] M. Papathomas. Concurrency Issues in Object-Oriented Programming Languages. *CUI, Université de Genève*, 1990.

[Per Brinch Hansen 78] Per Brinch Hansen. Distributed Processes: A concurrent Programming Concept In *Communications of the ACM*, Volume 21, Number 11, November 1978.

[Perihelion 89] Perihelion Software. The Helios Operating System. *Prentice Hall*, 1989.

[Saleh and Gautron 91] Hayssam Saleh and Philippe Gautron. A System Library for C++ Distributed Applications on Transputer. In *Applications of Transputers 91*, IOS Press, Glasgow (Scotland), August 1991.

[Shapiro 89a] Marc Shapiro, Philippe Gautron, and Laurence Mosseri. Persistence and Migration for C++ Objects. In *ECOOP'89*, Nottingham (GB), July 1989.

[Tomlinson and Singh 89] Chris Tomlinson and Vineet Singh. Inheritance and Synchronization with enabled sets. In *OOPSLA'89*, New Orleans (Louisiana), October 1989.

[Robert and Verjus 77] P. Robert and J.-P. Verjus. Toward Autonomous Descriptions of Synchronization Modules. In *Proceedings of IFIP Congress*, North Holland, 1977.

Object-Oriented Concurrent Reflective Architectures*

Satoshi Matsuoka   Takuo Watanabe   Yuuji Ichisugi
Akinori Yonezawa

Department of Information Science, The University of Tokyo†

Abstract

Reflection provides the abilities to reason and alter the dynamic behavior of computation from within the language framework. It is a practical scheme that offers a new perspective in constructing a malleable, large-scale system such as programming languages, operating systems, and window systems. Reflection is more beneficial in object-oriented concurrent/distributed computing, where the complexity of the system is much greater compared to sequential computing; this has been demonstrated through recent works in *Object-Oriented Concurrent Reflective (OOCR)* architectures. From a structural perspective, we can categorize OOCR architectures into *individual-based*, *group-wide*, and their hybrid (*hybrid group*). Through the introductive categorization of various OOCR architectures based on our previous and current work, we explore the characteristics as well as benefits and limitations of each.

1   Introduction to Reflection and Reflective Systems

Reflection is the process of reasoning about and acting upon the system itself[23, 15, 34]. In a conventional computing system, the *subject matter* of computation is external to the system, i.e., the computation is performed on data that represent or model entities that are external to the system. A *reflective system* takes a step further by allowing the subject matter be the system itself, i.e., computation can be performed on the system itself in a uniform way[15]. A reflective system thus 'opens up' the system by providing an appropriate abstraction on the internal (often implementational) detail of itself to the user program. Contrary to the misconception that 'reflection' is some difficult-to-understand, not-too-useful philosophical jargon, it is a practical scheme that offers a new perspective in constructing a malleable, large-scale system such as programming languages[14], operating systems[32], and window systems[22]. One can make an analogy of reflection to *inheritance*, which was derived from AI and incarnated into object-oriented programming languages, and now serves important roles in methodologies for system construction of

---

*An extended abstract of this paper appeared in [9]

†Physical mail address: 7-3-1 Hongo, Bunkyo-ku, Tokyo 113, Japan. Phone 03-3812-2111 (overseas +81-3-3812-2111) ex. 4108. E-mail: {matsu,takuo,ichisugi,yonezawa}@is.s.u-tokyo.ac.jp

user interfaces, operating systems, and database systems. We believe that, in the same manner, reflection can offer another clear architectural perspective, especially for the dynamic aspects of the system where inheritance is known to be somewhat ineffective.

To expose, or *reify* its internals, a reflective system contains data that represents or models the metalevel structural and computational aspects of itself within itself. Such data is said to be *reified*, and must be dynamically self-accessible and self-modifiable by the user program. Furthermore, when the user modifies such data, the modification must be 'reflected' to the actual computational state of the user program. This requirement is termed as *causal-connection*, and is satisfied by all reflective systems. When the requirement is satisfied, the meta-level data that provides the abstraction is called the *Causally-Connected Self-Representation(s) (CCSR)*. For practical purposes, the meta-relation is often that of implementation. In such systems, causal connection is automatically guaranteed. Although modifying the implementation may seem like a dangerous endeavor, it has been shown that modification can be confined to the local portion of the user program by some appropriate *Metaobject Protocol*, a scheme pioneered in CLOS[14].

Another requirement for reflective systems is that self-access and self-modification must be possible in a way that is little different from the base-level programming. In other words, appropriate abstraction of the internal program state must be provided by the system so that the user can perform the meta-programming of the system in a clean, concise manner that does not deviate significantly from 'normal' programming. For example, in 3-Lisp[23], one can program reflective computation merely by defining *reflective procedures* whose means of definition differ little from that of normal procedures.

2 Reflection in Object-Oriented Concurrent Systems — The Benefits

The benefits of *computational reflection* in sequential languages have been identified by many researchers: Previously, programming language functionalities such as debugging facilities, interfaces to external world, and exception handling were added to languages in an ad hoc and inflexible manner. In contrast, languages based on reflective execution models are powerful in providing linguistic mechanisms to use the above functionalities in a uniform and flexible manner via clean access of the abstraction on how the system is implemented[15, 14].

We claim that reflection is more beneficial in concurrent computing, for a concurrent system embodies multitudes of aspects that do not arise in sequential computing: scheduling, communication, and load-balancing, among numerous others. Those aspects are still considered to be mostly outside the scope of programming languages, and their control is only available in a fixed, ad-hoc fashion, with little possibility for user extensibility. This is a not favorable, since concurrent architectures are much more complex as compared to sequential ones, and the system must be *open* to structured dynamic extensions and/or modifications for adapting to new problems and environments.

Here, as were pointed out in [34] and [24], constructing a concurrent system with a reflective architecture could be beneficial to encompass such aspects within the programming language framework for the reasons mentioned above. The dynamic optimization is especially effective in a concurrent system because (1) as mentioned, the reflective architecture allows the programmer to control the computational aspects of concurrent system dynamically[1], and (2) both the reflective computation and the base-level computation can be performed in parallel[34, 17, 29].

3 Object-Oriented Concurrent Reflective (OOCR) Architectures

With the aforementioned observations and principles, our research proposed the use of reflection in the framework of *Object-Oriented Concurrent Programming (OOCP)*, with various *Object-Oriented Concurrent Reflective (OOCR)* architectures: languages ABCL/R[29] and X0/R[18] were based on the *individual-based architecture*, ACT/R[30] was based on the *group-wide architecture*[2], and the evolution of ABCL/R, the language ABCL/R2[17], was based on the *hybrid group architecture*. Each language differed in what meta-lingual features can be realized through reflection, i.e., what features particular to concurrent OO computing, such as object monitoring and migration, could be cleanly encompassed within the programming language framework. There, the evolution of the languages can be understood for the difference in the characteristic of their reflective architectures.

Although there have been works that discusses various aspects of reflection and classifies metalevel/reflective architectures from different viewpoints[16, 28, 6, 24], so far to our knowledge no work has existed that generally discusses reflection in the context of concurrent/distributed object-oriented languages. Nor, has there been work that classifies architectures dependent on characteristics that are *particular to object-oriented concurrency*, i.e., not becoming manifest in sequential object-oriented languages. It is our premise that the need for such a discussion and classification is becoming omnipresent — for as we argued above, the power of reflection can be best utilized in concurrent computation. Furthermore, we claim that in order for reflection to be put to practical use in concurrent/distributed systems, we need to analyze and evaluate the merits and weaknesses of each, and synthesize a new architecture suitable for practical use.

First, the two aspects of CCSR in OO languages are the (1) *structural aspect*, indicating how objects or group of objects in the base-level and the meta-level are constructed and related, and the (2) *computational aspect*, indicating how meta-level objects represent the computation of the base-level objects[6]. Altogether, appropriate construction of the *meta-level architecture* dictates what structural and computational aspects can be reflected and operated upon — this we believe is more prevalent in concurrent systems, for factors such as scheduling must be given appropriate meta-level abstractions in order for them to be effectively and efficiently accessed from the base-level.

The OOCR architectures can be categorized from the structural aspect, chiefly dependent on whether the architecture has the notion of *metaobjects*, which Pattie Maes introduced for sequential object-oriented language 3-KRS in [15]. It is often argued that providing explicit metaobjects in the architecture is conceptually natural with respect to the uniformity principle, "everything is an object." But, what do we really mean by a

---

[1]One of the interesting applications we will note is to change the scheduling policy of object execution dynamically [3] in distributed simulation based on the Time Warp Scheme[13].

[2]The original idea of the group-wide architecture was mentioned in the last sections of [29] and [34]

'metaobject'? It is pointed out that there has been great confusion on the usage of the term[7] — we first attempt to provide conceptual distinction in the terminologies.

A *meta-level object* is any object that resides in the meta-level of the object-level computation. *Metaobjects* are objects that reflects the structural and computational aspect of a *particular* base-level object; thus, a metaobject is a meta-level object, while the converse is not necessarily so. The relationship between the metaobjects and the base-level object they represent could either be one-to-one or many-to-one, i.e., there could be multiple metaobjects collectively 'representing' a single base-level object[10, 21]. The metaobjects must be unique to a single object in the base-level, that is, they are not shared.

There are several important criteria that metaobjects must satisfy that distinguish it from other meta-level objects:

1. *Identifiability of Metaobjects* — a base-level object must be able to identify its metaobjects intrinsically.

2. *Uniqueness of Metaobject Denotation* — metaobjects must be able to intrinsically and uniquely identify the base-level object it denotes.

3. *Causal Connection* — a base-level object and its metaobjects must be *causally connected.*

4. *Governing of Computation* — the metaobject must dynamically govern the computation of the object it denotes or represents.

By these criteria, the 3-KRS and ABCL/R 'metaobjects' are metaobjects as we describe later on, whereas the CLOS 'metaobjects' are meta-level objects in our terminology. Class objects in class-based languages such as ObjVLisp[4] are not metaobjects either, for (1) the denotation is not direct and/or not unique, and (2) classes are not "meta" in a computational sense[6], that is, they do not actually govern the dynamic aspect of object computation.

Given the distinction of metaobjects and meta-level objects, a reflective object-oriented system can basically be constructed in two ways:

- **Individual-Based Architecture:** Each object in the system has its own metaobject(s) which govern(s) its computation. By 'individual-based' we mean that an individual object is the unit of base-level computation that has a meaningful CCSR at the meta-level.

- **Group-wide Architecture:** In this architecture, a group of meta-level objects comprises the meta-level. The behavior of an object is not governed by metaobjects; rather, the collective behavior of a *group* of objects is represented as the coordinated actions of a group of meta-level objects, which comprise the *meta-group*. By 'group-wide' we mean that the entire object group is the unit of base-level computation that has a meaningful CCSR at the meta-level (as a meta-group); thus, there are *NO* intrinsic meta-relationships between a base-level object and a particular metaobject at the meta-level.

- **Hybrid Group Architecture:** The hybrid group architecture combines the individual based architecture and group-wide architecture. Each object has its own metaobject(s), while the coordinated actions of a group of objects, such as scheduling, are controlled by meta-level objects that comprise the meta-group. Both the individual object and the group have meaningful CCSR at the meta-level.

For sequential OO-languages, the representative of the individual-based architecture is 3-KRS, and the one representative of the group-wide architecture is CLOS. Below, we will give examples of each architectures for object-oriented concurrent languages in our research.

3.1 The Individual-Based Architecture — ABCL/R

An example of this architecture is ABCL/R[29]. Each object has its own unique metaobject, ↑x that can be accessed with a special form [meta x]. Conversely, given a metaobject ↑x, [den ↑x] denotes the object it represents. The correspondence is 1-to-1, i.e., [meta [den ↑x]] $\stackrel{\text{def}}{=}$ ↑x and [den [meta x]] $\stackrel{\text{def}}{=}$ x. The structural aspects of x — a set of state variables, a set of scripts, a local evaluator, and a message queue — are part of state variables of ↑x. A metaobject has its own metaobject ↑↑x as well and so on, conceptually forming an infinite tower of metaobjects (Figure 1).

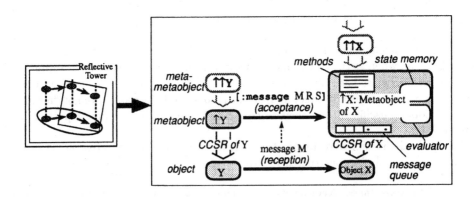

Figure 1: The Individual-Based Architecture in ABCL/R

The *arrival* of a message M at object x is represented as an *acceptance* of the message [:message M R S] at ↑x, where R and S are the *reply destination object* and the *sender object*, respectively. The interpretation of the script of x by ↑x is carefully designed so that the concurrent activities allowed within an object in the computational model are preserved. Causal connection and total governing are guaranteed as ↑x implements x. Figure 1 illustrates this. As are most individual-based architectures, reflective computation by an object in ABCL/R is basically performed by sending messages to its metaobject (or any other metaobjects in the tower); alternatively, the metaobject can immediately identify and send messages to its denotation.

Note that the individual-based architecture is independent from the issue of inter-level concurrency. As stated earlier, In a sequential OO-reflective architecture, there is only a single computation thread in the tower of metaobjects. This thread performs the interpretation of a certain level, and a reflective operation causes a 'shift' of this level. By contrast, in ABCL/R, there is internal concurrency within a single object as defined by the computational model of ABCL/1[33]: message reception/queuing versus the execution of the user script. The interpretation of x by $\uparrow x$ is designed so that the former is performed as a meta-level task while the latter is performed as a base-level task. Concurrency between the tasks is then preserved, because ABCL/R supports inter-level concurrency between the base-level object and its metaobject.

Other examples of individual-based architecture are Rosette[27], Merling III[5], Tanaka's actor language[3][26], and X0/R. The distinction here is the relationship between the object and its metaobject — whether the meta-object has a separate identity from the object it denotes:

- **'Unified' Identity:** when the meta relationship is that of total implementation as in ABCL/R. There is actually only one unique object in the tower; whether to regard it as an object or its metaobject (or metametaobject, ... ad infinitum) depends on from which level the object is being 'viewed' in the computation.

- **Separate Identity:** the metaobject has its own separate identity. Metaobjects in 3-KRS, Merling III, and X0/R are of this kind. In a class-based architecture, a metaobject is often an instance of class MetaObject or its subclasses.

- **Partially Self-Reifying Identity:** when there are no explicit metaobjects, but the snapshot of object state can be reified. We can consider the reified structure to be obtained from the implicit metaobject. T-Actor is an example of this.

The advantage of the separate identity over the first two is that the metaobject could be interchanged dynamically in order to change the basic behavior of the object, such as message reception. Although unrestricted alteration of metaobjects could be catastrophic to the integrity of computation, it nevertheless can be a powerful tool if employed in a controlled manner[18]. Dynamic alteration is more difficult for the first two, although possible for the unified identity by changing the behavior of the metaobject through its meta-metaobject. One major drawback of the separate identity particular to concurrency is the possible cost for maintaining causal connection. This becomes prevalent if the only way for the objects to communicate is via messages, because there is a natural delay for the transmission to occur. Then, the object and its metaobject must explicitly synchronize their activities in order to maintain the causal connection.

3.2   The Group-wide Reflective Architecture — ACT/R

ACT/R[30] is an Actor-based language that supports the notion of groups under this architecture. It is based on Gul Agha's Actor formalism[1] which models the state of *system S* of Actors as its *configuration*, C (a pair consisting of a set of Actors and a set of *tasks* in the system), and defines transitional semantics between the configurations, each transition being the computation of a task. Now, given a configuration C, We define the

---

[3]Unfortunately, this language does not have an official name; henceforth, we will refer to it as *T-Actor* for convenience.

metaconfiguration $\uparrow C$ as being a metalevel representation of a configuration by a system of Actors. A task $< t, m, k >$ in C where t is the *tag* of the task, m is the *target mail address*, and k is the *message value*, is represented in the metaconfiguration as a *meta-task* $< u, m_\theta, [:\texttt{task}\ \uparrow t\ \uparrow m\ \uparrow k] >$, where u is the task tag of the meta-task, m_θ is the mail address of the *task handler Actor* θ, and $\uparrow$ is the *handle function*[4]. Actors in the base-level have their specific information stored at the meta-level *database entry Actors*, which are accessed via the meta-level *database Actor* δ^S. The framework is conceptually illustrated in Figure 2. We formally prove that $\uparrow S$ is a correct representation of S by showing that the transitions in $\uparrow S$ faithfully represent transitions in S. The difficulty is that the atomicity of a transition in the base level no longer holds at the meta-level; we overcome this with a technique called *normalization*. For details, see [30].

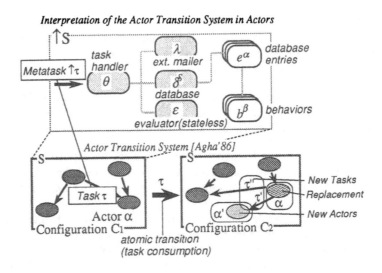

Figure 2: The Group-Wide Architecture in ACT/R

The essence of ACT/R is the lack of metaobjects, for the behavior of a single Actor is realized at the meta-level by coordinated action of multiple meta-level Actors. All reflective operations are performed solely via message sends, which are interpreted at the meta-level concurrently with interpretations of Actors in the base level. We claim that there are no metaobjects in ACT/R, although one could argue that the database entry Actors are so, for there is one entry Actor for each handle of the base-level Actors. They do not, however, satisfy our criteria, for (1) the denotation is not direct, and (2) the database entry Actor is not solely responsible for the computation of the corresponding Actor in the base level, e.g., the message reception is the responsibility of the task handler Actor.

Another example of the group-wide architecture, is the Muse distributed operating system[32, 31], although it has some features of the hybrid group architecture we discuss below. In Muse, the meta-level objects in the 'meta-space' 'support' the activity of the

---

[4]Not to be confused with the metaobject notation in ABCL/R.

objects of the base-level. There are specific meta-level objects responsible for various operating system tasks, such as message delivery, scheduling, memory management, etc. The reflective operation is performed by communicating with the meta-space via communication ports called *reflectors*. Muse is not a programming language, nor has an underlying monolithic base language, as is true for Genera[25] (which is Lisp-based). The system is nevertheless reflective, in that Muse has its own object model that can be realized by multiple object-oriented programming languages. Because of its language independence (being a general-purpose operating system), features that are highly language dependent, e.g., environments, are not handled in the Muse object model. However, Muse does support primitives for constructing some types of language features that are essential for the manipulation of the Muse object system, such as classes.

3.3 The Hybrid Group Architecture — ABCL/R2

In real-life concurrent language architectures, various system resources such as computational power, communication, storage, I/O, etc., are naturally distributed, and their availabilities are limited; computational power, for example, is limited by the number of CPUs in the system. For this reason, coordinated resource management is a fundamental problem in any concurrent architecture, but usually become little manifest at the language level. We made attempts to linguistically (namely, at the programming language level) formulate reflective features including resource management with previous OOCR architectures, and discovered the limitations of the architectures on their manageability of finite resources and their coordinated management. The primary reason was that such coordinations require the following abstractions to exist simultaneously in the meta-level: (1) (meta-level) object groups representing global computation, (2) object identity in the meta-level for the control of individual objects, and (3) proper abstraction of limited or bounded computational resources.

To solve this problem, we proposed the notion *hybrid group architecture* and the language ABCL/R2 based on this architecture[17]. By 'hybrid' we mean that the architecture embodies the architectural properties of both the individual-based and the group-wide architecture. Each object has its own (tower of) metaobject in the same manner as ABCL/R, and it also belongs to an ACT/R-like group. At the base-level, the structure of a group is flat in the sense that there are no base-level member objects that perform tasks specific to the group. Rather, analogous to the group-wide reflection, the structure and the computation of a group is explicitly defined at the meta- and higher levels of the group, by the objects called the *group kernel objects*. The group performs management of computational resources, called *group shared resources* by coordinating among the metaobjects of the members and the group kernel objects.

Groups can be created dynamically with the group creation forms. The creation process of a group is not intrinsic, but is given a concrete metacircular definition with ABCL/R2. As a result, not only that we have the tower of metaobjects, but we also have the tower of *meta-groups* as in ACT/R.

The key features of the language ABCL/R2 are as follows[17]:

- Heterogeneous Object Groups and Group Shared Resources

- Non-reifying Objects (objects that do not have metaobjects)

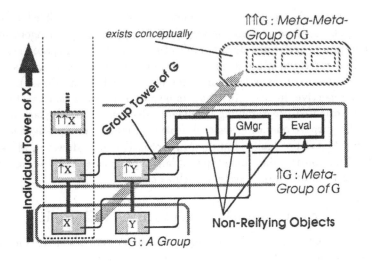

Figure 3: The Hybrid Group Architecture in ABCL/R2

- Meta-groups and Individual/Group Reflective Towers

The essential point is that these features are not ad-hoc, but are defined within the framework of our reflective computational model. As a result, reflective features of ABCL/R2 allow coordinated computational resource management to be effectively modeled and efficiently controlled — for example, the scheduling problem of the Time Warp algorithm[13] used in parallel discrete event simulations can be elegantly solved. Figure 3 is the pictorial illustration of the reflective architecture of ABCL/R2.

The hybrid group architecture also contributes feedback to the conceptual side of OOCR architectures and object groups by (1) showing that (heterogeneous) object groups are not ad-hoc concepts but can be defined constructively and lucidly, and (2) identifying that hybrid group architectures embody *two* reflective towers, instead of one: the *individual tower* that mainly determines the structure of the object, and the *group tower* that mainly determines the computation.

Our work on ABCL/R2 is still ongoing — the actual implementation of the compiler raises various interesting issues regarding optimizations. Also, there are still many aspects of concurrent computation we have not addressed in ABCL/R2. For example, there is a difficulty in the management of two distinct resources exhibiting collaborative behaviors; or, how to model the behavior of group of objects actively competing for the computational resource to solve a problem as a whole.

4 Future Directions — Towards Stronger Theoretical and Practical Foundations

Recently, there have been several interesting works on OOCR architectures other than the ones we have mentioned so far. These include AL-1[11, 12], OO||[2], and Actra[19, 20]. Although they could be classified as being an instance of the above architectures, each has interesting and unique architectural aspects that were not covered in this paper. For example, AL-1 is basically individual-based architecture; the novel aspect of AL-1, however, is that the CCSR of a single object can be 'viewed' in several ways, depending on how much the user wants to expose the underlying implementation of the object. This framework, called *multi-model reflection framework* in [12], allows the user to work with varying degrees of reflection by not restricting the user to a single model of CCSR.

Still, much more work needs to be done in order for reflection to be used generally in constructing malleable architectures. Figure 4 is a road map describing the relationships between our previous and current work, plus our future directions in search for a better OOCR architecture. Our current research topics include:

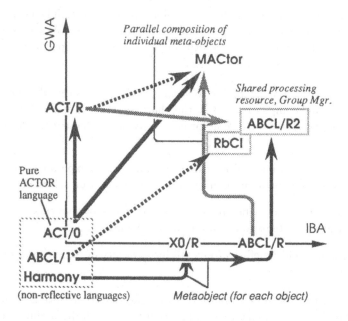

Figure 4: The Road Map of Our Previous and Current Works, Plus Future Directions

- To lay a more theoretical foundation for the hybrid group architecture — rather than giving direct formalization of ABCL/R2, we are currently taking an alternative approach by again using Actor transition system as the base computational model. The work is currently called *MACTOR*, and has a different formulation from ACT/R, more in line with ABCL/R2.

- To have an effective parallel implementation of ABCL/R2 — We are in the process of (1) constructing a prototype called Micro-ABCL/R2, which runs pseudo-parallel on conventional workstations, and (2) a full implementation on OMRON LUNA-88K, which has a shared-memory architecture and runs Mach. There are various technical intricacies, especially on how to efficiently and safely break the metacircularity in the compiler, as mentioned above.

- To construct and apply reflective system to real-world applications in concurrent/distrib systems — In parallel to the development of ABCL/R2, we are designing a language called RbCl (Reflection-based Concurrent language). The non-reflective features of RbCl are similar to that of ABCL/1; it is intended to run on a network of workstations and also on multicomputers such as iPSC/860.

We will briefly overview our latest language, RbCl, in the next section.

4.1 RbCl — A Hybrid Group Architecture Language for Practical Distributed Computing

The main motivation of this research is to develop a practically useful concurrent programming system that is easy to customize and become adaptable. We propose our object-oriented concurrent reflective language RbCl (Reflection-based Concurrent language)[10]. The goals of the RbCl system are as follows:

1. The system should be adaptable to various environments that differ in the architecture of parallel computers, and in the characteristics of applications. The system should also be able to evolve according to dynamic changes of execution environments.

2. The system should be used as a platform for various experiments on parallel languages to test linguistic mechanisms and implementation schemes.

3. The programmer should be able to access external environments (e.g., window systems, database systems, etc.) in a uniform manner.

4. The system should be efficient enough for a variety of parallel and distributed applications.

The requirements 1 and 2 are realized by the reflective computation facilities provided by RbCl. To make our language easy to program and practically useful, one of our goals of this research is to provide a *disciplined* scheme for the usage of reflective facilities that is analogous to the metaobject protocol (MOP) of CLOS[14].

The reflective architecture of RbCl is a practical incarnation of the hybrid group architecture. Each unit of metalevel representation models (or represents) a group of base-level objects, and such a group corresponds to the group of objects running on a single processor node. The RbCl metalevel architecture models the actual hardware configuration of a distributed computation system. Basically, the metalevel architecture consists of metalevel objects that form a metacircular definition (or, implementation) of the execution mechanism of base-level objects, just as ABCL/R2. Namely, the execution mechanism

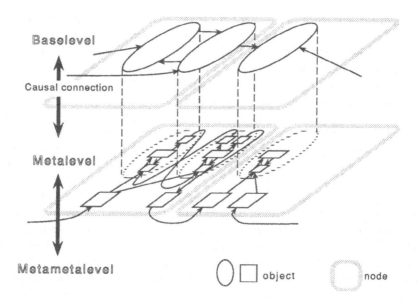

Figure 5: Overview of the RbCl Architecture

of a group of objects is represented by a (unit) group of meta-level objects. Reflective computation in RbCl is realized by the interaction between the base-level objects and the metalevel objects via message passing as in [29, 30, 17] (Figure 5). Our *metaobject protocol* (RbCl-MOP) to be designed provides a set of rules to customize and modify/extend metalevel objects in a disciplined manner.

One of the interesting characteristics of RbCl is the *linguistic symbiosis* with other object-oriented languages, namely C++, which does not offer reflective capabilities by itself. C++ objects and RbCl objects may coexist and communicate with each other within the RbCl system. Communication is transparent to each language due to the encapsulation property of objects: A RbCl object can communicate to a C++ object via the RbCl message passing protocol, which to a C++ object corresponds to a virtual function invocation. The converse is also possible, i.e., message passing expression in a C++ object to a RbCl object would correspond to a *now type* (i.e., RPC-like) message passing in RbCl.

The notion of symbiosis is different from simple "external language interface" schemes of previous languages. Neither C++ objects nor RbCl objects require little or no special programming to do the interlingual communication, because they cannot basically distinguish whether the receiver is a C++ object or a RbCl object in their message transmission. This is more difficult to realize than it seems, because the message passing semantics of the two languages are totally different. For example, a RbCl object could send an asynchronous message to a C++ object, which involves creation of a new thread of activity.

· The linguistic symbiosis in RbCl is realized with the metalevel architecture of RbCl. For example, the forking of the thread of activity is programmed in the meta-level as an coordinating action of the RbCl meta-level objects. In fact, both RbCl objects and C++ objects interdependently comprises the meta-level architecture of RbCl itself, allowing (1) efficient implementation of the RbCl language and also (2) enables the use of external systems (e.g., window systems and database system, etc.) via the C++ objects acting as an interface. Furthermore, linguistic symbiosis allows the programmer or the compiler to replace a RbCl object with an object coded in C++ with the same behavior.

Implementation of symbiosis in the meta-level introduces circular interdependency in the system, since it is the meta-level architecture of RbCl that enables the symbiosis of RbCl objects and C++ objects in the first place. We can show that this circularity is not a vicious one, however. In fact, the initial construction of the default RbCl meta-level system is designed so that objects communicate with each other only via the now type message passing. Together with the fact that all meta-level objects are initially C++ objects of the same behavior, this allows all message passings between objects to be directly realized with direct virtual function call for high efficiency. Only when a RbCl object is introduced into the meta-system, the lazy instantiation of meta-meta-level support for interlingual communication in the meta-level become necessary.

5   Conclusion

We have categorized and reviewed several OOCR architectures, mainly from our past and present works. Research in OOCR architectures has only yet to reveal only a portion of their power so far, and the possibilities they offer in construction of a clean and malleable systems are being actively investigated in many places. The past two ACM OOPSLA workshops on Reflection and Metalevel Architectures in Object-Oriented Programming[8, 9] have collected nearly 30 papers per year, and each paper therein addressed numerous issues and ideas of object-oriented reflection with respect to programming language design, system architecture, theory, and implementation.

In conclusion, we feel that works in OOCR languages should have strong emphasis on the architectural issues, for it is not the language itself but the language architecture that would contribute the most in solving the problems in practice.

References

[1] Gul Agha. *ACTORS: A Model of Concurrent Computation in Distributed Systems.* The MIT Press, 1986.

[2] Peter C. Bahrs. On Reflection in Object-Oriented Heterogeneous Environments for Concurrent Processing. In *Proceedings of the OOPSLA '91 Workshop on Reflection and Metalevel Architectures in Object-Oriented Programming*, October 1991.

[3] Christopher Burdorf and Jed Marti. Non-Preemptive Time Warp Scheduling Algorithm. *Operating Systems Review*, 24(2):7–18, April 1990.

[4] Pierre Cointe. Metaclasses are first class. In *Proceedings of OOPSLA '87*, volume 22, pages 156–167. SIGPLAN Notices, ACM Press, October 1987.

[5] Jacques Ferber. Conceptual reflection and Actor languages. In Pattie Maes and Daniele Nardi, editors, *Meta-Level Architectures and Reflection*, pages 177–193. North-Holland, 1988.

[6] Jacques Ferber. Computational reflection in class-based object-oriented languages. In *Proceedings of OOPSLA '89*, volume 24, pages 317–326. SIGPLAN Notices, ACM Press, October 1989.

[7] Brian Foote. Object-oriented reflective metalevel architectures: Pyrite or panacea? In *Proceedings of the ECOOP/OOPSLA '90 Workshop on Reflection and Metalevel Architectures in Object-Oriented Programming*, October 1990.

[8] Mamdouh Ibrahim, editor. *Proceedings of the ECOOP/OOPSLA '90 Workshop on Reflection and Metalevel Architectures in Object-Oriented Programming*, October 1990.

[9] Mamdouh Ibrahim, editor. *Proceedings of the OOPSLA '91 Workshop on Reflection and Metalevel Architectures in Object-Oriented Programming*, October 1991.

[10] Yuuji Ichisugi, Satoshi Matsuoka, Takuo Watanabe, and Akinori Yonezawa. An object-oriented concurrent reflective architecture for distributed computing environments. In *Proc. 29th Annual Allerton Conference on Communication, Control and Computing*, Allerton, Illinois, October 1991. (To Appear).

[11] Yutaka Ishikawa. Reflection facilities and realistic programming. *SIGPLAN Notices*, 26(8):101–110, August 1991.

[12] Yutaka Ishikawa and Hideaki Okamura. A New Reflective Architecture: AL-1 Approach. In *Proceedings of the OOPSLA '91 Workshop on Reflection and Metalevel Architectures in Object-Oriented Programming*, October 1991.

[13] David R. Jefferson. Virtual Time. *ACM Transactions on Programming Languages and Systems*, 7(3):404–425, July 1985.

[14] Gregor Kiczales, Jim des Rivières, and Daniel G. Bobrow. *The Art of the Metaobject Protocol*. The MIT Press, Cambridge, Massachusetts, 1991.

[15] Pattie Maes. Concepts and experiments in computational reflection. In *Proceedings of OOPSLA '87*, volume 22, pages 147–155. SIGPLAN Notices, ACM Press, October 1987.

[16] Pattie Maes. Issues in computational reflection. In Pattie Maes and Daniele Nardi, editors, *Meta-Level Architectures and Reflection*, pages 21–35. North-Holland, 1988.

[17] Satoshi Matsuoka, Takuo Watanabe, and Akinori Yonezawa. Hybrid group reflective architecture for object-oriented concurrent reflective programming. In *Proceedings of ECOOP '91*, number 512 in Lecture Notes in Computer Science, pages 231–250. Springer-Verlag, 1991.

[18] Satoshi Matsuoka and Akinori Yonezawa. Metalevel solution to inheritance anomaly in concurrent object-oriented languages. In *Proceedings of the ECOOP/OOPSLA '90 Workshop on Reflection and Metalevel Architectures in Object-Oriented Programming*, October 1990.

[19] Jeff McAffer. A unified distributed simulation system. In *Proceedings of the 1990 Winter Simulation Conference*, pages 415–422, New Orleans, LA, December 1990.

[20] Jeff McAffer. Variably Asynchronous, Reflective Tasks in Smalltalk. In *Proceedings of the OOPSLA '91 Workshop on Reflection and Metalevel Architectures in Object-Oriented Programming*, October 1991.

[21] Tatsuo Minohara and Mario Tokoro. Multiple meta-objects support an object. In *Proceedings of the ECOOP/OOPSLA '90 Workshop on Reflection and Metalevel Architectures in Object-Oriented Programming*, 1990.

[22] Ramana Rao. Implementational reflection in Silica. In *Proceedings of ECOOP'91*, number 512 in Lecture Notes in Computer Science, pages 251–267. Springer-Verlag, July 1991.

[23] Brian C. Smith. Reflection and semantics in Lisp. In *Conference Record of the ACM Symposium on Principles of Programming Languages*, pages 23–35. ACM Press, 1984.

[24] Brian C. Smith. What do you mean, meta? In *Proceedings of the ECOOP/OOPSLA '90 Workshop on Reflection and Metalevel Architectures in Object-Oriented Programming*, October 1990.

[25] Symbolics Inc. *Genera User's Guide*, 1990.

[26] Tomoyuki Tanaka. Actor-based reflection without meta-objects. Technical Report RT-0047, IBM Research, Tokyo Reserach Laboratory, August 1990.

[27] Chris Tomlinson and Vineet Singh. Inheritance and synchronization with Enabled-Sets. In *Proceedings of OOPSLA '89*, volume 24, pages 103–112. SIGPLAN Notices, ACM Press, October 1989.

[28] Frank van Harmlen. A classification of meta-level architectures. In Abramson and Rogers, editors, *Meta-Programming in Logic Programming*, chapter 5, pages 103–122. The MIT Press, 1989.

[29] Takuo Watanabe and Akinori Yonezawa. Reflection in an object-oriented concurrent language. In *Proceedings of OOPSLA '88*, volume 23, pages 306–315. SIGPLAN Notices, ACM Press, September 1988. (Revised version is in [33]).

[30] Takuo Watanabe and Akinori Yonezawa. An actor-based metalevel architecture for group-wide reflection. In *Proceedings of the REX School/Workshop on Foundations of Object-Oriented Languages (REX/FOOL), Noordwijkerhout, the Netherlands*, May 1990. (Also in number 489 in Lecture Notes in Computer Science. Springer-Verlag, 1991).

[31] Yasuhiko Yokote, Atsushi Mitsuzawa, Nobuhisa Fujinami, and Mario Tokoro. Reflective object management in the Muse operating system. In *Proceedings of the IEEE International Workshop on Object-Orientation in Operating Systems*, pages 16–23. IEEE Computer Society Press, 1991.

[32] Yasuhiko Yokote, Fumio Teraoka, and Mario Tokoro. A reflective architecture for an object-oriented distributed operating system. In Stephen Cook, editor, *Proceedings of ECOOP'89*, pages 89–106. Cambridge University Press, 1989.

[33] Akinori Yonezawa, editor. *ABCL: An Object-Oriented Concurrent System*. Computer Systems Series. The MIT Press, 1990.

[34] Akinori Yonezawa and Takuo Watanabe. An introduction to object-based reflective concurrent computations. In *Proceedings of the 1988 ACM SIGPLAN Workshop on Object-Based Concurrent Programming*, volume 24, pages 50–54. SIGPLAN Notices, ACM Press, April 1989.

Abstract Description of Distributed Object Systems*

Thorsten Hartmann
Ralf Jungclaus

Abt. Datenbanken, TU Braunschweig

P.O. Box 3329, D-W-3300 Braunschweig, FRG

E-mail: {jungclau,hartmann}@infbs.uucp

Abstract

In this paper we propose an abstract object-oriented model to describe distributed systems in an actor-oriented way. We introduce *Basic Object Structures* (BOS) with the basic concepts *base objects* to represent entities and *channels* as representations of communications between base objects. Objects are regarded as processes that can be observed. Based on these concepts we show how BOS can be uniformly described using an abstract language, the TROLL-kernel.

1 Introduction

It is rather straightforward to regard a (distributed) system as a collection of dynamic autonomous objects that communicate. This approach dates back to [Hew77] and has initiated different approaches towards a computational model for objects. The *ACTOR* model of computation [Agh86] promotes asynchronous communication between actors, whereas in POOL-T [Ame87] objects are considered as processes that communicate synchronously. Other approaches are ABCL/1 [YSTH87], that models objects as active entities with a single thread of control which may communicate synchronously and asynchronously, or *Abacus* [Nie90, NP90b], that uses a computational model of communicating agents based on CCS [Mil89]. The behavioral description of systems of communicating agents has been a vivid field of research since the presentation of CSP [Hoa85] and CCS.

In this paper we propose a more abstract view of dynamic object systems. We regard objects as units of concurrency encapsulating a single process without internal concurrency (this is known as the *trace model*). The state of an object is described by a number of (structured) attributes that take values from predefined codomains. The attribute values are determined by the history of the object — in this way advantages of process models are combined with data modeling capabilities. Mathematical models of objects in our sense are described in [SE90, ES91].

---

*This work is supported by Deutsche Forschungsgemeinschaft under Sa 465/1-1 and Sa 465/1-2.

Based on this view we develop *Basic Object Structures* (BOS) to serve as an abstract view of loosely coupled distributed systems. The only concepts supported by BOS are simple (non-composite) objects and communication objects representing communication channels between simple objects. The goal is to provide a suitable interface to implement BOS on a network of workstations.

BOS are the basis for high level abstractions like specialization, generalization, temporary roles, and complex (composite) objects. These abstractions are supported by a language called TROL particularly suited to the abstract description of interactive information systems [JSH91, JHSS91, SJE91]. Declarative TROL specifications will be decomposed into equivalent specifications of BOS described using a TROL-sublanguage, the TROL-kernel. In this sense BOS can be seen as a step towards implementation of distributed information systems. They provide a link between the conceptual model of the application area and the implemented system.

The advantage of this approach is basically the uniform language framework. In the process of describing a system we start with a consistent model of the application using language features of TROL. Then we will go on with transformations that do not violate the constraints given by this model. Each step can (at least in principle) be verified against the former step. The result of this procedure is a model of the system in terms of Basic Object Structures described with language features of the TROL-kernel.

In information systems, we typically have a huge number of *persistent* objects of which just a few are *active* (i.e. providing services and are given CPU resources) at one point in time [SE90]. Thus, the implementation of BOS will be supported by object stores managing the currently passive objects, object managers scheduling the active objects and several communication primitives. This viewpoint also provides a way to weaken the artificial boundary between active and passive objects.

The concept of object used as a basis for TROL and the TROL-kernel has been developed in [SSE87, SFSE89b, SE90] and [SFSE89a] which takes a temporal perspective of abstract object types and concurrency. This approach is accompanied by work on a categorical semantics [ES89, EGS90, ES91]. Based on this formal concept, work has been done towards a logical framework of structured theories over a suitable logical calculus [FSMS90, FM91].

The paper is organized as follows: In section 2 we describe the general concept of object in a formal representation. Then we introduce our notion of Basic Object Structures using a simple example of communicating objects. In the main section we describe the language features of the TROL-kernel used to model BOS providing a modeling of the simple communication example between a server and a possible client. In the last section we give some concluding remarks and state our future plans.

2 Formalization of Object-Oriented Concepts

In this section, we describe how a model, in the mathematical sense, representing a system as a collection of interacting objects is characterized. In our approach, emphasis is put on the representation of the behavior of objects through time and of their evolvement depending on their behavior resulting in a complete representation of structural *and* behavioral aspects.

Let us start with the characteristics of a mathematical model of single isolated objects, called an *object model* in the sequel. An object is in a certain state at any moment in time. Each state transition corresponds to an occurrence of an *event*, which is an abstraction of a method. A set of events may occur simultaneously, which is said to be a snapshot. A sequence of events starting from creating the object (*birth event*) and either ending with deleting the object (*death event*) or going on "forever" is called a *life cycle*. The possible behavior of an object thus is modeled by a set of admissible life cycles which is called a *process*.

Certain aspects of the object's (internal) state may be *observed* using *attributes* that represent *visible* properties of an object. The values of the attributes (an *observation*) depend on the object's state which is determined by the object's history, i.e. it depends on the sequence of state transitions occurred so far. The history is a finite prefix of an admissible life cycle.

Let us now sketch the formalization of these characteristics. Let X be a set of events.

Definition 2.1 *A subset $s \in 2^X$ is called a* SNAPSHOT *over X.* ∎

An object event alphabet is composed of *birth, death* and *update* events. We require the set of birth events to include at least one event.

Definition 2.2 *A set of events X is said to be an* OBJECT EVENT ALPHABET *iff $X = B_X \cup D_X \cup U_X$ such that $B_X \neq \emptyset$ and B_X, D_X, U_X are pairwise disjoint.* ∎

Snapshots can be classified according to birth or death events they contain. Birth snapshots contain at least one birth event and no death events, death snapshots contain at least one death event and no birth events.

Definition 2.3 *The set of* BIRTH SNAPSHOTS $\mathcal{B}_X$ *is defined as* $\mathcal{B}_X = \{s \in 2^X \mid \exists b \in B_X : b \in s, \forall e \in s : e \notin D_X\}$. *The set of* DEATH SNAPSHOTS $\mathcal{D}_X$ *is defined as* $\mathcal{D}_X = \{s \in 2^X \mid \exists d \in D_X : d \in s, \forall e \in s : e \notin B_X\}$. ∎

For the definition of life cycles we need the notion of finite and infinite life cycles. Infinite life cycles describe objects that will never be destroyed.

Definition 2.4 *The set of* FINITE LIFE CYCLES *over X is denoted as* $\mathcal{L}_X^* = \{s_1 \dots s_n \mid n \in I\!N \text{ finite}, s_1 \in \mathcal{B}_X, s_n \in \mathcal{D}_X, \forall i \in I\!N, 2 \leq i \leq n - 1 : s_i \notin \mathcal{B}_X \cup \mathcal{D}_X\}$. *The set of* INFINITE LIFE CYCLES *over X is denoted as* $\mathcal{L}_X^\omega = \{s_1 s_n \dots \mid s_1 \in \mathcal{B}_X, \forall i \in I\!N, i \geq 2 : s_i \notin \mathcal{B}_X \cup \mathcal{D}_X\}$. ∎

The set of life cycles over X is then defined as the union of the empty, finite and infinite life cycles. The empty life cycle ϵ describes the fact that an object has not been created yet.

Definition 2.5 *The set of* LIFE CYCLES *over X is defined as* $\mathcal{L}_X = \{\epsilon\} \cup \mathcal{L}_X^* \cup \mathcal{L}_X^\omega$. ∎

Now, we are able to define the behavioral component of an object model, determining it's possible *states*.

Definition 2.6 *A* PROCESS *P is a pair* (X, Λ) *where X is a set of events and* $\Lambda \subseteq \mathcal{L}_X$ *is the set of permitted life cycles over X such that* $\epsilon \in \Lambda$. ∎

We now formalize how a process determines the observations. Let A be a set of attributes. Associated with each attribute $a \in A$ is a data type $\text{type}(a)$ that determines the range of the attribute. Let $\Pi(\Lambda)$ be the set of all finite prefixes of life cycles in Λ and $\text{carrier}(\text{type}(a))$ be the carrier set for the data type $\text{type}(a)$.

Definition 2.7 *An* OBSERVATION STRUCTURE *V over a process P is a pair* (A, α) *where A is a set of attributes and* α *is an observation mapping* $\alpha: \Pi(\Lambda) \rightarrow obs(A) \subseteq \{(a, d) \mid a \in A \wedge d \in \text{carrier}(\text{type}(a))\}$. *A given prefix* $\pi \in \Pi(\lambda)$ *is called (possible)* STATE *of an object*. ∎

Note that by definition we allow for non-deterministic observations.

An object model is defined by putting together a process and an observation structure over that process yielding a complete description of possible behavior and evolution over time.

Definition 2.8 *An* OBJECT MODEL $ob = (P, V)$ *is composed of a process P and an observation structure V over P*. ∎

Thus, an object is an *observable process*. As a notational convention, the sequence of observations during the execution of a life cycle $\lambda \in \Lambda$ is denoted by $\omega \in \Omega$, the set of all possible sequences of observations.

Recall that a system is represented by a collection of interacting objects. Thus, we need a mechanism to relate object models. This mechanism is an *object morphism* [EGS90, ESS90]. A special case of object morphism is the *object embedding morphism*. It describes an embedding of an object ob_2 as an encapsulated entity into another object ob_1.

This implies that the set of life cycles of ob_2 must be preserved and ob_1-events must employ ob_2-events to alter ob_2's state. The latter requirement is captured by the concept of *calling*. If an event e_1 calls an event e_2, then whenever e_1 occurs, e_2 occurs simultaneously.

Let us now define an object embedding morphism between objects ob_1 and ob_2. Assume, ob_2 should be embedded into object ob_1. Firstly the events of ob_2 are included in the set of events of ob_1. For the life cycle of ob_1 we state that if we constrain a life cycle to the events of the embedded (or part) object, we have to obtain a valid life cycle of the embedded object. Secondly the attributes of ob_2 are included in the set of attributes of ob_1. For observations of ob_1 projected to the attributes of the part object, we must obtain the same observation as for applying the observation mapping of part object ob_2 to a life cycle of ob_1 restricted to the events of ob_2.

Formally, this is expressed in the following definition:

Definition 2.9 *Let* $ob_1 = (P_1, V_1)$ *and* $ob_2 = (P_2, V_2)$ *be object models. Then* ob_2 *is embedded into* ob_1, $ob_2 \hookrightarrow ob_1$, *iff*

$$X_2 \subseteq X_1$$
$$\forall \lambda_1 \in \Lambda_1 \exists \lambda_2 \in \Lambda_2 : \lambda_1 \downarrow\downarrow X_2 = \lambda_2$$
$$A_2 \subseteq A_1$$
$$\forall \tau_1 \in \Pi(\Lambda_1) : \alpha_1(\tau_1) \downarrow A_2 = \alpha_2(\tau_1 \downarrow\downarrow X_2)$$

∎

$\lambda_1 \downdownarrows X_2$ denotes life cycle restriction. All events that are not in X_2 are eliminated from the snapshots in λ_1 and only the sequence of non-empty snapshots is taken into account. A single arrow on observations like in $\alpha_1 \downarrow A_2$ only takes into account those attributes that are in A_2.

Usually, objects are classified. For this purpose, we introduce the notion of a class type.

Definition 2.10 *A* CLASS TYPE *$ct = (I, ob)$ consists of a set I of object identifiers and a (prototype) object model ob.* ■

The set I is the carrier set of an arbitrary abstract data type. Following this definition, each object of a class has the same object model as structure definition. This definition can be generalized to heterogeneous classes as proposed in [SSE87] and [JSS91].

Object classes in our setting are sets of objects of a certain type fixed by the corresponding class type. Thus, with each object class we associate one corresponding class type. A class type describes possible extensions of a class definition in terms of object sets identified by identifier values $i \in I$. Therefore, possible class populations are subsets of $\{\langle i, ob \rangle \mid i \in ct.I \land ob = ct.ob\}$. Usually, the term *object class* is connected with the current state of a class variable, i.e. a concrete current object population with current states for included objects.

Definition 2.11 *A state of an* OBJECT CLASS *$oc = (ct, O)$ consists of a class type ct and a set of instances O. Instances $\langle i, ob, \pi \rangle \in O$ are described by an object identifier $i \in I$, an object model $ob = ct.ob$ and a current state $\pi \in \Pi(ob.\Lambda)$. The identifier i identifies instances in O uniquely.* ■

In this way, an object class definition is extensional. Note that we use the "dot notation" to refer to components of structures.

Taking object models as objects and object morphisms as arrows, a category of objects is established. Models representing the system to be developed can be constructed using category-theoretic operations. For details see [EGS90].

3 Basic Object Structures

Before we describe BOS consider a tiny example. Suppose we want to model a stopwatch. With the start-event, the stopwatch is created and starts to count the time units. The passing of one time unit is indicated by an occurrence of the tick-event. The stop-event models the pushing of the stop-button. A deliver-event parameterized by a natural number delivers the count of time units and is only permitted to occur after the stop-event has occurred. Our kind of stopwatch can only be used once, the reset-event is the death event of a stopwatch. The two observable properties of stopwatches are the time being the count of time units that passed since the start and a flag stopped that indicates whether the stop-event has occurred so far. Each admissible life cycle starts with a start-event, continues with an arbitrary number of occurrences of the tick-event before a stop-event. There may or may not be a deliver-event after the stop before the reset-event. Using an informal notation, resembling the specification of an object model (see definition), this may be written as follows:

```
stopwatch = (  {  time:nat, stopped:bool },
               {  start, tick, stop, deliver(nat), reset },
               {  start → tick → stop → reset,
                  start → tick → ... → stop → reset,
                  start → tick → stop → deliver(1) → reset,
                  start → tick → tick → stop → deliver(2) → reset,
                  ...
                  start → tick → ... → stop → deliver(n) → reset,
                  ... },

            ...
            )
```

Note that we omitted the specification of the observation mapping and that the process description is incomplete showing only the intuitive behavior of the proposed stopwatch.

The basic mechanism to relate objects is *object inclusion*. Briefly, it is an embedding morphism between object models which allows to *include* an object into another without violating any of its properties (i.e. only local events may alter its state and the set of possible life cycles must be preserved, see above). Only inside such a composite object we may have *communication*. The basic mechanism for communication is asymmetric synchronous communication which is called *event calling*. If an event e_1 calls an event e_2 ($e_1 >> e_2$), then e_2 must occur synchronously whenever e_1 occurs, but e_2 may occur alone. *Event sharing*, denoted by $e_1 == e_2$, means that e_1 and e_2 always occur synchronously (i.e. they are identified).

Now let us turn to *Basic Object Structures* (BOS). In BOS, only two kinds of objects are known. Firstly, there are simply-structured *base objects* representing some kind of entity as stopwatches, customers, users and so on. The second kind of objects are called *channels* and represent the "communication channels" between base objects that communicate, for example communication buffers or message queues.

Basically, channels include events that model communications between base objects. A channel is *shared* by base objects which are specified to synchronize. This is modeled by including the channel into the communicating base objects. Thus, the base objects *know* about the properties of the channel objects. This way they can force events of the channel object to occur using the concept of calling or sharing. On the other hand also the channel objects may induce the occurrence of events of the base objects in the same way. Conceptually, the channels are considered to be *parts* of the base objects.

Consider an example. Suppose we have a type STOPWATCH that describes stopwatch instances as described above. As name space we provide an isomorphic copy of the set of natural numbers called |STOPWATCH|, where the operation STOPWATCH: nat → |STOPWATCH| takes a natural number to generate a unique surrogate. In general, we may identify instances by giving the classname and a natural number like e.g. STOPWATCH(15). Stopwatches, in this example the server objects, are used by a customer, the client. The customer is created and destroyed independently from stopwatches with the events pop_up

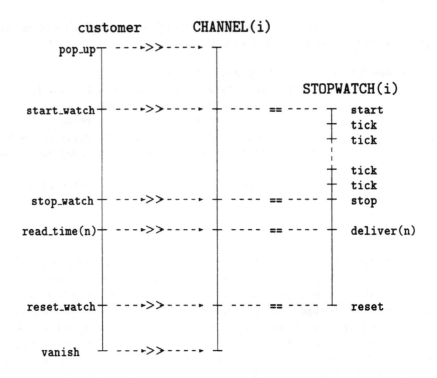

Figure 1: Communication of base objects through a channel

and vanish, respectively. Additionally, there are events start_watch, stop_watch, as well as read_time(nat) and reset_watch that correspond to the events of stopwatches.

Figure 1 shows how an instance of the class CHANNEL models the communication between customer and an instance of STOPWATCH. The CHANNEL object serves as a buffer between instances of clients and servers.

In this example events of the customer are immediately reflected in events of the CHANNEL and therefore also in events of the STOPWATCH, i.e. we have synchronous communication. Asynchronous communication may be modeled using channels with attributes, through which they are able to "remember" previous states. This kind of channel objects may delay service requests using queues for example.

In the following section, we introduce language features of the TROLL-kernel to describe *Basic Object Structures*.

4 Language Features to Describe BOS

The TROLL-kernel includes language features for abstract description of BOS. It is upward-compatible with the language TROLL that supports the description of information systems on higher levels of abstraction.

A specification of the structure of (prototype) objects is called a *template*. A template is structured as follows:

```
template [ template name ]
    data types        data types to be imported;
    attributes        attribute names and types;
    events            event names and parameter types;
    valuation         effects of events on observations;
    permissions       enabling conditions for events;
    obligations       completeness requirements for life cycles;
[ end template template name ]
```

Template names are optional and may be used to refer to separately defined templates, i.e. code reuse in class type definitions. Let us now describe the subsections of a template specification. In the data type section, the data types to be imported for the underlying data universe are indicated. The data types may either be chosen from a set of predefined types (like 'nat', 'string' or 'bool') or from a set of user-defined types specified using a language for abstract data type specification. Note that we also may import name spaces which are defined by an abstract data type (implicitly with the specification of a class type). Such name spaces are denoted by |OCT| for an object class type OCT. The type constructors (**list, set, record, bag**), known from abstract data type specifications, may be applied to construct complex structured data types. For example the constructor **set** applied to the predefined data type nat: set(nat) yields a complex structured data type representing sets of integers with operations like:

$$\begin{aligned}
\text{insert:} &\quad \text{nat} \times \text{set(nat)} \rightarrow \text{set(nat)} \\
\text{delete:} &\quad \text{nat} \times \text{set(nat)} \rightarrow \text{set(nat)} \\
\text{empty:} &\quad \text{set(nat)} \rightarrow \text{bool} \\
&\quad \ldots
\end{aligned}$$

In the **attribute-section**, the attribute names and the codomains are specified. In the **event-section**, event names and parameters are introduced. Event parameters allow for data to be exchanged during communication and for defining the effects of events on attribute values. The symbols introduced in the data type section, the attribute section and the event section make up the *local signature* of an object specification.

As an example, consider the local signature of the STOPWATCH-template:

```
template stopwatch
    data types nat, bool;
    attributes
        time:nat;
        stopped:bool;
    events
        birth start;
        tick;
        stop;
        deliver(nat);
```

               death reset;

        ...

      end template stopwatch

The signature defines the access interface for an object, that is, the external visible properties in terms of observations and possible event names. Another terminology for the signature of TROL objects would be visible state and possible operations. At this point nothing is said about the *correct* use, i.e. the underlying semantics of the object. Signatures (in this stage) can only be used for type checking but not for reasoning about object behavior and correct use [FM91, NP90a]. On a higher level of abstraction TROL allows to define special interfaces to objects, thus restricting the visible properties of an object to a proper subset [JHSS91, SJ91].

In the **valuation**-section of a template, rules that specify the effects of event occurrences on the attribute values are presented. The rules are implicitly universally quantified and invariant. A valuation rule has one of the following forms:

        [event] attribute = data_term;

or:

        [event] attribute_1 = data_term_1,
                 attribute_2 = data_term_2,
                 ...
                 attribute_n = data_term_n;

Such a rule denotes that the attribute **attribute** after the occurrence of the event **event** will have the value of the term **data term**. The data term is evaluated in the state *before* the occurrence of the event and thus corresponds to an assignment in imperative programming languages. The second form is added as 'syntactic sugar', denoting that after the occurrence of event **event** attributes 1,...,n will have the values of data terms 1,...,n respectively. Another way to look at valuation rules are simple postconditions to event occurrences. An implicit frame rule states that attribute values not being set by a valuation rule remain unchanged after an event has occurred.

As an example, consider the valuation rules for **STOPWATCH**-objects:

      valuation
        [start] time = 0,
               stopped = false;
        [tick] time = time + 1;
        [stop] stopped = true;

After the **start** event of the stopwatch the attribute **time** is initialized to zero and the attribute **stopped** is initialized to **false**. **Tick** events increment the counter attribute **time** and the **stop** event sets the 'flag' attribute **stopped** to true.

In the **permissions**- and the **obligations**-section, the set of admissible life cycles is defined declaratively by giving conditions to be fulfilled by each life cycle. These sections describe the *behavior* component of an object description.

Permissions state preconditions for the occurrence of events. Events are only allowed to occur if the precondition is fulfilled. Roughly, permissions correspond to safety conditions (here: restricting the *next* possible states) [Lam83]. In the TROLL-kernel, preconditions are formulae of a first-order logic, build upon attribute symbols and operations imported in the data type section.

Consider the permissions for STOPWATCHes:

> **permissions**
>   variables n:nat;
>   {not stopped} tick;
>   {not stopped} stop;
>   {stopped and n = time} deliver(n);
>   {stopped} reset;

These rules state, that tick and stop events are only permitted if the attribute stopped is bound to false. Note that the stop event, since it alters the attribute stopped, may only occur once.

In the **obligations**-section, conditions to be fulfilled by complete life cycles are stated. The conditions must be fulfilled before an object can be destroyed. For STOPWATCHes, we require the reset-event to occur:

> **obligations**
>   reset;

In this sense obligations correspond to *liveness requirements*, stating what *must* occur. **Obligations** are thus used to describe necessary events in the live of an object and, in case of passive objects, can be seen as guides for correct use by potential clients. For example, we may have specified a slightly different obligation, stating that a deliver event must occur in the life cycle of stopwatches:

> **obligations**
>   ((exists n:nat) deliver(n)) and reset;

This condition implies, that users of stopwatch objects (clients) must invoke a deliver operation before a reset, the death event of the stopwatch. Failing to do so is a violation of the *contract* between objects and its clients [Mey88]. This contract can be derived from the life cycle definition of stopwatches. Informally, it may be expressed as: Potential users of stopwatch objects, that issued start and stop events *must* issue a deliver event before destroying the stopwatch object with the reset event.

This view of the server object stopwatch is purely passive. The other way round, specifying the deliver event as an *active* event would state that the stopwatch can force this event to occur, that is, to behave like an active object. Following this line permissions correspond to input offers, whereas obligations correspond to output offers in the terminology of [NP90b, NP90a].

Let us now consider the specification of class types. We want to describe a *set* of objects with similar structure and behavior. Each object in this set or *class* must be uniquely identified. As identification space we use an isomorphic copy of the set of natural numbers. The class type STOPWATCH is specified as follows (compiling the former described specification fragments under the keyword **template**):

```
object class STOPWATCH
    identification
        number:nat
    template
        data types nat, bool;
        attributes
            time:nat;
            stopped:bool;
        events
            birth start;
            tick;
            stop;
            deliver(nat);
            death reset;
        valuation
            [start] time = 0,
                    stopped = false;
            [tick] time = time + 1;
            [stop] stopped = true;
        permissions
            variables n:nat;
            {not stopped} tick;
            {not stopped} stop;
            {stopped and n = time} deliver(n);
            {stopped} reset;
        obligations
            reset;
end object class STOPWATCH
```

With the definition of a class type an abstract data type (ADT) for object identifiers is generated implicitly. As a convention the name of this ADT is given by the class type name between vertical bars. Note that we may use the identification selector of an instance denoted by number in the same way as attribute symbols defined within the object template.

For the sake of completeness, here is the specification for customer. In the attribute uses we save the identifier of the STOPWATCH-instance that is currently used by the customer.

```
object customer
    template
        data types nat, bool, |STOPWATCH|;
        attributes
            stopped_time:nat;
            stopped:bool;
            uses:|STOPWATCH|;
        events
```

      birth pop_up;
      start_watch;
      stop_watch;
      read_time(nat);
      reset_watch;
      death vanish;
   valuation
      variables n:nat;
      [pop_up] stopped_time $= 0$,
           uses $=$ STOPWATCH(1);
      [start_watch] stopped $=$ false;
      [stop_watch] stopped $=$ true;
      [read_time(n)] stopped_time $=$ n;
      [reset_watch] stopped_time $= 0$,
             uses $=$ STOPWATCH(uses.number$+1$);
   permissions
      variables n:nat;
      {stopped_time$=0$} start_watch;
      {not stopped and stopped_time$=0$}stop_watch;
      {stopped and stopped_time$=$n}read_time(n);
end object customer

Customers use different stopwatches since stopwatches are destroyed after they have done their work, i.e. a **reset** event occurred. Every time a customer resets the currently used stopwatch and therefore removes it, the attribute **uses** is altered to the next possible stopwatch identifier. The dot notation **uses.number** is another notation for the operation **number(uses)** (yielding integer values) defined implicitly in the abstract data type |STOPWATCH|.

Up to now we have specified two different base objects. The next step is to tie together these base objects using a mediator object, a channel. This CHANNEL object handles the communication between the **customer** object and an instance of class STOPWATCH. Note that channels are identified by identifiers of STOPWATCH instances. We thus have one CHANNEL for each instance of STOPWATCH.

object class CHANNEL
   identification
      with:|STOPWATCH|;
   template
      data types nat;
      events
         birth set_up;
         startwatch;
         stopwatch;
         readtime(nat);
         resetwatch;
         death close_down;

end object class CHANNEL;

These **CHANNEL** objects only contain events, but this is not a general requirement. Recall that we may specify channels with buffer or queueing functions. Therefore attributes as a form of memory would be needed.

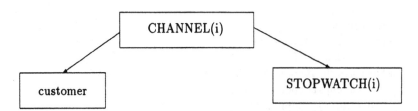

Figure 2: System of communicating objects

Figure 2 shows the relationship between the **customer**, an instance of **STOPWATCH** and the **CHANNEL**.

Now let us consider how the TROL-kernel can be used to model a system of communicating base objects. The **customer** must include all instances of **CHANNEL** after they have been created. Since all communications are initiated by **customer**, in the **interactions**-section of **customer** the calls to the communication events must be specified:

```
object customer
    including C in CHANNEL;
    template
        ...
    interactions
        variables n:nat;
        pop_up >> CHANNEL(uses).set_up;
        start_watch >> CHANNEL(uses).startwatch;
        stop_watch >> CHANNEL(uses).stopwatch;
        read_time(n) >> CHANNEL(uses).readtime(n);
        reset_watch >> CHANNEL(uses).resetwatch;
        vanish >> CHANNEL(uses).close_down;
end object customer
```

By definition, the operation **CHANNEL**, applied to an object identifier, yields the object itself. Recall, that referencing these **CHANNEL** objects is only possible because they are included in the **customer** object (see def. 2.9). This way the signature of **customer** objects also contains the event symbols of **CHANNEL** objects. Since we included a set of (possible) objects, we have to deal with *indexed* symbols. Indexing is denoted using the dot notation.

Similar to **customer** objects, an instance of class **STOPWATCH** must include the corresponding **CHANNEL** instance. Since each **STOPWATCH** instance is associated with exactly one CHANNEL instance, a slightly different including clause is used. Here a single instance of class CHANNEL is included. The notation SELF.identification denotes the instance of the data type |STOPWATCH| associated with the current instance. The condition C.with=SELF.identification thus binds the identifier C to the desired CHANNEL instance.

Since there are no name clashes between the signatures of CHANNEL and STOPWATCH we do not need to rename any components:

```
class STOPWATCH
   identification
      number:nat
   template
      including instance C in CHANNEL
         where C.with=SELF.identification
      ...
      interactions
         variables n:nat;
         start == startwatch;
         stop == stopwatch;
         reset == resetwatch;
         deliver(n) == readtime(n);
end class STOPWATCH
```

In contrast to the customer specification, we have sharing of events. This implies that the connection between CHANNELs and STOPWATCHes is stronger than between CHANNELs and customers because communication is *symmetric*.

Suppose the STOPWATCH is modeled as an active object, that is it can force events to occur by own initiative. These events will then be reflected in the CHANNEL due to the sharing equations in the interaction section and therefore in other objects possibly connected to it (that have included the CHANNEL).

In this case obviously there should be no other objects that use the STOPWATCH. We can reason that with this *communication structure* defined with the interactions between the base objects and the CHANNEL, the customer is not aware of events triggered in the STOPWATCH.

Consider for example another client 'connects' to the CHANNEL after some tick events occurred and forces concurrently to the former client the stop event. Note that this situation cannot be distinguished from an active STOPWATCH object, since the original client is not aware of concurrent use of the STOPWATCH by other clients forcing state changes of the STOPWATCH. The result is trouble within the original client: the STOPWATCH is stopped, but this state is not reflected in its stopped attribute.

Therefore, communication by calling is not sufficient here because events induced to the STOPWATCH from somewhere else may not be noticed by the customer. We should rewrite the specification of the communication structure between customer and STOPWATCH to:

```
object customer
   including C in CHANNEL;
   template
```

...

interactions
    variables n:nat;
    pop_up >> CHANNEL(uses).set_up;
    start_watch == CHANNEL(uses).startwatch;
    stop_watch == CHANNEL(uses).stopwatch;
    read_time(n) == CHANNEL(uses).readtime(n);
    reset_watch == CHANNEL(uses).resetwatch;
    vanish >> CHANNEL(uses).close_down;
end object customer

Now state changes of the STOPWATCH that coincide with state changes of the customer (for example the stop and stop_watch events) are reflected symmetrically in both objects. Now a correct use of the STOPWATCH from within the customer is possible, even if there are other concurrent requests to the STOPWATCH operations (even if this is not the desired use of a stopwatch).

5 Conclusions and Future Work

In this paper we have introduced a language for abstract description of Basic Object Structures. We have sketched a model of objects being regarded as processes observed by attributes. Then, we argued that distributed systems can be modeled using base objects and channels. Channels are objects that represent communication relationships between objects. Base objects can be regarded to be the actors in the system. Their behavior described using *permissions* and *obligations* can be used for reasoning about correct use by potential clients.

We think that BOS reflects the structures of distributed systems. Actors (base objects) and channels (communication lines) are described in a uniform way using the TROLL-kernel language. The models of specifications are object models as described in section 2.

Currently, we are starting to investigate how BOS can be implemented on a network of workstations. First ideas are that base objects that are currently active can be mapped to OS-processes. Therefore a more detailed notion of *activity* of objects is needed. Certain events may be specified as being active and can be executed by own initiative.

Channel objects may be mapped to specialized OS-processes performing communication with other processes. Whether this communication takes place between different machines using physical communication lines or between processes on one machine should be transparent, thus allowing objects to migrate. The uniform description of base objects and channel objects using one language framework appears to be the main advantage of this approach.

Another facet of objects in our sense is persistence. Instances may carry a lot of state information (attributes), thus we will need a database system to manage the state information of active *and* passive objects. These are only first ideas towards an implementation of abstract specifications of information systems.

Acknowledgments

We are very grateful to Gunter Saake and Cristina Sernadas who influenced significantly the language design of ꞮℜOℒ. Thanks also to the anonymous referees for providing very interesting ideas to our original workshop submission and not at last to all the participants of the workshop.

References

[Agh86] G.A. Agha. *ACTORS: A Model of Concurrent Computation in Distributed Systems*. The MIT Press, Cambridge, MA, 1986.

[Ame87] P. America. POOL-T: A Parallel Object-Oriented Language. In M. Tokoro and A. Yonezawa, editors, *Object-Oriented Concurrent Programming*, pages 199–220. The MIT Press, 1987.

[EGS90] H.-D. Ehrich, J. A. Goguen, and A. Sernadas. A Categorial Theory of Objects as Observed Processes. In J. de Bakker, W. de Roever, and G. Rozenberg, editors, *Foundations of Object-Oriented Languages (Proc. REX School/Workshop)*, pages 203–228, Noordwijkerhood (NL), 1990. LNCS 489, Springer-Verlag, Berlin, 1991.

[ES89] H.-D. Ehrich and A. Sernadas. Algebraic Implementation of Objects over Objects. In W. deRoever, editor, *Stepwise Refinement of Distributed Systems: Models, Formalisms, Correctness (Proc. REX'89)*, pages 239–266, Mood (NL), 1989. LNCS 394, Springer Verlag, Berlin, 1989.

[ES91] H.-D. Ehrich and A. Sernadas. Fundamental Object Concepts and Constructions. In G. Saake and A. Sernadas, editors, *Information Systems — Correctness and Reusability*, pages 97–128. Technical University Braunschweig, Informatik Bericht 91-03, 1991.

[ESS90] H.-D. Ehrich, A. Sernadas, and C. Sernadas. From Data Types to Object Types. *Journal on Information Processing and Cybernetics EIK*, 26(1/2):33–48, 1990.

[FM91] J. Fiadeiro and T.S.E. Maibaum. Towards Object Calculi. In G. Saake and A. Sernadas, editors, *Information Systems — Correctness and Reusability*, pages 129–178. Technical University Braunschweig, Informatik Bericht 91-03, 1991.

[FSMS90] J. Fiadeiro, C. Sernadas, T. Maibaum, and G. Saake. Proof-Theoretic Semantics of Object-Oriented Specification Constructs. In R. Meersman and W. Kent, editors, *Object-Oriented Databases: Analysis, Design and Construction (Proc. 4th IFIP WG 2.6 Working Conference DS-4)*, Windermere (UK), 1990. North-Holland, Amsterdam. *In print.*

[Hew77]   C. Hewitt. Viewing Control Structures as Patterns of Passing Messages. *Artificial Intelligence*, 8:323–364, 1977.

[Hoa85]   C. A. R. Hoare. *Communicating Sequential Processes*. Prentice-Hall, Englewood Cliffs, NJ, 1985.

[JHSS91]   R. Jungclaus, T. Hartmann, G. Saake, and C. Sernadas. Introduction to TROLL – A Language for Object-Oriented Specification of Information Systems. In G. Saake and A. Sernadas, editors, *Information Systems — Correctness and Reusability*, pages 97–128. Technical University Braunschweig, Informatik Bericht 91-03, 1991.

[JSH91]   R. Jungclaus, G. Saake, and T. Hartmann. Language Features for Object-Oriented Conceptual Modeling. In T. Teory, editor, *Proc. 10th Int. Conf. on the ER-Approach*, San Mateo (CA), pages 309–324, 1991.

[JSS91]   R. Jungclaus, G. Saake, and C. Sernadas. Formal Specification of Object Systems. In S. Abramsky and T. Maibaum, editors, *Proc. TAPSOFT'91*, pages 60–82, Brighton (UK), 1991. LNCS 494, Springer-Verlag, Berlin.

[Lam83]   L. Lamport. Specifying Concurrent Program Modules. *ACM Transactions on Programming Languages and Systems*, 5(2):190–222, April 1983.

[Mey88]   B. Meyer. *Object-Oriented Software Construction*. Prentice-Hall, Englewood Cliffs, NJ, 1988.

[Mil89]   R. Milner. *Communication and Concurrency*. Prentice-Hall, Englewood Cliffs, 1989.

[Nie90]   O. Nierstrasz. A Guide to Specifying Concurrent Behaviour with Abacus. In D. Tsichritzis, editor, *Object Management*, pages 267–293. Université de Genève, 1990.

[NP90a]   O. M. Nierstrasz and M. Papathomas. Towards a Type Theory for Active Objects. In *Object Management*, pages 295–304. Université de Genève, 1990.

[NP90b]   O. M. Nierstrasz and M. Papathomas. Viewing Objects as Patterns of Communicating Agents. In N. Meyrowitz, editor, *ECOOP/OOPSLA'90 Proceedings*, Ottawa, 1990. ACM, 1990. also in [NP90a].

[SE90]   A. Sernadas and H.-D. Ehrich. What Is an Object, After All? In R. Meersman and W. Kent, editors, *Object-Oriented Databases: Analysis, Design and Construction (Proc. 4th IFIP WG 2.6 Working Conference DS-4)*, Windermere (UK), 1990. North-Holland, Amsterdam. *In print*.

[SFSE89a] A. Sernadas, J. Fiadeiro, C. Sernadas, and H.-D. Ehrich. Abstract Object Types: A Temporal Perspective. In Banieqbal, Baringer, and Pnueli, editors, *Temporal Logic in Specification*. Springer, LNCS 398, 1989.

[SFSE89b] A. Sernadas, J. Fiadeiro, C. Sernadas, and H.-D. Ehrich. The Basic Building Blocks of Information Systems. In E. Falkenberg and P. Lindgreen, editors, *Information System Concepts: An In-Depth Analysis*, pages 225–246, Namur (B), 1989. North-Holland, Amsterdam, 1989.

[SJ91] G. Saake and R. Jungclaus. Specification of Database Applications in the TROLL Language. In *Proc. Int. Workshop on the Specification of Database Applications*, 1991. To appear.

[SJE91] G. Saake, R. Jungclaus, and H.-D. Ehrich. Object-Oriented Specification and Stepwise Refinement. In *Proc. International IFIP Workshop on Open Distributed Processing, Berlin*. North Holland, 1991. To appear.

[SSE87] A. Sernadas, C. Sernadas, and H.-D. Ehrich. Object-Oriented Specification of Databases: An Algebraic Approach. In P. Hammerslay, editor, *Proc. 13th Int. Conf. on Very Large Databases VLDB'87*, pages 107–116, Brighton (GB), 1987. Morgan-Kaufmann, Palo Alto, 1987.

[YSTH87] A. Yonezawa, E. Shibayama, T. Takada, and Y. Honda. Modelling and Programming in an Object-Oriented Concurrent Language ABCL/1. In M. Tokoro and A. Yonezawa, editors, *Object-Oriented Concurrent Programming*, pages 55–89. The MIT Press, 1987.

Design Issues for Object-Based Concurrency

Peter Wegner

Brown University

Abstract

We examine the design space for object-based concurrent programming, emphasizing high-level design alternatives in the areas of process structure, internal process concurrency, synchronization, and inter-process communication. We consider the role of abstraction, distribution, and synchronization in determining the granularity of modules, and introduce the notion of "relative persistence" of operations and data for functions, objects, and transactions. Our primary goal is to present design alternatives rather than to draw strong conclusions about how concurrent object-oriented systems should be designed. This work derives from [15] and complements work on fundamental models of concurrency such as [1, 4, 12, 17].

1 Process Structure

Design issues of process structure to be discussed include:

- shared memory versus object model
- styles of client/server interaction: tasks versus monitors
- styles of nondeterminism
- logical versus physical distribution,
- weakly and strongly distributed systems

1.1 Shared Memory Model versus Object (Process) Model

Process-oriented architectures discard the shared memory model that forms the basis of procedure-oriented programming and replace it by an object-model in which each object (process) is responsible for its own protection. Consider an operating system with READ, EXECUTE, and PRINT processes, where the READ and EXECUTE processes share an input buffer and the EXECUTE and PRINT processes share an output buffer [2, 3].

In the shared memory model, the data in the input and output buffers are unprotected. The READ and EXECUTE processes must cooperatively protect the data, for example by semaphores with request and release (P and V) operations that control access to shared data and ensure mutually exclusive access.

In an object-based model, the input and output buffers are server processes responsible for their own protection. The input and execute (client) processes no longer need to use low-level primitives for protecting the data in the input buffer. Remote procedure calls that rely on local protection of data in called programs may be used.

1.2 Client and Server Processes

Objects may be viewed as server processes that are activated by messages from their clients. We examine two distinct forms of interaction between client and server processes exemplified by Ada tasks and monitors [6, 7, 16].

1.2.1 Tasks with Rendezvous

Ada tasks have a single thread of control that may synchronize with incoming procedure calls at entry points determined by accept statements:

Task body T
    hidden local variables
    sequence of executable statements that include
    accept statements (entry points) synchronizing by rendezvous with
    remote procedure calls
    accept bodies that determine communication during synchronization
endtask

Task synchronization requires remote procedure calls of a calling module to rendezvous with accept statements of a called module. If a call (message) arrives before an accept statement is ready to accept it, the calling procedure suspends and the call is placed in a queue. If an accept statement is reached before a waiting call then the task suspends and waits for a call. When a rendezvous occurs the threads of the calling and the called module are temporarily merged, input parameters may be transmitted from the calling to the called procedure, the code specified by the accept statement is executed, and output parameters may be transmitted back to the caller. On completion of the rendezvous the calling and called processes resume separate concurrent execution.

Entry points for accept statements are defined in *ask specifications*. A buffer task with APPEND and REMOVE entry points may be specified as follows:

task BUFFER is
    entry APPEND (M: in MESSAGE)
    entry REMOVE (M: out MESSAGE)
end BUFFER

The task body has accept statements for accepting APPEND and REMOVE calls:

accept APPEND (M: in MESSAGE) do
    BUFF(IN) := M;

end

The code between the do and end is executed during the rendezvous. In this case no value is returned to the caller (M is an *in* parameter). However, the accept statement for REMOVE has an *out* parameter that returns the value of M to its caller as the final action of the rendezvous:

```
accept REMOVE (M: out MESSAGE) do
   M := BUFF(OUT);
end
```

1.2.2   Monitors with Internal Monitor Queues

Monitors [6, 7] have local variables and an interface of operations that are effectively entry points. They guarantee mutually exclusive access by clients to shared data, but their operations may suspend and later resume (like coroutines):

```
Monitor M
   hidden local variables
   operations (entry points) that include
   wait commands for suspending and signal commands for resuming operations
endmonitor
```

Monitors have an entry queue for incoming monitor calls and wait queues for suspended monitor calls. Suspension is realized by a command *wait(condition-name)* that suspends the current thread and places it on the named wait queue, from which it may be removed (reawakened) by a command *signal(condition-name)*. When a thread suspends then a waiting reawakened or entering thread may commence execution.

Monitors control the execution of threads more flexibly than tasks, allowing threads within a module to suspend and later resume. This requires greater complexity at the language level, with wait and signal commands, and greater complexity of implementation, with internal monitor queues. Scheduling priorities determined by the operating system arbitrate between the resumption of signaled threads in wait queues and incoming threads in the monitor queue: processes in wait queues usually have priority over incoming processes in the monitor queue.

1.3   Non-Determinism

Nondeterminism is a necessary feature of any client/server system because the demands made by clients for services cannot be predicted. Objects and monitors are at the mercy of clients to select the next operation to be executed. A BUFFER object cannot know whether the next operation will be an APPEND or a REMOVE.

Ada tasks accommodate nondeterministic behavior of clients through a select statement which selects among guarded waiting remote procedure calls (rpcs):

```
select
    when guard-condition1 then accept rpc1
    or
    when guard-condition2 then accept rpc2
    ...
    when guard-conditionN then accept rpcN
endselect
```

Select statement may be used to implement nondeterministic choice between APPEND and REMOVE operations of an Ada buffer task:

```
select
    when notfull then accept APPEND
    or
    when notempty then accept REMOVE
endselect
```

When the buffer is neither full nor empty, this statement chooses among waiting APPEND and REMOVE operations, and otherwise chooses the first to arrive. When the buffer is full executing REMOVE will unblock the buffer for APPEND. For an empty buffer executing APPEND will unblock it for REMOVE.

Ada's explicit select statement contrasts with the implicit nondeterminism of monitors, which consist of an implicit select statement with unguarded alternatives:

$$select\ op1\ or\ op2\ or\ \cdots\ or\ opN\ endselect$$

Guarded selection is realized in monitors by *wait* statements (wait(guard-condition)) that may suspend monitor operations during their execution. Monitors are more flexible than Ada tasks in allowing guards to occur not only on entering a process but at any point during execution of the process. They decouple nondeterministic entry from guard conditions that determine whether a process is ready for execution.

Nondeterminism is built into the fabric of object-based programming independent of concurrency. The nondeterminism of objects mirrors the real world where the sequence of events in which entities participate cannot be predicted. Since nondeterminism occurs even in the sequential case, the nondeterminism of object-based concurrency comes for free.

The nondeterminism of objects differs from that of traditional nondeterministic automata, where nondeterminism refers to the fact that a computational step in a given state can generate multiple next states. Objects have nondeterministic input to a computational step, while nondeterministic automata have nondeterministic output. The two forms of nondeterminism are is a sense dual and may be called input and output nondeterminism.

input nondeterminism: the next operation on an object or process is unknown
output nondeterminism: the output is a nondeterministic function of the input

Select statements arise because of the need to handle input nondeterminism of clients. They support output nondeterminism when several branches of a select statement are ready for execution. For example, if the select statement of the buffer task is reached when the buffer is neither empty or full, and both an APPEND and a REMOVE call are waiting to be executed, then output nondeterminism may be used to determine which action is actually performed.

1.4 Logical Versus Physical Distribution

A system of modules is logically distributed if each module has its own separate name space. Local data is not directly accessible to other modules, conversely modules cannot directly access non-local data, and must communicate with other modules by messages.

We distinguish between logical distribution defined in terms of properties of the name space and physical distribution defined in terms of geographical or spatial distribution of modules. Physical distribution usually implies logical distribution, since physical separation is most naturally modeled by logical separation. But logically distributed systems are often implemented by shared-memory architectures for greater efficiency. Object-based systems are logically distributed but are usually implemented on non-distributed computers.

Logical distribution supports autonomy of software components and thereby facilitates concurrent execution. Another important benefit of logical distribution is its support of autonomous interface modules, such as multiple windows. Autonomous interface modules allow the user to pursue multiple autonomous, conceptually concurrent, interface activities. Physical concurrency is not required and usually unnecessary. But conceptual autonomy is an important property of activities in the real world, and its realization at the workstation interface is one of the most important practical benefits of object-based programming.

1.5 Weakly and Strongly Distributed Systems

A system is weakly distributed if its modules know the names of other modules. It is strongly distributed if its modules cannot directly name other modules. In a strongly distributed system a given module knows only the names of its own communication ports. The names of modules with which it communicates are stored as data in its communication ports, and may be viewed as pointers to ports of other modules that cannot be dereferenced to determine the name of non-local ports. A module communicates by sending a message, specified as a data value, to a local port for transmittal to a destination.

Traditional object-oriented languages are weakly distributed. Objects can know the names of other objects and send messages to methods of other objects. The weak distribution reflects that implementation is usually in a shared-memory architecture. Strongly distributed systems better capture the the reality of physical distribution where connections among modules of a network are realized by physical channels and the topology of the network may change.

In strongly distributed systems like Nil and Hermes [13, 14], processes can refer to their own ports but not to ports of other processes. When a process Q is created, the creating process must supply Q with initial capabilities. The created process stores the initial capabilities by a receive command as in the program PR below, and can then make use of the capabilities to access its environment.

A newly created process finds its initial capabilities in the system-defined variable *init*. The program PR below for printing the message "Hello World" first executes the command "receive Port from Init", which stores its initial capabilities in the local communication port called *Port*. Then it calls the Putline component of its communication port with a message to print "Hello World". Finally it executes a return message that returns its capabilities to the caller, and allows the process to expire.

```
PR: receive Port from Init
    call Port.Putline ("Hello", "World")
    return Port;
```

Strongly distributed systems have greater overhead than weakly distributed systems but allow dynamic reconfiguration for anonymously communicating (*autistic*) processes.

2   Internal Process Concurrency

Processes of object-based concurrent systems may be internally sequential, quasi-concurrent, or fully concurrent.

Sequential processes are illustrated by Ada whose tasks have a single executing thread that may be suspended while waiting to receive an external communication but must run to completion once the external communication is accepted. Rendezvous causes temporary merging of the incoming and executing threads until the interaction of the two threads is completed.

Quasi-concurrent execution is illustrated by monitors, which have at most a single active executing thread but may have suspended threads in one or more wait queues. The ability to suspend threads internally provides flexibility while the fact that at most one thread can be active ensures mutually exclusive access to local data. Because of these advantages object-based concurrent languages like ABCL1 and Orient 84 [17] are based on quasi-concurrency, although their message passing protocols transcend the client/server mechanism of monitors. However, quasi concurrency gives rise to problems when the threads being executed represent transactions whose data may be accessed only when in a stable state. Suspension of threads when not in a stable state allows tampering with data that violates the conditions of transactions.

Fully concurrent processes are illustrated by Argus guardians [10]. Guardians do not synchronize incoming threads on entry, so that entry of a thread to a Guardian simply increases the number of executing threads. Synchronization occurs later when executing threads within a Guardian attempt to access shared data.

Consider an Argus mail system with MAILER, MAILDROP, and REGISTRY guardians that may be replicated at many physical locations. The Mailer is the user interface and allows users to send mail, receive mail, and add users to the mail system. The MAILDROP guardian contains a subset of the mailboxes and is invoked by MAILER to deliver mail to those mailboxes. The REGISTRY guardian specifies the maildrop for each user and must be updated when users are added or deleted from the system.

In this example, MAILER guardians may execute multiple threads freely since there is no shared data structure to worry about. MAILDROP guardians must synchronize for delivery and removal from a given mailbox but can concurrently interact with different mailboxes. REGISTRY guardians can permit concurrent lookup but must synchronize when adding or removing users. By delaying synchronization so that it occurs at the point of access to shared data rather than on entry to a concurrent module, we can realize greater and more finely grained concurrency.

3   Design Alternatives for Synchronization

We distinguish synchronization for unprotected and encapsulated data. For unprotected data, the work of synchronization must be performed by each process that accesses the data. Synchronization may require cooperative protocols: for example among semaphores to specify mutually exclusive access to critical regions. Protected data assumes responsibility for its own protection, removing the burden from the processes that access the data. Object-based systems focus on synchronization for protected data.

Three kinds of synchronization mechanisms may be distinguished:

- **rendezvous** synchronization between two threads (for sequential processes)

- **condition variables** controlled by wait and signal operations (for quasi-concurrent processes)

- **locking** synchronization between a thread and shared data (for fully concurrent processes)

The rendezvous mechanism for sequential processes may be viewed as synchronization between two threads, namely the calling and the called thread. Synchronization is symmetrical for the two parties that synchronize. But the calling and the called threads play different roles once synchronization has occurred, with the calling thread being passive and the called thread performing the task for which it was invoked. An Ada rendezvous causes temporary merging of the calling and called threads for the purpose of executing the accept body, and subsequent forking to permit concurrent execution of the calling and called process to be resumed.

Quasi-concurrent processes employ implicit rendezvous-like synchronization to define entry to the monitor, and use condition variables (guards) to model internal synchronization. They decouple synchronization for entry and resumption of threads by having different protocols for entry and resumption, specified by different language primitives.

Fully concurrent processes involve synchronization between concurrently executing threads and local, unprotected shared data. This is realized by locking the data and temporarily restricting access to the thread on whose behalf the data was locked. The locking protocol may itself be complex when an operation requires exclusive access to multiple shared data entities. Two-phase locking, which separates the phase of acquiring locks from the phase of releasing them, reduces the likelihood of thrashing in the competition of threads for multiple shared resources. Alternative locking protocols for distributed architectures are discussed in [5].

4 Asynchronous Messages, Futures, and Promises

Design alternatives for message passing include *synchronous, asynchronous* and *stream-based* message passing. Synchronous message passing, which requires the sender to suspend until a reply is received, is essentially remote procedure call. Asynchronous message passing allows the sender to continue, but requires synchronization if subsequent execution depends on the reply. Stream-based message passing supports streams of messages which likewise require synchronization at message-use time to check that replies have been received.

Asynchronously computed results may be handled by data structures called *futures* created at the time of message-send. Anonymous futures allow synchronization of operators for asynchronously computed arguments, and may be assigned to variables:

+(future(e1), future(e2))   *wait till both e1 and e2 are ready before adding*
define(x, future(e))   *x cannot be used till evaluation of e is complete*

+ requires *strict* (synchronous) evaluation that blocks till its arguments and the sum are evaluated. *define* permits *nonstrict* (lazy, asynchronous) evaluation that blocks only when x is accessed for further computation.

Asynchronous ·*send* may be viewed as a nonstrict operation that specifies a *reply-variable* at message-send time for synchronization at message-use time: In the example below, the value of x is specified to be the future reply from the asynchronously called process P, so that access to x must wait till the reply from P arrives.

send P(message) x(future(reply))   *access to x must wait for the reply from P*

Future objects are used in object-based systems like ABCL, Orient 84/K, and ConcurrentSmalltalk. They are used in the *streamcall* mechanism of the MIT Mercury system [9], which allows the sender to send a stream of messages along a call stream and the receiver to send a return stream of replies. Streamcalls are an efficient form of asynchronous communication for frequently communicating processes. Synchronization for streamcalls is realized in Argus by typed data structures called *promises* [11], which, like futures, are created at the time of call (message send) and can be claimed only when the promise has been fulfilled (the promised reply from the called process has been safely stored in the "promise" variable). Mercury supports synchronous, asynchronous, and stream-based message passing for heterogeneous, cooperating distributed processes:

call: synchronous remote procedure call
send: asynchronous send with return for exceptions
streamcall: pipelined stream of calls and returns

5   Inter-Process Communication

Design alternatives for inter-process communication include two-way interconnected distributed processes, one-way interconnected client/server processes, and dynamically interconnected strongly distributed processes.

In CSP communication requires two-way naming, with the sending process knowing the name of the receiving process and the receiving process knowing the name of the sending process. Two-way naming models hard-wired interconnection between processes. However, one-way naming, where the called process need not know the names of its callers, is more flexible and is the standard inter-module communication mechanism for procedures and synchronous message passing. Two-way naming is implemented in terms of one-way naming by passing the name of the caller as an argument to the called procedure.

Ada *accept* statements use one-way naming, requiring the caller to name the called task but allowing a task to be called by anyone who knows its name.

In strongly distributed processes, the names of non-local ports are stored as data in local port variables and the connection to to other processes is therefore dynamic. Channel interconnections are established by storing port values in port variables. A channel can be viewed as a cable with a plug at one end connecting it to its target and a socket at the other end into which the source can be plugged.

6   Abstraction, Distribution, and Synchronization Boundaries

Module boundaries in object-based concurrent systems are determined by the mechanisms for abstraction, distribution, and synchronization.

The *abstraction boundary* is the interface a module presents to its clients. It determines the form in which resources provided by an object may be accessed (invoked). It is an information-hiding boundary encountered by a client looking inward into a module. It limits what the client can see, hiding local data from access by the client. It is the unit of encapsulation and the fundamental unit of object granularity.

The *distribution boundary* is the boundary of accessible names visible from within an object. The abstraction boundary is encountered by a user looking inward, while the distribution boundary is encountered by an agent within a module looking outward. The distribution boundary may be coarser than the abstraction boundary, as in block-structure languages, or finer, when a large abstraction (say an airline reservation system) is implemented by distributed components. When the abstraction and distribution boundaries coincide, we say a module is *distributed*.

The *synchronization boundary* of a module is the boundary at which threads entering a module synchronize with ongoing activities in the module. For sequential processes the thread synchronization boundary is also the abstraction boundary. For concurrent processes the thread synchronization boundary is finer than the abstraction boundary. Conversely, the unit of abstraction can be coarser than that for concurrency, for example when the address space associated with a single thread can contain many abstract objects.

The boundaries for abstraction, distribution, and synchronization are in general independent. However, the special case when the three boundaries coincide is an interesting one. Processes for which these boundaries coincide are called *distributed sequential processes*. They are distributed because their abstraction and distribution boundaries coincide and sequential because their abstraction and synchronization boundaries coincide.

Distributed sequential processes are attractively simple both conceptually and in terms of their implementation. However, insisting on the same granularity for abstraction, distribution, and synchronization may reduce efficiency or expressive power. For example, large abstractions such as airline reservation systems need finely grained synchronization at the level of individual flights or even individual seats to execute efficiently. Conversely, a network of sequential computers with multiple objects at each node is naturally modeled by a unit of concurrency coarser than its unit of abstraction.

7   Persistence and Transactions

Data is persistent if its lifetime is long relative to the operations that act upon it: for example income tax data that persists from year to year. However, persistence is relative rather than absolute: if income tax were computed every hour (for fast moving stockbrokers) then data persistence would be measured in hours rather than years.

Modules may be classified in terms of the relative persistence of operations and their data:

functions: persistent actions on transient data
objects: operations and data with coextensive lifetimes
transactions: flexible relative persistence of operations and data

Functions and procedures emphasize the persistence of programs for transitory data. Objects partly redress the balance by supporting coextensive persistence for operations and their data, but are not flexible in supporting variable persistence of operations and data. Databases solve the data persistence problem by entirely decoupling programs from the data on which they operate and introducing transactions for flexible temporary coupling of operations and data.

Transactions are atomic, all-or-nothing actions that either complete or abort with no effect on the rest of the program. When executed concurrently on shared data, their atomic effect can be achieved by locking sharable data temporarily to the operations of a particular transaction, so that the data and operations form a temporary entity that is dissolved when the transaction is completed. The temporary entity may be viewed as a dynamically created object that temporarily binds data to the operations of the transaction. During execution of the transaction its data is accessible only to local operations, just as for local data of objects. Transactions may be viewed as dynamically created temporal modules that supplement textual modularity of programs in space by modularity in the time dimension.

Transactions allow shared data structures to be associated with operation sets of different transactions at successive stages of their life. Conventional objects bind data structures to operations in a permanent union, while in a transaction system data structures can be promiscuous, having a variety of different partners. Operations can be equally promiscuous, having temporary liaisons with many different data structures. The relative persistence of operations and data is flexible and dynamically determined.

Are transactions object-based? The answer is no if objects are viewed as fixed combinations of data and operations. However, if the notion of object is extended to include temporary associations of data and operations, then transactions may be viewed as extending traditional object-oriented notions to include dynamically created objects.

Should persistent storage be object-oriented, or should it reflect the transitory association of operations with persistent data. It may well be that persistent storage should support loose bonds between operations and data, and transaction-like mechanisms for temporary bonding. These issues are being debated by proponents of object-based and relational databases.

8   Conclusion

A primary dichotomy in examining design alternatives is the tradeoff between efficiency (or simplicity) and generality. This ubiquitous tradeoff appears in the following cases:

- shared variables versus distributed processes

- weakly versus strongly distributed systems

- tasks (single thread) versus monitors (one active and multiple suspended threads)

- internally sequential versus internally concurrent processes

- synchronous versus asynchronous communication

- static versus dynamic process interconnection

- independence of abstraction, distribution, and synchronization boundaries

- static versus dynamic relative persistence of programs and data

In each case the first alternative is simpler to implement and usually more efficient than the second. However, the second alternative allows more flexible forms of concurrency. There is no definite criterion that allows us to state that simplicity is to be preferred over generality, or vice versa. Each of the design alternatives mentioned has been explored in some concurrent object-oriented system, but no clear consensus has yet emerged concerning the best mix of features for object-oriented concurrency.

References

[1] G. Agha, *Actors: A Model of Concurrent Computation in Distributed Systems*, MIT Press 1986.

[2] G. R. Andrews and F. B. Schneider, *Concepts and Notations for Concurrent Programming*, Computing Surveys, 15 (1), 1983.

[3] G. R. Andrews, *Concurrent Programming: Principles and Practice*, Benjamin Cummings 1991.

[4] G. Agha, P. Wegner, and A. Yonezawa, *Proceedings of Workshop on Object-Based Concurrent Programming*, Sigplan Notices, April 1989.

[5] G. Graunke and S. Thakkar, *Algorithms for Shared Memory Multiprocessors*, IEEE Computer, June 1990.

[6] P. B. Hansen, Distributed Processes, *A Concurrent Programming Concept*, CACM, 1978.

[7] C. A. R. Hoare, Monitors, *An Operating System Structuring Concept*, CACM, October 1974.

[8] C. A. R. Hoare, *Communicating Sequential Processes*, CACM, August 1978.

[9] B. Liskov, T. Bloom, D. Gifford, R. Scheifler, and W. Weihl, *Communication in the Mercury System*, Proc 21st Hawaii Conference, January 1988.

[10] B. Liskov and R. Scheifler, Guardians and Actions, *Linguistic Support for Robust Distributed Programs*, TOPLAS 5(3), 1983.

[11] B. Liskov and L. Shrira, *Promises: Linguistic Support for Efficient Asynchronous Procedure Calls in Distributed Systems*, SIGPLAN Conference on Programming Language Design and Implementation, June 1988.

[12] R. Milner, *Calculus of Communicating Systems*, Springer Verlag 1980.

[13] R. Strom and S. Yemini, *NIL, an Integrated Language and System for Distributed Programming*, Sigplan Notices, June 1983.

[14] Strom et al., Hermes, *A Language for Distributed Computing*, Prentice Hall, 1991.

[15] Peter Wegner, *Concepts and Paradigms of Object-oriented Programming*, OOPS Messenger, August 1990.

[16] Peter Wegner and Scott Smolka, *Processes, Tasks, and Monitors, Transactions of Software Engineering*, July 1983.

[17] A. Yonezawa and M. Tokoro, *Object-Oriented Concurrent Programming*, MIT Press, 1987.

Panel: What Is An Object? *

Moderator: Peter Wegner   (Brown University)
Panelists: Robin Milner   (University of Edinburgh)
             Pierre America   (Philips Research Laboratories)
             Oscar Nierstrasz   (University of Geneva)
             Mario Tokoro   (Keio University / Sony CSL)
             Akinori Yonezawa   (The University of Tokyo)

1   Panelists Initial Presentation

Wegner: The closing panel is titled "what is an object". To provide a framework, I suggest that panelists consider what are the essential properties of objects. Are objects required to have the following properties:

classes	types
inheritance	state
identity	message
code	values
concurrency	persistence
views	reference/address

Figure 1:

Each panelist should address these questions in his presentation about "what is an object".

Yonezawa: I would like to answer the question of "what is an object" by listing essential features of *concurrent objects*, as I think the notion of objects should be inherently concurrent. The features are: persistent identity, as an object models some entity; encapsulated local state, which means access protection except by message passing; and state changes triggered by message receipt, or method invocation; autonomous thread(s) of control, that

---

*This panel discussion was held as the last session of the workshop, at University of Geneva on July 16, 1991. Transcribed and edited by Kohei Honda and Satoshi Matsuoka.

is, an object should not be a passive data entity just to be manipulated but an entity with independent activity; messages which can contain objects' names, implying dynamic topology among objects; and dynamic object creation at run-time. These features imply the dynamic nature of concurrent object-based computing.

Nierstrasz: I think three issues are important to understand the notion of objects, namely, what is an object? why are objects important? and how are objects realized? First, what is an object? A minimal definition is that an object encapsulates services made available through a message-passing interface. A client can make requests and obtain some kind of services. As side-effects of providing services, objects may change state, and so they are persistent entities. In addition, being persistent, an object has a kind of identity, though this does not necessarily mean that objects have unique identifiers. Second, why are objects important? Objects are useful as an organizational paradigm, that is, for *decomposing* large systems into manageable chunks, and they are useful as a paradigm for reuse, that is, for *composing* systems from pre-packaged, plug-compatible objects. For this purpose, we need standardization of service interfaces of objects. Third, how to realize objects? Essentially two things are needed: packaging and binding. For functions, packaging is λ abstraction, whereas binding is application. In object-oriented programming, we can find these two elements in objects themselves (packaging by objects and binding by message-passing), classes (by class definition and by subclassing), and generic classes (by parameterization and subsequent binding of type parameters).

Tokoro: I would like to address some fundamental issues. First, we understand that computation is simulation of a real/imaginary world. The world is naturally open, distributed, and concurrent. There are things which should be modeled as objects and things which are difficult to be modeled as objects. In this sense, there are objects and non-objects in the world. An object is a thing which is distinguishable from others with notion of inside/outside. Otherwise it is a non-object. Tables and chairs are objects, whereas water, sky and blue are not appropriate to be modeled as objects. Computation is achieved through concurrent communication between objects. We assume a single "self-consciousness" (or "thread") per each object, but they may be composed to define composite objects. For objects in the distributed world, sub-optimal objects allocation in the computational field model, distributed transactions, distributed constraint-solving, cooperation, dynamic modeling of other objects etc. are essential. Finally what properties should we look for in concurrent/distributed computing? In terms of composition of objects, strong compositionality in a synchronous world may be replaced with weak compositionality in the asynchronous world. In addition to properties like safety, liveness, etc., some kind of the equilibrium state beyond the boundary of an object or an objects group should be considered.

America: An object is a unit with a clear boundary. Data and functionality operating on data determine an object. My standpoint is to make the notion of "object" as simple as possible. If one feature can be delegated to specialized objects, don't include it as a basic mechanism in the object model (in real-world programming it can be introduced as "syntactic sugar"). For example, couldn't we delegate types, inheritance, and so on to some language mechanisms which disappear as soon as an object comes into existence? Classes, which in my terminology describe internal structure of the objects, and types, which says how the object can be used, are needed when you are programming, but when the program is running, mostly you don't need them any more. The same kind of thing may be true for other elements. But why is simplification necessary? Because in the near future we will see a lot of things which cannot be modeled with objects alone (e.g. the continuous phenomena Mario mentioned). So to integrate new concepts to model various aspects of the real world which we currently do not model with objects very well in future, we need to make our current framework of objects as simple as possible. The simplicity is the only way of being able to extend our present tools.

Wegner: What are the essential properties you retain after simplification?

America: The basic idea of an object is that it has its state or data, some way of operating on them, and independent activity. Other elements should be delegated to other elements than objects themselves. For example, types can be considered as filters by which to describe your system.

Wegner: Are state and identity fundamental?

America: Yes, and operations or activities in addition.

Milner: First, the idea of objects, or agents, as I call them, should be considered as a basis of models of computation. In studying semantics of concurrent programming languages, I realized that interaction and state are essential, which is not embedded in existing models of computing, e.g. functions. Thus, my first attribute to objects is that they should be a really basic model of computation. The model should consist of objects and as little else as possible. That is what I have been working for with CCS and π-calculus. Models for programming are not necessarily the same as the basic calculus but can be built on it. Second, in regard of composition/decomposition, decomposition to objects (of some system) should not be unique but obey some decent algebraic laws, the origin of process algebra. So objects are views, how we impose structures on the world. Another essential element is internalization. Hence two basic operators in basic process algebra, process composition and internalization. The last thing is theory. In theory we have another abstraction based on bahavioural equivalences. Then we have classification of objects based on these equivalences, to understand different kinds of objects which you use. Then theory will help us build type systems, which, agreeing with Pierre, are not concerned with structures of objects but behaviour when they are running.

2 Discussions

2.1 How much run-time information should objects retain?

Floor: As we have to consider the notion of objects which are intelligent, flexible, complex, and even self-adaptive, we need more information at run-time for flexible interaction among agents.

America: First, we ourselves, as human beings, do not have and do not need much information about our own internal structure in order to perform intelligent communication. Second, it may not be a good way if you do not know how to use the information.

Milner: Pascal programs run without type information because of compile-time type checking. But when they interact with the outside, they need the notion of classification information. So we may need both.

Floor: In relational databases, the schema is required for external use.

Wegner: Don't you believe in having types and classes as they are when they are needed (at run-time)?

America: Yes and no. I agree that, in open systems, there should be some kind of object descriptions around for run-time use. But I am not sure that the types humans use for programming and reasoning are the right information for objects to keep around when they communicate with each other.

2.2 Extension of the notion of objects

Floor: Are objects finite and bounded?

Nierstrasz: If you take the basic model of objects, objects are things that accept messages and render services. Then essentially everything you want to know is there in objects, except messages they will receive. This means there are some parts which are unknown, unbounded. Furthermore, as classes can be objects, it is possible to change

Milner: I doubt everything is an object.

Nierstrasz: Pure values and ports are not objects. But everything else can essentially be modeled as an object.

Floor: But you should have classes.

Nierstrasz: You do not have to. Classes can be regarded as templates or as types. When it comes to templates, there is no reason to introduce new concepts in addition to objects.

Wegner: So there is a criterion for being an object, something like providing service and operation when required. In that sense, classes are objects.

Nierstrasz: And types can be objects if we regard types as partial specifications of behaviour. A type, in this view, is just a very non-deterministic object. Refinement makes the specification more specific.

2.3 Identity and Persistence

Floor: (to Tokoro) What is the identity of water?

Tokoro: That is why I excluded water from being an object! If you put the water into a bottle, then we can identify it; it is an object.

Floor: Is the notion of unique identity fundamental in objects?

Milner: I am negative about it. Id's are channels. Channels can be used to distinguish, for example, you from your neighbors. But this is not the whole story about you.

Wegner: One example Robin gave us in his lecture yesterday was when composing several objects the identity of original objects disappears.

Milner: If somebody is addressing you and me together, we cannot be sure if he is addressing me or you.

Nierstrasz: You can interpret the issue of identity in another way. If objects can change state, this implies that they have some kind of "identity" since we can point at this state. But this is the viewpoint of "God" (who can see the state), not of the clients of the object. Clients cannot tell one agent processing messages concurrently from two separate agents who share the same name because direct comparison is impossible. So *within* a system we do not necessarily have the notion of identity.

Floor: Is identity related to the notion of persistence? Also I think that the notion of identity should be defined in terms of some equivalence which compares two objects.

Tokoro: For that purpose, you should pay the cost of checking the equivalence.

Nierstrasz: Consider objects in a tuple space. The tuple space is persistent, can change state, but tuples there do not assume any identity.

2.4 Behaviour-As-Objects and Persistence again

Floor: Do you consider behaviour as objects?

Milner: My answer is no. Equivalence classes are not objects. When the behaviour is coded into an expression, it becomes an object.

Floor: If behaviour is considered as a transition system of process calculi, then an object is behaviour, i.e. a transition relation. By the way, how can the notion of persistence be understood in the framework of process calculi?

Milner: Quite easy. Persistence is expressed as residuals, as in the lambda-calculus. An occurrence of a subexpression can be traced through the computation. That gives you the identity of the subexpression in the lambda-calculus. The same thing for process calculi.

Nierstrasz: That is from the viewpoint of God.

Milner: Yes, the idea of perception of identity from meta-level is quite different from keeping objects distinct in addressing objects. Communication at the system level is different from perception of structure at the meta-level.

2.5 Objects and Concurrency

Floor: Is concurrent object-orientation the same as the actor paradigm?

Wegner: The actor paradigm is a special case of concurrent object-oriented programming.

Milner: As an approximation, the two paradigms come to the same thing. I am surprised that object-oriented study can be *not* concurrent. If objects are persistent, then they can persist simultaneously and are therefore concurrent.

Wegner: So in the list of the features of object notion shown at the beginning (Figure 1), you put the concurrency right there as part of the basic properties?

Milner: Yes.

Tokoro: When we talk about objects, they are inevitably concurrent. And, furthermore, if we introduce the notion of objects, they should be distributed, because of the existence of boundary separating inside and outside of objects. Hence the notion of time, or distance, or asynchrony becomes important. Time and asynchrony are closely related.

Wegner: Pierre, do you have any comments, because this seems to go against your view that we should reduce the number of essential properties?

America: I think that we should simplify what we have, and simplifying is not throwing concepts away, but either unifying them or separating them to deal with them independently.

Milner: In that regard, Kohei and Mario's work is interesting, expressing asynchronous messages by making messages objects i.e. without introducing additional entities. Technically it is nice to reduce the number and kinds of entities.

2.6 Various Discussions

Floor: Objects should be regarded as views imposing structures on the world.

Floor: How can objects be mapped to processes?

Tokoro: The mapping from objects to processes can be quite difficult in traditional operating systems. In our Muse operating system, the situation is different.

Floor: What does an object have definitely?

Milner: (Checking each item of Figure 1) state, absolutely. Then identity (not unique, but in the sense of persistence, and in God's eyes), yes. Messages, yes. Code and values, yes. Concurrency, definitely. References/addresses, in terms of addressing in communication, yes. Others, like classes, types, inheritances, etc. seem somewhat inessential elements for object paradigm.

3 Closing

Wegner: Finally I would like to ask panelists their opinions about the future of Concurrent Object-Oriented Programming ten years from now:

Nierstrasz: My view is that the various concurrent programming paradigms, like concurrent objects, functional programming, and concurrent logic programming languages, will get unified little by little, at least conceptually. This will take time, but eventually the paradigms will merge.

Tokoro: We are just beginning to know about distributed computing in terms of objects, and the research in that area should continue. Nonetheless concurrent object-oriented languages will be in practice in a few years, because of the development of parallel processing hardware and distributed computing environments. There will also be fruitful interaction between practice and theory.

Milner: Apart from theoretical issues, I would like to say that programming languages are interface issues, because they should cope with the real world. Thus no unique language for concurrent objects will serve all purposes.

America: My prediction is rather pessimistic in that I believe that theory and practice will become more and more separated within these few years. People tend to use traditional languages and therefore there is very slow advancement.

Yonezawa: As a methodology for simulation of phenomena, concurrent objects will play a more and more important role. In that regard, however, we should note that objects can model entities very well, but not the relationship among them. Thus something like a constraint-based framework should be necessarily combined with the concurrent object paradigm that we know.

Wegner: I would like to thank both the panelists and the audience for the lively discussion.

Author Index

Lecture Notes in Computer Science

For information about Vols. 1–529
please contact your bookseller or Springer-Verlag